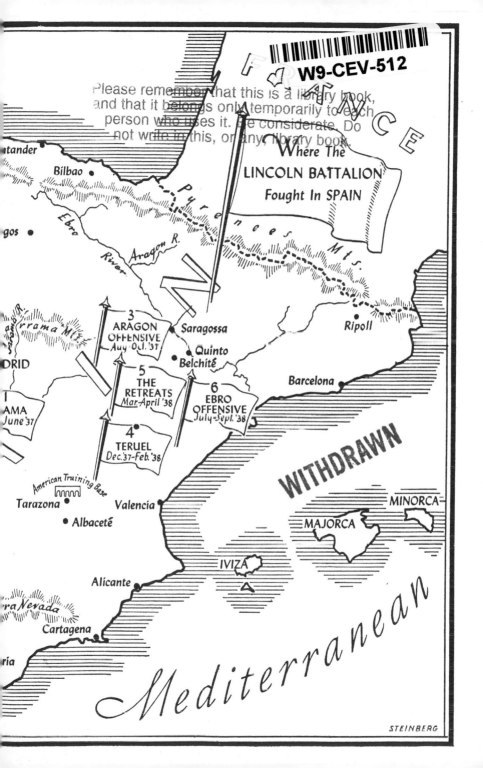

FRANCE

Where The
LINCOLN BATTALION
Fought In SPAIN

Santander

Bilbao

Pyrenees Mts.

Ebro River

Aragon R.

gos

Burgos

Ripoll

rrama Mts.

MADRID

3
ARAGON
OFFENSIVE
Aug-Oct. '37

Saragossa

Quinto
Belchité

Barcelona

1
JARAMA
June '37

5
THE
RETREATS
Mar-April '38

6
EBRO
OFFENSIVE
July-Sept. '38

4
TERUEL
Dec. 37-Feb. '38

American Training Base

Tarazona

Valencia

MINORCA

Albaceté

MAJORCA

IVIZA

Alicante

Sierra Nevada

Cartagena

ría

Mediterranean

STEINBERG

CRUSADE OF THE LEFT

THE LINCOLN BATTALION

CRUSADE
OF THE LEFT

N THE SPANISH CIVIL WAR

Robert A. Rosenstone

PEGASUS · NEW YORK

For Lolita,
who has made possible all the good things.

In the eighteen months between December 1936 and June 1938, some 3,000 young Americans sailed the Atlantic to France and then crossed the Pyrenees to take part as voluntary soldiers on the side of the Republic in the brutal civil war then raging in Spain. Virtually all of them joined the International Brigades, formed under the auspices of the Soviet-led Comintern and largely directed by Communists. Yet a large number of these men were not Communists, and the activism they showed in going to Spain did not spring from a desire to make the world safe for Joseph Stalin. Rather, these Americans who largely fought beneath the banner of the Abraham Lincoln Battalion of the XVth International Brigade were native American radicals who had been impelled by the domestic and international crises of the 1930's to defend what seemed to them to be the cause of Western civilization itself.

Thirty years later, one may wonder at the actions of militants who volunteer for a conflict thousands of miles from home. Yet the experiences of the 1960's should help us to understand them. In the past decade, we have become accustomed once again to the idea of the United States as a land of conflict as well as consensus. Student strikes and sit-ins, anti-war marches and demonstrations, black demands and ghetto revolts have reminded us that a native radicalism can flourish in America. It was the same in the thirties. The men who went to Spain came out of a radical subculture that emerged in the era of the Depression and the New Deal. This radicalism was a native plant, but it was also nourished from abroad. For in the thirties the menace of fascism was spreading like a cancer across Europe, and this gave an international aspect to many domestic problems. The threat of fascism to intellectuals, students, unionists, liberals, and leftists was so real that many came to believe it could only be stopped in open combat; the Americans who went to Spain sincerely felt that if reaction were not stopped in that country, eventually they would have to take up arms against fascism here at home.

Perhaps only older Americans now remember how pure seemed the cause of the Spanish Republic in the late thirties. Here was a legally elected government battling against a group of reactionary rebel generals who wished to do away with democracy and social reform. Here was a Republic kept from buying arms to defend itself by the Western democracies, while the governments of Hitler and Mussolini rushed men and material to aid its foes. It is no wonder that the struggle of the Spanish Republic for life came to symbolize the stand of everything that was good and just and decent in the Western tradition against the onslaught of barbarism and evil. Such a view may be overly simple, but it was exactly this view which sent thousands of foreign volunteers to Spain and caused millions to applaud their actions. Perhaps the closest parallel in the sixties is that of the early freedom riders, or the whites who literally risked life and limb by going South to help impoverished Negroes register to vote. To significant numbers of Americans, the actions of the Spanish volunteers had that kind of morality and nobility about them.

To study the history of the Americans who fought in the Spanish Civil War it is necessary to bury some of the shibboleths of cold war years and to remember that dissidence in the United States occurs in response to perceptions of reality on this side of the Atlantic, and not because of the wishes of men in the Soviet Union. After the experiences of the sixties this should be easier, even though some American political leaders still sound as if any domestic dissent is the product of an international conspiracy. By now, one should even be able to look sensibly at the role of the American Communist Party and its enterprises and see that its adherents were not inevitably evil men or dupes of the Kremlin, but were often honest, sensitive individuals responding to problems created by the malfunctions of our own socioeconomic system. The men of the Lincoln Battalion were genuine products of America and their story is properly a page in American history. In studying them, one can learn much about one kind of native response to the world of the 1930's and perhaps even something about the potentialities of modern man for thought and action in time of crisis.

Acknowledgments

In making this study of the Abraham Lincoln Battalion, I became indebted to many people for their time and help. Because numerous publications and pamphlets of the American left wing are not available through normal library channels, I must thank various individuals across the United States who generously opened their private collections to me; though some must necessarily remain anonymous, they nonetheless have my gratitude, as do Dan Bessie, Emil Freed, and Arnold Krammer. My thanks, too, to Moe Fishman of the Veterans of the Abraham Lincoln Brigade, who allowed me to go through his organization's collection of newspaper clippings and files of the *Volunteer for Liberty.*

Certain people went out of their way either to help me obtain material or to introduce me to others who helped. Alvah Bessie not only gave of his own time and library, but also let me use his invaluable diary from Spain and then wrote a lengthy critique to correct some of my historical errors. Mary Rolfe generously opened her library, her husband's papers, and even her home to my wife and me. George Sklar and Marvin Goldsmith both made valuable suggestions as to where materials could be found. Naturally, I am immensely grateful to all the Spanish veterans, named and anonymous, who allowed me to interview them.

I also wish to express my appreciation to three members of the academic community: George E. Mowry—under whose direction I began this study—who had the faith to urge me forward in a work that other historians thought could not or should not be undertaken; Daniel J. Kevles, who read and perceptively commented on parts of the manuscript; and Joseph Boskin, who provided cogent criticism, warm friendship, and moral support at times when things looked bleak. My thanks also go to Lucille Lozoya, who not only typed the manuscript both speedily and accurately, but also saved me from more than one grammatical error.

Naturally, whatever faults or mistakes in historical fact or interpretation I have committed have nothing to do with any of the above individuals. I can truthfully say that however good this book is, it would have been significantly less so without the help of the people I have named.

Finally, there is my debt to my wife, Lolita, whose ancestors lived in the country for which the men of the Lincoln Battalion fought, and who has a full measure of the mystery, beauty, and wisdom of the Spanish people. Not only did she brave the dust, heat, insects, and lizards of the Spanish countryside to visit remote places with me, but she also put up with the emotional storms that arose whenever she made her usual incisive criticisms into the content and style of this work. My debt to her is one which cannot be repaid in words.

Los Angeles
January 1969

Contents

MAPS AND ILLUSTRATIONS

A Note on the Notes

To avoid redundancy and a proliferation of numbers, the note references in this work appear—for the most part—at the end of either paragraphs or sections dealing with a particular subject. Thus a single note will sometimes contain all the references for the preceding couple of pages. Note references occur in mid paragraph only when it seems necessary to avoid a confusing reference. The reader on the track of the author's sources should have little difficulty in finding them if he keeps this in mind.

(Some facts about the men who appear often in this history of the Lincoln Battalion.)

Hans Amlie: 37; Wisconsin; brother of Progressive Congressman; mining engineer; veteran of Marine Corps in World War I; commander of the Lincoln Battalion at Belchite.

Bill Bailey: 27; New York City; seaman, participant in 1934 Pacific shipping strike, union organizer and editor of West Coast labor newspaper; sergeant and member of Lincoln machine gun company.

Alvah Bessie: 33; New York City; author of novel *Dwell in the Wilderness* (1935) and recipient of a Guggenheim Fellowship for creative writing; joined battalion during Spring, 1938 retreats and took part in Ebro offensive.

Joe Dallet: mid-twenties; New England; Dartmouth graduate from wealthy family; Communist Party organizer in Ohio steel mills; Mackenzie-Papineau Battalion commissar; killed at Fuentes del Ebro.

Dave Doran: 27; Albany, New York; left high school for sea at age 16; Communist organizer in South and National Trade Union Director of Young Communist League; XVth Brigade Commissar; disappeared during Spring, 1938 retreats.

Henry Eaton: 27; Los Angeles; son of former L. A. mayor; four years at military academy and two at UCLA; active in organizing citrus and aircraft workers in Southern California; company commissar; killed at Belchite.

John Gates: 23; New York City; son of small shopkeeper; joined Young Communist League at CCNY; party organizer in Ohio and Pennsylvania; last commissar of XVth Brigade.

Mike Goodwin: 21; Brooklyn; sometime CCNY student and member of Young Communist League; spent one year at CCC camp in Montana; captured in Spring, 1938 retreats and spent year in Franco prison camp.

Gabby Klein: 21; Brooklyn; office boy and bookkeeper with no union affiliations; night student at NYU in engineering and business; sergeant in Spain after almost two years of combat.

Samuel Levinger: 20; Columbus, Ohio; son of rabbi; Ohio State University student; member of Young Socialists; killed at Belchite.

Wilfred Mendelson: early twenties; New York City; CCNY student and militant member of Young Communist League; arrived Spain in summer of 1938 and was among last to join battalion; killed in Ebro offensive.

Robert Merriman: 28; Nevada; graduate student in economics at Berkeley; participant in San Francisco General Strike; first field commander of Lincoln Battalion, then Chief of Staff, XVth Brigade; disappeared in Spring, 1938 retreats.

Steve Nelson: 35; Pennsylvania; carpenter; longtime organizer for the Communist Party; ordered to Spain by CP to help boost morale of troops in Spring, 1937; commissar of XVth Brigade; seriously wounded at Belchite and repatriated.

George Poole: 21; Buffalo, New York; student; wounded in Spring, 1938 and repatriated.

Edwin Rolfe: New York City; one-time University of Wisconsin student; poet who had published *To My Contemporaries* (1935) and contributor to *Daily Worker, New Masses* and *New Republic;* editor of *Volunteer for Liberty;* footsoldier in Ebro offensive.

Donald Thayer: 26; Minnesota; descendant of West Point superintendent; sometime University of Wisconsin student; veteran of CCC camp; commander of all-Spanish company in Lincoln Battalion.

David McKelvy White: son of former governor of Ohio; instructor in English at Brooklyn College; served with Washington Battalion machine gun company at Brunete.

On November 8, 1936, Madrid was in chaos.

Its citizens awoke in the cold, predawn morning to the booming of artillery and the harsh noise of loudspeakers and radios crackling out messages announcing total mobilization of the population. The streets were filled with workers in blue *monos*, alone and in groups, some shouldering rifles and many without them, some hurrying on foot, others riding in trucks or cars with the initials of labor unions painted in large letters on the sides. There were children in the streets helping to tear up cobblestones and erect barricades, and taxis racing back and forth bearing military officers and messages. The city echoed with the shouted slogans, *"No pasarán"* and *"Madrid sera la tumba del fascismo,"* and everywhere, above the noise and confusion of men preparing for battle, loudspeakers were blaring with the voice of La Pasionaria, the Spanish Communist leader, calling on the Spanish women to resist their enemy to the death, saying: "It is better to be the widow of a hero than the wife of a coward." At 6:30 A.M., Madrid's transportation system began to function as usual, and more than one worker on that crisp fall morning kissed his family goodbye and mounted a streetcar as he did every day. Only on November 8, 1936, he was calmly riding to the front lines and to war.

For the Madrileños were preparing to resist what the outside world had already accepted as inevitable, the fall of the Spanish capital to the armies of the insurgent generals led by Francisco Franco. Newspaper correspondents had flashed dispatches around the globe the night before saying that Madrid was as good as lost. General Franco had already announced that the "liberation" of the capital was near, and Radio Lisbon had broadcast a description of him entering Madrid on a white charger and being greeted by joyous crowds. The preceding day insurgent troops had fought their way into the city, entering the Casa de Campo park on the west of Madrid, capturing the high point named Mount Garabitas.

There was little reason to suppose Madrid would not fall. The African armies of the rebel generals had in three months swept virtually unopposed from Seville north to Madrid, brushing aside the ill-organized Loyalist militia, stopping long enough to raise the siege of the Toledo Alcázar, and then moving easily onward to the outskirts of the Spanish capital. Loyalist counterattacks south of Madrid had slowed down the insurgent advance during the last week of October, but had not halted the rebel approach to the western gates of the city. General Emilio Mola had long since told newspaper reporters who asked which of his four military columns would take Madrid that it was the fifth column of supporters inside the capital that would do the job, and indeed rebel partisans were disrupting the city by firing from hidden windows and by hurling homemade hand grenades into crowds. Unknown to the world, but well known to the rebel generals was the fact that Nazi Germany's Condor Legion, totaling 100 fighters and bombers, 32 tanks, and 6,000 military men, was almost completely assembled at Seville and ready to go into full-scale action on behalf of the rebels. For the last two weeks, German Junker bombers had flown low-altitude bombing raids over Madrid, which contained no antiaircraft guns. The Spanish Loyalist government of Francisco Largo Caballero seemed itself to have given up the fight by fleeing the capital with all its officials, records, and files on the evening of November 6, leaving the city under control of a defense junta headed by General José Miaja.

Daylight on November 8 found rebel artillery battering the buildings of the University of Madrid, just inside the city, and the Moroccan troops and foreign legionnaires of the rebels pushing slowly through the Casa de Campo and into the streets of the city against stubborn resistance, when the first units of foreigners that were to become known to the world as the International Brigades marched through the Spanish capital. They were tough-looking men, French and Germans, English, Belgians, and Poles, clad in corduroy uniforms, wearing steel helmets, their rifles gleaming dully in the light of day. They marched from the railroad station along the tree-lined Paseo de Prado and turned left up the hill to the Gran Via, while the people of the city, thinking the Soviet Union had intervened at last, hung from the balconies and windows overlooking the boulevards, crowded the sidewalks, and cheered until the streets echoed with the cries, *"Vivan los rusos!"* Past the noisy crowds they swung, down the sloping boulevard west to the Plaza de Espana, and then on to the Casa de Campo.

By evening the 2,000 men of the XIth International Brigade were in position, some in University City, most under the trees of the great park, spread out among the militia. The park roared with the sounds of battle that night as the Internationals fought and died to help hold the enemy back from Madrid. For the first time in the war, rebel troops met soldiers equipped with good machine guns, soldiers who entrenched well and fired accurately and would not budge, and by early afternoon on November 9, rebel commanders found that their forces had run into a stone wall. That evening the Internationals fixed bayonets and mounted an offensive through the north end of the Casa de Campo, breaking through the ranks of the Moroccan troops and foreign legionnaires, taking a heavy toll of casualties as they pushed the insurgents back until Mount Garabitas was the only point in the Casa de Campo left to them. By then, one third of the Internationals were already dead, but the rebel assault through the park was at an end.

Two days later the XIIth International Brigade of Germans, Frenchmen, and Italians went into action at Madrid, and on November 15 the foreigners were called into the bloody battle of University City, where "The marching songs of the German Communists brought to the crumbling masonry of the laboratories and lecture halls a wild Teutonic sadness," and some men gave their lives defending a city they had never seen. For a week the battle raged through the university campus, from building to building, from floor to floor, and in hand-to-hand combat from room to room. Men built barricades out of library books, and one young Englishman found that those made out of volumes of Indian metaphysics and German philosophy "were quite bullet-proof." November 23 saw both exhausted armies digging trenches and building fortifications. The troops of the rebels had been halted, and Franco and Mola had been forced to call off the assault upon Madrid.[1]

There is no doubt that the International Brigades did not alone save the Spanish capital. Most of the troops committed in the battles of Casa de Campo and University City were Spaniards, militia of all parties, tough fighters from Madrid's Communist Fifth Regiment, and some 3,000 Anarchists who had marched in from Catalonia. Yet the 5,000 foreigners played a crucial role in helping to break the back of the rebel attempt to storm the capital. Arriving at a moment when Loyalist lines seemed stretched to the breaking point, fighting almost to the last man to maintain untenable positions, they had bolstered the ranks and morale of the Spaniards. Once the Internationals had arrived, the Madrileños knew that they were no longer alone in their struggle, and from the examples of the foreigners they learned to fight without giving ground and then to take the offensive in counterattacks. Whether the victory belonged to the populace of Madrid or to the foreigners remains debatable, but when the news of the battle of Madrid was reported, the International Brigades had so much caught the fancy of the correspondents that a Spanish censorship official grumbled, "The International Brigades figured in the press dispatches as though they were the sole saviours of Madrid. . . . I found it unjust that the people of Madrid . . . were forgotten. . . ." [2] Beneath towering headlines, the exploits of the foreigners in Madrid flashed through the newspapers of the Western world.

The population of the outside world already knew what was happening in Spain, already had been touched by the struggle of the Loyalist government, already had chosen which side to support in the conflict that from its very beginning symbolized so much of the crisis of the 1930's. From the outset of the war, intervention on the rebel side by Hitler's Germany and Mussolini's Italy was a secret shared by most of the world. As early as July 30, two weeks after the rising of the generals against the Spanish Republic, three Italian Savoia bombers on their way from Sardinia to Spanish Morocco were forced to land in French Morocco, where investigation clearly established they were part of an expedition to aid the insurgent cause. On August 1, the *New York Times* reported the arrival of 18 Italian aircraft in the Spanish Moroccan city of Melilla, and two days later it carried a story about the bombing of a Republican cruiser by an Italian airplane. In following weeks, Italian aircraft and pilots began to arrive on the mainland in the rebel stronghold of Seville. Meanwhile, in late July, 20 German heavy transport planes were engaged in an airlift that ferried the 15,000 African troops of the Spanish Army over the heads of the Republican Navy from Morocco to Seville. When the Loyalist cruiser *Jaime Primero* used its anti-aircraft guns to interfere with the operation, it was put out of commission by bombs from a German Junker.[3]

At the outset of the conflict, the French Popular Front government of Léon Blum reacted positively to Spanish Prime Minister José Giral's July 20 plea for military aid. By the first week of August, Air Minister Pierre Cot had sent some 50 airplanes—all of them obsolete by 1936 standards—across the border. But Blum, whose cabinet was split over aid to Spain, who did not wish to weaken France militarily in view of increasing German rearmament, and who was afraid that the strong French right wing might itself foment civil strife, was quickly forced to retreat under

25

English pressure. For the Conservative British government of Stanley Baldwin, instinctively favorable to the Spanish right wing, warned Blum that England would not come to France's defense if involvement in Spain led to war with Germany. Faced with this prospect, Blum proposed non-intervention of the European powers in the affairs of Spain, hoping that all the governments would agree and the war would quickly end for lack of armaments. Even before his idea was everywhere accepted, he closed the frontier on August 8, at a time when Germany and Italy were stepping up aid to the rebels. By the end of the month, 27 European nations had committed themselves to the Non-Intervention Agreement—which kept the Spanish government from buying arms on the world's markets, as it was legally entitled to do—the small democracies of the continent tamely following the lead of the big powers. Soon a Non-Intervention Committee was meeting regularly in London. Yet in spite of their adherence to the pact, Italy and Germany continued their military aid to Franco.

When the generals rose against the Spanish Republic on July 18, large segments of the population of the Western countries were immediately pro-Republican. In France, both Socialist and Communist labor unions demanded that their government support Spain with arms, while the French liberal middle classes who had supported the separation of Church and State, and who could still remember the Dreyfus Affair, looked askance at the alliance of the Church and the military that Franco represented. In England, Labour was pro-Republic, though its pacifist leaders acquiesced in nonintervention in the sincere hope—soon to be shattered—that it would be observed and peace would be restored.[4] As the Republic fought back against the uprising, the anti-fascists of the continent felt, according to George Orwell, "a thrill of hope. For here at last, apparently, was democracy standing up to fascism." And though Orwell quickly recognized that Franco was not comparable to Hitler and Mussolini, that his uprising represented the traditional forces of Church, aristocracy, and military, the thrill did not fade. For the principles of democracy and liberalism, insofar as they were embodied in the governments of the world and the League of Nations, had taken too many beatings in recent years: the Japanese invasion of Manchuria, Hitler's takeover of Germany, Dollfuss's crushing of Austrian social democracy, Mussolini's brutal war against the helpless Ethiopians. With the resistance of the Republic in Spain, "It seemed—perhaps it was—the turning of the tide." [5]

With the news of Italian and German intervention in Spain, all people in the Western countries who did not like fascism, Nazism, and the sort of world order they envisaged, who did not like the bombing of synagogues, the concentration camp, the tramp of boots, and the knock on the door in the middle of the night, began to support the Spanish Republic. Long before the broadcast of Radio Madrid on November 8, many people in the Western countries agreed with the sentiments of the Spanish Republican deputy, who proclaimed, "Madrid is the universal frontier that separates liberty and slavery. It is here that two incompatible civilizations undertake their great struggle: love against hate, peace against war, the fraternity of Christ against the tyranny of the Church. . . . It is fighting for Spain, for Humanity, for Justice, and, with the mantle of its blood, it shelters all human beings!" [6]

Enthusiasm for the cause of Loyalist Spain took many forms in the cities of Europe, from the newspaper editorial to the soapbox oration to the mass meeting, with demands for an end to Italo-German intervention and for aid to the Republican government. Yet among the many liberals and left-wingers in the countries of the West—England, France, and Holland, Sweden, Switzerland, and Belgium—there were men too committed to the ideals of the Popular Front against fascism, too impatient or too wise to stay at home and work for a change in their country's nonintervention policy. In these countries there also resided a large number of political exiles from Eastern lands that specialized in ignoring the voice of the people or in silencing it, refugees from Germany and Italy, Poland, Austria, Hungary, and Yugoslavia. For these activists, who had lived through a

27

right-wing takeover in their own country or had watched the right sweep over much of Europe, the rising in Spain provided a conflict where they could confront their enemy with rifle in hand for the first time. By fighting in Spain, many of the exiled hoped to find the road back to their own homelands. As one Italian said, he wanted to show his own countrymen living under Mussolini that "one could and should die for liberty."[7] If enough men did so, the regimes of the right might everywhere be toppled.

So the Eastern exiles and their Western comrades went to Spain. The last two weeks in July, hundreds of volunteers poured over the Franco-Spanish border to Barcelona, where they enlisted in various militia units. There were Socialists, Communists, Anarchists, and Republicans among these first volunteers, and in early August they marched out into Aragón with Catalan troops who occupied town after town, but were stalled short of their main objective, Zaragoza. Soon the foreigners formed their own centuria, military columns of a hundred men or more. Each had a distinctive name: "Thaelmann" for the Germans, "Gastone-Sozzi" for the Italians, "Paris" for the French and Belgians, with Slavs and Englishmen scattered in all the groups. By late August there were enough English to form their own centuria, and a second Italian unit, composed largely of Anarchists, was in the field.

Across Spain, in the Basque country, in late August rebel troops closed in upon Irún to cut the Loyalists off from the French border. Here a large number of Poles, French, Belgians, and Czechs threw themselves into a bitter battle which was watched by spectators from the French side of the border, the foreigners being among the last troops to retreat across the frontier. Soon these same volunteers were back in Spain, with the foreign centuria in Catalonia. In September, as the Army of Africa raced toward Madrid, some of the centuria left Catalonia to join the Communist Fifth Regiment near the capital. On September 11, the Gastone-Sozzi column was wildly cheered as it marched through Madrid, and soon it was fighting with Spanish militia units in several ill-fated attempts to stop the rebel thrust at the Spanish capital.[8] So it is obvious that long before Soviet Russia approved the formation of International Brigades, long before the first group of Frenchmen under the sponsorship of the Comintern arrived in the provincial capital of Albacete in mid-October, and long before French Communist André Marty assumed control of the International base there, foreigners were crossing the Spanish border and offering their lives to defend the cause of the Spanish Republic.

The appeal of Spain to the liberals and left-wingers of the world has nowhere been better described than by W. H. Auden, in his poem "Spain, 1937." Here is a picture of the call to arms being heard in the remote corners of the globe, on "sleepy plains" and in the "corrupt" hearts of cities. And then comes the response of the volunteers, answering the call, clinging to trains, floating across oceans, and hiking through mountain passes to defend Spain. As Auden put it, "Madrid is the heart," the heart of a civilization, of a world, and of an ideal, that 35,000 men from 53 foreign lands would put their lives on the line to protect.[9]

Across the Atlantic Ocean, over which so many volunteers were to journey to Spain, the United States lay still sunk in the worst economic depression in its history, its political leaders grappling with domestic issues, largely oblivious of the world beyond. And although no European war ever seemed quite real to the people of the United States, at least until they were in it, this war had already touched them more than most, and some looked upon Loyalist Spain as "a beacon of hope in a continent darkened by increasingly ominous clouds."[10] For American writers, artists, intellectuals, or simple democrats, sensitive to the world around them, the Spanish struggle had quickly become the most important international event since the world war and the Russian Revolution. To writer Malcolm Cowley, the Spanish War brought two opposing systems of life face to face for a showdown. On one side were the privileged few, the landlords, the Church, the military, and the large financial institutions. Facing them Cowley saw the workers, peasants, and artists who were guiding "a poverty-stricken people toward more knowledge, more freedom, more of everything." And Cowley was only one of many who feared the dictators lurking in the wings, feared that if Franco won in Spain the second act might see fascist-inspired uprisings repeated "in Czechoslovakia, in France, in all the free nations of Europe." [11]

Across the United States, in towns where the Spanish language had never been heard, people closely followed news of the war. In mining communities like Coeur d'Alene, where exploitation was more than a memory, in the grimy waterfront bars of San Francisco, where longshoremen well remembered the feeling of National Guardsmen's bayonets pressed against their bellies, in Minneapolis, where 65 teamsters could show the scars from policemen's bullets, the news of the workers of Spain being armed by the government must have brought a thrill of envy. Soon came the horrifying accounts of rebel atrocities, like those at Badajoz, where 2,000 civilians were reported slaughtered in the bull ring after the Army of Africa captured the town on August 14. In late October, the first bombings of the civilian population of Madrid occurred. Then the pulses of many Americans quickened when they read of the heroic stand before the capital city, and men carrying the radical conscience of America smiled at the blows being struck for the underdog in a far-off land. [12] Throughout the country there were men who felt a kinship with the Spanish militia, struggling to save their Republic, and some yearned to travel to the site of the conflict. But Spain was more than an ocean away, and the journey there, which for a European might be simple and brief, was long and too expensive for most Americans interested in making the trip.

Yet some Americans did manage to make it to Spain on their own in the early days of the conflict. Two of the first were professional soldiers and probably men of little ideology. In August, completing enlistments in the French Foreign Legion, they crossed from Africa to Spain to join the Loyalist forces. A few others reached Barcelona in the same month, joined Catalan militia units, and took part in skirmishes on the Aragón front. One of them was Rosario Negrete, a leader of the American Trotskyist Revolutionary Workers' League, who joined a column of the Communist POUM. (POUM stands for Partido Obrero de Unificación Marxista. This anti-Stalinist party has often been labeled "Trotskyist" though in fact Trotsky did not support it.) On October 10, a month before rebel forces reached the gates of Madrid, Humberto Galleani, a naturalized American who had fled Mussolini's Italy and was editor of the New York anti-fascist newspaper, *La Stampa Libera*, arrived in Spain to defend its government. And the same month an American engineer, Lee Fleischman, who, according to the *Daily Worker*, had been in "close contact with the workers' movement for years," was killed while serving in the Loyalist armies.[13]

When the siege of Madrid began in November and it looked to so many foreign observers as if the Spanish capital were about to fall, American Louis Fischer, European correspondent for *Nation*, after a life devoted to reporting world events, decided to contribute "work as well as words" to the cause of the Spanish government. He enlisted in the newly formed International Brigades, became the quartermaster at Albacete, and explained his action by saying: "A nation was bleeding. Machine guns were being mounted on the ivory tower. It was not enough to write." For a few weeks Fischer was in charge of distributing arms, food, and clothing to the Internationals who were pouring into Albacete from all over Europe. His situation was difficult, for he never had enough supplies for all of them, and once an angry battalion commander sent troops to arrest Fischer for not delivering promised equipment. Soon Fischer quarreled with brigade chief André Marty, and as a result he resigned his post and went back to writing about the war.[14]

Reports of Americans fighting in Loyalist ranks began to trickle back to the United States, appearing in American newspapers from time to time during November and December. Usually, correspondents could find only two or three Americans in Spain, though in reality there were more than that. The news fanned interest in the war, particularly in radical circles, and more Americans began to consider the possibility of enlisting in the Loyalist Army.[15] For some of them the chance came soon, and toward the end of December 1936, the first large, organized group of American volunteers for the International Brigades was slowly gathering in Manhattan. Its members knew little of warfare or of what was happening at the front lines, but they had been told to go to Spain prepared, and most of them were making forays into Army and Navy Supply Stores, buying boots, blankets, mittens, and heavy jackets, snapping up military equipment they might need, ammunition belts, canteens, first aid packs. Some of them browsed through New York bookstores, purchasing volumes of tactics and strategy, finding a few dog-eared copies of old American Army training manuals.

Ninety-six men, most of them in their early twenties, boarded the SS. *Normandie* on a sunny Saturday, December 25, 1936, bound for Spain, though it is unlikely that any of them had listed that country as his destination when applying for a passport. Ostensibly they were tourists or students, on their way to visit overseas relatives or to study at the Sorbonne or to complete their educations with a grand tour. On board they acted like any other passengers, loafing on the decks, playing cards, reading in the lounges, or sleeping in their cabins. But unlike the other tourists, some of these men devoted time to studying military manuals. The ship docked at Le Havre on New Year's Eve. The men scattered to a number of hotels, then strolled the town's streets, stopping at small restaurants to order meals in halting, high-school French, learning with amazement in the red-light districts that French prostitutes carried union cards.

On the afternoon of January 2, they went by rail to Paris, and after only an hour in the French capital, boarded another train. In its compartments they met volunteers from all over Europe—Poles and Germans, Italians and Yugoslavs—and the Americans attempted to talk with them in a *mélange* of broken languages. They sat, cramped and uncomfortable, on the hard third-class benches through the night and until noon the next day, when the train steamed into Perpignan, where the brightly colored buildings and red tile roofs already looked like Spain. That same night they mounted into old buses and were driven to the Pyrenees border. There French border guards in their blue uniforms saluted them with the clenched fist of the Popular Front and then waved them on. It was only a short ride to the Catalan town of Figueras, where the buses stopped and the volunteers stepped on Spanish soil for the first time.

For two nights the Americans slept in the old fortress on a hill overlooking Figueras. Then, on slow trains, they were carried down through the mountains to Barcelona, along the coast south, the blue gleam of the Mediterranean stretching on their left as far as the eye could see, through the orange groves of Valencia and then inland again to Albacete, halfway between Madrid and Valencia, in the ancient region of La Mancha, where Don Quixote had once tilted against his foes. They spent only 48 hours in this once-sleepy town, now bustling with activity as the new International Brigade headquarters. Then they rode in Russian trucks across countryside that to two men from Wisconsin "looked and smelled like home," until they were deposited in Villanueva de la Jara, a small village that was the site of the first American training base.[16]

From the moment the Americans arrived in Villanueva, they were virtually cut off from the outside world. In Albacete, brigade commanders had their hands full, trying to rush fresh soldiers and equipment to the front lines to fill the thinning ranks of the four International Brigades that were now in the field. Around Madrid a bitter struggle still raged. Stalled at the western gates to the city, the troops of Francisco Franco were engaged in a series of flanking maneuvers designed to carry them around the northern edge of Madrid, thereby cutting the capital off from its water and power supplies which originated in the Sierra Guadarramas. Until mid-January the battle swayed back and forth, while three International Brigades lost one third of their men.[17] By the time the Republic had successfully stalled the rebels, the Americans had been stewing away in Villanueva for two weeks, unaware of the important battles near Madrid, unable to understand why they had received virtually no supplies from Albacete.

The men at Villanueva were unhappy and discontent. A few of them had been designated military leaders at Albacete but had been given no rank. Quarrels broke out, grievance committees were set up, Communists held meetings and argued over what was to be done. Finally, the leaders at Albacete got wind of the trouble and tried to straighten out the situation by appointing James Harris military commander and Robert Merriman his adjutant. Harris, who claimed experience with the U. S. Army, quickly showed himself to be an incompetent leader. Grumbling occurred in the ranks because his lectures were incoherent and because the men suspected him of using company funds for his own needs. Things improved when Merriman, an ex-University of California, Berkeley, teaching assistant in economics, who had four years of college ROTC and several football letters behind him, took over actual leadership of the base. As the ranks quickly swelled to 400 men and they voted to use Abraham Lincoln as their unit designation, military training began. For the most part it was not very thorough. Merriman and the few others with some military experience gave lectures on strategy, mapping, scouting, and fields of fire, teaching the raw recruits something of the theory of warfare. There was practical work, too, exercise and marching and the digging of trenches, but rifle practice, the most necessary training for infantrymen, was sorely lacking. Republican Spain was still short of military supplies, and the few rifles spared for Villanueva were ancient. They usually jammed after the first shot, and most of the men never fired a round throughout the training period.

Still unaware of what was going on in Spain and the rest of the world, the men of the Lincoln Battalion tried to console themselves by making friends with the people of Villanueva de la Jara. Suspicious of the soldiers, partly because the preceding French battalion had engaged in drunken brawls, the villagers were happily surprised when the Lincolns, led by a few Spanish-speaking Cubans among them, systematically began to improve relations. The Americans donated money to the local Red Cross, showed films for both the children and adults of the town, and the battalion doctor held clinics, treating the townspeople without charge. During the long afternoon siesta and on their free evening hours before lights out at nine o'clock, the new soldiers gathered in the town's little cafés to sip wine and write letters, or they dropped in on the homes of their new Spanish friends, to talk in sign language and haltingly acquire a few phrases of the unfamiliar tongue.

On the afternoon of February 15, the Americans were told to gather their belongings and climb into waiting trucks. A rumor circulated among the men that they were being transferred to another training base. The trucks took the road back toward Albacete, where the Lincolns were marched into the bull ring. They stood in formation on the brown sand, bored and restless, a cool breeze blowing, and listened to André Marty and Peter Kerrigan, British commissar of the International Brigade base, deliver long speeches. When the words began to get through to them, when they found they were being exhorted to defend the causes of liberty, freedom, justice, and humanity, the Americans knew for the first time that they were being sent into action. The speeches done, commissions were bestowed by brigade officials, Harris and Merriman being named captains, five other men receiving lieutenant's bars. The officers began to inspect their men, and it soon became apparent that something had unnerved Captain Harris. He began talking wildly and incoherently, until many of the men thought him drunk. Ordered out of the bull ring by a commissar, he returned after a while, then wandered away again. Before evening, brigade sent down word that Merriman was now in charge of the battalion. Shortly after nightfall trucks rumbled into the ring and the Americans were issued steel helmets, cartridge belts, ammunition, and rifles that were still sticky with packing grease. Only the officers knew the battalion's destination when the men climbed aboard and the trucks rolled out of Albacete into the darkness of the Spanish countryside.[18]

In spite of its sketchy training, the Lincoln Battalion was being rushed into battle because of the gravity of the military situation. Still determined to seize Madrid, rebel forces on February 6 had launched an attack through the Jarama River valley southeast of the capital with the objective of reaching the Madrid-Valencia road, the last main highway connecting the city to the rest of Spain. If the insurgents were successful, the lifeline of the beleaguered capital would be severed and it would soon fall into rebel hands. Though Valencia now housed the Spanish government, the bitter struggles in the Casa de Campo and University City had given rise to slogans and rallying cries which proclaimed Madrid the heart of the struggle against fascism, and the Loyalist government felt the city had to be defended at all costs.

With 40,000 troops led by tank companies and closely supported by German aircraft, rebel forces broke across the Jarama River and fought up the valley to a point above Arganda, where they brought the Valencia road under fire. The Loyalist command rushed brigade after brigade into the breach, and by February 12 had contained the thrust. The rebels then shifted the attack farther south, and fighting began to center in the vineyards and olive groves on the five miles of rugged hills between the Jarama and Tajuña river valleys. Already, insurgent troops had seized Pingarrón, the highest peak in the area. Now there were only a few more ridges between them and the long slope down toward Morata, beyond which lay another segment of the Valencia road. As the casualty lists lengthened, the Loyalists rushed all available men into the lines. On February 12, the British, the Franco-Belgian "Sixth of February," and the Balkan "Dimitrov" battalions of the newly formed XVth International Brigade were thrown into action to help stop the rebel drive. Of 600 members of the British battalion who climbed a hill on February 12 to defend it, only

225 were unscathed at the end of the day.[19] With still more troops needed for defense and possible counterattacks, the Lincolns—with one section of Cubans and another of Irish attached to them—had been called to the front and incorporated as the fourth battalion in the XVth Brigade.

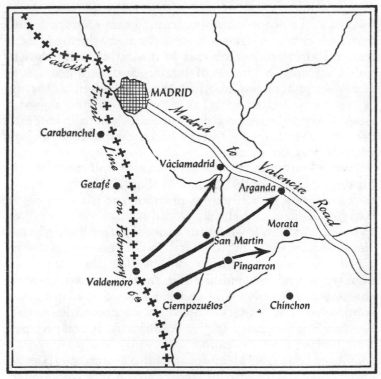

JARAMA

Cramped and half-dozing in the trucks, the Americans knew nothing of the military situation, knew only that out beyond the dark hills artillery boomed and rifle fire echoed amid the screams of men dying in the night. And here, in the jolting trucks, among the muffled whispers of their companions, they gripped the rifles that they had never loaded or fired, that they did not know how to sight or zero, gripped them for comfort and wondered what the dawn would bring. Once there was a stop, and the whispered warning came down the line that any man showing a light would be shot. Overhead there was the drone of aircraft. The Lincolns held their breath, clutched their rifles tightly, and felt somehow reassured by the weight of the cartridge belts around their waists. Jack Kalleborn, leader of a 40-man section in one of the two rifle companies, relaxed as the drone subsided, leaving him with the feeling that the war which had seemed so far away during training was real after all, and he was in it at last. As the convoy rolled on and the noise of heavy guns rumbled in the distance, he was reminded of the time when at the age of ten he had climbed onto a log and floated down an ice-filled creek only because someone had said he didn't dare do it. For some reason, he had the same feeling about what he was doing now.[20]

Before sunup the trucks ground to a halt and the men tumbled to earth in the gray light. Captain Merriman gave them the order to fire five practice rounds against the barren hillsides, so that they would have some idea of how to use their rifles. Pressed for time, short of the necessary cleaning rags, the Americans had to use their shirts to wipe the sticky grease from the weapons. The shots sputtered, then rippled out through the hills, and in the half-light the sharpness of his own rifle and the roar of so many others sounded strange to Jack Kalleborn's virgin military ears. For him, as for many of the Americans, it was the only time he had fired a weapon.

There was no real sleep for the Lincolns on the sixteenth either, save for those who could catch a few winks as the convoy joggled northwest along the dirt road, passing troops and military vehicles, batteries of artillery and peasants working in the fields, stopping from time to time when a truck broke down. On the outskirts of Morata, the sun already gone and the sky darkening into night, there was a stop for food. As the men stretched their legs, lit cigarettes, and wandered about, rebel aircraft roared into view and swooped to attack. The Americans dropped to the ground and hugged the earth as the machine-gun bullets hissed into the earth and the dusty streets of the town, and clattered off the tile roofs of nearby houses. As the Lincolns trembled under fire for the first time, government airplanes appeared and drove off the attackers, leaving the Americans shaken but uninjured.

It was dark now. Back into the trucks went the troops, and the convoy turned west and slowly climbed into the hills toward the Jarama Valley. When they stopped this time it was near a crossroads hut that served as brigade headquarters. While the men dismounted and formed into companies, Merriman received his instructions. Russian tanks, on their way back from the front, rolled swiftly past the Lincolns toward Morata. Orders were given and officers led the troops forward in the darkness, across a railroad embankment and up the steep side of a hill that must have seemed like a mountain to men struggling under the weight of a full pack. Word came for them to dig in, and the question spread through the ranks, "How?" For there were only 35 picks and shovels among the more than 400 men. Their first real military lesson was that of field expediency. As they began to dig at the stony earth with helmets or bayonets, small points of light flashed on unseen hills, followed by the noise of rifles and occasional machine-gun bursts.

In Jack Kalleborn's section, the men were tired from the long truck ride. They could not tell if the enemy fire was directed at them, but as rounds began to snap angrily overhead, some instinctively dropped to the ground, and it took all of Kalleborn's courage to keep from doing the same himself. He urged his men to keep digging, and soon they were ignoring the fire, though it made them work more furiously. By one o'clock their trench was finished, and after Kalleborn assigned guard shifts, most of his men dropped wearily into the trench and fell asleep. Feeling snug and safe behind the dirt parapet just thrown up, Kalleborn was enjoying his last cigarette of the day, smoked beneath the cover of a blanket, when a runner arrived with an order for the section to move to another place on the hill. He was still enough of a civilian to question the wisdom of moving his tired men to dig another trench, but no army ever supplies answers to such questions. He woke his troops, drugged with lack of sleep, and they stumbled to their new positions and painfully began to dig again.[21]

The Americans who did get to sleep that night awoke to find the morning gray and cold. Their blankets were soaked with dew. The two infantry companies and one machine-gun company were stretched out on the north and west slopes of the hill in secondary positions. In the dawn light the men could see down a valley and to hills where the other battalions of the brigade held the front lines. Beyond were the high ridges occupied by the rebels, among them Pingarrón. Everywhere there were rolling hills with open brown patches of earth amid clumps of scrub brush. Scattered about were groves of olive trees, planted in straight lines, their limbs gaunt and gnarled and scarred with bullet and shrapnel wounds. It was not long before the Lincolns named their position "Suicide Hill," for early on the first morning they learned that their ridge was a perfect target for artillery and aircraft. As the enemy unlimbered his field guns and the hillsides began to shake with their thunder, one American is supposed to have snapped angrily, "What are they trying to do, kill us?" Then Charles Edwards, an observer in a forward trench, shouted to the men around him to keep down and peered over the edge to see what was happening. Suddenly he fell back, a bullet through his head, the first member of the battalion to be killed.

For three days the Americans remained on Suicide Hill, learning how helpless infantry can feel beneath aerial and artillery bombardments, learning, as Jack Kalleborn put it, that their hillside "wasn't exactly a health resort." Young New Yorker Eli Beigelman wrote home, "It did not take us long to realize we were in a war, a life very much different from that at the base." Here the Americans were digging real trenches, working to deepen and extend them, and learning to make use of the protection they gave against the indirect fire of artillery. Enemy aircraft were a worse problem and the soldiers learned the feel of dirt in their faces as they pressed against the ground while Heinkels and Junkers wheeled and dropped their loads of bombs, the world erupting into smoke and noise and flying dirt, and then they waited the long minutes as the aircraft swung slowly around and dived toward earth with machine guns blazing. Because enemy airplanes had a nasty habit of appearing just when food was being brought up to the lines, there were often empty stomachs among the Americans. But they were learning to be soldiers, were becoming accustomed to the noises of the battlefield, were finding out that aircraft attacks caused few casualties. Soon Kalleborn could scoff at rebel air superiority, writing, "Their planes never did any more than scare the livin' daylights out of us. . . ." When the Lincolns changed positions on February 21, only two men had been killed and a handful wounded.[22]

The new trenches were on different slopes, but not far from the old ones, and the view of olive groves and hills was much the same. As they settled down the first night, Captain Merriman was called to brigade headquarters. During his absence, the wayward Captain Harris suddenly reappeared and startled everyone with the announcement that he had been sent to reorganize the battalion and take command. The other officers were dubious, but there were no phone connections to headquarters to check on his story, and with Merriman gone, Harris was the ranking officer. He issued orders for the battalion to move, took charge of one company himself, and led the Lincolns out to stumble through the dark hills. Machine guns blasted at them. Harris led the battalion forward, then began to speak wildly to the men nearest him, saying he was going to lead an attack on enemy positions. As the other officers began to realize he must be drunk, delirious, or insane, Merriman, who had returned to find his battalion gone, caught up with the Lincolns, took charge, and had the raving Harris removed quietly in an ambulance. He was never heard of again by the men of the battalion. Strangely, only one man had been wounded on what they ever afterward referred to as the "Moonlight Walk."[23]

Crouched in their new positions on the Jarama front, the men of the Lincoln Battalion slowly learned one of the truths of the common foot soldier. Though they were shifted from one set of trenches to another, though they suffered from bombardments and aerial attacks, though their food often tasted of mud and there was never hot water to shave or wash in, they had not the slightest idea of how the war was progressing or even of what role they were playing in the Jarama campaign. In fact, they had only the vaguest notions of the importance of the struggle for the Valencia road. While they waited and wondered about the war, the tide of the Jarama battle turned a few miles to the north of the hills they held, when tank-led Republican forces counterattacked near Arganda on February 17 and pushed the enemy back until the Valencia road was once again safely in Loyalist hands. Essentially the battle of Jarama was over, its outcome a stalemate, and all along the front both armies began to entrench themselves solidly. But General Gal, commander of the division to which the XVth Brigade was attached, was not satisfied with the positions of his troops. He was determined to capture the high ridges that the rebels held and, if possible, push them back across the Jarama River. What Gal did not know was that the heights he faced were the most heavily reinforced of all the points on the Jarama front. On the nineteenth he sent his men swarming up Pingarrón, and for a brief moment they overran the summit, only to be pushed off it by determined Moroccans. Undaunted, the general planned another assault, and this time he picked the untested Lincolns to take part in the attack.[24]

The Americans moved again on February 23, the 400 men advancing cautiously in sections down from the scrubby hills, across a dirt road, and up into new trenches. It was a quiet afternoon at Jarama as the Lincolns settled into their new positions. Word came down the line almost immediately that they were to ready themselves for an attack, and before the men had time to begin worrying, the signal to go was given. At three o'clock on that gray afternoon the Lincoln Battalion scrambled from its trenches and charged down a long slope dotted with olive trees. On hills to the left the Dimitrovs were advancing, while on the right flank a Spanish battalion moved forward. As they went through the trees, with the Cuban and Irish sections on the left of the battalion, enemy fire was light, yet Lieutenant Rudolfo de Armas was struck and killed almost immediately. Now the enemy turned his full fire against them, the battlefield rocked with noise, and men began to drop to the ground, some hit, some to take cover behind a mound of earth, an olive tree, or a clump of withered grapevines. They came out of the trees, looked up toward the enemy ridge still a few hundred yards away, and began scattering across an open field. Under raking machine-gun bursts they tried to advance, then dived for cover, digging with bare hands in the earth to throw up protective piles of dirt. A tank supporting the advance was hit by a shell and it burst into flames, glowing in the darkening after-noon, as one soldier put it, "like a huge bonfire."

Paul Burns, a Boston labor newspaper reporter, moved out of the olive grove and found himself unable to advance through the barrage. He knelt behind a tree on the slope. To his right, he could see men digging in, and below him in a hollow was Captain John Scott, his company com-mander. Charley Donnelly of the Irish section joined him behind the tree, and they both worked their bolt-action rifles until the barrels began to burn their hands. Then Burns saw Captain Scott rise to wave his company forward and immediately fall beneath a hail of bullets. Some men went over to drag his body away, but Burns, Donnelly, and most of the others left their shelter and began to charge up the long hill toward the rebel ridge. They dashed forward until their own machine guns stopped hammering because they were jammed, and suddenly the Lincolns were pinned to earth, unable to advance farther, with dusk already dropping on the land. For a while after darkness the firing continued, and men near the still-burning tank moved away for fear of being seen by enemy gunners. Slowly the noises of battle subsided, and the troops were surprised to find themselves being called back to their

43

starting positions. As they returned, one stumbled over a soft form in the darkness and found it was a pale young soldier who had cowered in the trench beneath his blanket all day long. Some of the soldiers were lost in the darkness and huddled in the fields until morning, not knowing their comrades had pulled back. Others blundered about the hills and managed to find the trenches sometime during the night. One was shot down by the enemy as he tried to sprint back to the lines the next day. While stragglers continued to return, the men in the trenches were told by the officers that their advance had been fine, but the attack had bogged down because supporting battalions had not moved up, making their assault impossible for lack of flank support. In truth, their attack had kept a large number of rebel troops busy for the afternoon, while a little to the south and west other Republicans had stormed to the top of Pingarrón, only to be again swept off it again by counterattacking rebels.[25]

The next day, February 24, the battalion moved to another new position on the endless Jarama hills. Battalion strength was down, for 20 men had been killed the day before and 40 wounded evacuated to the hospitals. Then, on the twenty-sixth, some 70 fresh volunteers appeared to fill out the ranks. The new men had had no military training at all. Half of them, like seventeen-year-old Robert Kirby, who had lied about his age to get to Spain, were still wearing the civilian clothes in which they had crossed the border only three days before. They had been rushed directly from Albacete to Jarama with orders that they be given training behind the lines. Rifles, helmets, canteens, packs, and blankets were found for them, and the week-old veterans of war tried to fill them in on the fundamentals of being soldiers. Kirby, who had done a lot of street fighting on Manhattan's Lower East Side, had never handled a weapon before. Now, in one confusing day, he was supposed to learn how to take a rifle apart, how to load and sight and fire it, at the same time that he tried to remember all sorts of other strange, new facts about throwing hand grenades, infiltrating in short dashes, watching for section leaders' signals, taking cover properly, and learning how to protect himself from various kinds of enemy fire.[26]

The basic training of the newcomers was over almost before it began, for General Gal was still determined to push the rebels back. Evidently, he could not stand having the enemy in higher positions than his own, and in spite of the heavy casualties in the attacks of February 19 and 23, he called for another assault on Pingarrón Hill. The enemy was well dug in on its rocky heights and had covered its approaches with three lines of machine-gun emplacements. The last 500 yards to the summit of Pingarrón ran uphill at a 30-degree angle and the terrain was completely open, with not so much as a tree or a fold of earth for cover, making it a suicidal point to attack. But the general was a stubborn man, and since he considered the Lincolns his freshest troops, he picked them to lead the assault. Battalion and company officers were told about the attack in the early hours of February 27. They were promised a heavy artillery barrage for cover, the support of tanks, and at least 20 aircraft to bomb and strafe rebel trenches and pave the way for the infantry. The advance was to begin in mid-morning when a Spanish battalion moved up on the right flank of the Lincolns.[27]

The twenty-seventh dawned wet and cloudy on the Jarama front. Crouched in their trenches, the men of the Lincoln Battalion waited for the big guns to shatter the false calm of morning. They were tense and nervous, their mouths dry. Breakfast had consisted of canned sardines and milk, and Neil Wesson of Detroit attributed the strange feeling in his stomach to that unusual combination of foods. When the artillery began, it was not the massed roar the Americans had expected, and as battalion officers looked through field glasses, they could see the few shell bursts were wide of Pingarrón. As the day brightened and sun broke through the clouds, no friendly aircraft filled the morning sky, no tanks rumbled up to lead the assault. Over the folds of earth Captain Merriman could see the

Spanish battalion leave its trenches, advance a short distance, and then pull quickly back as many men fell beneath enemy fire. Merriman was nervous. He knew that without the cover of artillery and the support of the Spanish battalion on his flank it would be suicidal to ask his men to leave their positions. Transmission lines had just that morning been completed, and Merriman picked up the phone to headquarters. He asked the whereabouts of the tanks and aircraft and received an order to attack without them. He tried to explain that unless the Spanish moved too, this was impossible, and was told the Americans should go forward alone as an example to the Spanish. Excited and unnerved, he began to shout into the phone that if the Americans advanced without support, it would be a massacre. But the order came back to take the enemy position "at all costs."

It was close to noon when Merriman ordered the Lincolns to advance. The soldiers hopped from the trenches a few at a time and darted forward like scared rabbits. The sun was hot now and the enemy machine guns swung toward them and poured a rain of fire down from the hilltops. Men were already hurtling across the fields when bullets began to spray the trenches and many in the second wave were hit climbing the parapets and fell back on those who had not yet left. Captain Merriman, angry and upset over the senseless order to advance, watched his men go toward what seemed to be certain death or injury. Then he leaned forward and waved his arm above the parapet in a signal for another group to move out. He was knocked back into the trench as a bullet drilled through his left shoulder. Just a few feet in front of the trenches his adjutant, Douglas Seacord, already lay dead.[28]

Robert Kirby crouched in the trenches waiting the signal to advance, his limbs trembling. The noise of the battlefield was so deafening he could not hear the shouts of the men around him. Suddenly someone was pushing him up, and then he found himself blindly running forward, stumbling over grapevines. He crashed to earth, picked himself up, ran a few steps, and realized that people were shooting at him and dived for cover behind an olive tree. Around him soldiers were advancing in little rushes and Kirby began to do the same. After several dashes forward he noticed men firing their rifles, and only then did he consciously remember that he was carrying a weapon. Momentarily safe behind a small ridge, Kirby pointed his rifle in the general direction of the enemy lines and began to fire. After a couple of shots, the weapon stopped functioning. It was jammed and Kirby had no idea how to get it working again. All across the Jarama hills, inexperienced American soldiers were breaking down in tears of frustration as their old rifles jammed and would not come unstuck.[29]

Jack Kalleborn led his section from the trenches and began "running like hell" into a storm of enemy fire. A hundred yards out, someone seemed to kick him in the leg and he crashed to the ground. He jumped to his feet and flopped to earth again, realized he had been hit, and dragged himself behind a tree for safety. It was a clean wound and he lay there waiting for the first aid men, but none came. To make the time pass, he dragged himself into position and began to fire at some clumps of bushes that concealed rebel machine guns. His right arm suddenly seared with pain as a bullet grazed across it and then he could use his rifle no more. He flattened himself against the ground and lay quietly, listening to the beating of his heart, waiting for the afternoon to pass.

Elsewhere on the rolling hills of the battlefield, in the dips of earth and through groves of trees, the men of the Lincoln Battalion were slowly and painfully moving upon Pingarrón. They were going forward into a curtain of steel as the blue sky of Spain sang with death. As they went, hidden machine guns high on the right opened up with a deadly crossfire. Still they blundered on, the enemy's guns piling up a heavy toll as man after man slumped to earth, some dead before they hit the ground, some almost sliced in two by the intense fire. Those with bodies shredded by machine-gun bullets writhed on the ground and screamed for the first aid men who could not reach them through the barrage. Those who were still untouched deafened their ears to their comrades' cries as they pressed forward, advancing in little rushes from mound to olive tree to fold of earth, moving toward the enemy with an audacity later called "insane." The bravest and luckiest of them even reached the naked approaches to the crest of Pingarrón.

As the afternoon went on, the volume of enemy fire never slackened. The shadows of the olive trees lengthened over the hillsides and then the Lincolns were no longer moving forward. Or at all. They had lost the unequal contest of flesh against steel. With the slow dusk and the welcome darkness of evening, the Americans began to straggle back to the trenches, blundering across the battle-scarred no-man's-land, some of the wounded like Jack Kalleborn crawling hundreds of yards on their bellies to safety. A few of the Lincolns were still out in the fields, wandering dazedly through the night, and one of the wounded was found still alive three days later lying among the corpses on the battlefield. When the healthy Americans returned to their own lines, they left 300 comrades dead and wounded on the slope toward Pingarrón.[30]

That the attack had been a useless one, that, in Ernest Hemingway's words, General Gal's plans had been "idiotic," that one day a historian would call the general's orders "an act of monumental stupidity," would have mattered little to the shocked survivors of the debacle, lying weary and shattered in their trenches at the end of that long day.[31] For that matter, had the attack been a success, as later official publications claimed it to be, had it really been the final blow that stopped the rebel Jarama offensive, it would have mattered just as little.[32] After February 27, praise came to the Americans from all quarters, and even the rebel general wrote that he had never seen government forces assault more bravely.[33] But this meant nothing. For the men of the Lincoln Battalion were ill with a sickness that only those who had been through such a bloodbath could really know, one composed of horror and shock and fear, the loss of so many friends, and the terrible realization that they were frail and mortal and alone.

The Americans in Spain had undergone their baptism of fire, and that night, among the few who were not injured or too tired to walk, there were a number of desertions. Bob Kirby, who had gone through the day without a scratch, and two friends with whom he had arrived in Spain one week before, decided that this sort of war was totally ridiculous, not at all the sort of thing they had come to Spain for. At least they had expected to have a chance to hit back at the enemy, but this day's battle had made it seem as if the war in Spain was no more than a confused, hopeless slaughter. Deciding they wanted none of it, Kirby and his friends stumbled off through the hills in the darkness with no real destination, no objective other than the overwhelming desire to get away. They wandered through the night, and in the light of the next day, the horror of combat already fading and the fear of falling into enemy hands growing, they began to see things differently. When they found the Lincolns again, battalion officials looked the other way, asked no questions, and the three were quietly accepted back into the depleted ranks.[34]

With the end of the battle of Jarama, the rainy season began. The sky was black with clouds almost every day and the rain filled the trenches with seas of mud. The men awoke in the morning to find themselves soaked, and they spent their days bailing out their positions, eating cold meals, grumbling about the lack of cigarettes, and slowly recovering from the trauma they had undergone. As the cold rain of Castile fell and the winter winds sliced down from the Guadarrama Mountains, the men of the Lincoln Battalion hunched inside their coats and awaited the coming of spring.[35]

The men who fought and died in the Jarama hills in February 1937 were the vanguard of some 3,000 Americans who would cross the Atlantic to join the International Brigades. To a later age, such volunteering for duty in a foreign war may appear inexplicable. But to the men who went to Spain the journey was a most natural one to make, and to a significant number of observers the action of the volunteers seemed quite commendable. Indeed, publications as politically diverse as the *Nation, Life,* and *New Masses* could agree that the men of the Lincoln Battalion were idealistically motivated. Even those who did not wholly approve of the volunteers might say, as did one morning paper, that after all they did go to Spain to fight for ideals that "you . . . must admire and respect."[1]

To understand how volunteering for a foreign war can emerge from ideals homegrown in America, one must look closely at the 1930's, an age of ferment and upheaval for the United States and the Western world. Moreover, one must look at the radicalism that flourished in America in response to the conditions of that era, radicalism that would allow conservative critics to tag the thirties the "Red Decade." The title is a misnomer. Both friends and enemies of radicalism have tended to overexaggerate its importance, and there is no doubt that the overwhelming majority of

Americans never wavered from middle-class beliefs during the depths of the Depression—certainly support for radical movements was always miniscule compared to support for the New Deal. Yet there is little doubt that class politics were more important during this decade than they usually are in the United States, and among certain groups a radical subculture flourished. Some of the radicalism was of an undifferentiated sort, neither of the left nor right, but there was enough with a Marxist tinge to allow the "Red" label to stick. It is this kind of radicalism that helps to explain the presence of Americans in Spain, but it would be most misleading to wrench it out of the context of upheaval all over the American scene: the impulse that made some men Marxists grew out of American conditions, and the problems that concerned these American radicals were far from phantoms imported from abroad.

To understand American radicalism of the thirties, one must start with the Depression, as severe a collective trauma as the United States has ever undergone. In the months after the stock market crash of November 1929, social unrest in the country was at a minimum. Depressions were after all nothing new in the United States, and naturally nobody could foresee the eventual depths of misery that this one would reach. So when the economy began to run down like a tired clock, there was little radical protest from the American people. Instead, men continued vainly to look for work, while some ended on street corners, selling the inevitable apples, and others, unable to face the families they could not support, simply wandered away from home. Hundreds of thousands rode the rails aimlessly from one section of the country to another, while many people—dispossessed because they could not meet rent or mortgage payments—went to live in the packing crate and tar-paper clusters known as Hoovervilles that blossomed on the outskirts of every town. For a while, millions existed on relief payments, but public welfare agencies, dependent upon shrinking tax revenues, had to cut rolls and then benefits until large families lucky enough still to be eligible were living on no more than $2 a week.

As the winter of 1932–33 approached, 100 major cities had no money at all left for welfare, and the most sanguine of Americans had difficulty in believing the repeated bland assurances from the White House, the empty promises that prosperity was on its way. Most Americans remained passive, but for many the image of what had been called the American Dream had become terribly "flawed and cracked."[2]

Yet the docile acceptance of the Depression by the American people should not be overemphasized. As the crisis ground through its third year, as unemployment figures spiraled, and as feelings of hunger became commonplace for significant numbers of people, mutterings of discontent became audible and in some areas translated themselves into action. Spontaneous and ill-organized, the protests were reactions to the desperate conditions in which men all over the country found themselves. In West Virginia, 1,500 hungry miners marched unsuccessfully on the state capital in the summer of 1931 to demand food from the governor, while in several Oklahoma towns, mobs stormed into grocery stores to steal food. Farmers in half a dozen Midwest states armed themselves with pitchforks to prevent sheriffs from carrying out foreclosures, and demonstrations of unemployed turned into riots in Detroit and Cleveland, Toledo, Seattle, and New York.[3] Protest became national in the summer of 1932, when the 12,000 veterans of the Bonus Expeditionary Force marched on Washington, only to be denied the payment of their bonus by Congress and to be dispersed by the tanks and bayonets of General Douglas MacArthur's troops.

Accompanying these actions were voices articulating discontent. Some were those of unimportant people, the Pennsylvania miner's wife telling a reporter, "I'm a Bolshevist, and so's my man and my four kids. What of it? You'd be a Bolshevist, too, if you didn't have enough to eat." Or the leader of the West Virginia hunger marchers saying to his followers in public, "All that stands between you hungry people and food are a few plate glass windows; no state has a right to call you criminal if you take what you must have to live." More important people sounded much the same. Governor Theodore Bilbo of Mississippi could say, "Folks are restless, Communism is gaining a foothold. . . . In fact, I'm getting a little pink myself," while Senator Reed of Pennsylvania stated: "I say that if this country ever needed a Mussolini, it needs one now." Significant was the testimony of A. N. Young, president of the Farmers Union of Wisconsin, to a Senate committee: "The farmer is a naturally conservative individual, but you cannot find a conservative farmer today. . . . I am as conservative as any man could be, but any economic system that has it in its power to set me and my wife in the street, at my age—what can I see but red?"[4]

Perhaps one should not make too much of these manifestations of discontent, for during these years radical political parties were able to make little headway with the American people. The most radical of them, the Communists, after furious activity did manage to double their membership between 1930 and 1932, but only to a meager total of about 15,000.[5] Obviously, then, the riots and farm strikes, marches and demonstrations, and the voices of despair were not fully representative of the feelings of Americans. But at least they must be taken as symptomatic of a growing alienation from America's traditional values. If the United States was not ready for a revolutionary political movement in its pre-New Deal Depression years, there can be little doubt that certain segments of society were looking forward to substantial political, social, and economic change.

For many people this change came with the New Deal. Pragmatic and eclectic, tacitly promising all things to all men, this movement may never have solved the economic problems of the Depression, but in its sense of purpose and thrust, above all because of President Roosevelt's own buoyant optimism, it quickly dispelled the air of apathy, despair, and foreboding that hung over the United States in the winter of 1932–33. Suddenly America was filled with a climate of hope, and a revolutionary spirit was abroad in the land. Indeed, during the New Deal era social turbulence was to characterize the United States, and much of it would be channeled into movements outside the normal two-party system.

The pattern for turmoil was set by labor, by workers who had long been at the bottom of America's economic totem pole. Encouraged by Section 7a of the National Industrial Recovery Act, which guaranteed labor's right to collective bargaining, union organizers in 1933 began to undertake successful membership drives by claiming, "The President wants you to join a union." Quickly, however, it became apparent that many employers felt the organization of labor would be disastrous for their interests. Through hastily formed company unions, industry attempted to blunt labor's new drive. When this tactic failed, certain "fundamentalist employers" adamantly refused to recognize unions, and instead hired police and spies and bought weapons, "prepared to fight it out, if necessary, on the barricades." [6]

Frustrated when unions were not recognized, workers called strikes. On the picket lines, goaded by scabs and strikebreakers, union men exploded into violence. In 1934, clashes on the labor front broke out all over the map. In Milwaukee, streetcar workers tore down electric trolley poles in their battle for recognition, while Philadelphia drivers set fire to 100 of their taxicabs. In Toledo, Ohio, pickets at the Electric Auto-Lite Company and the Edison Company battled police and National Guardsmen until two were dead and hundreds wounded. Striking textile workers in September 1934 fought with troopers and Guardsmen from Georgia to Rhode Island, and six union organizers were shot down by deputies in South Carolina. The general strike, that revolutionary instrument of class war, hit Terre Haute and San Francisco. In May, another such strike in Minneapolis found police firing into a crowd of workers, wounding 67 and killing 2.

Despite the violence, or maybe because of it, labor won only a few victories in 1934. In San Francisco the longshoremen were recognized, in Minneapolis the teamsters smashed that city's tradition of the open shop, and in

Toledo electric workers brought employers to the bargaining table under federal mediation. But in many basic industries, steel and auto, rubber and textiles, unions recorded failure. This was due to management's stubborn defense, the fact that local and state governments sided with industry, and also to labor's own weaknesses, the timidity of the leadership of the American Federation of Labor, and its distaste for organizing unskilled workers.[7] Organization of many industries had to wait until the AFL schism and the rise of the CIO, dedicated to furthering the interests of industrial labor. In 1936–37, that militant organization would begin with sitdown strikes and a new round of violence would commence.

Turbulence in the United States in the New Deal era may have been most persistent in the area of labor, but it touched far more than that. For a few years, large segments of society seemed to be in upheaval. Quiet university campuses became storm centers as students quarreled with administrators, demonstrated against war, or went on strike because students or professors with radical views were dismissed. The most traditionally individualistic of men—artists—organized leagues and demanded a voice in which of them would be selected to work on WPA projects. Poets crowded together in stuffy halls at writers' congresses to discuss proletarian literature and wrote odes to political leaders rather than nightingales.

Naturally enough, the unrest in American life spilled over into the realm of politics, and though the Democrats won overwhelming victories at the polls, radical movements began to blossom like hothouse flowers. Suddenly it seemed as if everyone had a plan for reforming America. In June 1934, the Los Angeles Utopian Society filled the Hollywood Bowl for a program of tableaux portraying the coming social order in which the profit motive would vanish and "production for use" would reign. From the West, appealing to breakfast table patriotism, the "Ham 'n' Eggs" movement of militant older Americans demanded early retirement and "thirty dollars every Thursday." Then came kindly Dr. Townsend of Long Beach, calling on the state of California—and then the nation—to print special pension money for oldsters. Soon spreading across the country, the Townsend Movement had formed 1,200 local clubs by 1934. The next year it claimed control of two governors, and the legislature of seven Western states, while the only candidate supporting the Townsend Plan in Michigan won election to Congress as a Republican.[8]

More politically serious were the activities of the Detroit Catholic priest, Father Coughlin, whose millions of radio listeners nodded approval to his calls for social justice and sent in their money to support its pursuit. By 1934, he was receiving more mail than anyone in America, in spite of his increasingly open anti-Semitism and his attacks on the New Deal that would end with Coughlin labeling Roosevelt a "Communist." Dead serious too was Huey Long, virtual dictator of Louisiana, whose plans to make every man a king and share the wealth won him not only the support of his home state, but of a national following large enough to worry President Roosevelt as the 1936 elections approached.

On the left wing was Upton Sinclair's End Poverty in California (EPIC), calling on the state to open the idle factories and lands to the jobless to produce goods and food for their own needs. This movement won the novelist the Democratic nomination for governor in an open primary, and only a violent smear campaign and the endorsement of the Townsend Plan by his Republican opponent kept Sinclair from going to Sacramento. More successful was Floyd Olson, onetime Seattle longshoreman and member of the Anarchist Industrial Workers of the World, who was elected governor of Minnesota on a Farmer-Labor ticket. Olson delighted in styling himself a "radical" rather than a "liberal," and even after calling for public ownership of industries he was reelected to serve a second term. In neighboring Wisconsin, the sons of Bob La Follette put together a Progressive Party that captured the state. Here newly elected Governor Phil La Follette could claim, "We are not liberals! Liberalism is nothing but a sort of milk-and-water tolerance. . . . I believe in a fundamental and basic change," while Progressive Congressman Tom Amlie flatly stated, "Whether capitalism could be kept going for another period of years or not, it is not worth saving."[9]

Obviously the people who joined the Townsend clubs and sent part of their meager savings to Coughlin, and those who acclaimed and voted for Long, Olson, Sinclair, Amlie, and others with similar views, were among vast numbers who did not think that the New Deal had gone far enough toward solving America's problems. Although reform legislation had been passed, many Americans were going back to work, government was smiling on the organization of labor, and farm income was improving, not everyone agreed that the crisis was over. Though national income was rising, in 1934 it was only slightly more than half that of 1929, and while unemployment was down by 2 million jobs, more than 10 million people—one fifth of the labor force—were still looking for work. Obviously the problems of joblessness and hunger and insecurity had not ended for all. There were still hoboes riding the rails, millions whose stomachs were never quite full, men sleeping on park benches, children without milk, and young men whose college degrees would not buy them a loaf of bread. Long after the legislative achievements of Roosevelt's Hundred Days, long after the Second New Deal and the enactment of Social Security, the Depression lingered on for many Americans. As late as 1935, the young poet Edwin Rolfe, who was later to fight for the government of Spain, could write of the Depression winter:

> *This is the sixth winter;*
> *this is the season of death*
> *when lungs contract and the breath of homeless men*
> *freezes on restaurant window panes . . . .*[10]

Throughout the decade such "homeless men" would remain a constant of the American scene, as the New Deal never did fully solve the problems of unemployment. In this nagging dichotomy between promise and reality one can find a prime source of the era's continuing social turmoil; here, too, is one source of the alienation from capitalism that affected certain groups for much of the decade.

The economic catastrophe of the Great Depression, the sharp decline in living standards, the myriad bank and business failures, the hope engendered by the New Deal, the inability of FDR's administrations to solve the problems of full production and employment, the organization of labor, the pension plan movements and Utopian schemes, and the rise of new charismatic leaders are all part of the climate in which a Marxist-oriented radicalism was to flourish in the second half of the 1930's. But American conditions alone cannot explain the growth of this left-wing subculture. The kind of radicalism that sent men off to fight in Spain can be understood only by also looking at Europe, for the rise of new leaders and ideologies there helped to crystallize and shape the American left fully as much as did the Depression itself.

Europe of the thirties, indeed of the whole interwar period, seems in retrospect a sick and decaying society, a civilization vainly pursuing memories of a lost time of peace. The few faint hopes of government by the people that had issued from Versailles were already dimming in the twenties. Then the shock waves that spread from the American stock market crash collapsed the fragile prosperity supporting a civilization. Perhaps liberalism, the faith of the nineteenth century, had really died in the trenches of the world war; perhaps it lived on until November 1929. Certainly, whenever the *coup de grâce* came, it had been administered by 1930. For the sounds of that fourth decade of the century are not those of reasonable voices debating in parliament, but rather the strident tones of men with glib answers, posturing on balconies.

The pattern had been set by Italy. One of the Allies and ostensible victors in the world war, this nation in the early twenties turned from the parliament which had governed her since independence and delivered herself into the hands of Benito Mussolini, who scorned democracy, snuffed out opposition, and organized a totalitarian state according to the tenets of fascism, his own nonphilosophy of action. Square-jawed and belligerent, Il Duce glorified combat and set to work to build up Italy's military strength. Though for a long time his armies did not march, Mussolini seemed to have reactivated his country through his programs and style, through chauvinism, militarism, and bluster. Soon he had imitators. One by one the fragile buffer states of Eastern Europe began to give up the parliamentary democracy that had never taken deep root in them. They, too, turned to strong men and the military for leadership and protection. Hungary, Poland, Lithuania, and Bulgaria went first. With the onset of the Depression, Greece, Yugoslavia, and Rumania marched down the same road to dictatorship and militarism. In Austria, where left-wing workers were an entrenched, strong minority, a rightist government rolled up field guns to blast down their comfortable cooperative apartments on the outskirts of Vienna, to bury the Social Democratic Party, and allow the 4'11" Engelbert Dollfuss to tower over the nation and rule by decree.

The smug, older democracies of the West were not untouched by this upsurge of the right. In France, reactionary parties proliferated and splintered in typical Gallic tradition. In February 1934, when members of various right-wing groups marched to the Place de la Concorde and battled wildly with police all night long, a government was forced to resign. In traditionally peaceful Belgium there were the Rexists, and in Holland and Sweden, Norway, and England, there were small but militant groups of pro-fascists, each with its own military garb, its Roman salute, its plans for military ventures, its own would-be dictator. For a long time, democrats of the West had been able to consider fascism a middle European phenomenon. But by the mid-thirties, when street clashes were disrupting the streets of London, Paris, and Brussels, they were beginning to worry about how long their own parliaments could continue to function smoothly in an atmosphere of terror and violence.

Even with the rise of the right in Europe, such doubts

might not have been entertained had not Germany delivered herself into the hands of Adolf Hitler in 1933. Sometimes thought a comic figure before his accession to power, Hitler quickly showed himself to be a leader one could not afford to laugh at. Reports out of Germany in the mid-decade showed a brutal regime of pogroms, purges, book burnings, and concentration camps that led sensitive Westerners to view the Third Reich with loathing as a kind of "medieval hell." Soon the dark shadow of this ex-postcard painter brooded over Europe, and even as far away as the United States, in Paul Jacobs's words, "Hitler was everywhere and forced us to talk continually about politics."[11] Meanwhile many Americans, provoked and enraged by events in Germany, flocked to groups that opposed the rise of fascism and Nazism throughout the world. That such groups were backed by Communists mattered not at all. For many men it was a time for choosing sides: Nazism was the touchstone, and few would inquire into the credentials of those who wished to oppose the spread of barbarism.

Taken together, the continuing effects of the Depression in the United States and the rise of fascism and Nazism in Europe help to explain left-wing radicalism in the United States at the time of the Spanish Civil War's outbreak. Of course, such radicalism flourished on different levels, from the book-lined studies of college professors to the grimy forecastles of itinerant coal freighters. Though the denizens of each had been raised in different milieus and had widely divergent experiences of the Depression, they would come to share much in their attitudes toward the world: for each, Marxism—more likely watered down than pure—would explain both the trials of capitalism and the rise of fascism, and political parties based on Marxist theories would seem to hold the key to the future.

The loss of faith in capitalism is understandable. In 1929 the economic system seemed to have collapsed, and as the wounds of the Depression were too deep to be healed by the first remedies of the New Deal, the questioning of

American society it called forth was not ended when the Democrats passed reform legislation. Such ideals as the sanctity of free enterprise and the virtues of rugged individualism were deeply questioned and criticism of the social and political order was widespread. Indeed, there was more than criticism, for the troubles of the decade brought forth Cassandras galore. As Murray Kempton has pointed out, during the thirties there came to be numbers of Americans "of significant character and talent who believed that our society was not merely doomed, but undeserving of survival, and to whom every one of its institutions seemed not just unworthy of preservation but crying out to be exterminated." [12]

For many American intellectuals—writers, artists, professors, journalists, and critics for highbrow publications— the Crash and Depression came as a vindication of their longstanding quarrel with American life. In the twenties, intellectuals had been alienated from the world of George F. Babbitt. Disgusted with a business civilization, they fled to Greenwich Village, or its colonies in Paris, Antibes, or Pamplona. From these havens they had heaped scorn upon America, and now its economic troubles seemed to justify their position. In the words of Edmund Wilson, "One couldn't help being exhilarated at the sudden unexpected collapse of that stupid gigantic fraud." [13] Soon after the Crash, the intellectual exiles came home and joined those who had never left in listening to the voices of Depression America and considering solutions to the problems the country faced.

When the New Deal began, a large number of intellectuals went to Washington, where they helped to design its programs and administer its agencies. But many felt that patching up the old social order was no real solution, and the first two years of Roosevelt's administrations confirmed their doubts about the efficacy of reform. Central, national planning of the economy seemed a necessity to those who were repelled by the slapdash pragmatism of the New Deal. John Dewey—the leading living pragmatist—repudiated FDR's so-called experimental approach, arguing that the "experimental method is not just messing around nor doing a little of this and a little of that in the hope that things will improve. Just as in the physical sciences, it implies a coherent body of ideas, a theory, that gives direction to effort." In the New Deal, Dewey could find no coherent theory, and so he concluded that ultimately it had to fail. Committed to social planning, Dewey maintained, "no . . . compromise with a decaying system is possible." Others agreed that old-style liberal solutions would not work, and for them the future looked bleak. As one of the gloomiest of them, the theologian Reinhold Niebuhr, stated, "Next to the futility of liberalism we may set down the inevitability of fascism as a practical certainty in every Western nation."[14]

Paralysis over the inevitability of fascism was not a common state of mind, however, even for intellectuals. To those who could not accept the New Deal but still sought answers to the breakdown of capitalism at home and the rise of fascism abroad, it was Marxism that spoke in tones most loud and clear. Its critique of the inner contradictions of capitalism, the boom-and-bust cycle, and the final inexorable rise of fascism seemed borne out by recent history, and its leading propagandists, the Communists, with their iron laws of history, spoke with a self-assurance that proved contagious. James Wechsler, a writer who joined the Young Communist League for a brief period, was one of many who saw a vivid contrast between the "frustration and emptiness" that liberals expressed and the attitude of the Marxists, who "came breathing certitude and salvation."[15]

Certitude and salvation—this is what many intellectuals were looking for, and this is what they found in adopting Marxism, which had answers for every problem. Of those who flirted with this system of thought, many—like Niebuhr—soon found it irrelevant to the American situation. But others, like Malcolm Cowley, were exhilarated that Marxism could offer "a sense of comradeship and participation in a historical process vastly bigger than the individual." For Marxists, there was an alternative to both the

New Deal and possible fascism in the United States. There was, in the words of one group of intellectuals, the possibility of "a truly scientific economy under a genuine workers' democracy. . . ." [16]

Marxism in the thirties was of course more than an idle theory. Halfway around the globe in the Soviet Union it was getting a trial run, and from America it looked as if things in Russia were going very well indeed. Intellectuals had been journeying there since the twenties, when men like John Dewey had been impressed by the great experiment the Russians were undertaking. After depression struck the United States, it was the Soviet's smooth-working Five-Year Plan that convinced American thinkers of a need for similar social and economic planning at home. Excusing the negative aspects of Russia—the lack of civil liberties, the terrorism of the regime—on the grounds of tradition and revolutionary necessity, even nonideological observers were impressed by the full employment and purposeful productivity of the Soviets. And many were convinced that if Marxism could make Russia function so well, it could do the same for the United States. [17]

One thing more must be said about American intellectuals who became Marxists at this time: most of them in no way thought that doing so meant a total abandonment of traditional American values. As Arthur Koestler put it for Western intellectuals in general, Marxism seemed "the logical extension of the progressive humanistic trend . . . the continuation and fulfillment of the great Judeo-Christian tradition—a new fresh branch of the tree of Europe's progress through Renaissance and Reformation, through the French Revolution and the Liberalism of the nineteenth century, toward the Socialist millennium." [18] Intellectuals became Marxists because they cared for man and hoped to free him from the shackles of economic exploitation and deprivation that seemed to have bound him for too long.

If men who devoted their lives to ideas were impressed by the Marxist analysis in the mid-thirties, it is not surprising to find less intellectually sophisticated people following their lead. Just how the ideas diffused through America cannot be systematically documented. If few outside the intellectual world bothered tackling Marx himself, popularizers and interpreters like John Strachey and Harold Laski reached wide audiences, while Lincoln Steffens's autobiography convinced many that progress was only possible in a society like Russia. College students were affected by their teachers, as well as by the student movements under control of left-wing parties. Who influences clergymen other than divine powers cannot be said, but fully 28 per cent of more than 20,000 responding to a poll in 1934 found socialism "more consistent with the ideals and methods of Jesus" than capitalism. Of course, it is likely that most of the 5,879 clergymen who plumped for socialism did not consider themselves Marxists, but they must be counted fellow travelers to that ideology. Certainly, estrangement from capitalism was shown when the Methodist General Conference called the American system "unchristian, unethical and antisocial because it is largely based on the profit motive," or when the general council of the Congregational Christian Churches asked for abolition of "the profit-seeking order." [19]

Beyond clergymen and students, it becomes hard to trace how Marxism filtered to the American people, especially to members of the working class for whom reading books is an uncommon pastime. Certainly in a simplistic form it was carried by the proliferating left-wing publications, and to the expanding readership of older journals like the *Daily Worker* and the *New Masses*. Obviously, Marxism was part of the intellectual baggage of Communist organizers as they went through steel towns and oil fields, into auto plants and onto the docks to organize industrial unions. Yet it probably distorts the picture to search for the influence of Marxist intellectuals on the workingman. For the left-wing world view that some workers and their unions embraced seems to have been the product of fermentation in the ranks of labor, a kind of spontaneous growth in fields made fertile by the Depression, the surge of unions, and the backlash of employers committed to the open shop. More important, one hesitates to designate the workers' beliefs as "Marxism." Though their ideas were left-wing, and often couched in such Marxist terminology as "class struggle," they were too unsystematic and even extemporaneous to come under that label. Above all, few workers seem to have had any vision of a fully articulated socialist society; they used Marxist language because that was the political vocabulary of the thirties, but what interested them most was recognition of unions rather than the coming of socialism.

The beliefs of workers were not wholly different from those of many students, clergymen, white-collar workers, or even intellectuals. Men in all groups used Marxist concepts to protest conditions in the United States rather than to agitate for revolution. In the atmosphere of the mid-thirties there was arising a whole complex of left-wing feelings, ideals, and beliefs that came to pervade large segments of society. Wherever workers marched in picket lines, or students gathered to plan rallies against the Japanese invasion of Manchuria, or writers met to discuss the "collective novel," these ideas could be heard. Important was the thought that no man is an island, that the persecution of a man in Germany threatened people in New York, that the lynching of a Negro in Georgia was a call to arms in Seattle. The new left-wingers glorified "labor" and were against "capital," were for "the people" and against the business interests and politicians who supposedly misled them. They saw a new world coming, in which there could be an end to prejudice and strife and workingmen would have the full fruits of their labor. They looked for their heroes to a radical American past, to the violent Molly Maguires of the Pennsylvania coal fields, the labor leader Joe Hill who was shot by the "copper bosses" and died with the word "organize" on his lips, the anarchists Spies and Parsons put to death for the Haymarket bombing, and above all to Sacco and Vanzetti, the idealists supposedly murdered for their beliefs by the American system of law. Above all, the leftists' ideas were cataclysmic. They saw Armageddon fast approaching, with Hitler, Mussolini, and their cohorts personifying all the evil forces in the world. Years later, such ideas might be dismissed as naïve. Writer Murray Kempton could with an ill-concealed sneer dub them "the myth of the thirties," and point out that they were fostered by political parties of the American left.[20] But in the context of the times, large numbers of union men, college students, even writers making a good living, knew that such beliefs were no mere "myth," for they had a firm basis in the reality of the world and in men's fears and aspirations. A more sympathetic retrospective view would term these ideas "the conscience of the thirties," and would respect the sincerity and even idealism of those who shared that conscience.

Such a conscience was not at all a passive one. The men and women who shared it usually wished to see their beliefs used to change conditions in the world. Impelled to action, they joined labor unions, student groups, and artists' leagues, marched on picket lines, demonstrated before German consulates, boycotted stores selling Japanese merchandise. Many also joined Marxist-oriented political parties. Though there were several of these to choose from, Socialists, Trotskyists, Lovestoneites, and other tiny splinter groups—and though all of them grew during this decade—there can be little doubt that the American Communist Party benefitted most from the new interest in the left. Before one can understand the success of the Communist-sponsored movement of volunteers to Spain in 1937–38, one must look at the factors which made the CP the most popular of American Marxist parties by the middle of the decade.

Asked in 1932 to discuss the merits of the Communist and Socialist movements, John Dos Passos wrote, "Becoming a Socialist right now would have just the same effect on anybody as drinking a bottle of near-beer."[21] Here Dos Passos put his finger on a major weakness of the Socialist Party during the Depression decade; for many young radicals the old guard leadership of the Socialist Party seemed to have a sentimental rather than an activist interest in Marxism, seemed content to wait for change rather than to agitate for it. Clearly, such leadership was out of step with the times. When a Young Militant wing organized within the party, membership rose—reaching about 20,000—but the ensuing internal factional disputes paralyzed the party from within and disgusted many of its adherents. Then, when members of several left-wing splinter groups entered the party in 1935, fully 7,000 members resigned, leaving the Socialists more impotent than before.[22]

What was true of the Socialists was even more true of the dozens of Marxist groups that rose and splintered time and again during the decade. Trotskyists, Lovestoneites, Gitlowites, Fieldites, Zamites—all of them were hopelessly sectarian and seemed more interested in maintaining the purity of their doctrine than in accomplishing social change. Even within the tiny Trotskyist movement, one could distinguish the following groups: Ohlerites, Schachtmanites, Cannonites, and Marlenites, the last reaching a grand total of seven members.[23] Though all these groups could agree that Stalin had betrayed the Russian Revolution, the doctrinal differences between them were so marginal or esoteric that often members did not really know what they were. With such a situation, small wonder that people interested in social reforms looked elsewhere for parties to join.

While other groups were splintering and involving themselves in internal disputes, the Communist Party was growing steadily. Those who quarreled with its doctrines found they could not change the party from within, and so they departed to join other parties or form their own. Aside from the internal weaknesses of other radical parties, the CP enjoyed one great advantage in the competition for members: it was allied with the Soviet-led Comintern, and thus it was heir to all the feelings of goodwill that Americans generated toward the experiment in Marxism that was going on in Russia.

Russian successes were important, but the appeal of the Communists was based on more than that. Part of it was certainly the image of dedication and militance they projected. Probably this is what Sherwood Anderson was getting at when, asked the difference between a Socialist and Communist, he answered: "I guess the Communists mean it." [24] Members of the CP did seem wholeheartedly committed to the doctrines they espoused. Those involved in organizing unions, planning conferences, and setting up demonstrations against war and fascism found that CP members were willing to work more days, go with fewer hours of sleep, hand out larger numbers of leaflets, do with less food, march longer distances, and brave colder weather than the average radical activist. If it was such activity which allowed Communists to gain control of many movements in which they were a tiny minority, it was also such dedication which won them admirers among the uncommitted, and which reasonably enough led many to think that a movement that brought out such selflessness in men must have something to be said for it.[25] Even so, immense dedication cannot alone account for the party's growth. Such dedication always existed among Communists, and yet the party did not grow at an even rate during the Depression. Like other political groups, the American Communists have seen periods when the stands they took on issues were right in the mainstream of society's beliefs and desires: the late thirties was such a time, and because this was so, membership in the CP grew most rapidly between 1935 and 1939.[26]

Basic to understanding the appeal of the Communist Party is a knowledge of what the party seemed to be to the people at the time of joining. Studies of this have shown that most people did not join because of its long-range revolutionary goals, but because they were vitally interested in short-range goals for which Communists agitated on specific issues. Put another way, in the thirties people did not become Communists because they wished to build barricades in the streets or to storm Capitol Hill. Rather, they joined the party because it defended Negroes like the Scottsboro Boys or Angelo Herndon, because it organized the unemployed or industrial unions, because it objected to anti-Semitism both in the United States and Germany. This phenomenon could occur because CP journals that reached the public, such as the *Daily Worker*, rarely spoke in the language of Marxist-Leninism. Violent revolution, class struggle, the dictatorship of the proletariat—none of these reached the pages of the *Daily Worker*. The man who joined after exposure to that paper, or similar popular journals, had no more than "identified himself with a rather pallid champion of generalized virtue," and not with a revolutionary movement with plans to reshape the world. This is important because not more than 28 per cent of the Americans who joined the party had even been exposed to more esoteric, long-range goals, such as "dictatorship of the proletariat." And even of this small number, few had really registered or accepted such goals, for often they could not understand or were bored by basic Marxist writings. The goals of the party perceived by Americans joining were more often those of "general social improvement and bettering of conditions than as specifically socialist aims." Most typically, an American party member would say of his decision: "I didn't worry through the thick books on Marx. I joined the party when it moved a widow's evicted furniture back into her house. I thought it was right. That's why I joined." [27]

Since the public goals of the party were the ones that caused people to become members or support its activities, it is to those that one must look to find the increased attraction of the CP after 1935. Here the reasons are at once apparent, for while Communist doctrines were harsh and alien to American experience before 1935, they seemed well within the liberal tradition in the years to follow. From the Sixth World Congress of the Communist International in 1928 to the Seventh in 1935, Communist Parties of the world were in the so-called third period of revolutionary attainment, in which the contradictions of world capitalism were expected to deepen and its collapse was thought to be imminent. To hasten its downfall, Communist tactics took a turn to the left. Party programs in this period called for dual unions, refusal to collaborate with other left-wing groups, and open hostility to liberals, trade unionists, Socialists. Thus Social Democrats were termed "social fascists," and in Germany the CP not only refused to help others oppose the rising Nazis, but actually combined with Hitler's followers to destroy the Weimar Republic, hoping that communism would be its heir. In the United States, the CP set up the Trade Union Unity League as a rival of the AFL and agitated for Negro "self-determination." The epithet "fascist" dotted the pages of the *Daily Worker*, being applied to such groups as the AFL, the NAACP, and the Socialist Party, while such diverse people as Fiorello La Guardia, Norman Thomas, and Dave Dubinsky of the ILGWU were similarly denounced. More important, in terms of its isolation from the mass of Americans, the CP regarded the New Deal as "a government serving the interests of finance capital and moving toward the fascist suppression of workers' movements." To a public wanting relief from the Depression, the NRA did not seem like a "slave program" nor the Wagner Act like an "anti-strike" measure. That the Communists could label them as such is an indication of their alienation from the masses they hoped to influence.[28]

While the American Communist Party remained militant through the early thirties, it remained fairly well estranged from even the most liberal segments of society. The change came in the summer of 1935, at the Comintern's Seventh World Congress, when Georgi Dimitrov announced the beginning of the fourth period by calling on Communists to enter a worldwide "united front" against the menace of fascism, "the open terrorist dictatorship of the most reactionary, chauvinistic and most imperialist elements of finance capital."[29] Obviously the tactics of the third period had failed, resulting in isolation both for native Communist parties and for the Soviet Union. Nazi Germany was becoming more formidable and frightening every day, and now the party was ready to admit that Adolf Hitler might be more of a threat to the workers of the world than Norman Thomas. To counter this threat, a Popular Front of Communists, Socialists, liberals, and all other "progressive elements" was called for, while the Soviet Union joined the League of Nations and signed a mutual defense treaty with France.

Within the United States, the new line meant that the CP could abolish its own unions in the TUUL, while its organizers happily poured into the newly formed CIO. It meant not only that the Communists could cozy up to the Socialist Party, proposing joint action on various issues, but that the CP would also admit to having unfairly slandered the Socialists in the past. The fourth-period policy even allowed American CP leader Earl Browder to try to take advantage of the radicalization of politics in America by saying nice things about such movements as Upton Sinclair's EPIC or the Townsendites. Most important for its integration into American life, the CP could now align itself with the New Deal and its reforms. Not only could Browder applaud such things as higher wages, unemployment relief, and public works, but after Roosevelt's smashing electoral triumph in 1936, Browder could say of the New Deal coalition: "This new party that is beginning to take shape before our eyes, involving a majority of the population, is what we Communists have in mind when we speak of—the American expression of the People's Front. . . ." In other words, the New Deal and the Popular Front against fascism were now considered one and the same. For the first time since the birth of the American Communist Party, one of its members could be a good Communist and at the same time give wholehearted support to the dominant powers on the national political scene. This Americanization of the party is surely a major factor in its rapid growth after 1935.[30]

Since, during this fourth period, a person could join the party without in any way alienating himself from America, some people who had previously admired the party but had been repelled by its tactics now felt free to become members. Granville Hicks, an editor of *New Masses* since 1934, belonged to this group. Though he may not be typical, Hicks's reasons for joining can tell much about others who became Communists during the Popular Front.

Sympathetic to communism, Hicks had previously been put off by the CP's attacks on other leftist groups. When Dimitrov's speech changed all that, he was "delighted," and soon he joined the party. His reasons for doing so are instructive. As he wrote years later:

> When I joined the party, it was not because I wanted to help Russia, though I had friendly feelings toward the Soviet Union both as an example of working socialism and as the chief enemy of fascism. Nor was it because I desired the overthrow of the government of the United States: toward that government as currently constituted I was sympathetic, both officially as a Communist and in my personal convictions. If a violent revolution came, I believed, it would be led by native fascists, and I would support the government against them. . . . I joined the party because, as a convinced Marxist, I was in agreement with what I believed to be its ultimate aim—the socialization of the means of production—and especially because it seemed to be leading the struggle against fascism.

Apart from the statement that he was a "convinced Marxist" and the belief, flowing from that, in the ultimate "socialization of the means of production," these might be the words of anyone who joined the CP during the Popular Front. Friendliness but not slavish devotion to Russia, support for the American government as "currently constituted," and above all the desire to stop fascism—these attitudes were most typical of those who entered the party between 1935 and 1939. Even for Hicks as a Marxist, the ultimate aim of socialism seemed a long way off and definitely took a back seat to the current "struggle against fascism" that the Communists were leading.[31]

In this period of the Popular Front, it was the opposition of Soviet Russia to Hitler's Germany, as well as that of the world Communist parties to fascism, that was foremost in bringing people into the ranks of the American Communist Party. Domestic policies were important, but much less so than before, for in this era world fascism seemed to threaten whatever gains progressive groups might make at home. This might happen either through external aggression, or because native fascists felt encouraged to emulate the successes of Hitler, Mussolini, and other strong men in Europe. After the Comintern decision for an antifascist Popular Front, American Jews, whose coreligionists in Germany were suffering from the scourge of Aryan supremacy, flocked to the CP. Other Americans were drawn to the Communists for similar reasons—students and teachers, artists and intellectuals because of the book burnings and purges of universities, unionists because of the way fascism had smashed labor movements.[32] And to many a sensitive democrat it was not simply the overseas variety of fascism that drove him left, but the portents of fascism within the United States. As William Leuchtenberg has pointed out, "The success of Huey Long seemed evidence that fascism could come from within, not through a coup d'etat, but with the acquiescence of the people." The growth of the Silver Shirts of William Dudley Pelley, the fact that Gerald Winrod, who blamed communism on the "international Jew," could poll 53,000 votes in a Kansas Republican senatorial primary, the revelations that gangs of right-wing hoodlums roamed the streets of New York like Mussolini's *squadristi*, beating Jews and other "undesirables," all made the possibility of domestic fascism seem very real.[33]

The belief has been persistent in America in the cold war years that people joined the Communist Party not because of political issues but because of defects in their own personalities, such as feelings of personal inadequacy or submissiveness. Granting that some Communists were undoubtedly neurotic, one can still assert, as did John Gates after he left the party in 1957, that it was not at all personal aberrations that drew men to communism, but rather the "aberrations of society." The things Communists concerned themselves with and protested against, the unemployed workers, the starving children, the Hoovervilles, and the threats of militant fascism in Europe, were all terrible realities. All posed problems for which the CP had solutions that seemed reasonable. Studies which affirm the existence of a special Communist personality type—and there are those which deny it as well—are weakened because they do not compare CP members with those of other political groups; perhaps men even joined the Republican Party for neurotic reasons. Moreover, they imply that the party was revolutionary and alienated from society, which was certainly not at all the case during the Popular Front. After all, men who joined the CP did not think they were entering a conspiracy, but only a strongly reformist party. Most important, to ascribe certain personalities to Communists is to ignore the short-term reformist goals of the party, the ones that caused people to join it. As the historian Earl Latham has put it, "Presumably the psychotics and psychoneurotics were not less in number or proportion in 1933 than in 1936 or 1938," yet in the latter years, after the proclamation of the Popular Front, far more people became Communists than in the former. As Latham goes on, "This suggests that the membership variable was more than likely the change in party line and not a sudden increase in weak personalities."[34]

While the CP made its greatest membership gains between 1935 and 1939—it claimed 100,000 in the latter year, though this was undoubtedly exaggerated—its influence was made wider by the many Popular Front mass organizations that its members joined and often controlled. To catalogue them would require a separate book; let it simply be said that whatever group suffered from injustice, real or imagined, in American life, there was sure to be a Popular Front organization catering to it. For Negroes there was the National Negro Congress, agitating for equality. Workers too poor to hire lawyers might be defended in court by International Labor Defense. Students could join the American Student Union, which sponsored strikes against war and promoted the Oxford Pledge. Largest and most impressive was the American League against War and Fascism, which changed its name to American League for Peace and Democracy in 1937, when Communists and other supporters began to feel that some wars, such as those against fascism, were justified. Meanwhile, in this period, CP organizers were plunging into the organizational drive of the CIO and were being welcomed by John L. Lewis, who recognized them for the dedicated workers that they were. Soon the Communists had solid footholds in some of the major CIO unions, the Pacific Maritime Federation, the United Auto Workers, the National Maritime Union, and the Transport Workers Union.

In later years it has become rather common to adopt either a cynical or an ironical attitude toward Popular Front organizations that were joined by tens of thousands and which enlisted the support of hundreds of thousands more. Both attitudes stem from knowledge of the Stalin-Hitler pact, in which the Soviet Union sold out the Popular Front. Thus, adherents of its mass organizations appear in retrospect as people manipulating others for the good of the party, or as dupes being manipulated for the same ends. Yet the cynicism of the Comintern cannot be transferred to the front organizations in America, or even to the majority of party members. The people who attended rallies against fascism, solicited funds for the relief of strikers, raised money to help refugees from Germany, or passed out leaflets denouncing the jailing of strike leaders were not motivated by cynical reasons. Even the Communists were not necessarily being cynical—though some of the leaders surely were—for the bulk of CP members were people who entered the party for the express purpose of achieving the ends that the Popular Front organizations were dedicated to. Admittedly, people may appear as dupes, or at least misguided, because it is hard to see exactly what the Popular Front accomplished. Except in the realm of labor organization, where the success of the CIO owes something to the CP and its supporters, the front seems to have failed. Perhaps it did help some victims of injustice—Negroes, union organizers, a few Jewish refugees—but, a critic might argue, everyone knows that it did not stop fascism, that a world war was necessary for that. True. Yet this seems to prove that adherents of the Popular Front were not mistaken, but especially farsighted. If more people had joined the front, or at least if Western governments had earlier adhered to the anti-fascist policies it favored, perhaps war would not have come, or would have come on terms more favorable to the West. If one approves of the necessity of stopping fascism, one can hardly condemn those who joined Popular Front organizations for taking stands against it when they did.

Selfless idealism was the finest component of the men and women who supported front organizations, as of those who joined the CP. Yet beneath this shining surface flowed dark currents that must be mentioned if the picture is to be complete. In a larger view, one that focuses on more than the fourth period alone, it can be seen that the Popular Front was a Communist tactic, an attempt to broaden the base of support for CP enterprises. At the same time it was an attempt to win worldwide friends for the Soviet Union. Every front organization not only pursued its particular objectives, it also supported the Soviet Union when it could. While working for social equality, an organization would pass resolutions lauding Russia as a land where Jews and Negroes never met discrimination; while criticizing unemployment one could point to the Soviet Union, where everyone had a job; while attacking fascism, a group could point to Russia as the chief bulwark against Germany. Some of these things might be true, such as the Soviets as standing against Germany—at least for the time being. Some might be false, such as lack of discrimination against Jews in Russia. The point is that truth or falsity were often not important to leaders of Popular Front organizations—only defense of Russia mattered. While proposals for a front against fascism would have been popular if no American Communist Party had existed, and while the social climate of the thirties was such that large numbers of Americans were willing to accept reforms of the kind that various front organizations sponsored, still much of the tone of the front was set by Communist leaders.[35]

What was true of the Popular Front was even more true of the party itself. Many who joined because they believed in social reform and defense against fascism soon left because they found the CP different from what it had appeared to be. Even during this fourth period, when the party was least committed to long-range Marxist ends, it could be described by one member as a kind of "revolving door" through which many streamed. On an average, members remained in the CP no more than two to three years. They left for as many reasons as they joined. One might go because he was expected to give up too much of his free time to the party (though in the Popular Front period this was rare). Another might start reading Marxist works and find that Trotsky's criticisms of Stalin made sense. Many found that CP meetings were simply too dull to sit through and decided they could work for the same ends in more interesting front organizations. Others were simply repelled by the lack of democracy within the party.[36]

From a distance of thirty years it looks as if the best reason for leaving the CP during the Popular Front era should have been the Moscow Trials, when Stalin rid himself of so many of the Old Bolsheviks. Though some did quit the party for this reason, there was not a general exodus. Once more, Granville Hicks probably gives the best reasons for this:

> Again and again, between 1935 and 1939, I was troubled by events in Russia, especially the trials for treason of men who had been held up to us as heroes of the revolution. I felt that if the Old Bolsheviks were guilty, then corruption had gone deep in the Communist party of Russia; if they were innocent, the trials were outrageous. Yet it was true, I thought, that Russia was the bulwark of anti-fascism in Europe and that the Communist party was leading the fight against fascism in America, and I convinced myself that I had no right to let my private doubts interfere with this great struggle against evil.[37]

The many who stayed in the party, like the thousands more who joined in these years and the hundreds of thousands who supported Popular Front organizations, had their gazes diverted from Moscow by the threat of fascism. The struggle against that force, so long expected, became a reality after July 1936 when civil war erupted in Spain. The sounds of conflict from the Iberian Peninsula drowned out any voices of doubt that the Moscow Trials raised, for German and Italian arms were attacking Spain, and Russia alone, of all the world powers, was defending her. Here was the first country, the first people to take arms against fascism, and if the Soviet Union was helping the Spanish Republic, who could doubt that Russia was on the side of the angels?

Spain in the 1930's—perhaps as always—was an anomaly. While all the countries of Europe were sliding toward the right, Spain for one of the few times in her political history was moving toward republicanism. In April 1931, parties supporting King Alfonso XIII were so overwhelmingly defeated in municipal elections that the last of the Bourbons announced he could see he no longer enjoyed the love of his people. Rather than attempting to retain power, the king stated, "I am determined to have nothing to do with setting one of my countrymen against another in a fratricidal war." Exiling himself, Alfonso left Spain in the hands of political leaders who were to draw up a constitution and hold democratic elections. When they did so, the Second Spanish Republic was launched into the agony of its brief life.

All the years of the Republic were troubled ones, even those before the war came. Labor unrest, bitter political disputes, and violence in the streets showed that Spain after all shared much with the rest of Europe. To foreign observers and to natives, the Spanish scene was a bewildering kaleidoscope of parties, factions, and interest groups, all tugging in separate directions. The basic split was between parties favoring the Republic and those desiring a return to traditionalism and monarchy. Yet opposition to the Republic itself was only a part of Spain's troubles. Among the groups supporting the form of government, there was little agreement on even the most elementary kinds of public issues. Anarchists and Socialists, bourgeois Republicans and Radicals, Catalan and Basque separatists, Stalinist and anti-Stalinist Communists—each of these groups had its own ideas about agricultural lands and labor, about education and the problem of the Church. Suppressed through long years of monarchy and the military rule of Primo de Rivera, few of these groups were willing to wait for the social change that comes through the give-and-take of parliamentary bargaining. Impatient to bring Spain into line with its own passionately held vision of the modern world, each party and labor union was willing—if elections did not bring what they wanted soon—to carry its arguments into the streets. What was true of parties backing the Republic was equally true of its enemies; Monarchists, Carlists, Catholic Party members, and those who belonged to fascist groups like the JONS or the Falange Español—all proved themselves ready to use illegal violence to achieve their ends.

The first government of the Republic, mildly left-wing, had to suppress a rising of the army in August 1932, and then an Anarchist revolt in the province of Cádiz. The second government, conservative and more traditional, was faced with a general strike in October 1934. Though armed uprisings of workers in Barcelona and Madrid were quickly put down, bitter resistance to the government continued in the mountainous Asturias, where miners had set up a workers' soviet and had burned churches and convents. To crush this rebellion, the government had to call in Foreign Legion and Moorish troops from Africa, under the command of General Francisco Franco. After the fighting ended, hundreds of miners were summarily shot and jails were filled with political prisoners. Then came the elections of February 1936, when a coalition of liberal and leftist parties, grouped together in a Popular Front, won a resounding triumph in parliament (278 to 134 seats), though its popular vote was only slightly more (4.1 to 3.7 million) than that of the opposing National Front of conservative and rightist groups. Most ominous was the way support for center parties dwindled from 167 to only 55 members in the 470-seat Cortes. In a country where men were ready to appeal to violence, such polarization boded no good.

With its own followers, the Popular Front coalition got off on the right foot by opening the jails to free political prisoners taken by the last regime. But, although acclaimed by leftist parties, this action only served to widen the split between supporters and opponents of the government. Soon its leaders found that the Popular Front program could not paper over the splits among its own followers, and disputes between Anarchists, Socialists, Communists, and Republicans were not long in reappearing. Now there was an increasingly strong and militant right-wing party to contend with, the Falange Español, a group which emulated Mussolini's fascists in what passed for ideology and also in techniques of disrupting the city streets. Fights and brawls between right and left multiplied until by the spring of 1936 they were a daily occurrence. Meanwhile, disturbed by the disorder and the Republic's inability to quell it, disgusted by what they considered the left-wing tendencies of the government, a group of high-ranking, conservative military officers laid plans for something quite traditional in Spanish history, an uprising of the army against the regime.

To the outside world, the internal troubles of Spain did not seem as real or as pressing as they actually were. What was apparent was that Spain, after centuries of being cut off from Europe, at last had a government that seemed to be moving it into the mainstream of Western political development. This government had taken education out of the hands of the Catholic Church; it had expropriated some, but by no means all, of the vast Church lands; it had made a tentative start toward breaking up the large, landed estates, with compensation paid to their owners; it had raised the wages of laborers and had legalized divorce. To democrats of the West concerned about such things—and probably few of them were—Spain provided a heartening contrast to the rest of Europe, which seemed to be relapsing into the Dark Ages.[38]

When the Spanish generals, supported by their Monarchist and Falangist allies, rose against the Republic in mid-July 1936, the sympathies of those committed to constitutional government in the Western world were naturally on the side of the government. Then, with the quick and virtually open armed intervention of Germany and Italy on the side of the rebels, the cause of the Spanish Republic suddenly became the most popular one of the decade. For those who had reason to hate the resurgent right already, Spain became a testing ground for the battle against fascism. Not just Socialists, Communists, or radicals, but all Americans of a liberal political persuasion supported Loyalist Spain. Partly they backed it because they believed its Republican ideals preferable to those of government by an alliance of the military and the Church. But mainly they supported the Republic because it stood for a worldwide resistance to fascism that seemed sorely needed.[39] Here was the "conscience of the thirties" active again. Many Americans, as they rode crowded morning subways into Manhattan or clung to cable cars precipitously dropping toward Market Street, as they grabbed hamburgers in coffeeshops on State Street or started lunch with martinis at the Brown Derby, read their newspapers and came to believe that the battle lines before Madrid were personally important to them. But their concern was not completely altruistic. To some of them the fear was real that if the forces of reaction were not stopped in Spain, they would soon engulf Europe and prepare for battle with the United States. The verse of Kenneth Fearing summed up this attitude well:

ACT ONE, *Barcelona, Time, the present*
ACT TWO, *Paris in springtime, during the siege*
ACT THREE, *London, Bank Holiday, after an air raid*
ACT FOUR, *A short time later in the U.S.A.*[40]

For those already active on the left, in the Communist or the Socialist Party, in a labor union or a Popular Front organization, the Spanish conflict became a time of excitement and hope. In the past few years there had been only defeat and frustration. The swift triumph of Hitler in Germany had left Communists, Social Democrats, and liberals squabbling over who had been to blame. Meanwhile, Dollfuss had crushed social democracy in Austria. Across the world the Japanese had been slowly swallowing Manchuria, while in Africa Mussolini's forces had bombed the helpless Ethiopians as the League of Nations, in Orwell's phrase, "Made pious noises 'off'." Now the nations were still looking the other way, but parties of the left were burying their differences to join the Popular Front against fascism. The issue was squarely drawn again and, as James Wechsler wrote, there was the feeling that "this time it would be different. . . . In Spain . . . the air was clear and the battle lines were clearly marked." For people not yet committed to the left, the Spanish war often became the catalyst once it was obvious that Soviet Russia and world Communist parties were providing the only substantial aid to the Loyalist government. Of all the issues the American Communist Party ever took a stand on, the cause of Spain was the most popular; both the party and the Popular Front organizations benefited enormously in terms of members and support because Russia made Spain the test case for anti-fascism.[41]

Support for the Spanish government and opposition to Francisco Franco and his allies took many forms in the United States. From almost the beginning there were protests lodged against the un-neutral neutrality of the European powers, who stopped aid to the Loyalists but apparently winked at German and Italian intervention. By January 1937, there was the American embargo of Spain to be decried, and Loyalist adherents bombarded representatives and senators, cabinet members and the President, with letters calling for it to be lifted.[42] In cities there were rallies to attend, sometimes featuring speakers from the Spanish government or reports from Americans who had visited the battlefields. There were dances at colleges where the proceeds went to aid the Loyalists, and parties were given in private homes where the money for every Scotch and soda went to buy ambulances or milk for the underfed children of Spain—if one could get pleasantly drunk and know he was aiding the cause at the same time, so much the better. And for those who wished to do something more than write letters or dance or drink for democracy and freedom, for those few who wished to cross from the shadow world of idealism to confront reality in its most urgent and brutal form, there came the opportunity of reaching the front lines in Spain.

One day early in 1937, Jack Lucid, a recent graduate of the University of Washington, fidgeted in a chair in a dingy Seattle office strewn with left-wing leaflets and copies of the *People's World*. Though Lucid had been raised as a Catholic, he had recently joined the Communist Party because of the "harrowing sense of impending doom" he felt over the spread of fascism in Europe, the apparent indifference of Americans to this phenomenon, and the fact that only Soviet Russia was opposing fascism in the one place where it seemed to count, on the battlefields of Spain. Lucid was a tough young man, in good physical condition because of the long hikes he liked to take through the Cascades. Normally rather belligerent, he was now trying to conceal his impatience from the small group of men questioning him. "Why do you want to go to Spain?" they kept asking, apparently unsatisfied with his answer that he was damn angry at Hitler and his fascist friends and wanted to get back at them personally. "Wouldn't it be better for you to stay in Seattle and help to build the Popular Front in the United States?" they wanted to know. Lucid kept insisting that he could do more good in Spain, all the while wondering why it had taken so many weeks to process his application and call him for this interview, thinking of what he could do to make them believe he was a good Communist who would acquit himself well in the armed struggle against the forces of reaction and oppression.

In many ways, Jack Lucid was typical of his generation. Raised in a devoutly religious home, he had stopped attending church when the Depression seemed to pose questions for which religion had no answers. Graduating high school, he had spent two years at the Jesuit-run Seattle College before going on to the University of Washington for a degree in liberal arts. At the university he heard faculty members criticize capitalism and watched students demonstrate against war and for various social reforms. Still, he did not become involved in politics himself until Spain became the catalyst. Lucid had always been more fearful of the rise of the right in Europe than concerned over the Depression at home; now across the Atlantic he saw the naked aggression of "fascism" against liberal democracy, and he was impelled to join the Communist Party, partly in the hope that it would help him get to Spain. Oddly, at first the CP seemed to be standing in his way. But a few weeks after his interview, the recruiting committee did accede to Lucid's wishes. Before long he was in the war, much to the dismay of his devout mother, who enjoyed attending church-sponsored anti-Loyalist lectures throughout the course of the conflict.[1]

The case of Jack Lucid was not an isolated one. Many a devoted young Communist who desired to join the Lincoln Battalion found his application being turned down by fellow comrades sitting on a screening committee. Some party members who tried to volunteer were never allowed to go, while others reached Spain only after applying for duty several times.[2] Apparently paradoxical, the reason the CP could turn down its own members becomes quite clear when one understands the nature and purpose of the International Brigades.

These brigades must be seen as part of the total picture of Soviet support for Loyalist Spain, which did not commence until the fall of 1936. Anti-fascist as they were, the Russian leaders refrained from aiding the Spanish Republic in the first few weeks of the war, evidently hoping that nonintervention might actually curb German and Italian aid to the rebels. At the same time, the Soviet press presented a picture of the war as an international fascist attack upon a democratic government, and Russian workers responded with hundreds of public meetings of support for the Loyalists, donating more than $2 million to buy food and medical supplies for Spain. When the Non-Intervention Commission, sitting in London, quickly proved to be ineffectual in stopping fascist aid to Spanish insurgents, Soviet spokesmen said they would consider themselves no more bound by the Non-Intervention Agreement than were other signatory powers. And in October, Russian ships began carrying military equipment—trucks, airplanes, and tanks—and some advisory and technical personnel to Spain.[3]

Exactly who first thought of recruiting International Brigades nobody really seems to know, but the French Communist leader Maurice Thorez and the party member Tom Wintringham, an early English volunteer, were both ardent advocates of the idea. The Soviet Union's motives in directing and supporting the brigades, as well as its aims in sending other military aid to the Spanish Republic, are still the subject of much historical debate.[4] Even the relationship of Joseph Stalin to these decisions is unclear. Certainly, whoever made the decision for the brigades was aware of the propaganda value of defending the legal Spanish government. By making use of and organizing the volunteers already in Spain, and by helping to transport more young men to the Iberian Peninsula, Russia could obviously make the large numbers of people in the West who were enthusiastic for the Spanish cause look favorably and sympathetically upon the Soviet Union. Since Russia at this time was hoping to stop Western appeasement of fascism and perhaps to get England and France to agree to some sort of collective security against both Germany and Japan, such widespread support could only do her good. Another component in the support of Spain was genuine Soviet idealism. Some Russian leaders found in

Spain a fire that rekindled their faith in revolution; others who thought their own revolution was being betrayed at home wished to partake in this new, pure struggle. Whatever their motives, it must be remembered that Russia had no real economic or strategic interests in Spain. Above all, she did not want a Communist Spain, for this would interfere with attempts to establish collective security with the Western powers. Thus Soviet propaganda throughout the war emphasized the bourgeois nature of the Spanish government, and within Spain the CP played the role of a conservative party, subordinating revolution to the fight against Francisco Franco.[5]

By the time the Soviets decided to form the brigades in September 1936, the Spanish Republic's need for military assistance was all too apparent. When the war had begun in July, almost the entire regular army—both officers and men—went along with the uprising of the rebel generals, and the Republic had to improvise its military machine with only a few army regulars as a nucleus. On July 19, the government had, somewhat reluctantly, distributed arms to the Spanish workers. The militias of various labor unions and political parties had then shown great enthusiasm and bravery in putting down the original risings in major cities, storming through machine-gun fire to capture the Montaña Barracks in Madrid and the Atarazanas Barracks in Barcelona. But when it came to open field warfare, the untrained militias could not stand up to the regular Spanish Army of Moors and foreign legionnaires. Unused to modern techniques, men who were fearless in street fighting often broke and ran under artillery shelling or bombs dropped from the air. The situation was made worse by the Spanish attitude toward war. Prime Minister Largo Caballero was typical in saying that it was beneath a man's dignity to hide in a trench and fire at the enemy. So all along the southern front, as rebel armies marched inexorably from Seville toward Madrid, they easily pushed past militiamen who refused to dig defensive trenches and chose to die standing up. An offer by the Italian Republican exile Randolfo Pacciardi to form an Italian legion to aid the Loyalists was turned down by Largo Caballero in early September. But with continuing disasters on southern battlefields and the approach of the enemy toward Madrid, the idea of using foreign troops to buy time for the Republic looked better and better. So the Communist offer of International Brigades was accepted. Besides, with the Soviets providing the only outside military aid to Spain, the prime minister and his government were not in much of a position to turn down the Russian offer.[6]

With the decision to form the brigades made, the Comintern set about getting recruits. Evidently quotas were assigned to local Communist parties, and an underground railway for transporting volunteers to Spain was set up, its European headquarters at the *Maison des Syndicats* in Paris. Throughout the world, the CP began to channel men toward France, its main recruiting theme based on the slogan: "Make Spain the grave of European fascism." Yet in line with the Popular Front idea, the Communists were interested in enrolling many nonparty members in the brigades. Georgi Dimitrov, the Bulgarian head of the Comintern, told American correspondent Louis Fischer in Moscow that he hoped the United States would send many more non-Communists than party members to Spain, stressing the wisdom of enlisting Socialists, liberals, and "Jewish nationalists" so that "We can then build the American Popular Front on the Spanish battlefield." Probably the Russians were also afraid of depleting the ranks of communism in the various countries of the world, and this led to scenes like the one in Seattle, where honest young Communists with a burning desire to get to Spain were questioned at length, stalled for months, and sometimes even refused permission to leave for the front-line struggle. Some were threatened with expulsion if they were to go to Spain against party wishes, though in one case there was a sudden change of heart when the volunteer offered to pay his own way.[7]

In the United States, recruiting began quietly. Orders went out to units all over the country to enlist men for

Spain, but there was apprehension over possible violation of American laws or government retaliation, and no publicity was given to the venture in the party press. The first mention of it did not appear in the pages of the *Daily Worker* until December 21, 1936, just as the initial contingent of 95 Americans was preparing to leave New York. On that day the newspaper printed a speech which Earl Browder had delivered to the national committee of the CP earlier in the month. It quoted the party leader as commenting that "the movement toward volunteering for the armed defense of Spanish democracy is affecting all strata of serious democratic people in America." Browder then urged the party to encourage "honest democratic people to go to Spain."

Five days later, the first group of Americans secretly sailed away from New York on the SS. *Normandie.* But the day before Christmas the lid on recruiting for Spain had been blown off by the Socialist Party. In the pages of the *New York Times* the executive secretary of the Socialist Party in New York was quoted as saying that the Socialists were organizing a 500-man Eugene V. Debs Column. Supposedly they already had enough volunteers for the military unit, and all that was needed was $50,000 to cover transportation costs. For the next couple of months Socialist publications continued to write about the proposed column, while a committee was created to raise funds for it, rallies were staged in New York, and advertisements for money and recruits were placed in magazines like the *Nation* and the *New Republic.*[8]

Little seems to have come of the Socialist Party's efforts, for the Debs Column never appeared in Spain. But the publicity and the ensuing negative reactions of some government officials did annoy and upset the Communists, engaged in their own recruiting. Several senators were already talking of revoking the citizenship of anyone who went to Spain to fight, and when Congress convened in January 1937 there were more such rumblings on Capitol Hill. Legislation to revoke the citizenship of Americans involved in combat in foreign wars was finally introduced into the House of Representatives, but it died in the Committee on Immigration and Naturalization. Similarly, an FBI investigation of recruiting for Spain and threats from the Attorney General's office to prosecute violators of American laws did little to interfere with the Communist Party's recruitment. Indeed, calls by congressmen for the Department of Justice to apply the section of the Criminal Code providing a $3,000 fine or a year in prison for enlistment in a foreign war served only to reaffirm the beliefs of some volunteers that they were doing the right thing in going to Spain. If American "reactionaries" were against them—the reasoning ran—then their course must be just.[9]

The fact that Americans were fighting in Spain in the Abraham Lincoln Battalion first became known to the general public only after the Jarama battles of late February 1937, and the bloodbath at Pingarrón. Newspaper accounts of the action brought so much publicity to the Lincolns that Constancia de la Mora, a Spanish censorship official, began to grumble about dispatches in which "it almost appeared as though the Americans had single-handedly held back the enemy at Jarama." Complaining that the "Americans had been very few compared to the Spanish troops," she more generously went on, "We were all so proud of the Americans who had come so far and fought so well for democracy . . . [that] a little exaggeration was surely pardonable."[10]

The publicity which the Lincolns received made the task of recruiting easier. Now Earl Browder could openly say such things as: "One of the greatest achievements that our Party has ever made is the building of the . . . Battalions of the International Brigade." Now the party press could openly report and glorify the actions of the Lincolns. In this task it was helped by the national wire services, a good part of the general daily press, the small liberal magazines, and even mass circulation publications like *Time.* Now publications like the *Daily Worker* and *New Masses* could openly solicit funds for the Friends of the Abraham Lincoln Brigade (FALB), an organization formed in the spring of 1937 for the purpose of collecting money to send cigarettes, chocolates, and reading material to the boys in Spain and also of helping with the rehabilitation of wounded soldiers. Not so incidentally, the FALB sometimes served as a screen for recruiting activities.[11]

Though a good section of the American press wrote favorably about the Lincoln Battalion, and though many of the country's most famous journalists—Herbert Matthews, Vincent Sheean, Martha Gellhorn, Ernest Hemingway—penned glowing portraits of them, it was the Communist press that sang their praises most highly. The view of the battalion portrayed by the CP was that of a group of young, idealistic heroes who had gone off to Spain to save the world from the scourge of fascism. At various times they could be described as the "Real League of Nations" or as "comrades-in-arms defending all that is best in contemporary life." Frequently they were compared to the "International Brigades of 1776," the Lafayettes and Kosciuskos who had come to America to help win her own struggle against "tyranny." Allusions were often made to Jefferson and his desire to aid libertarian movements around the world, and American memories were evoked as actions were compared to Gettysburg and Valley Forge. Putting the Lincolns in the mainstream of American history, the *Daily Worker* pictured them as "The living embodiment . . . of the grand traditions of the U.S.A. in the fight for human liberty." Such CP appeals to the American past and to democratic principles were common during the Popular Front era, and they were not necessarily cynical or insincere—though undoubtedly they were sometimes both. After all, foreigners had come to the aid of the Thirteen Colonies, Jefferson had wished to apply libertarian principles to the world, and Americans had given lives for human liberty. Many men in the late thirties could believe that the Communist Party—and especially the men fighting fascism in Spain—was simply continuing a worldwide historical struggle toward liberty, equality, and fraternity.[12]

There were times when the Communist press did overstretch itself in its desire to idolize the Lincoln Battalion and the Spanish cause, times when its stories must have tested the credibility of the truest believer. Certainly none but the most blindly dedicated Communists could swallow the report that after the February battles, "the dead were recovered with their arms stiff in the revolutionary salute." Similarly strange was the *New Masses* story of the tough, Anarchist Army commander breaking down and weeping openly because "rich Americans" were coming all the way to his country to help defeat fascism. Especially farfetched in view of the Anarchists' cold-blooded penchant for burning churches and occasionally carving up their inhabitants, this tale was simply impossible because the Anarchists always maintained an intense dislike for the Communist-dominated International Brigades. Obviously such a story was an attempt to show the camaraderie and solidarity of all Loyalist parties. Like various other reports early in the war, it seems to have emanated from the New York offices of the party rather than from Spain. Belonging to a similar category are the stories of groups of Chinese and Arab comrades that appeared in the party press in early 1937.[13] Since such internationals never arrived on the battlefields, it seems certain that they were no more than the brainchild of some propagandist. Evidently, adherence to the truth was unnecessary to the party when it was selling a worthy cause.

Stories about Spain in the Communist press obviously served the dual function of reporting events and creating enthusiasm for the Loyalist government. Also underlying some of them was the hope that they would cause men to enlist in the International Brigades. Yet enlistment was never openly urged. The closest the party press came to open recruiting was in a memoriam to Ben Leider, a Communist, a pilot, and one of the first Americans killed in Spain. Written by Leider's girlfriend, Ruth McKenney, the article was both a cry of anguish and a call to arms. Leider, Miss McKenney wrote, had gone to Spain because he believed the struggle there was a "life and death fight for world democracy." Now he was gone and, she went on portentously, "Now what will you do for Spain? What will you, who still live, while Ben lies dead, what will you do to make sure that fascism does not pass?"[14]

Publicity and propaganda about Spain and the International Brigades were obviously useful in getting volunteers, but the CP did more than report the war and await enlistments. Recruiters across the country were active in making personal contact with men in labor unions, Popular Front organizations, and college campus groups. Acting under CP aegis, the recruiters nonetheless maintained a pose of independence from parties, though in left-wing circles everyone knew for whom they worked. On its own and through front organizations, the party sponsored hundreds of public meetings about Spain. People gathered in union halls and YMCA auditoriums to hear speakers—often fresh from the battlefields—paint glowing portraits of the struggle of the Spanish people toward democracy. Sometimes motion pictures about the Lincoln Battalion were shown or the crowd was entertained by such groups as the No Pasarán Singers, performing Spanish Civil War songs. Though no one at the meeting spoke of volunteering, handbills might be distributed with the name and address of a person to contact if one wanted to "do something more" for Spain.[15] One did not have to be especially perspicacious to know what that "something more" meant.

In certain circles a myth has grown up which alleges that aside from hardened revolutionaries, most of the young men to cross the Atlantic to the Iberian Peninsula were somehow tricked or swindled into volunteering. Years later, FBI Director J. Edgar Hoover asserted that "American communists [sic] used glittering promises, underhanded tricks and downright fraud to coax young men to go to Spain." Among the tricks he mentions are promises of lucrative positions, large cash rewards, and sumptuous travel accommodations. Most interesting is his idea that "A young girl would entice unsuspecting men; in return for her favors they would promise to enlist."[16] Apart from this rather odd picture of young Americans being so sexually desperate that they would journey across the Atlantic and enter a foreign war just for a woman's "favors," and the startlingly high standard of honesty that would keep them from reneging on their promises once the "favors" were at an end, the FBI director's description falls short on other counts. For only the illiterate would not have known the news that all daily papers carried, that Spain was a brutal, dangerous place where thousands of soldiers were being killed weekly, and only the childishly romantic would have imagined war as something in which there were lucrative positions and fine accommodations.

Other charges made against CP recruitment claim that some men who volunteered for noncombatant positions—such as ambulance drivers—were, once in Spain, put into the ranks of the Lincoln Battalion. This was supposed to have happened to Don Henry, a University of Kansas student, but since he spent his time as a first aid man, his desire for noncombatancy does not seem to have been violated.[17] Yet if Henry's case does not fit into this category, others do. As Edwin Rolfe noted in his diary, one soldier told him that "many men, who came here to be technicians, were fooled, tricked into becoming infantrymen, then killed in action."[18] Exactly what is meant by "technician" is not clear. Since it is preceded by a complaint to Rolfe that the battalion had the bad policy of making all volunteers infantrymen "without regard to special capacities, abilities, etc.," it might mean that men who had previous training in some specialty, say artillery or first aid, considered themselves "technicians" and were disappointed to be put into trenches with a rifle. Yet disappointments of this sort are common to any army.

There is another possible explanation for such complaints. Perhaps some recruiters in the United States, zealously trying to sign up as many men as possible, made promises about certain kinds of positions without the authority to do so. Certainly several thousand miles away, with a pressing need for men in the front lines, International Brigade officials would ignore such promises, assuming they even knew about them. Yet this sort of mixup could not have happened often, and one suspects that Rolfe's informant, in saying this happened to "many men," either did not know what he was talking about or was exaggerating. There simply was no need for recruiters to lie to men about what they would be doing in Spain because there were many more people trying to enlist than the Communist Party could ever handle. Observers noted that recruiters were often approached by total strangers, seeking to make their way to the war. Murray Kempton, no friend of the Communists, has estimated that "ten times as many as ever got there wrote the Spanish Embassy asking to enlist." Spanish diplomats in the United States indirectly confirm this by claiming they received "countless" unsolicited letters from young Americans wishing to fight for the Loyalists. Though it was naturally in their interest to make such a claim, it seems likely that they were telling the truth. For the desire of men to volunteer for Spain often preceded their knowledge of how to go about enlisting. Before he even knew the party was recruiting, a CP member like John Gates was overwhelmed with envy when he heard of the Lincoln Battalion, and he wished to join it. Typical was the reaction of twenty one-year-old Edward Robel, of Lewiston Orchards, Washington, who had wanted to fight fascism from the opening of the war and who found the opportunity of going to Spain presented by the CP "too good to be true." [19]

With the formation of the International Brigades, the Spanish Civil War became a moment in history when many of the desires and aims of the leaders of Soviet Russia coincided closely with those of liberals and democrats in the Western world. The Popular Front of all democratic and leftist parties against fascism had been a Communist idea, and in Spain it was meeting its first test. That the Russians manipulated and tried to use the enthusiasm for Loyalist Spain to their own ends was inevitable, but there would have been no International Brigades at all if Western democrats, liberals, and radicals had not seen their own countries turn their backs on Spain's pleas for help and go on doing nothing about the intervention of the fascist powers. Bereft of government support at home, Westerners touched by the plight of Spain welcomed Russian support and the Communist Party leadership of the International Brigades. On their part, the Kremlin leaders did not arbitrarily conjure up the brigades; the early appearance of foreign volunteers in Spain shows that they merely took advantage of and exploited some deepseated emotion in the Western world.[20] That such emotion was widespread, even in the United States, is shown by the fact that it was not a Communist publication but the liberal *Nation* which editorialized in early 1937: "The supreme test of an antifascist today is not what he says but what he does for Spain." And it was not the *New Masses,* but Henry Luce's mass-circulation *Life* which in 1938 ran a feature article on the Lincoln Battalion entitled "Americans Have Died Fighting for Democracy in Spain."[21]

There is no doubt that the Americans who journeyed to Spain to fight beneath the banner of the Abraham Lincoln Battalion were genuine volunteers who knew what they were getting into. At least they knew as much as anyone can know who has never dashed across a naked field lugging a rifle, the angry whine of machine-gun bullets filling the world, as much as a man can know who has never huddled in a trench, his mouth dry with fear as the sky splits into a million pieces of shrapnel, as much as a human being can know who has never joked with a comrade and taken a swig from his canteen and suddenly seen him slump forward in the posture of death. The Americans who went to Spain were no dupes of the Kremlin, for they knew what Soviet Russia was doing, knew precisely that it was the only power supporting the legal Spanish government, were perfectly aware that the Communists controlled the only road to Spain. And that was the road they wished to travel.[22]

Shortly after the end of the Spanish Civil War, a propagandist for the victorious General Francisco Franco, writing about the Lincoln Battalion, said: ". . . its human material was disastrous. The soldiers were Negroes from Broadway, Chinese from the ports of New York and Los Angeles, gangsters from Chicago and militants from the Communist sections of Philadelphia." Obviously not meant to flatter, this description bore only the faintest resemblance to reality. But the picture of the Americans who went to Spain usually drawn by their friends was also hardly an accurate portrait. Typical was a pamphlet written by the *Daily Worker* reporter Joe North. Entitled *Men in the Ranks,* the work presented the view of the Abraham Lincoln Battalion that the Communists wished the world to see. Here the men were portrayed as a representative cross section of the "best elements" in the United States. There was one chapter on a former Boston altar boy, and another on the farmer who did not "want to see shrapnel bursting on Iowa's rich fields." Mention was made of college teachers, university graduates, and wealthy men who nonetheless had social consciences. North wrote of men from the "grimy working class" areas of New York, of Negroes who viewed Messerschmidts as "lynch law on wings," of workers in the steel factories, and sailors who were always first in "big social and progressive movements." The individual stories he told may have been true, but the overall impression that farmers and workers and intellectuals, poor men and those from wealthy backgrounds, Catholics, Jews, and Protestants, Negroes and whites had all marched off to Spain in numbers approximating their percentage in the American population was a long way from the truth.[1]

Three thousand Americans crossed the Atlantic to Spain, and the average volunteer—if one can talk about such a creature—was a man between the ages of twenty-one and twenty-seven who lived in an industrial, urban center where labor unions and radical political parties were most active—New York, Pittsburgh, or Cleveland, Detroit, Milwaukee, or Chicago. If he did not work in a factory or on the docks, he might very well be a seaman, struggling to organize a union, or a college student active in the League Against War and Fascism. Like all Americans, he had suffered from the Depression, and he well knew what it felt like to walk the streets, hungry, looking for a job. But unlike the majority of his fellow countrymen, he probably came from a working-class home where deprivation predated the stock market crash. He was more likely to be foreign-born or a first-generation American than to come from old stock, and though not interested in religion, he probably had some attachment to the secular faith of Marxism. But like all human groups, the Lincoln Battalion was composed not of ideal types but of men with individual skills and accomplishments, fears and wants and hopes. To find out what kinds of Americans went to Spain, it is of course necessary to look at the men themselves and see who they were.

All wars draw their share of adventurers and the Spanish conflict was no exception. Yet despite the romantic concept of men from all over the world fighting together in a cause, the Spanish struggle drew no more than its share, at least from America. One of the few was twenty-six-year-old Peter Campo, who on his return to Bridgeport, Connecticut, in June 1938 admitted that he had gone to Spain only because he was "out of work and looking for adventure." Another was John C. Pitzer of Oklahoma City, for whom the trip was just another lark. In 1934, at the age of twenty, Pitzer had gone over the side of a boat on which he had stowed away for China. He then floated on a raft in the Pacific for several days before being rescued. The next year he made his way to China, then returned to America, stopping in Hollywood to become a movie extra until leaving for Spain in June 1937, still what the Oklahoma City *Times* could call a "boy adventurer." [2]

When Communist publications tried to show that the middle and even upper classes were contributing to the ranks of the Lincoln Battalion, there was truth in what they said. While most of the volunteers came from working-class homes, there were many from comfortable middle-class backgrounds, and even a smattering of men from wealthy families. Pittsburgh produced Ralph Thornton, a member of one of that city's "oldest families," while from Massachusetts came twenty-eight-year-old Owen Appleton, a 1932 honors graduate of Harvard and a member of a banking family considered "one of the most prominent" in Springfield. David McKelvy White, a wispy, bespectacled Brooklyn College English teacher, whose father had been governor of Ohio and manager of Cox's presidential campaign in 1920, made his way to Spain along with David Thompson, nephew of the novelist Kathleen Norris and member of a wealthy northern California family. [3]

Among the volunteers were also a number of men from families that were well known, if only in their local communities. Robert Thwing, son of the mayor of Murdo, South Dakota, and Henry Eaton, son of a former Los Angeles mayor, served together in the ranks. With them were Hans Amlie, brother of the Wisconsin congressman, and Roy Mouton, nephew of a Louisiana congressman, great-great-grandson of Alex Mouton, onetime Democratic governor of Louisiana, and a member of the same family as Confederate General Alfred Mouton, described as "one of the most widely known . . . of Teche county." [4]

The best-known name in the battalion belonged to James Lardner, son of author Ring Lardner. A graduate of Andover, Lardner had spent two and a half years at Harvard before quitting, apparently because he did not find formalized education very stimulating. He worked for three years as a reporter on the *New York Herald-Tribune*, then wearied of the routine stories that are a young newspaperman's lot and went off to the Paris edition of the newspaper. Lardner was well read, with a questioning mind, a man who was interested in the world around him. Though never a member of the Communist Party, he became vitally interested in the Spanish War, and in April 1938 went to Spain on his vacation for a firsthand look at what was going on. He rode down on the train from Paris with Ernest Hemingway and Vincent Sheean and stayed with them in a Barcelona hotel. After a few days he told them of his intention to enlist in the Lincoln Battalion. Because it was late in the war and the cause of the Republic already seemed doomed, Hemingway and Sheean tried to talk him out of his desire, arguing that it was as important to have good reporters as good soldiers. But, as Sheean observed, Lardner had reached that state of mind, "familiar to all newspaper reporters who take any interest in their living material," in which the whole practice of merely reporting events seemed "futile and silly." He went off to join the fighting troops and a few weeks later wrote of his reasons for doing so: "The cause is so plainly a worthy one that the question which the young men of the world should be putting to themselves is what justification they have for staying out of the struggle." He had put it even more simply earlier, when making his fateful decision, by saying the situation in Spain was such that "somebody had to do something."[5]

A look at the occupations of the men who went to Spain shows that the union battles for recognition in the 1930's were a breeding ground for volunteers. More than 1,000 of the Lincolns had seen violence and death on the picket lines long before they reached Spain.[6] They were used to police swinging clubs, to tear-gas bombs exploding, and to the chilling sound of pistols being fired into crowds. For this was the era when workers were seeking to unionize the great American industries and when many employers were resisting to the bitter end, utilizing "private police, strikebreakers, thugs, spies and agents provocateurs . . . tear gas, machine guns and fire arms."[7] While some major companies like United States Steel recognized unions without a fight, it took sitdown strikes at General Motors to win recognition for the United Auto Workers, and giants like Ford, "Little Steel," and Armour held out for a long time, while police and workers battled, sometimes to the death. Most men involved in the organizational struggles of America's blue-collar workers had seen friends killed or injured, or had been hurt themselves. Once they became convinced that the rebel forces in Spain were the same "reactionary" ones that had fought unionization in the United States—as Communist propaganda never tired of saying—it is hardly surprising that they were ready to take arms against any enemy, even one thousands of miles away.

The blue-collar workers who went to Spain came from everywhere. There were auto workers from Detroit's many factories and from subsidiaries like the large Fisher Body plant in Cleveland, and some 100 men from the mills of Youngstown, Gary, Bethlehem, Pittsburgh, and other steel centers. More than 100 came from the waterfront areas of the country, from New York Harbor, and the steaming ports of the Gulf Coast, with a large contingent who were veterans of the bloody Embarcadero battles of the San Francisco General Strike and members of the new ILWU.[8] Miners volunteered from the coal fields of Pennsylvania and Ohio, along with at least one who had dug metal ore in Utah and another from Coeur d'Alene. Men who cut timber in the dense forests of Minnesota and lumberjacks from the rainy Pacific slopes joined the battalion, as did needle-trade workers and fur dyers from the Yiddish-speaking garment district of New York, and truckers who might call any part of the country home. Altogether, unions from the docks and from the auto, steel, mining, lumber, garment, and trucking industries sent over 600 men into the ranks of the Lincoln Battalion.

The largest single group of workingmen to go to Spain consisted of seamen, and the National Maritime Union claim that 500 of them took part in the struggle is not at all exaggerated; indeed, the figure is more like 600.[9] Why the kind of radicalism that sent people off to Spain flourished among sailors is open to various interpretations. Some sociologists think that sailors—like lumbermen—tend to be radicals because they live in their own communities, shut off from the moderating influence of a middle-class environment. Left-wingers who have gone to sea like to think it is "natural" for sailors to be radicals, because they have so much time for reading and thinking about the world and because they are exposed to many ways of life and thus see various forms of "exploitation." Certainly their radicalism in the thirties was partly attributable to the wretched conditions on board ship. Years later, a sailor like Ben Sills, who left CCNY in his senior year to go to sea and who joined the IWW in the Gulf Region in 1935, would recall the long hours of work, the filthy food, the low pay, and he would remember the struggle to form new unions, the company spies, the organizers beaten and fired. Communists explained the large number of sailors in Spain by speaking of the "titanic struggle" of maritime workers against "the lords of the open shop." According to the party, after they had won their own battle, the sailors went off to Spain to safeguard the future of their new unions by defeating "fascism which has destroyed democracy and workers' organizations, where it has come to power." The Communists were not exaggerating the struggles that did take place, but one has the feeling they were lauding the sailors chiefly because the party wielded so much influence in their new unions. Whatever their individual reasons, it was against this background that seamen both flocked to the Communist Party in the thirties and made the decision to go to Spain.[10]

One sailor who volunteered was Bill Bailey, a huge, powerful man, born in Jersey City in 1910. Bailey went to sea at the age of fourteen and a half, and except for slack periods during the Depression, he was a sailor from then on. The union in Bailey's early seafaring days he later remembered as being run chiefly to line the pockets of its leaders. When the "strictly left wing" Marine Workers Industrial Union was formed, Bailey became active as an organizer. His travels had taken him to Spain in the early days of the Republic, where he liked the people and the way of life, and also to Hitler's Germany, where he got a "first-hand idea of what was taking place under fascism." Angry at an incident in which an American sailor had been pulled off a ship in the Elbe, imprisoned, and beaten supposedly for carrying anti-Nazi propaganda into Germany, Bailey and a group of others climbed aboard the German ship *Bremen* in New York Harbor one day in 1935, tore down the swastika flag from the bow, and threw it overboard. They were dragged away by police and, in a well-publicized trial, allowed to go free by a Jewish judge. When the Spanish conflict erupted, Bailey enlisted because he believed that if fascism could be defeated in Spain, it might collapse in Italy and Germany. In his own words, he did not like to see the Spanish people being "pushed and kicked around."[11]

Not all of those who went to Spain were employed, for in the United States in 1937 9 million people were still looking for jobs. Many of them had backgrounds like that of Frank Rogers, who wrote, "I am a coal miner's son who knew poverty from my childhood. . . . Smoke and dust was my childhood diet." Unable to go to college, though he wanted to become a teacher, Rogers added, "I've worked, hard and diligently. . . . Somehow the system caught up with me. I was fired, depressions [sic] hit my employer. I may not be an expert on economics but I know something is wrong with the system that treats hard working people in this manner. . . . Perhaps it is true that if I had a job and money I would not have gone to Spain. . . . But it wasn't adventure . . . I believe the world can be made into something better than it has been."[12]

Employment in heavy industry, participation in labor

violence, or the inability to find a job, were far from being the only backgrounds of the men who went to Spain. The occupations represented were wide-ranging. The ranks of the Lincoln Battalion contained skilled electricians and carpenters, an ex-policeman and a youngster who resigned his job with the FBI to make the trip, several newsboys and taxi drivers, some members of the International Typographers Union, plumbers, at least one baker, one butcher, and one motion picture projectionist. Three of the volunteers had owned small restaurants, a couple were salesmen, others worked for railroads or canning factories. Waiters joined the ranks along with elevator operators and a few petty white-collar workers like clerks and bookkeepers. Two of the Lincolns had supported themselves as vaudeville dancers, one had made a living as a professional wrestler, several were musicians, and one had barnstormed the United States as a stunt pilot.

Similarly, though 83 per cent of the Americans came from eleven states, and usually from the large urban centers within them, every state of the union was represented in the battalion and some of the smallest, least-known American communities sent native sons off to war. Along with the many volunteers from New York City, Chicago, San Francisco, Cleveland, Detroit, Pittsburgh, and Milwaukee were men from Wilburton and Luther, Oklahoma; Naugatuck, Connecticut; Missoula and Cascade, Montana; Pueblo and Leadville, Colorado; Hoquiam, Washington; Angora, Minnesota; Janesville and Suring, Wisconsin; Turtle Creek, Pennsylvania; Monterey, California; and Denison, Iowa.

If attending a university or college can be considered an occupation, then students were the second largest occupational group to make their way to Spain. Five hundred young Americans who were going to school or had recently graduated joined the Lincoln Battalion. Students are always an unruly group, many of them tending to the left in politics, and in the thirties they were certainly affected by the upheaval in American life and around the world. The energy that normally went into student activities was channeled elsewhere in the Depression years as college men gathered to discuss labor strikes rather than line plunges, and hung Hitler in effigy rather than a losing football coach. It is not that all normal college activity in these years ceased, but rather that students concerned with the questions of politics, economics, and peace came more into their own and, because of the tenor of the times, were given more of a hearing. Certainly one reason that their fellow students were ready to listen to them was the fact that the Depression had intruded into the normally comfortable academic world by swallowing up the summer jobs and part-time work which supported so many college students. As one lamented, "A generation without money in its jeans has trouble getting a girl friend. A generation that couldn't find work found little solace at home and often less understanding." Typical was Donald Thayer of Rochester, Minnesota, a descendant of the third superintendent of West Point, who was in and out of the University of Wisconsin more times than he could remember because he could never earn enough money to attend more than one semester in a row. When he had no money to do anything else, Thayer went off to the libraries, for they were free, and much of his reading was in the field of economics, where he began to adopt the socialist ideas of John Strachey. The ideas of Marx and his disciples were floating around the campuses, too, often under the sponsorship of the Communists, who either controlled or set the tone for many of the student movements.[13]

There is no real pattern to the students who went, either in type of university or major field of studies. Some were studying literature and Romance languages, others sociology, economics, or history. A couple were majoring in agriculture or premedical studies, and there was at least one in physics, another in mathematics, one in physiology, and another in archeology. They came from schools all over the United States, a few from small colleges like Swarthmore and Oberlin, more from the great state universities of California, Wisconsin, Iowa, Kansas, Washington, Texas, Pennsylvania, and Missouri, a number from the Ivy League campuses of Cornell and Harvard, many from the city schools of New York, CCNY, NYU, and Brooklyn College, and here and there one from Howard, Rice, New Hampshire, Arizona, Wayne State, or Pittsburgh.

Undoubtedly, some were glad to flee poor academic records and stern professors for the safety of the trenches, and many were more at home holding a rifle than a book, less frightened by an enemy than by the prospect of writing an essay on the causes of the American Revolution. But a number had excellent academic records. George William Lighton had won honors at the University of Louisville, while John Field had a high scholastic rating at the University of Rochester. Benjamin Kitler of New York probably found little use for the Phi Beta Kappa key that was delivered to him in the trenches one day during a lull in fighting. Graduate students—generally thought to be a responsible lot—went too, like John Cookson of the University of Wisconsin, working toward a Ph.D. in physics; Edward Melnicoff, in classical studies at the University of Pennsylvania, or Ralph Wardlaw, an M.A. in English, who was working on a doctorate at Columbia.[14]

Probably the most common denominator among the students was the feeling that their academic studies bore little relationship to the "real" world around them. Events in the thirties were hurried and important, and the knowledge of books too unreal to satisfy their desires. Great social changes seemed to be in the offing, and it was more important to be part of them than to listen to lectures and read books about the institutions of a vanishing society. Young men are always impatient to begin "life," and the thirties exacerbated this impatience. One of them who could not wait for graduation day was Sam Levinger, the son of a rabbi, who left Ohio State University at the age of twenty-one and was killed after nine months of combat in Spain. Levinger was from Columbus, born into a comfortable, bourgeois home that did not smother his social conscience. Always sent off to school with a huge lunch, Levinger often gave most of it away to students who had nothing to eat. In high school one day he tagged after some Ohio State students off on a lark to watch picketing coal miners, and he landed in jail because he talked back to a deputy sheriff. He joined the Young Socialists, and after entering the university, spent more time away from campus marching with workers on picket lines than in the library reading books. Levinger was a young man who enjoyed life very much, but the rise of European fascism seemed to threaten his world and the revolt of the rebel generals left him with the feeling that "the cause of Spain was the cause of America." In January 1937 he enlisted in the International Brigades with little posturing or fanfare, making the simple statement that he was going to Spain "to give the fascists what they've asked for." [15]

Among the members of the Lincoln Battalion were many whose college days were behind them, men who left various professions to journey across the sea. The largest group of these were teachers, usually from the public schools, a few holding minor university posts. Several lawyers left their practices for Spain along with a couple of engineers. More than 30 surgeons, physicians, and dentists made the trip to care for the medical needs of the fightingmen. Newspapermen went in significant numbers, too, probably more interested in making news than reporting it. Superficially a most unlikely soldier was Evan Biddle Shipman, erstwhile expatriate and friend of Gertrude Stein, a sports columnist later described as "one of the world's greatest authorities on thoroughbred and harness racing and breeding," a man more interested in horses than politics. Shipman started for Spain to deliver a couple of ambulances purchased by his friend Ernest Hemingway, and he stayed to enlist in the Lincoln Battalion. Certainly none of the soldiers had a more all-American background than twenty-eight-year-old Pennsylvania reporter Cy Podolin, onetime gridiron hero, whose ability to outrun opposing halfbacks had once gained him a football scholarship to Muhlenberg College. [16]

Though artists are usually thought to be individualistic creatures, in the 1930's they were collective-minded too, and painters, sculptors, actors, and composers joined the ranks of the regimented in the Spanish struggle. Even though they were not all Communists, they all probably would have agreed with the *New Masses* article which claimed that in times like these creating works of art was not enough for the serious artist. Because art depended upon freedom, it was necessary for every artist, "whatever his political affiliations, if any," to ally himself "in the cause of man's liberation." [17] The cause in this case was that of the Spanish Republic, and the artists went, not just because of the CP line but because they knew what had happened to art and artists in Germany and Italy—in fact, there was enough truth in what the *New Masses* said to make them do more than pause and wonder.

Since writing and romanticism are supposed to go hand in hand, it is not surprising to find writers flocking to Spain, and among them the sort of men who had not written anything yet, but were in the process of gathering material for a book that would someday startle the world with its truth and poetry.[18] But there were serious writers in the Lincoln Battalion, too, men who had published novels or books of poetry, who had won literary fellowships or some critical recognition. Sensitive men, revolted by the pogroms and book burnings in Germany, some writers had felt themselves impelled to join the Communist Party because of its opposition to fascism. When the war erupted in Spain they became volunteers, not consciously to further party interests, but for the same reason they had joined the Communists in the first place.[19]

The novelist Alvah Bessie went to Spain late in the war for reasons that may seem idiosyncratic, but were probably no more so than those of anyone else making such a decision. Like all good Americans, he had been taught to get ahead and prosper, to seek "distinction and preferment." Like all writers, he was used to working alone. Now there was a different climate in his world, and he wished to "submerge" himself in a mass of men, to destroy his middle-class training and achieve "unselfishness," to reconstruct his life so that it would "be geared to other men and the world-events that circumscribed them." By lending his strength to "the fight against our eternal enemy—oppression," he hoped to achieve a personal and artistic self-integration as well as rid the world, or a portion of it, of a system that threatened free men everywhere. Edwin Rolfe, a poet with a physique as frail as a couplet, a young man who published verse that smoldered with a hatred of the Depression that gripped America, where "we do not play, we may not work/ and sleep escapes us," lamented the fact that the "soft office voices" had stolen the country the workers had built. Rolfe had studied at the University of Wisconsin before going to the staff of the *Daily Worker* and then the *New Masses,* and one book of his poetry had already been published. A Marxist and a Communist, Rolfe had written of the necessity for renouncing "the fiction of the self and its vainglory," and he had once called for "the miracle of deeds performed in unison." [20] For him, Spain became the chance for that renunciation and that miracle.

Ethnically, the Lincoln Battalion was as much of a *mélange* as the United States itself, and it included men of many cultures, Irish from the East and Scots-Irish from the South, Finns, Swedes, and Germans from the Middle West, Polish and Italian-Americans from New York, Greeks and Yugoslavs, a few men with American Indian blood, Negroes from both the South and North, and a number of men who claimed pedigrees stretching back to the Revolution and earlier. The only groups that seem to have been missing from its ranks were Mexican-Americans and Chinese, while a single Japanese-American made the trip to Spain.

Communist propaganda often spoke of the Negroes with the Lincolns, usually exaggerating their numbers, probably to emphasize the party's concern with equality and its desire to attract more Negro members. Though the poet Langston Hughes once put the figure of his fellow Negroes fighting for the Loyalists at 200, it is unlikely that their number even reached 100. [21] For the Negro who went to Spain, fascism represented the extremes of racism from which he already suffered in the United States. As one wrote, in Spanish fascism he saw "those who chain us in

America to cotton fields and brooms." But whereas in the United States the Negro had no real way of fighting back in the thirties, in Spain he could hit out directly at the enemy. Hughes saw this and he wrote home after a tour of the battlefield a description of fascists as "Jim Crow peoples." Then he added triumphantly, "here we shoot 'em down." The Lincoln Battalion offered another appeal to the Negro, as did the Communist Party in general, for these were two of the rare places in American life where he might rise to whatever level his talents would take him, regardless of the color of his skin. For a period until his death, the battalion was commanded by Captain Oliver Law, probably the first Negro ever to lead a body of primarily white American fightingmen into action.[22]

In religious backgrounds, the Lincolns showed the same heterogeneous composition. Even two sons of ministers found their way into the battalion's ranks. In spite of general Catholic support for the cause of Francisco Franco, a goodly number of American Catholics journeyed to Spain to battle against his "crusade" for the Church. A young man like Robert Raven might say, "I won't have my priest tell me I'm fighting religion when I'm supporting the Loyalists. . . . I can't believe that the Moors are fighting for Christianity," but one suspects that Raven and his Catholic comrades were not much interested in Christianity either. A *Daily Worker* story about one young Catholic who regularly attended church services, and even received a leave from the trenches to attend Easter services in Madrid, contained more enthusiasm than truth in view of the fact that Catholic churches in Republican Spain were closed throughout the war.[23]

By far the most significant ethnic imbalance in the Lincoln Battalion came from the fact that at least 30 per cent of the men who joined had been born into Jewish homes. In view of Hitler's brutal treatment of their fellow Jews, his spreading of the Aryan myth, and the presence of some of his troops in Spain, this hardly seems surprising. Almost any Jewish volunteer when questioned would reply as William Harvey did to a *Life* reporter: "I know what Hitler is doing to my people." Yet many of the Jews who went off to Spain were not at all religious, were the sort of people who remain Jewish only because the world identifies them as such. They were the same Jews who flocked to the Communist Party, not only because it was opposing Hitler but, as Nathan Glazer has pointed out, because it promised to break the old forms of society that had traditionally meant oppression for them, because—as for the Negroes—it offered them a community in which all men were equal, in which they could shed the limitations of their social reality and "join in a fraternity that transcended the divisions of the world." Like the Communist Party, the International Brigades were another such fraternity.[24]

The men who went from the United States to Spain were young men, but they were hardly adolescents. While there was at least one seventeen-year-old among them, a good 70 per cent were between the ages of twenty-one and twenty-eight, with their numbers pretty well distributed in between. The oldest man in the battalion was "Pop" Kowalski, fifty-four, a veteran of the Argonne in World War I; and while most of the men beyond forty did not enter combat, he was for a while a leader of a machine-gun company. There were a few other world war veterans, too, some like Sheldon Jones holding the common opinion that he and millions of others had been made fools of in that earlier "crusade." Military experience of one sort or another was in the background of probably 100 of the Lincolns. Few had seen as much military life as had Roe Burkett, an Oklahoman who had been in the American Navy from World War I until 1929, before going off to China to see action in the Sino-Japanese fighting. Thirty-eight-year-old Edward Wills of Muncie, Indiana, was another volunteer with years of military experience. Entering the U. S. Army in 1921, Wills retired as a staff sergeant in 1936, was recruited by the Socialists for the Debs Column, and wound up in the Lincoln Battalion. Other Americans who had never seen active duty had spent time in the National Guard, the Army Reserves, or ROTC.[25]

Inevitably, with the Lincoln Battalion, one comes down to politics, for the Spanish Civil War was above all a time of intense and bitter partisan politics. Surprisingly, there were people in Spain who were not much interested in the subject, people to whom the name Marx might mean Groucho rather than Karl, but they were very few indeed. One young drifter was boozing it up in a Seattle bar one day when he fell in with a bunch of seamen who were going off to Spain, and because they were such good drinking pals, he volunteered to go along. A few others could be described by their comrades as "having no political awareness at all," men who had no more complex reasons for coming to Spain than that they had heard the underdog was getting kicked around.[26]

Communist publications of the period liked to give the impression that there were hordes of regular Republicans and Democrats in the ranks, but this seems little more than wishful thinking. For the vast majority of the troops were political radicals, formally enrolled in or sympathizers with America's most left-wing political parties. Some were Socialists, but not many. A few who had enlisted in the much-heralded Debs Column actually made their way to Spain. Others, like Sam Romer, onetime managing editor of the *Socialist Call,* probably found their way into the Lincoln Battalion with the help of the Communist Party. The scarcity of Socialists can be partly explained by the fact that in 1937 membership in the Socialist Party had sunk to an all-time low of 6,500. Moreover, the Communists were not really very anxious to have Socialist Party members in the battalion, for the Trotskyists had temporarily merged with the Socialist Party and it was hard to tell them apart. Also in the ranks were a few from the minute sect of anarcho-syndicalists, and a couple of Wobblies from the once-boisterous Industrial Workers of the World, which hovered on into the thirties like an unwanted ghost.[27]

So it comes down to the fact that the overwhelming majority of young men who entered the Lincoln Battalion either belonged to no political party at all or were members of the American Communist Party. To try to sort them out, to decide who was a Communist and who was not, to assign percentages, is as easy as counting grains of sand on a beach and about as useful. Herbert Matthews and John Gates could claim that 80 per cent were Communists, Earl Browder 60 per cent, and Hans Amlie 25 per cent.[28] But none of them really knew; none was making better than a guess, for there were no records of political affiliations ever kept by the battalion. When the men formally enrolled in the International Brigades at Albacete, their political party was put down as "anti-fascist," a designation that would at that time cover the political spectrum from Martin Dies to Joseph Stalin, leaving a rather broad area for ideological differences.

To say that a man who went to Spain was a Communist is not to say everything about him; it is more like saying nothing at all. Since the proclamation of the Popular Front in 1935 the party had loosened up its structure, become more flexible and less dogmatic about issues, had for the first time tried to Americanize itself by advising its members to become interested in local political problems like sewer bond issues. Moreover, the Communists had dropped their eternal seriousness, had learned to relax, and were sponsoring social gatherings, cocktail parties, dances, picnics, and moonlight cruises up the Hudson River; some people are known to have preferred the CP to the SP simply because the Communists gave better parties. Many of the newer members—and a high percentage of the Communists in Spain fell into this category—were not familiar with the old socially stifling, humorless party atmosphere. They could accept Communists as a species of extreme liberal.

Another reason the label tells little of the man is that while it is easy enough to discern the party line on issues, it is almost impossible to tell how closely any individual's beliefs followed that line. Many people were joining the party during the Spanish Civil War because of its stand on fascism. This does not mean that they necessarily agreed with traditional Communist positions. Indeed, many of the old shibboleths were not even being mentioned during the Popular Front period, and a newcomer would not have occasion to come to grips with many of them. In the late thirties, anti-fascism was *the* issue, and naturally all could agree on that.

Most important, to say a man who went to Spain was a member of the Communist Party is not to differentiate him ideologically from nonparty members in the ranks, especially with regard to issues surrounding the war. There was a community of belief among the men who went to Spain; all shared in one way or another in the "conscience of the thirties." Socialist and Anarchist, Communist or just plain liberal, all believed that the rise of the right in Europe was a threat to the workingman of America and all saw the war as a means of hitting back at the fascism they abhorred. A few, a very few among them also saw Spain as a way of hastening the "inevitable" day of social revolution that would change the world and usher in a new era. But most of them believed Spain was only a defensive action, a means of stopping fascist aggression rather than of spreading socialism.[29]

Young non-Communist liberals who went to Spain were the same people who in another era would be going on freedom rides, registering Negro voters in Mississippi, or demonstrating against the Vietnam war. They were probably too individualistic to accept the discipline of the Communist Party rather than wise enough to criticize its basic premises. Though not committed to Marxism, they certainly had absorbed much of the Marxist intellectual atmosphere of the decade and most of them saw the eventual arrival of socialism as more or less inevitable. If they themselves were not prepared to hasten the day of its arrival, they were certainly not going to build roadblocks to hold it back.

The Communists who went to Spain do not at all fit the stereotype of the hardened, bomb-throwing revolutionary. Tending to be the younger members rather than the old warhorses who had been active in Communist causes for years, they had little familiarity with the upper echelons of the party and few of them were officials. Their experiences as activists were recent, and not particularly soul-searing. The young Communists had paraded on May Day, marched in picket lines, clashed with the police, and sometimes ended up in jail for a few days. Typical of them was twenty-four-year-old John Gates, the son of a small shopkeeper in New York, whose early years were quite middle class. As a youngster, Gates was passionately interested in baseball statistics, and he would often cut high-school classes to watch the Yankees play. He had what he considered to be a "happy childhood," but sometime in his teens he learned that the world is bigger than Yankee Stadium, and at City College of New York he joined the Young Communist League. There he engaged in agitation and demonstrations against ROTC and the imprisonments of Tom Mooney and the Scottsboro Boys. Becoming an organizer and leaving New York City, his "revolutionary" activities brought arrests in Warren, Ohio, for "making a loud noise without a permit," and in Newcastle, Pennsylvania, for "littering the street." For Gates, the desire to go to Spain preceded his knowledge that the party was sending men, and he was glad he was allowed to leave his post. It is true that occasionally the Communist Party ordered an older, experienced member like Steve Nelson—who had spent some time in Moscow—to Spain, usually for the purpose of maintaining discipline or boosting morale, but for the most part it was content merely to accept volunteers and even discourage them in favor of nonparty members.[30]

Volunteer and CP member Saul Wellman has suggested reasonably that it was the rebels rather than the revolutionaries among the Communists who went to Spain. Another confirmed this indirectly by saying that the men who went over from the party "did so out of a kind of frustration with the radical movement, with too much sitting around and discussing how to better the world, with distributing leaflets and running mimeograph machines and writing articles. . . . Now they wanted to act."[31] For a real revolutionary, dedicated to a distant but inevitable cause, the mimeograph machine would have been as important as the rifle. But the Communists who went to Spain were not the type to think so.

If, during the Spanish Civil War, you had asked a member of the Lincoln Battalion why he was fighting in Spain, he would say, "Spain is fighting the world battle against fascism," or "I'm here to fight for democracy," or "I want to stamp out fascism before it gets to America." If he were more eloquent, he might reply as did a writer in the *New Republic* after his return, "With us it wasn't a question of being either brave or damn fools, though some of us were either or both. We knew and still know that democracy has to be saved. We knew and still know that the war in Spain is of the first importance in saving democracy for the whole world." Some might give more idiosyncratic reasons, like the Detroit newsboy who said, "I went to Spain because I was hungry. . . . I had taken part in a strike of newsboys in 1937 and had been discharged, so I had no money. I got to thinking about this war in Spain and decided that at least I could get something to eat over there." A strong union man might say, "to take up the fight here was a logical step from our battles on the picket lines." Once in a while, there was someone whose thought processes were complex enough to admit "mixed motives" and to say, as did Robert Bready of Chillicothe, Ohio, "We were anti-Fascist, we wanted to see first-hand what was going on, and undoubtedly most of us wanted a thrill." [32]

All the reasons they gave were valid ones. Those who find it hard to believe that a Communist could be interested in fighting for what he called "democracy," or to stamp out fascism, are ignoring the tremendous wellsprings of idealism that brought people into the movement and are in retrospect seeing only the cynical opportunism engaged in by some of the CP leaders, whose actions tell the story of the organization but never speak for what the rank-and-file member felt about the world. Herbert Matthews, a long way from being a Communist, said the party members in the battalion "have as high a percentage of culture, cleanliness, sincerity and ideals as any other political section of society."[33] No evidence exists to dispute his testimony.

Though the Americans may have given valid reasons for going to Spain, they hardly told the whole story. Antifascists they were, and though Franco was a complete stranger to them, it was his supporters they objected to. For many of them the commitment had really been made earlier, when they involved themselves in the social struggles preceding the war. Spain merely reflected the depth of their commitment to a cause, for there the issues of the decade seemed to have come to a head. There is no doubt that most of the men who went there were already involved in labor unions, political movements, or student action groups, and certainly decisions to go were influenced by the prevailing viewpoint of their organizations, by lecturers who appeared, and publications that were circulated. There was a companionship and perhaps even a social pressure generated by discussions of Spain within various organizations; the desires of some men reinforced the tentative plans of others, and often out of friendship they would enlist in groups. Though few openly admitted it, the desire of youth for adventure, to find out about the world, to test itself in the burning crucible of experience, was a factor in the decision to go.

As should be apparent by now, the men who went to fight under the banner of the Abraham Lincoln Battalion came from a wide variety of occupational, ethnic, and social backgrounds. If the organization's composition was not a true version of American social groupings in miniature, if there were too many men from the big cities, too many industrial laborers and too many students, it is still true that most strata of society were represented. And if one were to probe beneath the surface of individual groupings, still more variety would become apparent. Among the students, for example, were men from solid, middle-class backgrounds like Thane Summers of Washington, whose father was a successful Seattle attorney, along with Wilfred Mendelson, who had to work at a variety of menial jobs to put himself through CCNY. Even among

CP members there were men as diverse as Joe Dallet, a Dartmouth graduate and accomplished pianist who had once lived a life of ease on his parents' money in Paris, and Irving Goff, whose working-class father had joined the American CP when it was first formed and who had been in the YCL as long as he could remember. Or there was John Richard, self-described as "a sheltered boy from a wealthy family," whose only care during college days at Stanford was how fast he could swim 100 yards, side by side with Archie Brown, whose schooling took place in hobo jungles, Oakland hunger marches, the Salinas lettuce strike, and waterfront struggles in San Pedro and San Francisco.[34]

All these men, from diverse backgrounds, were now binding themselves together in a common enterprise. All of them were shouldering arms, were leaving behind the traditional American middle way in politics, were committing themselves wholeheartedly to an ideological cause. Yet the search for a real ideology among them bears little fruit. Certainly there was a body of ideas that they shared, and certainly many of them were vocal about the ideas. They were anti-fascist and pro-labor and a good number of them had misgivings about the viability of capitalism. Yet they were for the most part not at all familiar with the intellectual underpinnings of their left-wing ideas. Moreover, most of them had newly adopted these ideas or were just in the process of adopting them, and the issues of the Spanish War were themselves a factor in pushing many of the Lincolns left. Vincent Sheean once called their journey to Spain "a reflex of the conscience of the world," and there is much to be said for his statement.[35] They were joining the struggles of the decade as a kind of reflex action to the world around them, the American Depression, the organization of labor, the threat to their actual or potential freedom posed by the bellicose and expansive fascist powers, which were anti-labor, anti-Semitic, anti-intellectual, and almost anti-civilization. In this sense the Americans who went to Spain were not much more ideological than their countrymen. They had not adopted a body of ideas and then set out to defend them. The defense and the adoption went hand in hand. No man—with the exception of a few party leaders—went to Spain because he had joined the Communist Party. Rather, the impulse for doing both was the same.

In spite of whatever movements these young Americans belonged to, in spite of whatever talks they had heard and whatever they had read, the decision was a lonely one to make. Each individually had to weigh the values of life and death and decide alone whether he would go to Spain. More than one observer noted that the men in Spain were restless, lonely men, and one wisely observed that they went "by their own choice and out of . . . the same lonely impulse that made them Communists or radicals in the first place . . . a combination of alienation and the search for adventure."[36] This is not to deny that the issues of the war were deadly important. But millions of people in the United States recognized their importance, and only thousands were ready to journey to the battlefields. Of course, in any such historical crisis there are far more people who recognize the importance of the issues than are willing to pick up a rifle and go to the barricades. The men who went to Spain were the second sort, yet it is doubtful if even psychology can give the reasons why one man acts while another is content to sit back and merely applaud his action.

There was one thing that all the volunteers seemed to share—that was the disturbing feeling that time was running out for the world, that problems had to be met and issues resolved now, or there would be no tomorrow. One who best expressed this feeling of the pressure of hurrying events wrote that the world was no longer for the artist or the historian; now it was a world for the activist.[37] Perhaps more than any other man, Robert Merriman, commander of the Lincolns at Jarama, a man who was universally liked and respected, had behind him a career that exemplified this point. Within Merriman's whole life there was a terrific tension, as the impulses of scholarship and activism warred within him, the battle finally being decided by the temper of the times.

Born of Scottish-American parents, his father a lumberjack and his mother a writer, Merriman had to work part-time through his high-school days. He then began to travel around the western United States, working in logging camps and paper mills. He was a big man, 6 feet, 2 inches, with broad shoulders and a strong back, but he was shy and intellectual, and the logging camps did not satisfy his desire for mental exercise. Enrolling in the University of Nevada, he joined a fraternity, majored in economics, and earned money partly by playing end on the varsity football team and partly by belonging to ROTC, which paid $7.50 a month. During summer vacations he put his muscles to use at jobs such as ditch digging and harvesting on ranches and farms. Finishing at Nevada, he went on to postgraduate work at the University of California, Berkeley, where a teaching assistant's salary allowed him to eke out a meager existence. While studying economics at Berkeley and observing the Depression world around him, Merriman evidently came to the conclusion that Marx's critique of capitalism was sound. In his spare time he launched back into action. Too much of an individualist to join the CP, he began to work for the International Labor Defense, one of its front organizations, taking part in the defense of the Imperial Valley strikers in 1933 and playing the role of public relations man in the San Francisco General Strike. Again, action alone did not fully satisfy him. His intellectual background won him a traveling fellowship in economics that took him to the Soviet Union in 1935 to study Marxism in action. He was there for eight months, living on collective farms and taking notes on their methods of operation. Then he went off to compare Russian farms with those in Eastern Europe, traveling through Greece, the Balkans, and Hungary. The outbreak of the Spanish Civil War found him in Moscow again, writing a book on his findings, a book he was never to complete. For the Spanish War was the event that pulled him back from the world of thought to that of action again. He was to serve with distinction for a year and a half, rising to the rank of major and being wounded several times before his disappearance during a retreat in the spring of 1938.[38]

Merriman's internal tensions exemplified the feelings of many men in the 1930's, torn between personal desires and the feeling that the time was not ripe for self-indulgence. Edwin Rolfe, who shortly before the war found himself unable to enjoy a quiet vacation in the country, expressed this feeling by writing:

> *This silence is deceptive, the flowers a fraud*
> *the stream polluted. To live here is a lie.*

It was a lie because the world with its rampant fascism was too much with that generation. As Rolfe went on,

> *Escape from chaos is impossible;*
> *The world's too muddled, the skies thunder*
> *with guns, projectiles dealing death* . . . .[39]

Like Rolfe, the men who went to Spain were only making the conscious decision to embrace that chaos before it swallowed them.

It started with the decision, made among a group of
friends drinking beer together after the union meeting,
where the lecturer had told the membership that their new
union would not be safe if the wrong side won in Spain.
Or after a young man stood on a street corner handing
out leaflets for the twelfth Sunday in a row, watching the
people glance at them, crumple them up, and toss them
away into the gutter, and began to wonder if there wasn't
something more real he could do for the cause. Or after
a student returned from the rally where the short film had
shown the battalion training and the blind veteran had
made an impassioned plea, and one of the brochures
contained the name of a man who could give more information about what "you" could do for Spain. Perhaps he
propped it up against the mirror and looked at himself and
tried to imagine what he would look like in uniform. Then
he looked at the brochure again before turning off the lights
and going to bed. And sometime before morning the
decision was made.

Finding a recruiter for Spain was easier than being
accepted by one. The prospective soldier would have to
get friends in a union or student group, a Popular Front
organization or the Communist Party to vouch for his
reliability. He was interviewed by a committee, perhaps

more than once, and though he didn't know it, his background was then investigated. This cautious approach by Communist recruiters was to keep "weak" and "unreliable" people from reaching Spain. More important, it was to make sure that people were politically "sound," that is, to make certain that no Trotskyists slipped into the battalion, for the CP viewed the followers of Trotsky much as a medieval churchman looked upon agents of Satan.[1]

Once accepted, a candidate was given a physical examination, though of a most perfunctory sort. Many men never stripped below the waist, and Joseph Chimowlowski, who had had a wooden leg since childhood, passed the physical, reached the front lines, and engaged in three months of combat until his artificial limb was shot off and battalion authorities learned of his handicap. Even then he might have remained, but nobody was able to find him a new wooden leg to replace the old one. The medical examinations were given by doctors presumably friendly to the cause, and though much of this work was done free, some of the physicians wished to be paid for their services. In Detroit, doctors examined recruits and billed the city for the service under the guise that they had given tuberculin tests to indigents, for which the health-conscious city fathers were happy to pay.[2]

Passports were a necessity, and since more often than not the recruit had no money, the party supplied the $10. Nobody put down Spain as a destination, for passports were being stamped not valid for travel to that country. Men under twenty-one had to obtain parents' signatures, not always an easy thing to do, and many false names and birthdates were filled in on questionnaires, and many false addresses given so that families would not know what their sons were about. One young man named Gabby, because he was from a family sympathetic to the left and to the cause of the Spanish Loyalists, did not think of lying on his application. But his mother intercepted the envelope bearing the passport and sent it back to the government with a note saying it was not really needed. Angry and bewildered when he found out, Gabby rushed to the committee that had interviewed him, told the story and asked for advice. The members said they did not know or care what his name was. Taking the hint, he applied again for a passport, this time under a fictitious name, "Klein," and at the address of a friend who was not at all motherly. When he did get to Spain he was always known under his new name. The mother of twenty-year-old Abraham Eisenberg of Brooklyn took even more drastic measures. When she would not sign his passport application, Eisenberg applied under a false name. Learning of this, his mother informed federal authorities, who arrested the youngster for falsifying his application.[3]

The trip began for some men with a bus ride. For those from the West Coast like Bill Bailey, it was a long, tiring bus ride past desert, cornfields, and forest, until the towers of Manhattan loomed against the sky. For Samuel Levinger of Columbus, Ohio, it was a much shorter ride, and for George Poole of Buffalo, the trip took almost no time at all. In New York City the volunteers lived in the bare rooms of the YMCA and ate simple meals at cheap restaurants or at the homes of friendly party members. New Yorkers like Gabby Klein or Mike Goodwin, who had just returned from a CCC camp in Montana, had only the impatient wait, once they were selected, until a group gathered and travel arrangements were made. They went in small units of 15 or 20 men, with one party member designated as the official leader. On embarkation day they gathered and, behind a group leader such as Joe Dallet, climbed the gangplank and went down into third-class cabins, each to put his one suitcase away. From the decks the young men watched the tugs nose the liner into the harbor and were silent as Manhattan slipped slowly by, the towers of midtown, the Empire State Building, the tall structures of the Wall Street they disliked, the island where so many of their parents had landed in America, the green statue representing the liberty they thought was fading from the world, the tip of Brooklyn, the beaches of Coney Island that many of them knew so well. And then America was dropping away, a piece of land in a world of sea and sky, and at last there was nothing but the sea around them, the Atlantic Ocean stretching away to everywhere.

Time passed slowly, too slowly for the anxious young men on board ship, as they strolled on the decks and breathed the ocean air, slept long hours in their cabins, read novels and magazines, played shuffleboard or poker for small stakes, and drank endless bottles of cheap beer in the ship's lounges. Edwin Rolfe did all these things, and his poetic sensibility was alive to the changing beauty of the sea, the greens and blues and grays of its many moods. Still he was endlessly bored on this unreal world of an ocean liner, and he felt suspended and detached from the reality of the social struggle he had left behind and the angry battlefields he had yet to see. Others seemed to enjoy the Atlantic crossing, and Wilfred Mendelson, who would be in one of the last groups to make the trip, later described it as "marvelous," militantly adding, "For me it was an introduction to the splendid life all of us will lead under Socialism when the voyage will be for the many and not restricted to the few. . . ."[4]

At times there might be 100 volunteers bound for Spain on board ship, but to keep from arousing suspicion they were cautioned by their leaders to gather only in small groups and for the most part to keep away from each other. To Mike Goodwin, however, it seemed quite obvious that many of the other passengers knew who they were and where they were going. Steve Nelson, who prided himself on never discussing Spain even though the topic was often brought up by the regular tourists over meals, was disconcerted to have one of his table partners, a middle-aged businessman, wish him good luck in Spain at the end of the voyage and slip him an envelope containing $10. Still, the would-be soldiers maintained the fiction until they marched down the gangplank in Le Havre, a large group of young men each carrying only one suitcase, while all the other passengers were struggling with cameras and bags, trailed by porters bearing the rest of their luggage. As the realization struck the Americans that this was a dead giveaway, the French customs officers, loyal themselves to the idea of the Popular Front, waved them by with a smile and maybe even a few words of encouragement. The leaders would then hurry them on, worried that the customs men might be reactionary provocateurs.[5]

They went to Paris by train, but never had time to get to know the French capital. They were there for one or two or three days at most, staying in dingy hotels, eating at workers' cooperative restaurants, grinning at the public *pissotières* that adorned the broad boulevards, or, like Edwin Rolfe, wondering what that strange contraption in their hotel room was and being told, "It is for the ladies . . . afterwards, for a douche." They would attend a lecture given by the International Brigade Committee and be informed that though the French people were behind the Spanish Republic, the government of the Third Republic had closed the border and was trying to stop volunteers from reaching Spain. They would also be told to watch their step in France, to pretend they were tourists, to drink moderately and avoid prostitutes, for there were fascist spies lurking everywhere. At the union building where the lecture was given, Alvah Bessie's group ran into a wounded American veteran on his way home who called them "suckers." The men with George Poole met a shell-shocked Negro and were startled by his incoherence. Poole explained their surprise by saying this was their "first contact with the grim reality of the war we had come to fight."[6]

Finally, word would come to them in their hotel to wrap the few most essential belongings in paper, to leave their suitcases with the committee, and to get ready to go. Sometimes the Frenchmen on the International Committee, worried over the fact that the volunteers looked too American, would advise them to alter their clothing in some way. Irving Fajans was with a group that was told to get rid of their hats and buy berets. This they did in their last few hours in Paris, as they purchased cigarettes, chocolate bars, sandwiches, and bottles of cognac to prepare for the long night on a train without a dining car.

At 7:30 in the evening a large number of young men carrying identical parcels wrapped in paper and packages of food, their berets bobbing conspicuously, appeared on the platform in the huge, dingy black barn that is the *Gare de Lyon*. They avoided each other and clustered in little groups, but more than one of them was struck by the humor of the situation, by the fact that they looked more than ever like volunteers for Spain. Many would agree with Fajans's estimate that "Anyone mistaking us for tourists could also be convinced that Americans visited the Folies Bergère for cultural purposes." They scattered through the train, and as it clacked across the darkness of the countryside, they smoked and tried unsuccessfully to doze, played cards and drank from their flasks, nibbled at sandwiches and huddled together to keep out the coldness of the French night. When Sam Levinger made the trip, the compartments were so crowded that some volunteers climbed into the baggage racks to sleep, and the first casualties of the war that he saw were men "who fell off . . . onto somebody sleeping below."

The slow morning light found the Americans bleary-eyed and tired, peering out the windows at the rich, green fields of France, watching as the rolling, wooded hills flattened out and the earth became less fertile, as vineyards and olive trees appeared and clumps of rocks began to push through the thin soil. At last the leaders would give the signal and it was time for the volunteers to leave the train. They stretched and shook the kinks out of their legs and descended to earth as the baggage porters backed away, incredulous at the dozens of men who were leaving the train, all without so much as an overnight bag in their hands.[7]

Gathered on the platform of the station, the Americans waited for the cloak-and-dagger game to go on, many of them feeling, like George Poole, that things were a little too melodramatic to be serious. Yet sure enough, a man with a yellow sweater, or one with a flower in his buttonhole, would make a small gesture and quietly leave the station, and the Americans followed him in knots of two or three, trying vainly to look inconspicuous, quite conscious of the fact that their group stretched out for several hundred yards through the town, which might be any one of a number in southern France—Béziers, set on a hilltop; or Narbonne, with its archbishop's palace; Perpignan, where the kings of Mallorca once made their home; Toulouse, with its broad boulevards and gray buildings making it a miniature Paris; or some small town, where the buildings were painted bright colors and had red tile roofs. Soon they were safe in a hotel which quartered Internationals from all over Europe. They slept and ate simple meals and waited, perhaps as little as a couple of hours, usually as long as two or three days. Occasionally they might be kept waiting longer. Donald Thayer, some-time student at the University of Wisconsin, was with a group that stayed in a hotel for several weeks, playing cards and studying Spanish grammar books, all the time worrying that they had been completely forgotten. George Poole's group was shifted about several times, moving at night from one hotel to another, then being taken into the countryside, where they hid in barns during the daylight hours. Each day a Frenchman would come to tell them it was still too dangerous to move. But for Poole's group, as for all of them, a taxi, truck, or bus would arrive at last to pick them up and take them to the jumping-off point for Spain.[8]

Some American volunteers, a very small number, made the journey by ship, on liners from Marseilles or small fishing craft from harbors close to the Spanish border that carried them past the patrol boats of the Non-Intervention Commission. But water seems to have been an unlucky way to get to Spain. On May 30, 1937, the liner *Ciudad de Barcelona* was sunk by a torpedo off the Spanish coast just north of the city for which she was named, and many young men on their way to join the International Brigades drowned.[9] Two months previously, 25 volunteers—17 of them Americans—were removed from a little fishing smack by a French patrol ship. Since the story that they were tourists seemed a little odd in view of the fact that they had all been crammed into the hold of the ship, the group's leaders—Joe Dallet and Steve Nelson—decided to admit

they had been on their way to Spain. Charged with violation of a recent law that forbade people to cross French
territory to enroll in fighting forces in Spain, the Americans
were held in jail 17 days before being tried. The trial took
place in Ceret, in the shadow of the Pyrenees. The Americans were defended by a French Socialist lawyer, an
adherent of the ideals of the Popular Front, who pleaded
for clemency on the grounds of the nobility of their cause.
The court handed down a verdict of 21 days' imprisonment
and banishment from France. This meant only 3 more days
in jail, then 8 days in which to leave the country. After
being freed, the volunteers lounged openly about the cafés
of Perpignan—the first Internationals able to do so—and
then one by one they slipped away to cross the Pyrenees
into Spain.[10]

Other Americans were also apprehended by French
authorities, though of the 3,000 who made it across the
border, fewer than 100 saw the inside of a French jail. On
April 14, 1937, two days before the release of Dallet's
group, half a dozen volunteers were tried in the same
courtroom, receiving sentences of one month in prison. Ten
days before, on April 4, 29 Americans were arrested in
Toulouse. They received the stiffest penalty of all the
offenders, being sentenced to 40 days in jail.[11] Yet these
halfhearted attempts of French officialdom to enforce the
nonintervention laws provided only the slightest of dams
to stop the flow of volunteers. In view of the fact that the
movement of volunteers around southern French towns
was, as Mike Goodwin observed, "pretty obvious" to
everyone despite the elaborate secrecy precautions, it
seems that the French Popular Front government was for
its own reasons not really interested in stopping the foreigners from reaching Spain. Perhaps this was Léon Blum's
way of salving his conscience for having sponsored non-
intervention.

Aside from the few who traveled by water, the great
majority of the volunteers made the crossing to Spain the
hard way, on foot over the formidable mountain barrier
which has always cut the Iberian Peninsula off from the

rest of Europe. It usually began just after dark, as they rode in taxis or buses up into the foothills of the Pyrenees. A few went like Steve Nelson, who clung to the back of a motorcycle driven by a Frenchman at breakneck speeds down the narrow country roads of southern France. The man stopped the cycle and Nelson dismounted and hid in an irrigation ditch while a large group of men of all nationalities slowly assembled. Sometimes the committee in charge saw to it that the men were supplied with *alpargatas,* rope-soled Spanish sandals that tied around the ankles and would not skid on slippery mountain trails. The men waited and whispered, the sounds of the farmland muffled in the growing darkness, an occasional cow lowing, the whir of insects' wings, the sigh of the evening breeze through the underbrush. All were tense, and none more so than Gabby Klein, who in his twenty-two years had never been farther away from Manhattan than Jersey City. On the train riding south he had begun to get the feel of open spaces, but still the endless empty fields dotted by farmhouses made him nervous and disoriented. To Klein there was something homey about a skyscraper, and all through Spain he was to long for the dirty gray streets of New York.[12]

Out of the darkness a guide appeared. He was a little man who knew the mountain trails because he normally made his living smuggling things across the Franco-Spanish border. The volunteers started out single file, clutching paper-wrapped packages of belongings to their chests, across the fields and small streams, until the ground began to rise under their feet and they brushed against bushes in the dark, losing sight of any trail at all and keeping their eyes on the back of the man before them. Suddenly they were going up a steep incline, the rocks of the ground slipping under their feet and making them stumble, their breath already coming short. Steve Nelson slipped on the damp ground and pitched full length into mud. He pulled himself out, tried unsuccessfully to brush himself clean, then plunged ahead up the trail. The volunteers were sliding down a slope now and then going up again, a steeper hill this time, looming black against the stars that filled the sky. Soon they lost track of the number of hills they had climbed, knowing only that every time they came to the top of one, there was another, bigger one beyond it. They were breathing hard and pains were beginning to stab at their calves, when a halt was called and they sprawled on the ground and grabbed the bitter pleasure of a cigarette. It was cold when they stopped, and flasks of cognac were passed from hand to hand, the men gulping down the liquid to warm their bellies and limbs.

The rest was all too short and soon they were on their way again, sometimes holding hands because there was no trail, the hills growing ever bigger, numbness in their chests and legs and heads now as they heard dogs barking faintly in the distance. Alvah Bessie walked off the path in the dark, fell forward, and rolled down an embankment until he crashed to a stop against a tree. His hat was gone, and as he searched for it he could hear the men going on up the trail, oblivious of his predicament. Afraid of being left behind, he hastily scrambled back toward the path to follow the column of volunteers.

Sometimes it would rain in the mountains and their feet would pull out heavy from the muddy earth. In some seasons there was wind-driven snow stinging their cheeks and the wetness soaked through the rope sandals, numbing their toes. There was a second stop, and this time it was almost impossible to get up and move on. As the night lengthened, the volunteers lost all sense of time and place, for the only reality was their body, the hard pains in the chest, the mechanical plodding of the feet, the brain too fuzzed with lack of oxygen for them to notice the solemn beauty of the night, the small clusters of lights that were the French towns twinkling below, the frosty splendor of the moon and stars. They went on and up, and occasionally men fell exhausted to the earth. Ed Rolfe dropped to the ground several times, on each occasion thinking he could not possibly take another step. Yet a helpful hand would pull him to his feet, and in spite of himself he was moving forward again. Some men who fell had to be dragged along by stronger comrades, and Joe Dallet found himself carrying one youngster on his back. When there was nobody to carry them, some unfortunates were left lying on the trail, a few never to be heard of again. The night seemed endless, yet suddenly, wonderfully, the sky would begin to pale, and at last there were no more hills to climb and the volunteers were above the timberline, moving among huge boulders and patches of snow, an icy wind and the first light of day narrowing their eyes. They stumbled forward in a run to the stone marker that read "Francia" on one side and "España" on the other, and then collapsed to earth, their faces dirty and streaked with sweat, their clothes torn, the heaving of their chests turning to wild laughter or open sobbing.[13]

Before the volunteers lay Spain, a peaceful-looking countryside, a barren land with endless rugged hills and far-off rivers silver in the morning light. It was a thrill to look down on the wild land before them; Neils Kruth of Albany felt like a weary traveler who had at last reached what was to be his home "for many months, perhaps years, perhaps forever." The sun came up and dazzled the Americans. Alvah Bessie looked at the men around him, most lying on the ground, some standing in heroic postures, hands to their foreheads, gazing at Spain. It was windy on the mountaintop where he stood, and he had to lean forward to keep his balance. He could see no houses, no clouds, not even a bird in the morning air. His imagination took hold of him and he envisaged the place where they stood as "the top of the world and the end of it." In that calm sunrise he felt "in the presence of Time and Death," and imagined that if he put his arms out he could "soar into the face of the wind like a sail-plane, circle and bank and gently float to earth."[14]

The sight of the country they had come to defend quickly revived the exhausted men, and at this point the Communists among them seemed to feel it obligatory to shatter the calm scene with their voices raised together in the "Internationale." Soon they were moving again, this time downhill, passing an occasional farmhouse, perhaps seeing a few peasant women dressed in black and exchanging the greeting *"Salud."* Sometimes the Americans went through a small village like Sietecasas, which George Poole described as "a pitiful, dirty, bad-smelling place," with "narrow streets . . . oozing with mud. . . ." [15] Soon they would get to know such towns well, but from the first day all of them were struck with the "appalling poverty" of Spain, a poverty they would never really get used to. They went down until they reached a road where two Spanish soldiers stood guard. The Americans crowded around the soldiers, who wore the red star of the Republic on their caps, and offered them cigarettes. Those who knew a few words of Spanish tried to carry on a conversation, while others sat on rocks, and some stretched out on the ground and tried to sleep. In a while, trucks arrived and the Americans climbed aboard for a hair-raising ride at full speed down narrow mountain roads—past peasants working in the fields or riding in wagons pulled by donkeys—until they were rolling over an open, green plain. The ride ended as the trucks took them up a hill toward a stone castle, across a moat filled with waving grass, and into immense stone-floored courtyards.

They had arrived in the Castillo de San Fernando, a fifteenth-century structure above the Catalan town of Figueras, the receiving base for all Internationals who crossed the border into Spain. Built of huge rocks the color of sandstone, the walls of the fortress circled the crest of a hill. Inside were endless rows of two-story stone buildings surrounding parade grounds, athletic fields, and training areas. The fortress had been completely taken over by the International Brigades and it was staffed by men of a dozen nationalities. While its commanders awaited transportation to keep the flow of volunteers moving south, they confined the men to the grounds of the base. Figueras was in the heart of Anarchist country and to those individualists the International Brigades posed a threat of Communist takeover. Anxious to avoid any unpleasant confrontation between Internationals and Anarchists, and also to shelter the volunteers from some of the complex political realities of the war, the base commanders kept the volunteers busy at Figueras.

As soon as they arrived, the Americans were shown to their bunks in the long, barren rooms of the stone buildings. They were built of planks and covered by straw-filled mattresses. In small rooms off the sleeping quarters were the smelly latrines, no more than small holes in the floor. Almost immediately the volunteers were marched into the mess hall for a hot meal of stew and potatoes washed down with red wine. The food was bad, but after the 14-hour hike anything would have tasted good to the famished men. Finished eating, they listened to a welcoming speech by the base commandant, delivered in German, then translated into French, Polish, and English. Then the volunteers were free for the rest of the day. Some collapsed into bed in the chilly barracks to sleep off the effects of the hike. Edwin Rolfe, too excited to sleep immediately, sat on the edge of his bunk and removed his rope-soled sandals. When he took out the regular shoes he had carried with him, he found that his feet had swollen so much from the hike that he could not get them on. He relaced the sandals and joined the many other men wandering through the endless grounds of the castle, climbing the ramparts to look down on Figueras and across the green valley to the blue mountains beyond. Others were relaxing in the reading rooms with the *Daily Worker*, or *Life, Punch* or *The* (London) *Times*, or if they could read foreign languages, with *Frente Rojo, L'Humanité*, or *Rote Fahne*. Many men were playing checkers or chess or writing letters home. There were crude murals on the walls, pictures of Lenin and La Pasionaria, Marx and Spanish President Azaña, and the slogan: "Workers of the World Unite!" was painted in French, Russian, German, Italian, and Polish as well as English. Alvah Bessie found everyone smiling and friendly, men from all over the world trying to speak to one another and laughing over the mistakes they made in each other's languages. The camaraderie born of the ordeal of the hike and the common cause they had come to defend with their lives seemed already to be welding them into a truly international army.[16]

Their stay in Figueras was a short one, three days at most, but before they left they were already on a military schedule, rising early in the morning, cleaning the barracks, hearing lectures on military theory, learning the rudiments of marching. Some, like George Poole, were given guard duty at night, watching the fleet of American trucks in the motor park. In the evening there was group singing in many languages, or lectures on the politics and nature of the Spanish War. There was discipline at Figueras, but of a very casual sort. Joe Dallet was happily surprised to find the base officers eating at the same tables as the volunteers and joining them in the songfests at night. He found that no salute was necessary, only a friendly "Hello, comrade" when he passed a superior on the parade ground.

The Americans left the fortress with little regret. Many, like Sam Levinger, had found it a "grim place," with its dungeon-like barracks and stinking latrines. All of them were volunteers who were anxious to begin fighting a war. In the Figueras station they crowded into a dilapidated train and tried to adjust their limbs to the wooden benches. The train pulled out slowly and never picked up much speed. The Americans watched the Spanish landscape moving by them, the flat fields, the earth bright red, the terraced hillsides shored with stone, the towns the color of mud blending into the earth as if they had grown out of it, clustering around a large church which dwarfed all the other buildings. To Alvah Bessie, musing on the beauty of the countryside and the wretched squalor of the towns, the rich and heavy masonry of the cathedral and its commanding location were symbols of the age-old domination of the Spanish people by the Church, which Bessie was happy had at last been ended by the Loyalist government. There were innumerable stops in the little towns of Catalonia, and at each station ragged, hungry-looking children and adults surrounded the train, shouted and cheered the volunteers who shouted and cheered back, exchanged wine for the cigarettes of the Internationals or merely begged for food, and then waved the young men on to the next town, where the performance was repeated. Finally, the train descended through craggy mountains to the sea, and for hours it ran between the hills and the beaches, where Sam Levinger saw trenches in the sand and an occasional piece of artillery pointing at the Mediterranean. By the time it steamed through the smoky, industrial suburbs of Barcelona, seven to ten hours after leaving Figueras, the Americans were cramped and tired from the long hours in the crowded cars and they were cranky from the lack of solid food.

Sometimes when the train arrived in the middle of the night, tinned food and bread was distributed to the volunteers, and then they would move on. At other times, they would descend and march through the streets of Barcelona, past many flower stalls to a military barracks. Joe Dallet's group went from the air-raid-alert darkened streets into the brightness of a dining hall hung with flags and posters and filled with the noise of a military band. They ate and listened to Spanish labor union officials and army officers make speeches, were deafened by the band playing revolutionary songs, and then joined their voices in the "Internationale" before returning to the station. Then the train was moving again, so slowly that it was maddening, parallel to the beach, with rocky hills rising inland, on the left the sea as blue as the sky. When it was night the shades of the train had to be pulled down for fear of air attack, and the men sang to pass the time or tried to sleep sitting upright in the smoke-filled cars. Somewhere they might see combat troops moving, with tanks and machine guns on flatcars, and the war would seem closer than ever. Now they were passing through citrus country and the people at the stations gave them oranges and they bought bottles of cognac or wine, but Alvah Bessie and his companions found it more and more difficult to work up any enthusiasm as they stopped at endless numbers of small towns.

Valencia was like Barcelona. Bessie's group marched through the streets to a luxurious house, sat on the cold, marble floors for two hours awaiting a meal that turned out to be meager, then waited two hours more before the march back to the station. Already Bessie was beginning to realize the truth that all soldiers soon come to know, that a good deal of warfare consists of no more than waiting around. Other troops merely sat in Valencia until the train was moving again, this time inland, and soon the darkness of another night was coming on. Weariness had drained almost all emotion from the volunteers by now and they stared vacantly out of the windows at a landscape that was turning bleak and rocky, or tried to satisfy their hunger by opening tins of watery beef, chewing on stale bread, munching glumly on endless oranges. They were dirty, disheveled, unshaven, and wretched from the 48 hours in cramped railroad cars when the train at long last slowly steamed into Albacete, the headquarters of the International Brigades.

Somehow, their enthusiasm returned. Maybe it was the crowds on the platform, the peddlars selling knives and cigarette lighters, the brass band blaring military songs, the groups of Internationals everywhere, or the clenched-fist salute of the Popular Front that was the standard greeting. Shambling and out of step, the volunteers went through the town, while kids ran alongside begging for bread or tobacco and girls watched from the doorways, waving timidly. As he marched, one volunteer found himself throwing his shoulders back and straightening his spine. It felt good to be striding in front of Spanish people, and "a wave of vindication, of justification, of grim determination and of happiness swept over [him] because [his] 4,000 mile journey was being understood, appreciated by these people." The Americans went into the courtyard of a large building, where the flags of many nations were draped from the second-story balcony and brightly colored posters and banners were hung everywhere. The band played national anthems, the *Marseillaise*, the Star-Spangled Banner, God Save the Queen, and the Spanish *Hymno de Riego*, and when uniformed soldiers around them came to attention, clenched fist to forehead, the Americans quickly learned to do the same. In the brassy noise of the band, Alvah Bessie felt a stirring in his heart, a joy in life, a happiness that he had come. He felt light on his feet, "exhilarated, eager to do something, anything." When the music stopped, officers made speeches of welcome in a variety of languages. The came a hot meal, and finally the business of induction into the army began.[17]

The volunteers did not stay long in Albacete. They were only there long enough to fill out the lengthy questionnaires that are the hallmark of any army, to throw away their civilian clothes, take hot showers, and receive their army uniforms. Only with the International Brigades these should truly be called "multiforms," for rarely did two soldiers draw an issue of clothing whose items matched each other. There were all colors—greens, grays, olive drab, and khakis. Some men were given long pants, others breeches and puttees, some received short jackets, others long overcoats, some had caps with earflaps, others no caps at all. Even extensive swapping hardly helped make the new recruits look much more like soldiers than when they had arrived. Sometimes supplies were depleted to the point where no underwear, socks, or coats were issued, and usually men went off to training camp wearing the *alpargatas* in which they had hiked the Pyrenees or the shoes they had carried with them.[18] Also in Albacete the Internationals turned in their passports for safekeeping, and that was the last some of them ever saw of those precious documents.[19]

When the confusion of receiving new clothes and trying to get better fitting ones was over, the volunteers were lined up and a call was made for men with previous military experience and special skills. Some, like Sandor Voros— and these were mostly foreign-born Americans—were sent off to an artillery training base, and a few others were picked out to be cooks, truck drivers, and mechanics. But the great majority of them were destined for the infantry. Trucks took them to the permanent training base at Tarazona, a small town 20 miles northwest of Albacete, which lay amid the bleak plain that is La Mancha, on the small river Valdemembro—no more than a stream in the hot summer months. They were quartered in what had been private houses, sleeping on straw mattresses with only one blanket on the hard stone floors, having to wear all their clothes through the night in the cold months of the year. Tarazona was a poor town, with dirt streets that became impossibly muddy during the rainy season. On those streets and in the fields surrounding the village, the English-speaking Internationals—the British, Canadians, and Irish, as well as the Americans—began to learn the rudiments of soldiering.

In charge of the base at Tarazona were various experienced fighting officers who would stay for a while and then move back to combat posts. Robert Merriman was one of these, with the American Major Allen Johnson and English Captain T. H. Wintringham also there for periods of time. Training at Tarazona usually left much to be desired. In the early days of the International Brigades there was a terrible shortage of instructors and equipment, for experienced men and war materials were needed to fight the battle of Madrid. Even the Americans, who came later than any of the other nationalities, ran into this problem, and some young men were rushed off to the front with no training at all. Even when training became better organized, there was always a shortage of equipment. Guns and ammunition were the scarcest commodities, and Gabby Klein, who shot off half a dozen rounds in Tarazona, was considered one of the better-trained riflemen to leave for the front. At certain periods, men were forced to use sticks rather than rifles, and many would have agreed with one of their number who said, "When we finished training we didn't even know how to take our rifles apart and clean them. We had been shown how, but had had no time to practice. God forbid that we actually would have had to take them apart; we couldn't have done it to save ourselves." [20]

The ability to fire a rifle is the most important of a soldier's skills, but not the only one. As the war went on and the International Brigade organization became more efficient, training time lengthened until volunteers spent more than two months at Tarazona. The men exercised, marched, and double-timed to toughen their muscles. They attended lectures, and Edwin Rolfe dutifully penciled diagrams about how five-men squads were to advance. Then he went out with the men in his section to practice infiltration against simulated fire. Rolfe was told about trenches, that they were never to be dug in a straight line, and he was taught the age-old lesson that when making camp the first thing to do is dig a latrine below the water supply. He heard lectures on the nomenclature of the rifle and was told how to fire it, squeezing carefully and holding his breath while the round went off. Classes were given in map reading and the use of the gas mask. Some of the troops were taught specialties like first aid and the art of laying transmission lines. Finally, there were day-long maneuvers, in which companies marched across the countryside, deployed as if under fire, and attacked supposed enemy positions. Some men especially proficient in their new trade, like Chicago's Frank Rogers, found themselves being sent at the end of their training to a four-week course at NCO school. There he learned more about rifles and became acquainted with other weapons, machine guns, trench mortars, grenades, and bayonets, and he was taught how to lead men into battle. All this training was rugged, but most of the Americans thrived under it. As Ed Rolfe wrote, "Life here is hard (especially for white-collar workers, of which there are many) but enjoyable, vigorous and strengthening. One uses muscles that have been inactive for years."

The routine in Tarazona was much the same as in any army: reveille at 6 A.M.; exercise followed by a breakfast of bread and some dark, hot fluid purporting to be coffee; flag-raising in the town plaza at eight o'clock; instruction until noon; a lunch of thin soup, stew, beans, bread, and wine; classes through the afternoon; a dinner much like lunch except there would be no wine; and then free time in the evening until lights out at nine o'clock. The recruits were paid 100 Spanish pesetas every ten days, and given one package of black French cigarettes every week. There was little to spend the money on. In the ill-stocked canteen the perpetually hungry soldiers could sometimes buy ham sandwiches for 1.5 pesetas, or cups of coffee for half a peseta, or drinks of rum, vermouth, or anise, all of which tasted vile. Occasionally a bar of soap might buy a meal at a peasant's house, or a few eggs, but usually there was no extra food and no tobacco to be found in Tarazona. Some of the young men, bored with the lack of excitement, dealt with the inevitable bootleggers, in this case selling wine, and the drunks that turned up were confined to barracks for three days and fined 30 pesetas.

Brigade officials were well aware that Tarazona was far from an exciting town in which to be stationed, and the commissariat devised activities to keep the men busy in their free hours, to prevent them from becoming drunks or discontents. Often in the evening lectures were given. Sometimes Ralph Bates, the Anglo-American writer who was commissar of the XVth Brigade, told of the early days of the Spanish War, of the heroism of the Spanish Communist Party executive committee, which had fought in the Madrid trenches on the night of November 7, 1936, and of the first Internationals, who in a few short months were already legendary for having helped stop Franco at the gates of Madrid. Merriman, who spent a long time at the base after his Jarama wound, described the formation of the Lincoln Battalion and its February actions. Some nights performances were given by the men, who became acrobats, singers, and comedians for a couple of hours, and often the evening would end with a community sing. On weekends, sports competitions took place, foot races and softball games, volleyball and horseshoe and soccer matches. All these things helped to entertain the troops but could never completely fill the Saturday evenings and long Sunday afternoons that were the loneliest part of their life, the poignant hours when they remembered past weekends with friends and loved ones. These were the times when a young, sensitive man like Sam Levinger wanted to be alone, or at least away from the eternal horseplay, shouts, and rough kidding of his comrades, when he wanted to pull off his uniform and wander through a city in time only to his own inner cadence. He could feel close to home by rereading letters until they fell apart at the creases, but this only worked for a while. He could only write so many letters to loved ones describing the routine of training, and he could never give vent to the loneliness he sometimes felt because he did not want those who were thousands of miles away to worry more about him than they did already. Levinger could put on his uniform and wander on a Sunday afternoon through the dusty streets of Tarazona, nodding at the villagers, patting children on the head, acknowledging the greetings of his comrades, until the cluster of buildings was behind him and he was standing in a field of stunted grapevines alone, watching the yellow hills grow blue in the distance and merge into the sky, pondering on the destiny in battle that awaited him.[21]

Tarazona was a school for the volunteers in more than military subjects; in some ways it was a school in life. For here the Americans learned that human beings act, after all, like human beings, despite whatever bonds of ideology hold them together. During the crossing of the Atlantic, the hiding in southern France, the hike over the Pyrenees, and the arrival in Albacete, the men had felt welded together in a crucible of danger and ideology. At Tarazona, during periods of boredom and inactivity that accompany army training, they learned, as one man put it, that coming to Spain "did not make an ass into a good guy or a hero . . . he remained an ass." Sometimes at the base there was friction between the soldiers, quarrels and arguments that were settled by fistfights. Mike Goodwin blamed this on the fact that "A lot of the guys were not 100 per cent dedicated," and Donald Thayer thought it was due to the "anarchistic" spirit that infused some of the men.[22] To the outside observer, the stubborn realities of human nature serve to explain fights and quarrels among the Americans at Tarazona. And their importance should not be exaggerated, for the strict discipline of the CP members and the strong ideological bonds that did exist meant there was less human friction than in other such groups.

Human nature was at work in more things than just starting quarrels. One youngster found that because the

Americans came from such varied backgrounds, because some were laborers and others college students, some in their teens while others were mature men, often they had little in common, and the dissimilarity sometimes led to indifference or hostility. Brigade officials recognized this problem and combated it as best they could by assigning men to sections with their friends and fellow workers. In the American battalion there were often sections of seamen and of Irish-Americans. But there was no real segregation, for organizational as well as ideological reasons made that impossible.

There were of course volunteers who were disliked by others simply because of their personalities. At Tarazona, Alvah Bessie met one New Yorker who was loud and self-assertive and was shunned by everyone. Appointed a sergeant in training, he bullied his men until their widespread, open objection caused him to resign. Bessie knew another man, a Californian with a glib tongue who virtually talked his way into NCO school, smoothing the path by the judicious gift of cigarettes to some of his superiors. Naturally he, too, had few friends among his fellow trainees. Other men than Bessie found that they could not unreservedly like all their comrades-in-arms, but this picture of tension in the ranks should not be overdrawn. For the most part the Americans in Spain did like each other and, as Mike Goodwin said, there was a "solid spirit among the men, one of good comradeship." As in any army, this spirit would assert itself most strongly in times of crisis and danger, and be weakest during periods of boredom and inactivity.[23]

Another lesson learned at Tarazona was one that many of them knew already, that politics worked in the International Brigades as in all other organizations. Men who were Communists with good party records were sometimes put into leadership positions while non-Communists with better potential were bypassed. Perhaps it was natural enough for the Communist leadership of the brigades to look to their own comrades first, and certainly there were always enough non-Communists like Robert Merriman in high positions to avoid the charge that only party members got ahead. Yet even some of the party members were rankled by the promotion of others on the strength of their party work in the United States.

One volunteer who got ahead for such reasons was Joe Dallet, leader of the group that spent 21 days in the Perpignan jail. He was also an example of another phenomenon in Spain, the low-level leader suddenly thrust into a position of great responsibility without quite knowing how to act in his new role. Dallet was a strange sort of Communist. The son of wealthy New England parents, he had graduated Dartmouth, was an accomplished pianist, and had in the late twenties toured Europe in style, staying at the finest hotels and eating at the best restaurants. Sometime during the Depression he had revolted against his former way of life and had joined the CP. Soon he was a steel organizer working in various Ohio towns, idealizing the "workers" and showing great contempt for nonworkers. He dressed like a laborer and affected deliberately profane, ungrammatical speech. Some perceptive comrades like Steve Nelson saw through this studied, workingman pose, but everyone found Dallet devoted, self-sacrificing, and intelligent.

In early May 1937, after a few days at Tarazona, Dallet was yanked out of his company and sent to an officers' training school for a few weeks. When he returned to the training base in June, it was as commissar of the newly formed Mackenzie-Papineau Battalion. As commissar, Dallet worked hard to keep his men happy, sponsoring sports competitions and entertainment programs to fill their idle hours. Yet he was a disciplinarian with monastic ideas of how soldiers should live, and he forbade his men to play cards or visit wineshops and brothels, and severely punished violators of his regulations. He wrote home proudly to his wife that he had lost his "rank-and-file" tendencies, and though at Figueras he had approved of the easy camaraderie of officers and men, he now began to enjoy the greater luxury available to him as an officer, living in his own room, receiving a larger salary, sporting a pistol 24 hours a day. Dallet was sensitive enough to know that a gulf had opened between him and his former comrades, who now, according to Sandor Voros, found him "a pompous and overriding autocrat who gloried in his power over them." Others thought he was only trying to do a good job of instilling discipline, but was too high-handed in his ways. Obviously, Dallet was a victim of the fact that he did not know how to exercise power easily. As time went by, he became more and more isolated from his men, who increasingly complained about him. Totally alone, he even agreed to having his wife join him in Spain, though at first he had refused on the grounds that it would be bad for the morale of his men. To himself and to those who would listen to him, he justified his discipline on the grounds that it was for the good of the troops, so that they would be thoroughly ready for the rigors of trench life. Dallet promised that he, too, would show himself a good, disciplined soldier when the battalion went into action.[24]

There came a time when the routine of training palled for the soldiers, when they seemed to have learned all the theory they could, when one like Archie Kessner of Los Angeles would write home, "We are pretty sick of the same daily grind." They would read the newspapers and try to guess what was really happening at the front, for the war news was always disguised in a kind of double-talk. "Fighting with unusual brilliance, our troops retired to previously determined positions," might mean a minor pullback or a major retreat; it was hard to tell. As in all armies, rumors continually raced through the training camp about what was happening. If training suddenly seemed more intense, the rumors multiplied. When at last orders arrived, every man became, as George Poole wrote, "as sensitive as a racehorse."[25]

Men were called from Tarazona to the battle lines in different ways. Usually a group of them, perhaps 100 or 200, would be sent to the front to fill up the depleted ranks of the Lincoln Battalion after a major action. Supposedly those with the longest training went first, but Gabby Klein, who had earned his first name by not hesitating to complain loudly about things he did not like, found himself being called to the front before others who had spent more time at Tarazona, and Mike Goodwin had a similar experience. Some men who drank too much, talked back to officers, or were mildly insubordinate also were shipped off to the front before their turn had come. But the ones who went usually considered themselves lucky. They had come to fight a war and now they were going to do so, and Alvah Bessie noticed that as a group marched off to the front there were no serious, thoughtful faces; a "universal smile lit them all." Those left behind were often the ones to complain. After NCO school, Frank Rogers was assigned to the base to train other recruits, and he worried that "If I did not get the chance to prove my courage I would be ashamed to return to Chicago and to my friends." Edwin Rolfe was asked if, with his journalistic background, he wished to go into the press office. He said he wanted to fight, and was disappointed to find himself bundled off to Madrid to become editor of the XVth Brigade newspaper, the *Volunteer for Liberty.* Twice during the course of the war, in June and again in September 1937, Tarazona was emptied as entire battalions, the Washington and then the Mackenzie-Papineau, left intact for the battlefields.[26]

In spite of the rumors, it would come unexpectedly. Alvah Bessie was awakened by the lights going on earlier than usual in the barracks one morning and orders being shouted for the men to ready themselves quickly. The troops stood in formation and roll was called as they shivered in the darkness and watched the stars fade from the sky. Then one by one they went into the battalion office, where Bessie was asked one question: "Are you fit to go to the front?" Hurriedly, their tools of war were distributed, rifles, cartridges, belts, ammunition, sometimes bayonets and gas masks. Rations were given out, cans of beef and jam, loaves of bread, and packages of cigarettes. By now it was light and the town was an uproar of men hurrying back and forth, jostling each other. Many of the villagers turned out to wave and cheer the soldiers off, making Sam Levinger feel warm and happy, prompting

A Troop Train Getting Ready to Move to the Front

him to think, "We did not realize quite how well we had fitted ourselves into the life of that . . . town." Finally, they mounted into trucks or the boxcars of a train waiting at a nearby station, and they were so crowded together that Levinger wrote, "We were to learn that often the worst thing about a battle is the ride getting to it." The volunteers rode away to the shouts of those left behind, and on the journey—which lasted for hours or for days—they sang sentimental songs for companionship, while each wondered within himself whether he could live through combat. Somewhere on the way Alvah Bessie's group saw their first real bomb holes and, as he wrote, "They put the fear of God into us." Bessie noticed his comrades were more sober than he had seen them before; as they approached the front there was for the first time little horseplay among them. The troops had not the slightest idea of their destination, but finally they would arrive at some hills or a grove of olive trees and would learn, much to their surprise, that this was the front line. The first night sleeping was difficult, for the men were too tense and excited. Rolled in his blanket on the ground, Sam Levinger heard occasional bullets squealing overhead, and once in a while a shell exploded a long way off. At each noise of war, he found himself wondering whether anyone had been killed. Death was closer than ever now, and Levinger was learning that he was not a good sleeping partner. Yet after a while he stopped listening to the sounds of war, and then he fell asleep.[27]

March 1937 was a cold, wet month on the Jarama front. It rained almost every day, and there was no way of keeping dry in the muddy dugouts where the Lincoln Battalion lived. Men were already soaked and cold when they woke up in the mornings. The coffee that had to be carried a mile up a path to the trenches was tepid, and all the food they ate tasted of mud. One soldier was so angry at the weather that he wrote home from Jarama, "And by the way, who was the s.o.b. who invented the phrase 'sunny Spain'? It's rained for four days out of the last week. Rain is one thing when you're in New York and another in this proletarian army where you have only the clothes you wear and you wear them till they're worn out. . . ."[1]

After the February 27 assault on Pingarrón the Jarama front had stabilized. On March 14 there was a small action when the enemy seized some trenches to the left of the Lincolns, and on April 5 the Americans helped to recapture them. Commanding the battalion in these skirmishes was Martin Hourihan, a Catholic and a native of Towanda, Pennsylvania, who had arrived in Spain with the first group of Americans. Hourihan had a background as a seaman, longshoreman, union organizer, and teacher, but it was his three years with the U. S. Army in Texas that qualified him to lead the Lincolns. After April 5, the front he commanded was very quiet. There were nightly patrols and sniping duels, occasional bursts of machine-gun fire or artillery, but for the most part the Americans looked endlessly from their trenches toward those of the enemy, waiting in vain for something to happen.[2]

Elsewhere in Spain important events were taking place. At Guadalajara, northeast of Madrid, the Republic claimed a great victory in mid-March when the Italian contingent of the International Brigades was instrumental in defeating another rebel attempt to encircle Madrid, killing 2,000, wounding 4,000, and capturing 300 of their fellow Italians serving in Mussolini's expedition to Spain. Though pro-Loyalist correspondents like Hemingway termed the action one of the "decisive battles" of world history, it was really no more than a stand-off like Jarama; its greatest value was in the field of propaganda, for it gave clear proof to the world that organized Italian units were being used by the rebels. Yet newspaper reports of the action made it seem for the first time as if well-equipped fascist troops could be beaten by ill-armed Republicans, and in the United States the news from Guadalajara made more young men wish to enlist in the International Brigades. Some who joined at this time worried that they might not be able to get to the front before the war ended with the defeat of fascism.

With the Madrid front now stalemated on all sides, Francisco Franco turned his attention to the north of Spain and began systematically to reduce the Basque provinces, moving toward Bilbao, which remained loyal to the Republic in spite of its inhabitants' fanatical Catholicism. On April 26, 1937, came the infamous German bombing of the nonmilitary town of Guernica, where 1,654 civilians were killed and 889 wounded. Then between May 2 and 5 occurred a civil war within the Civil War, when Anarchists, Trotskyists, and Communists all built barricades and fought it out among themselves in the streets of Barcelona for three days before the government restored order.[3]

Camped at Jarama, the men of the Lincoln Battalion read

Soldiers Entertain Themselves as They Move Towards Front in Boxcars

the news of what was happening almost as if it were another war, for here they suffered more from the elements than from any human enemy. Their trenches ran along the crest of the hills two miles west of Morata, and the Lincolns looked through a grove of splintered olive trees and across the naked branches of a vineyard to the mounds of earth that were the enemy's position. Behind their own lines the Americans could see down into the peaceful Tajuña River valley. Olive orchards and vineyards surrounded Morata and climbed the slopes toward the trenches, and there were fields where peasants behind donkeys plowed the earth slowly and calmly. The soldiers were impressed by the stark beauty of the land and they wrote about it in letters home. Ed O'Flaherty of Boston noted with amazement how every possible inch of ground was under cultivation; even the sides of the steepest hills were terraced and planted. Used to summer vacations in Maine, he missed the thick green forests and the rippling mountain brooks of that state. Indeed, all but the Westerners among the Americans were startled by the lack of trees on the Spanish landscape, by the hills that were barren and windswept beneath an immense sky.[4]

In April the weather began to improve. Sun came through the clouds and days were warm, though the nights were still cold. In no-man's-land the vines sprouted green and the olive trees blossomed. A road was cleared almost to the trenches and the Lincolns began to enjoy hot food. The dugouts they lived in were enlarged, thatched roofs appeared on some, and one was made into a library with magazines, newspapers, and books. A radio with a loudspeaker was procured, and men in the trenches now enjoyed music while on duty. The battalion staff began mimeographing a daily bulletin with news of the world, and wall newspapers made their appearance, with poems, cartoons, short stories, and jokes. There were more than 400 Lincolns now, as men were brought up from the training base. When the weather became warm enough, the commissariat procured ping-pong tables and baseball equipment, and in the flat areas below the crest of the hills, sheltered from the trajectory of enemy small weapons fire, the troops spent their free hours playing these games, along with soccer, checkers, and chess. The men found things to laugh at, too; the story of the volunteer whose unemployment check reached him in the front lines; the signs put up at intervals on the parapets by some tenderhearted soul who liked the flowering vines, which read: "Care for the grapes! They suffer when you hit them."[5]

Spring was the season when newspapermen broke through the *cordon sanitaire* that General Gal had thrown around his whole front, and at last reached the trenches to tell the United States the firsthand story of the Lincoln Battalion. To the lines came Ernest Hemingway, whose fame and whose devotion to the Loyalist cause heartened the young Americans, and he was followed by correspondent Martha Gellhorn and novelist Josephine Herbst. George Seldes of the *New York Post* appeared in the middle

Resting at Jarama

of April, noted the lack of tension of the troops between the occasional bullets, and commented on the attire on that warm day, writing, "A rifle, socks and shoes, underpants and a helmet are what the well dressed soldier frequently wears." Herbert Matthews of the *New York Times* was there, too, and he wrote of the snugness of the trenches, of their great depth that easily hid his 6'4" frame. He described the Lincolns as a "healthy, happy lot with plenty of zest for fighting." Only Virginia Cowles was unimpressed with the Americans, saying they "looked strained and sick . . . they struck me as a pathetic group."[6]

In spite of the favorable comments of their friends, Miss Cowles caught some of the truth of Jarama at this time. Many of the Americans were weary, on edge, and sick, weary of the dull routine of trench life that all the games in the world could not alter, sick still with the ugly remembrance of February 27, with what seemed like the incompetence of their commanders, with the memories of the friends who had died so quickly and those that lingered on as shattered wrecks in Madrid hospitals. They may not all have been unnerved, but "demoralized elements" were prevalent in the ranks.

Beside general conditions, there were also many specific things that bothered the men of the Lincoln Battalion at Jarama. They complained about the food, greasy with olive oil, and about irregular mail deliveries. They grumbled at the bitter, black tobacco of the French cigarettes they were issued, terming them "one of the horrors of war," and they were annoyed because cigarettes sent from home never seemed to reach the front lines. Above all, they were angry over the fact that for a long time few of them received any leaves from the front or passes into Madrid.[7]

The demoralization of the Lincoln Battalion which followed the February attack lingered on into the spring and even infected newcomers. It was later admitted by at least one official publication, which said that during this period at Jarama, "Some begged for leave; some took it without asking." Back in the United States, Communist Party officials were so worried over the state of affairs in Spain that they intensified their drive for recruits and even ordered some seasoned party members to go over to straighten things out. To the CP, the problem in Spain was a political one, the grumblers and deserters "victims of neglected political work rather than conscious offenders," and its solution could thus be accomplished politically. Leading party officials like Robert Minor, James Hawthorne, and James W. Ford came out to speak to the men in the trenches, but were unable to quiet complaints.[8] The Communists were to learn there was more to keeping a soldier happy than telling him of the ideological reasons for which he was fighting.

Veteran Communist organizer Steve Nelson, called from the hard coal fields of Pennsylvania to Spain, in his own words, to "patch up" the Jarama situation, reached the Lincoln Battalion on April 31, the day the men had been pulled out of the lines and sent to Alcalá de Henares, just north of Madrid. He was the new commissar of the battalion, then commanded by an old friend of his, the Negro Oliver Law, who had taken charge when Hourihan moved up to a position on the XVth Brigade staff. The next day Nelson marched with the Lincolns in a May Day parade through the streets of Alcalá, and he stood with Americans still muddy from the Jarama trenches in an open field, while a smartly dressed General Gal reviewed them from horseback and made a lengthy speech.

From his first moments with the battalion, Nelson could not help but notice all the grumbling that was going on. At Alcalá the men criticized Gal for looking so spotless while they were dirty and full of lice. Then they complained when they were ordered back to Jarama the same night, only 24 hours after leaving the front. Back in the trenches, Nelson found all sorts of demoralized men. In a battalion of 200, 30 soldiers were on punishment details under armed guards, digging with picks and shovels to improve the trenches; most of them had committed only small infractions of military rules. Nelson's first impulse was to lecture the men into a better state of discipline and morale, but he did so only once. Soon he knew that talk was not enough, and he went to work to improve the conditions in which the Americans lived.

In his position of commissar, Nelson could do much for the Lincolns. He could not move the battalion out of the lines, but he could give passes to Madrid. He could not improve the food supplies, but he could make someone with cooking experience take charge of the kitchen. He could not raise the dead, but he could talk patiently and sympathetically with men who had seen their comrades killed. He could not end the need for extending trenches, but he could do away with the punishment details, explain that the job of digging was a necessary one in the army, and make everyone take his turn. Nelson was quickly learning what every political commissar in Spain sooner or later learned, that the problems of the International Brigades were not entirely political, that morale was a human problem, that it was constructive action, not words, which improved the lot of the soldiers and made them happy.[9]

The role of the political commissar in the Spanish Loyalist Army was unusual, and it has been much misunderstood. The post was created by the Spanish government initially to smooth any problems that might occur between regular army officers who remained loyal to the Republic and the revolutionary-acting militiamen who were their first troops, who often objected to the little, formal niceties of military life, like saluting and obeying orders, and who were distrustful of the professional military. When the Loyalists in 1937 adopted a unified command and their forces began to change from uncoordinated political militias into regular army brigades and divisions, the commissars became even more necessary, for with Anarchists, Communists, and liberals fighting in the ranks together, there had to be someone to unify political factions by explaining the government's policies and actions.[10] In a normal army, where the civilian soldier is fighting for his homeland, there is usually little need to explain the issues of the war; patriotism takes care of morale. In Spain, where a liberal might be fighting to defend the Cortes, an Anarchist to do away with government, a Socialist to set up cooperatives, and a Communist for dictatorship of the proletariat, patriotism alone would not do the job.

Within the ranks of the Americans in the International Brigades there were no such problems. The men ranged from liberals through Socialists to members of the Communist Party, but in coming to Spain under the aegis of the Comintern they had all more or less willingly accepted Communist leadership. They might not like everything the Communists said and did, but as adherents of the antifascist Popular Front, they were not about to quarrel over the politics of their officers.

There was a commissar assigned to every level of command, the company, battalion, brigade, division, and army. He was equal in rank to the commanding officer but subject to his military commands; if the officer were killed in action, the commissar stepped in to replace him until a new military leader was assigned to the unit. Throughout the Spanish Army the commissars were, by and large, Communists. Some people have suggested that the role of commissar was primarily that of a political watchdog, whose job it was to keep the army under Communist domination and loyal to the party line. Certainly as good Communists they did follow the party line, but a study of their actions—especially in the International Brigades— shows the commissars to have had much wider ranging functions.[11] Some Internationals have said that the commissars were party members largely because only Communists were willing to take on the burdens of the job. There was some truth in this. Certainly there is no doubt that the Communist Party was always the political party most interested in discipline and a vigorous prosecution of the war. Dedicated Communists were happy to take on commissar posts to help follow the party's policies, while liberals or Socialists were often less willing to assume leadership roles.

Within the International Brigades the commissars were Communists almost to a man. Though on the lower levels this may have been because only CP members would take the responsibility, in the higher places it was undoubtedly due to the fact that the leaders of the brigades wanted party members in these posts. Though in the Lincoln Battalion at least one Socialist was a commissar for a time, he was the exception rather than the rule.

The role of the International commissar was best explained by Vincent Sheean, who wrote that he was "guide, philosopher and friend to the men in his unit; he is responsible for their political education, their morale, their spirit; he has to explain the government's actions to them, and see to it that they have a very clear idea of why they are fighting." Keeping up morale and spirit was at times a difficult task. Steve Nelson at Jarama was not the only American to find that it was more than a matter of laying down the "correct" political line. Joe Dallet at Tarazona found himself talking to literally hundreds of men "on subjects ranging all the way from foot blisters to the fact that their girl was not writing to them." More than politics, Dallet found that morale depended upon "proper food and proper clothing, and bandages for the feet when the shoes rub, and soap and towels and newspapers and cigarettes . . . and seeing that the canteen carries the favorite drink of each and that the toilets flush and sufficient disinfectant is on hand, etc., etc., etc., etc., etc." In the field, where there were no toilets and often little enough clothing or bandages, the commissars had to improvise, and wall newspapers, mimeographed bulletins, magazines, concerts behind the lines, a shower truck, a regular food supply, and stories and lectures were the means of helping to keep morale high.[12]

The activities of the commissar were not rigidly defined by regulations. He was free to try new things, and there is much truth in the statement that "the importance of his role varied according to his personality." The headquarters of the commissariat of the International Brigades itself urged that commissars should do more than just apply directives issuing from headquarters, that they should freely adapt them to the exigencies of their own units with their very different social compositions. Saul Wellman took such advice perhaps too literally when, after listening to the complaints of his men for a long time, he went to brigade headquarters and insisted that the Americans could no longer smoke the strong French cigarettes that were the normal issue because their throats were not as tough as those of the Europeans. The head commissar of the brigades angrily denounced Wellman as a *petit bourgeois* chauvinist and sent him back to the front.[13]

It was also the commissar's job to ferret out enemy agents who were supposedly trying to undermine the discipline and morale of the Internationals. In the International Brigades, concern over fascist spying began right at the top, with André Marty, who is said to have been even more suspicious than Joseph Stalin. The commissars were repeatedly told, however, to distinguish carefully between "justified criticism" and "continual, unjustified and whispering protests of those who try . . . to set the soldiers against the commanders"—for the latter were considered enemies of the people and the government.[14] In the ranks of the Lincoln Battalion, however, the commissars seemed to uncover no spies, evidently considering the endless grumbling of the Americans as something quite normal and within the boundaries of "justified criticism."

In the early days of the Lincoln Battalion, between February and May 1937, the commissars inspired little confidence in their men, and the epithet "comic star" was hung on them, though later it became a term of affection rather than derision. A good party record was the chief qualification for the job in those days. Yet these good party men, however well they might be able to harangue against Franco and fascism, showed a propensity for being away from the front lines in times of military action, and it is not surprising that their lectures about the need to defeat fascism on the battlefields of Spain were less than convincing. As the war went along it became obvious to the leaders of the International Brigades that to live up to the motto of the commissars, "The first to advance, the last to retreat," one needed something more than a good party record. Increasingly, men were chosen commissar after they had shown they were good soldiers, though intelligence, understanding, and the ability to speak well were also qualifications. And, as in the case of Nelson and Dallet, the jumping of Communists into commissarships never entirely ceased.[15]

While the human services that the commissar performed increased in importance as the war went along, the word "political" in his title was never to be forgotten. In lulls between fighting, he was in charge of the constant political discussions that went on. He might be called upon to lecture on the background of the Spanish War, the nature of fascism, or the "Peace Policy of the U.S.S.R." He would have to explain the shifts in policy of the Spanish government, and there is no doubt that his explanations always followed the CP line. Before an offensive, it was his duty to define both the political and military reasons for and the objectives of the action. It is true that often the commissars talked too much, that often their political tirades only served to weary already tired soldiers. Yet Vincent Sheean looked upon the political education of the troops as their "main strength," and one of the Lincolns said that the "political consciousness" of the Americans, drummed into them by the commissars, allowed them to perform actions that could not have been done with military prowess alone. After the war, 95 per cent of the Americans agreed that their understanding of the political and military reasons for their actions, as explained by the commissars, helped improve their discipline and made them more effective fighters.[16]

Sometimes the commissars were called upon to make exceedingly complicated political explanations, when either the Spanish government or the CP engaged in one of their periodic about-faces. Steve Nelson was called upon to make such an explanation shortly after his arrival at Jarama. After the Barcelona street fighting of early May 1937, when each Loyalist party blamed its opponents for the trouble, the Spanish CP demanded the dissolution of the POUM. When Prime Minister Largo Caballero refused to dissolve it, two Communist ministers walked out of the cabinet and precipitated the collapse of the government. The Communists were happy to get rid of Largo, with whom they had been at odds over military policies for prosecuting the war. Now the party set out to destroy his reputation. American Communist leader Robert Minor hurried out to Jarama to speak to the Lincolns. He denounced Largo, saying he had been in league with the POUM, who supposedly started the Barcelona trouble under the direction of Italian and Nazi secret agents. This of course implied that Largo was a fascist himself, or at best a tool. Minor topped off his harangue by saying the former prime minister had kept good firearms from going to the Internationals and had given them to Trotskyists instead, and he ended up by endorsing the new government of Prime Minister Juan Negrín.[17] He then left Commissar Nelson with the difficult task of explaining to the Lincolns how Largo Caballero—whom the Communists had termed the "Spanish Lenin," who had formed the first cabinet in Western European history that included Communist ministers, and whose government had until now been named the "Government of Victory"—could suddenly become such a traitor to the cause. Whether Nelson himself believed the new line on Largo, which was little more than a pack of lies, was not important; it was his job to see that the Lincolns did.

For the Americans the war went on, or failed to go on, much the same under the new Spanish government. They might occasionally fire a few rounds across the vineyard at the enemy's positions, but it was more like target practice than warfare. Sometimes the still nights were shattered as the front line burst into wild firing that would cease as suddenly as it had begun, and a soldier would remark, "Some guy must have seen an olive tree move." [18] With the strain of waiting for an enemy that never came, more than one Lincoln began to see trees moving at night.

While the battalion held the Jarama lines through the late spring, the Loyalist government reformed its forces, changing them from a ragged collection of disparate militia units no larger than battalions to an army with a centralized command, with brigades and divisions and army corps. At the same time, each International Brigade received a Spanish battalion and each battalion one company of all-Spanish troops. In the north, Franco's forces cracked the supposedly impregnable "ring of iron" that the Basques had constructed around Bilbao. On June 19, rebel tanks rolled into that important city, while the Basque armies retreated toward Santander. At about this time the base at Tarazona was so overflowing with Americans that a second battalion—the George Washington—commanded by Yugoslav-American Mirko Markovicz, moved up to reserve trenches on the Jarama front and was incorporated into the XVth Brigade. Commanding one of its infantry companies was Hans Amlie, a mining engineer who had served as a sergeant in the Marines in World War I and was brother of the Farmer-Laborite congressman from Wisconsin, while Negro Walter Garland headed the machine-gun company. The Americans left behind at Tarazona were formed into another battalion, named Mackenzie-Papineau after the two architects of Canadian independence, largely to honor the Canadians who were scattered through all the American units. Commanding this battalion in training was Robert Merriman, his wounded arm still in a cast. His commissar was Joe Dallet.[19]

In late June, the Lincoln Battalion was recalled from the Jarama front after spending four long months in the trenches. As the veterans marched down the slopes toward Morata they could sing for the last time (to the tune of "Red River Valley") the song that had become most popular with them:

> There's a valley in Spain called Jarama;
> It's a place that we all know too well,
> For 'tis there that we wasted our manhood
> And most of our old age as well.

The men of the battalion were sent to Albares, a town farther up the yellow Tajuña. A group of them quickly dropped in on the local wineshop to relax. The only thing to drink there was anise, and they drank it until the hostility they had not been able to work off against an enemy at Jarama made them turn upon each other in a brawl that wrecked the shop. Disciplined and sentenced to five days in the brig by the battalion staff, the men were released after only one day because the understanding villagers interceded on their behalf.

There were less antisocial ways of relaxing at Albares the Americans set up a diamond and played baseball, and trooped down to the river to swim in its muddy waters or lie for hours on its banks, soaking up the hot Spanish sun. To maintain discipline, officers conducted classes in military problems and the use of various weapons. At night, the commissariat sometimes brought in movies from Tarazona and entertainers from Madrid. There was also the eternal male quest for females to enliven the stay in Albares, but in this field of battle the Americans enjoyed singularly little success throughout the war. One soldier wrote home sulkily: "The guys who bragged all along that they would put Don Juan to shame are still virgins." It seems to have been not so much the language problem as the Spanish custom of the chaperone, or even the multi-chaperone, which defeated the Lincolns time and again. The story was told of the soldier who got a date to the movies with the prettiest girl in one small town and then found himself marching to the show with an army of relatives, including the grandparents, five little brothers and sisters, several unmarried aunts, two older brothers home on leave, and the mother and father. The Lincoln had to buy tickets for all of them, and then he found himself inside the theater, sitting between a spinster aunt and the grandmother. The story may have been a trifle exaggerated, but the fact that it was told often shows that it contained some hidden truth that amused the troops. That such things went on was confirmed by the soldier in Albares who grumbled that it was not the girl's grandmother who bothered him, "I don't mind her tagging along. . . . Only I do wish they'd leave the goddam burro at home once in a while!" To the Americans, the Spanish girls remained untouchable for a reason best defined by the volunteer who wrote home simply that their motto was. *"No matrimonio, no pasarán!"* [20]

After loafing for a few days, most of the Lincolns turned out to help the villagers harvest their barley crop, probably under the prodding of the commissariat, which was always interested in promoting good relations with the Spanish. The joy of the farmers at receiving help with their hard labor turned quickly to dismay as they watched the Americans, totally unused to farm labor, blunder through the fields, trampling the grain underfoot and wasting much more than they harvested with their sickles. Dismay was probably mutual, for the volunteers were soon blistered and aching, and everyone seemed happy when the Spaniards, always a tactful people, begged that the "brave soldiers" trouble themselves no further with peasants' work. There were other attempts to help the villagers that were more successful, including a picnic for the town's children held on the banks of the river, and the clinic where the battalion doctors treated the ailments of the townspeople without charge.

The stay at Albares ended abruptly. On July 2, the church bells began to peal loudly and word went out for the Lincolns to pack their gear and get ready to move. It was a hot day and the men sweated as they rushed to and fro, stood in formation for roll call, and then piled into waiting trucks, clutching their rifles again. They were happy now, the time in the village, the swimming and loafing and drinking, having done more for morale than an entire army of commissars. As the trucks rolled onto the plain of Castile, the villagers shouted goodbyes and clenched their fists in the Popular Front salute. Then the Americans settled back. They did not yet know they were going to take part in the first government offensive of the war.[21]

Like most provincial capitals of Spain, Albacete was in the 1930's a stagnant town of dusty streets and tree-shaded squares where old men drowsed. Its 40,000 inhabitants seemed lost in the backwash of time. Contact with modern life was minimal, and carts pulled by burros filled the streets. Yet by the early summer of 1937 all that had changed, and Albacete was fully a part of the contemporary world. Swollen to three times its normal size, it was jammed with men from all over the world, and dozens of languages were to be heard in its overflowing cafés and wineshops, hotel lobbies and numerous houses of prostitution. Burros and carts could still be seen, but they were being crowded off the streets by trucks, ambulances, and military staff cars. The International Brigades had come to Albacete, and for the next year and a half it would be a thoroughly cosmopolitan center.[1]

In the fall of 1936, Albacete had been chosen as headquarters for the brigades because it was far from the front lines yet more or less halfway between Valencia and Madrid, with which it had good lines of communication. That Madrid's Communist Fifth Regiment already had a training base there was another factor in its favor. The first group of Internationals arrived on October 14. Soon the influx of volunteers was too great for the town to handle, and training bases for the different nationalities were set up in the surrounding villages, Tarazona, Madrigueras, La Roda, and Mahora, with an officers' school for all Internationals at Pozorubio. Albacete itself housed the headquarters of the brigades, offices representing all the nationalities fighting in Spain, the chief supply depots, hospitals with international staffs, repair shops for automobiles and trucks, a small factory that manufactured hand grenades, and the postal department, which had the task of censoring mail in 40 languages.

The base was run by three men. Supreme Commander was André Marty, hero of the Black Sea mutiny, slavish Stalinist, and a cruel, suspicious man whose liquidations of alleged spies earned him the title the Butcher of Albacete. Italian Communist Luigi Longo—under the name Gallo—was inspector general, and his countryman Giuseppe di Vittorio—using the name Nicoletti—was chief political commissar. While all these foreigners were in charge of the training, housing, discipline, and political education of the Internationals, orders for the troops' use in combat came from the supreme Spanish command of the Loyalist Army, which was itself very much under the influence of foreign Communist—often Russian—advisers. In action, the brigades were always under the direction of the division and army chiefs in their sector.[2]

The American contingent in Albacete was headed in the summer of 1937 by Bill Lawrence, a prematurely gray CP district organizer from New York. He had two assistants who were in charge of the files and personnel records of the Americans in Spain. In May they were up to their ears in work just trying to track down the location of their countrymen, for in the early, confused months of the brigades, records of their disposition had been haphazardly kept. Americans were scattered all over the map, some in hospitals in Madrid and elsewhere, others serving as truck and ambulance drivers in Spanish units, or in vehicle repair shops or as medical lab technicians.

The largest groups of Americans not with the Lincolns

had already been located. Some 60 men who had arrived at the end of February had been combined with English, French, German, Austrian, Polish, and Czech volunteers into the 86th Mixed Brigade and sent off at the end of March to the mountainous Córdoba front in the south. Commissar of the American company was twenty three-year-old John Gates, and its commander was Rollin Dart, who had spent four years as a pilot in the U. S. Army Air Force. After a few skirmishes, the men of the 86th saw as little action as the Lincolns at Jarama, and their morale was not much better.[3]

Three other Americans were part of a special guerrilla warfare section, operating largely behind enemy lines, blowing up railroad tracks, mining roads, contacting anti-Franco Spaniards, and organizing resistance movements. One of them was Irv Goff, who had spent his last five years before coming to Spain as an acrobat and apache dancer on the vaudeville stage. Active in the Young Communist League for many years, Goff had first been made a driver in Albacete, then was chosen to take part in the guerrilla outfit, which operated largely in the regions of Andalusia and Estramadura. The most successful operation in which Goff took part occurred later in the war, when the guerrillas went behind rebel lines to open the prisoner of war camp in Motril, allowing thousands of Loyalist prisoners of war to escape.[4]

Forty more Americans, largely men of foreign birth with previous artillery experience, were stewing away in the stagnant town of Almansa, halfway between Albacete and Valencia, having been assigned for training to the John Brown battery. Unfortunately, the unit did not possess a single gun, which made its commander's lectures something less than useful. As a substitute for training, Sandor Voros found himself having to listen to endless political lectures, but these did little to overcome the demoralization of men who had come to fight fascism and found themselves unable even to train properly. At the same time, half a dozen volunteers from the United States were going through the newly established officers' school at Pozorubio, while at Fuencarral, near Madrid, another group was serving in a transportation regiment.[5]

Trying to keep tabs on these various American units from his offices in Albacete, Bill Lawrence began to have the vague hope of consolidating all of them into one, neat military outfit. But the exigencies of war kept his desire from ever being realized. Eventually, however, in late summer of 1937, the Americans in the Córdoba region were brought back to Albacete and then sent on to serve with their countrymen in the XVth Brigade.

Steve Nelson came by Albacete for a couple of weeks on his way to join the Lincoln Battalion, and he found it a place of chaotic confusion. Besides the men attached to all the headquarters, thousands of soldiers crowded the cafés and squares of the town. Many of them were recovering from wounds, too well to be in the hospitals, not well enough for the front, unable to find themselves a post in Albacete or the officials who would discharge them and pay their way home. All of them had complaints of some sort and they filled Albacete with their grumbling from morning to night. By brigade officials, these men were referred to as the "demoralized elements," and because nobody knew what to do about them, they were allowed to hang about the town.

Yet many of these demoralized men had problems that could have been solved by an efficient organization with sufficient resources. In his first hours in Albacete, Nelson ran into one American who fitted into this category, and he proceeded to help him. The soldier was Joe Gordon of New York, who had lost one eye at Jarama. Now Gordon had pains in his other eye, which he feared was weakening. The French doctor in charge at the Albacete hospital said nothing could be done, and though Gordon had heard of a specialist in Barcelona, the doctor would not give him a pass to go there. Nelson went to the hospital and forced the doctor to sign a release for Gordon to go to Barcelona; shortly thereafter the specialist saved his eye.[6] Undoubtedly, there were many demoralized men with similar problems who never got to see someone like Nelson, and who could not get their medical or psychological needs attended to.

Not all of this was due to incompetence or indifference on the part of the International Brigade staff. Unlike regular military organizations, which have channels of communication and clearly defined lines of command, the International Brigades possessed only a hastily thrown together organization, staffed by men unused to office procedures. A continual shortage of material, including medical supplies, exacerbated the situation. While Nelson was at Albacete, the second in command of the artillery battery at Almansa breezed into the office, complained because he had no guns, and ran through a long list of other supplies that his men lacked, including rangefinders, pistols, field glasses, telephones, slide rules, and compasses. Wanting to help, Nelson found he had little authority; though he tried, he could not even get through to the base military commander on the phone.

The confusion in Albacete was made even worse by the language problem, and Nelson found that someone's reference to the town as a Tower of Babel contained little exaggeration. Attending a meeting of the base commissars, held regularly to transmit political decisions down the line to the men in the trenches, Nelson found the officers arranged in language groupings, each with an interpreter. When a speech began, a dozen interpreters began simultaneously translating to their own group in loud voices. If the speech were in a less-used language, like Hungarian, it had to be translated into Spanish before the interpreters could put it into their own tongue. The number of nuances lost in such a process must have been appalling, and for this reason alone—though there were of course others— brigade political propaganda had to be kept simple and direct.[7]

Language, mixed with nationality, caused other problems at Albacete. Because the French had gotten there first, many of the permanent staff posts of the headquarters had fallen into their hands. Chauvinism, theoretically absent from such an international assemblage, often raised its head.

Louis Fischer found that André Marty treated the American party leaders with "calculated rudeness," and some of his countrymen seem to have followed suit.[8] In the auto repair shops, Americans sometimes squabbled with their French chiefs, the arguments degenerating into childish assertions about the general shortcomings of the other's country. There were quarrels at other levels, too, and Americans were surprised and hurt when their complaints would be viewed by East Europeans as evidence of American "softness," or when a Latin American would say they were no better than agents of American imperialism. Such lapses of understanding were not the rule. They just showed that overworked men, harassed by lack of materials, worried over the progress of a war that was going against them, denied the comforts of home and the companionship of loved ones, sometimes exploded into anger at the state of the world and took their troubles out on whomever happened to be at hand.

Even less savory than any nationalistic squabbles was the hidden atmosphere of terror and intrigue which pervaded Albacete, and which John Richard found both stifling and depressing. After his basic training at Tarazona, he had been appointed a truck driver and was stationed just outside Madrid. Often he came to Albacete for supplies or to have his truck repaired, and always he was happy to get away as quickly as possible. Part of this atmosphere was undoubtedly due to Marty, whose activities in wiping out supposed spies and Trotskyists were widely rumored throughout the town. And part of Richard's reaction must have been that of a man who was risking his life to the relatively soft existence of a base, where meals were regular, women plentiful, and physical danger almost nonexistent.[9]

As in all armies, there was a split in the International Brigades between the front-line soldiers and the headquarters staff, whom the men in the trenches contemptuously felt were not really exposing themselves to danger. Of course, the infantry knew there had to be a base staff, but this knowledge in no way endeared its personnel to them. Even a man like Mike Goodwin, who was terribly afraid of getting bogged down in a desk job at the base, still begrudged the comforts of Albacete and Tarazona to the men who were there. Joe Dallet, whose wife wanted to join him in Spain, had to keep her from doing so for several months because rumors about high living among base officers were already disrupting the Americans at the front, and he did not want to give substance to them.[10] The gulf between the troops was most apparent when a headquarters commissar, cleanly shaven and wearing a fresh uniform, came out to the trenches to lecture to lice-covered men on some such topic as the need for learning Spanish or digging better trenches. When such a commissar left, the men sneered and went on about their business, deliberately ignoring what he had said. Soon the commissariat realized what was happening, and lectures were transmitted through the company commissars who lived in the trenches, for they were listened to with care.

The disdain of the front-line soldier for the headquarters personnel was serious, but it was best expressed in the humorous rhyme of an anonymous volunteer, who wrote:

> *On the Front of Albacete*
> *Meet the Generals of the rear.*
> *Oh! They fight the grandest battles*
> *Though the shells they never hear.*
> *For the wind is in their make-up*
> *You can hear the generals say*
> *"Yes, we're going to Cordoba,*
> *Mañana or next day."*
>
> *Albacete's Generals charging*
> *And the field is red with gore,*
> *As they spill their glass of wine*
> *And the red wine's on the floor.*
> *See them strolling in the evening*
> *To the grog shops for their wine*
> *For they are the brave defenders*
> *Of the Albacete line.*[11]

If the antagonism of the field soldier for the headquarters personnel was to some extent natural, there were occasional actions at Albacete that exacerbated the situation. At one point, a base commissar began cutting certain political articles out of the American magazines sent from home. As he told John Richard, it was "for the good of the troops" that they not be allowed to read things detrimental in any way to the cause, and presumably any other approaches to the war than that of the CP could be construed as detrimental. But Richard found the men at the front furious over the excisions in their magazines and at the Albacete authorities for okaying such censorship. Eventually this commissar was prevailed upon to stop his activities, but only after a lot of ill-will had been generated.[12]

Another thing that nettled the men in the trenches was the fact that though vast quantities of cigarettes were sent regularly by the Friends of the Abraham Lincoln Battalion, they rarely found their way to the trenches. The mystery of where they were sidetracked was never solved, but the fightingmen knew that somewhere in Albacete, Valencia, Barcelona, or Madrid, somebody was smoking their mild cigarettes, while their throats burned with the harsh, black tobacco that Europeans claimed to love. For American cigarettes, the Lincolns often had to depend upon the few that were stuffed into letters by wives and friends. Even then they did not always get through, and one wife made a practice of adding a P.S. to the censor, requesting that he not steal the enclosed cigarettes. Her husband eventually received an indignant note from the censorship office saying that officials never stole cigarettes, but the men at the front were too wise to be impressed by the note's tone of wounded innocence.[13]

Just because there was a split between combat troops and headquarters personnel, it must not be assumed that either group was not dedicated to the cause and to victory in the war. Administrators are as necessary to an army as infantrymen, though it seems inevitable that the latter will have little respect for the former. Among the Americans in Spain the situation was improved in the fall of 1937, when John Gates, after eight months as a commissar on the Córdoba front, took over Lawrence's post as chief American commissar. His assistants were all men who had seen considerable amounts of action or who had been wounded. No longer could the Americans in the trenches say that the men at headquarters had never risked their lives to defeat fascism. But long before Gates was to appear in Albacete, the eyes of all the Americans serving there were turned west of Madrid, and the headquarters personnel waited anxiously for news of how their countrymen were faring in the first Loyalist offensive of the war.

EIGHT

At the beginning of July 1937, the armies of Francisco Franco still lay around three sides of Madrid. Artillery batteries on top of Mount Garabitas shelled the city almost daily, terrorizing the inhabitants and reducing block after block to rubble, while in the north, rebel forces were slowly but surely swallowing the Basque provinces, pushing toward the last major center held by northern armies, Santander. With this situation in mind, the Loyalist government, its armies now unified under a central command, felt itself strong enough to launch its first offensive of the war, with the dual purpose of relieving pressure on the northern front and raising the siege of Madrid. The starting point of the drive was to be the El Escorial-Madrid road, to the northeast of the capital in the foothills of the Sierras. Its aim was to sweep down the flat plain west of Madrid toward the sleepy village of Brunete, cutting off the besiegers of the capital from behind and either crushing them or forcing them to withdraw from the gates of the city, where they had been ever since the International Brigades had helped to stall them in November. A secondary attack was to start from the south of Madrid, with the hope that its troops would push north and join up with the main offensive units coming down from El Escorial. The government had gathered 50,000 men for the offensive, with 150 aircraft, 128 tanks, and 136 pieces of artillery to support them. The XVth and XIIIth International Brigades, under the command of General Gal, now made up the 15th Division, which belonged to one of two army corps in the action.[1]

At the beginning of the offensive the XVth Brigade was commanded, as it had been since its inception, by the Yugoslav Communist, Vladimir Čopic, a man who entertained and sometimes bored his men by singing entire operatic arias in the trenches whenever the spirit moved him. Larger than normal, the brigade contained six battalions, divided into two regiments. The Dimitrovs, the Franco-Belge, and a Spanish battalion made up one regiment, while the British, the Lincolns, and the Washingtons were grouped into another under the command of English Major "Jock" Cunningham. His adjutant was the former Lincoln commanding officer, Martin Hourihan. Each of the American battalions consisted of about 500 men, with a scattering of Canadians, Cubans, and Irish still in the ranks. The battalions were divided into four companies, three infantry and one machine-gun company equipped with five heavy Russian machine guns. Oliver Law was still commander of the Lincolns, with Nelson as his commissar, and Mirko Markovicz led the untried Washington Battalion.

On July 3, the American battalions were making a long hike across the burnt plains north of Madrid. On the American national holiday they rested, were fed an extra large dinner, and received a double ration of chocolates and, for a change, American cigarettes. The troops were relaxing, looking forward to celebrations planned for the evening of July 4, but before they could begin, orders were given for the battalion to move out. For two nights the Americans marched, resting during the day of July 5 in a grove of trees. The roads they went over were crowded at night as other military units, trucks, and tanks moved toward the front. As they went, the land rose under their feet, the plain giving way to the foothills of the Sierras, and then they were going through heavily wooded land cut by occasional streams. The countryside looked unlike any part of Spain they had yet seen, with farm buildings of gray stone rather than earth-colored brick. Hans Amlie found the nights cool as he led his company along the road, winding sometimes through steep hills, past the old stone walls of great estates; in the bright moonlight he could see carefully tended fields broken by ghostly outcroppings of rock. The forced march went on, as silently as possible, and when the battalions stopped for occasional rests in ditches, Amlie allowed his men to smoke only if they hid the glow of their cigarettes beneath their coats.[2]

The commissars had already told the Americans where they were going, had let them know they were taking part in the government's first offensive, and as they went along the road the troops were nervous and excited on the night of July 5. Neil Wesson, wounded February 27 at Jarama, was marching with the Lincolns again, feeling spunky and looking forward to the next day's events. Twenty-seven-year-old Henry Eaton, whose father had been mayor of Los Angeles in the 1890's, was happy to be going into action at last. A left-wing ideologue who thought of himself as fighting to make the "great world dream of the workers a reality," Eaton found the march to the front with an army of men from all over the world a "thrilling experience." The farther the troops went, the more the suspense and anxiety mounted, until everyone talked only in whispers and even sergeants giving orders did not raise their voices. The march went on through the long night, the quick pace never slowing. Steve Nelson felt his eyes and jaws aching from staring endlessly into the blackness and gritting his teeth in anticipation. Finally, the sky began to pale above the hills, and the Americans could see the haze lifting from the vast Guadarrama Valley below them. As they hurried forward the last mile, the Republican offensive began to get under way.[3]

Dawn came clear on the sixth of July, and from the hills the men of the Lincoln Battalion could see the treeless, barren ochre plain spread out before them like a map, the small villages scattered on it looking like a child's toys. Brunete was slightly to the right and a few miles ahead, and the town of Villanueva de la Cañada was directly before them. Off on the far right was Quijorna, and to the

left a few miles away was Villanueva del Pardillo, with
Boadilla del Monte a speck in the distance. They could
see the sandy ribbon where the Guadarrama River sliced
through the plain and the land beyond it rolling up into
hills. And it was good in the early light to see columns
of troops advancing toward each of the enemy towns, to
watch government tanks roll across the landscape, while
overhead Loyalist aircraft filled the sky. There was something solemn and beautiful about the sunrise that day. For
David McKelvy White, weary from marching, the calmness
was suddenly shattered with "the roar of great guns, the
clean, swift sound of the shells passing overhead, like the
quick ripping of silken sheets, the distant boom of the
explosions in the valley below and the great plumes of
black smoke rising. . . ." Suddenly the toy villages were
vanishing in the dust and smoke of an artillery barrage
and the bombs dropped from Loyalist airplanes. From a
distance White found that war looked "very exciting," and
"the spectacle and the thought of really getting down to
business" chased the fatigue from his body and made him
wish to get into the fight.[4]

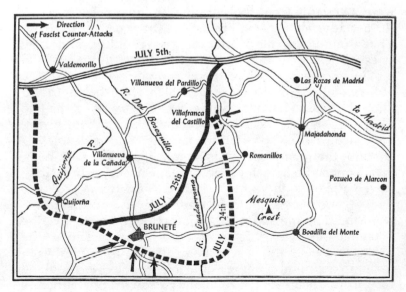

BRUNETE

While the Washingtons went down to the battlefield early in the morning, the Lincolns waited in the hills for several hours like nervous spectators, straining to see what was happening. Then Oliver Law received orders to lead his men toward Villanueva de la Cañada to help other battalions take the town. Squinting into the sun, Steve Nelson clambered down the hillside toward the plain. Stretcher bearers carrying wounded men passed them on their way back to field hospitals, and Nelson wondered how many men had already been hit. When he reached the bottom, Nelson found that the plain that had looked so flat from above was rolling and cut by gullies. Following the depressions in the earth for cover, the Lincolns went forward up the gently rising land toward Villanueva, where the Washingtons and English were already pinned down by enemy machine guns mounted in the high tower of the church. From that point the rebels commanded all approaches to the village, and as the Lincolns came over the folds of earth they began to draw fire from the tower and from rebel troops in trenches surrounding the town. The men dropped to their bellies and inched forward until they were 400 yards from the outlying buildings. Then, when further advance became impossible, they began to dig in. The ground was hard and the sun broiling, and they sweated heavily as they scratched at the earth, threw little mounds of dirt up before them, and cringed beneath the bullets of the enemy, some of which were beginning to find their mark. The machine-gun company set up its five weapons behind a raised road and unlimbered them, giving the Lincolns some protection. On the other side of Villanueva, the men of the Washington Battalion were lying in an open ditch in the fierce Spanish sun, where they stayed all day without food or water, unable even to raise their weapons as a storm of fire raged around them.

By the time the sun was dropping into the foothills, the Lincolns were well dug in. As the firing slackened, the exhaustion of the long march and the day's battle began to numb their limbs. Hungry and thirsty, they were looking forward to their evening food and to a night of rest before

On the Move at Brunete

an assault on Villanueva. Steve Nelson went out to talk to the machine gun crews. When he returned to the command post, Oliver Law was away, checking on the rest of the battalion. That left Nelson temporarily in command. He felt confident. The troops were spread out and well protected, the wounded had been evacuated, and food was due shortly. Villanueva was surrounded, and it was obvious that after a good night's sleep it would be easy to clean up the town in the morning. As Nelson relaxed in his position, a runner came up from brigade headquarters. He was carrying an order saying Villanueva had to be taken that night. Nelson was angered and shocked by this sudden change of plans, and he was worried that the soldiers were too weary to attack. But he sent out runners to the companies and the Lincolns readied themselves in the growing darkness. Firing began off on the left as the Dimitrovs launched the attack, and then suddenly seven battalions, the Lincolns and Washingtons among them, left their positions and rushed forward, stumbling over enemy sandbags and through trenches into the streets of the town, swarming over its outnumbered defenders. By ten o'clock that night, Villanueva de la Cañada was in Loyalist hands, though in a few buildings enemy snipers held out until the next morning.[5]

When the Lincolns formed up after the battle, the houses of the town were gutted and still flaming from artillery fire, throwing their shadows like giant specters in the flickering light. The torn bodies of dead townspeople and soldiers sprawled awkwardly in the streets, and Henry Eaton was sobered and numbed by the sight. Until that moment he had all his life "retained illusions about the glory of war." Now, with the ugly face of death all around him, he saw no more glory. He was drained of his human qualities, and Eaton felt that he and the men around him were turned into "automatons, unable to feel because horror had surpassed our ability to meet it. . . ." From less sensitive Americans there were other reactions that night. One was totally exhausted, but "exalted and thrilled" by the day's battle and its victory. Another, nineteen-year-old Francis Feingersh, a loyal Communist who had been wounded in the leg that day, wrote that when he had seen the Internationals advance he had thought, "This is what Marx wrote and dreamed about—an army made from the working class of the world—UNITED."[6]

For one day the American battalions rested, reorganized, and buried their 30 dead in an orchard just outside Villanueva, while rebel artillery began to shell the town. Back at headquarters there was bitterness and recrimination. The English-speaking units were not supposed to have been sent against Villanueva, but were to have bypassed it and been used to press the offensive onward against shattered rebel lines. Now the Americans were finally ordered forward, but precious time had been lost and it was already too late, for Franco's commander in the area, General Varela, had already reestablished his lines. Meanwhile, the secondary, southern half of the offensive had proved totally ineffectual, and its troops were stalled after having made almost no gains. Brunete and Quijorna, however, were already in Loyalist hands when the Lincolns and Washingtons marched swiftly east across the naked, baking plain on July 8, deployed as if on maneuvers, and pushed the enemy advance posts back across the Guadarrama River. The Americans plunged down the sandy banks, crossed the narrow trickle of water, and climbed onto the plain beyond, where the land rolled up and then folded itself into a series of ridges where the enemy had entrenched. They moved so quickly that Neil Wesson saw many of his comrades collapse in the heat, and he himself could barely stand up when at last a halt was called.[7]

In the Washington Battalion, Harold Smith led the first squad of the first company across the stubbly Brunete plain. He had to keep yelling to his men to spread out, for as a few bullets whined overhead, they closed together, and Smith had learned at training camp that it was disastrous for men to bunch up under fire. As they went up and down the gentle swells in combat formation, Smith could hear the sound of heavy firing in the distance, but he could not see the enemy. All he could see were the hot yellow hills and the men of the battalion going up and down them as they had done in training so many times. When they rested beneath the crest of a ridge, Smith felt the dragging weariness of all the marching of the last three days. Combat still did not seem real to him. Aside from the brief storming of Villanueva, it had been mostly marching in the summer sun and watching planes fly overhead. For the rest of the afternoon it was more of the same, aside from the time his men had to scatter into ditches while enemy aircraft roared over, dropping bombs. When they flew away, Smith's men moved on again, chasing an elusive enemy that was just getting ready to make his stand.[8]

By the evening of July 8, the battalions of the XVth Brigade had outrun their supply lines. No food came up to the Americans resting in temporary positions and preparing for an assault. By this time Franco had rushed 31 fresh battalions and 9 batteries of artillery to reinforce General Varela, whose defenses were anchored on the Heights of Romanillos and Mosquito Crest, the ridge that the Americans were about to attack.[9]

The morning of the ninth, a bloody battle began with Russian tanks rolling up the slopes toward the rebels. The

Americans rose from their positions and charged up the hill behind them, but the tanks went too fast. They topped the heights and disappeared, and suddenly the soldiers were falling beneath a heavy machine-gun barrage. It was Pingarrón all over again, the hills naked, the Americans dashing spasmodically, singly and in groups, up the slopes, the enemy machine gunners firing directly down at them, the casualty list lengthening as the day went on. Going up toward the rebels, Harold Smith at last learned what warfare was like. He waved his squad on until they were within the enemy's range, and then suddenly he was thinking about his men no longer. Climbing that hill, Smith found, was like going into a heavy storm, where bullets "beat down and across the slope in sudden, vicious squalls." It was an agony to advance, to leave shelter and spurt forward into the enemy fire, and at the end of each short dash his body wanted to bury itself into the ground. He drove himself on and then lost control of his bodily functions, felt urine running warmly down his leg, found himself swearing violently, senselessly, aloud, and he kept on advancing without really knowing why.[10]

Though they made a number of brave assaults, the Americans never reached the top of the rebel ridges, and when those heights held, the town of Boadilla del Monte behind them remained in rebel hands and the government advance toward Madrid could go no farther.[11] The struggle for the ridges guarding Boadilla was to go on, but on the evening of July 9 the Americans were already spread thin at the base of the hills, digging positions half a mile from the enemy and below him. Twenty-eight had been killed and 110 wounded in the two battalions and there were no reserves to take their places. The troops were worn out from the rapid advance and the murderous attack, but they were to have little rest. Though they were not called upon to assault the impregnable enemy positions, they received orders to hold what they had already won, and because they were entrenched below the rebels, this was not to be an easy job.

The American Internationals scooped hollows out of the

hard ground, pressed themselves flat against the earth, and waited for the enemy to come. Once rebel infantry did charge down the slope in a counterattack, but Loyalist fire stopped them. Zealous brigade officials ordered the Americans to chase them, but the machine guns were still on the crest of the hills and nothing could move against them. So the Americans hugged the earth and waited, lay beneath the enemy positions, and suffered until they lost all sense of time and place, until the only realities were heat and dirt and the awful noises of modern war.[12]

In one sense the offensive was working too well, for Franco had shifted the German Condor Legion from the northern front to Brunete, and by now the Luftwaffe pilots had chased the Loyalist aircraft from the sky and were free to pound government infantry at will. They flew bombing raids over the Americans until, as one wrote, the earth "heaved and rocked and swayed and roared and smoked, and the bombs kept coming down, and every time you heard the whistle and scream you knew there was a shaft pointing at the small of your back and the bomb would hit you right there and blow you to a million pieces." Snipers took their toll, but enemy artillery behind the crest could not hit the Americans in their trenches down in the valley. Yet the aircraft, the machine guns, and the artillery could all play havoc with the Loyalist lines of supply, and the Americans went without many a meal. Trucks could not get anywhere near them, and the only way of bringing up food and ammunition was on the backs of mules. The supply teams came down the hills behind the Lincolns under cover of darkness, running a gauntlet of machine-gun and artillery fire that tore many mules and men to pieces.[13]

Planes and artillery were bad enough, but for the Americans hanging beneath Mosquito Crest the weather was the worst enemy of all. The heat was suffocating and the rocks of the plain seemed slowly to catch fire. It was so hot that for hours during midday nothing at all moved on the battlefield, which stank of dead men and animals cooking in the sun. As the Lincolns lay on the parched ground and waited, their throats and mouths tasted of dust. While his men grew almost mad with thirst, Steve Nelson led teams of men back to the Guadarrama River, only to find that it was living up to its Arabic name, the River of Sands, for it had dried up since the Americans had first crossed it. The men dug feverishly into the riverbed until they were a few feet down and water seeped into the holes they had made. It tasted muddy and bitter, the taste of dead mules, but they drank it, for it was the only water they had.

When the Americans were pulled back from their positions beneath the enemy, Villanueva del Pardillo had fallen to the Loyalists, but Boadilla was still in rebel hands. Essentially the offensive had stalled, with the government having gained a bulge of land 7 miles deep and 10 miles wide on the open plain. Oliver Law was dead, having been shot in the belly in an assault up the hills, and Steve Nelson was now commanding the Lincolns. The soldiers had become so weary that they could no longer fight effectively. On one occasion a group of Americans who had just dug a trench had seen some Moorish troops within very close range. With a great effort the Americans had managed to get their weapons into position, but their hands were trembling so much they could not take aim accurately. Their first shots were all wild, and the enemy troops took flight and escaped unharmed.[14]

Withdrawn from battle, the Americans recrossed the dry river and collapsed. One young trooper complained, "I have fought, slept, crawled through mud . . . worked and sweated in the same clothes for the last ten days. . . ." A Negro soldier was still unnerved from his recent experience of returning toward friendly lines only to have a battalion of Spanish troops open fire on him, evidently mistaking him for a Moor. When he shouted at them in English they must have thought it Arabic, for their volume of fire increased, and he had to crawl on his belly hundreds of yards past them to the American trenches. David M. White— whose time teaching classes at Brooklyn College had done little to prepare him physically for the long days he spent at Brunete lugging boxes containing 500 rounds of machine-gun ammunition—was so tired from the heat, so fed up with the "bleak, bare" plain over which they were fighting, that he found himself wondering from time to time "why it wouldn't be more sensible to let the fascists have the place. . . ." White was learning strange, new lessons in this war, things he could never have learned in books. As he wrote to a friend, "I did not know what a dead mule looks like, stiff and bloated, or what a dead man smells like when left to ripen between the lines under two or three days of this Spanish sun." For Henry Eaton, the thrill he had felt marching to war on July 5 had vanished. Since the attack on Villanueva he had slept little, marched a lot, and learned that war drained his intelligence and sapped his feelings to the point where he was capable of only one thing: destruction. During a meal a comrade had been shot dead next to him by a sniper, and he had not stopped eating while the body was dragged away. In an air raid, when a soldier had been torn to bits by a bomb and the ragdoll body had landed on Eaton's back, he had felt nothing. Writing to his sister, he explained his inhumanity by saying, "I have no emotions left to drive me crazy." [15]

By now the ranks of the battalions were very thin. Casualties had taken 50 per cent of the Washingtons and a large number of Lincolns. The toll of officers had been very high, for besides Oliver Law, Regimental Adjutant Hourihan had been shot in the leg, and brigade commander Čopic had been evacuated with an injury. Company commanders Hans Amlie and Paul Burns were out with wounds, and company commissar Harry Hynes was dead. Harold Smith knew quite a bit about warfare now, but he was in a hospital with a shattered hand. There were so many gone from the ranks that on July 14 the Lincolns and Washingtons were merged into one battalion under Captain Markovicz, with the hyphenated name "Lincoln-Washington" that never really caught on. The next day, in their reserve positions, the Americans were visited by the brigade hygiene truck, and the men who for days had been thirsting for water now suddenly had enough in which to take showers. [16]

The Lincoln Battalion did not rest for long. By July 14, rebel forces were counterattacking and the Americans were among many Loyalist battalions who had been used as shock troops in the offensive and now were called on to hold the lines, a job for fresh reserves that the government did not possess. The attack was led by enemy aircraft, now overwhelmingly superior, and the Americans arrived in the lines near Villanueva del Pardillo just in time to bear the brunt of it. They huddled in the trenches all day as wave after wave of Heinkels filled the sky, bombing and strafing endlessly. When the planes vanished late in the day, strangely enough there were few American casualties and the battalions were still strong enough to repel enemy infantry. The Lincolns stayed in those positions for two more days, then were withdrawn when a Spanish brigade was brought up to take their place.

Beginning on the eighteenth, the rebels launched a full-scale counteroffensive along the entire Brunete front, and after that the Lincolns were caught in the confusion of a fluid and crumbling sector. The brigade was moved rapidly from position to position as headquarters tried to contain the thrust. There were forced marches at night, some battles during the hot days, always the enemy aircraft commanding the skies, always a lack of food and water to plague the Americans. From many points along the front the tired soldiers could see through the yellow haze of the plain to the bulk of the Sierras, where the offensive had begun, and the thought of cool pine groves and streams rose up to mock them. When they were finally pulled out of the lines, the last of the original offensive units to withdraw, it was just daylight, and on their dusty march to the rear, the Lincolns were dogged by enemy aircraft. It took six long hours to reach reserve positions in a grove of trees 10 miles from the lines of action.[17]

Some of the Lincolns immediately went to sleep, others waited for chow, stretched their legs, and smoked, really relaxed for the first time in days. Evening brought food to fill their stomachs and a cool breeze to begin blowing away the hot memories of the past two weeks' action. It

The Battalion Marches Towards the Front

was completely dark when a dispatch rider on a motorcycle arrived with a message calling the XVth Brigade back to the front lines immediately. The battalion commanders and commissars gathered and told the brigade commander that their men were too tired and worn to return to the battle. But in Spain, as in any army, orders came from the top, and Steve Nelson had to go out to explain to the tired Americans why they were being recalled. He stood on top of a boulder under the branches of the trees and watched the cigarettes of the men glow in the dark. The brigade Commanding Officer read the order and departed, leaving Nelson to calm the rising wave of resentment among soldiers who were, in David M. White's words, "close to a major revolt." It was an impossible explanation to make, but Nelson made it, saying that if they did not march back to plug up a hole in the front that night, they would either be surrounded in the morning or fleeing in a full-scale retreat. His talk was met with catcalls and then an ominous silence settled over the crowd. Finally, one voice said softly in the night, "You're right." And that was all. The men dispersed in the dark, wearily gathered their equipment, shouldered their rifles, formed into companies, and began to march. A few hundred yards down the road they were met by a motorcyclist with new orders; the rebels had been stopped and the brigade was to stay where it was. The Americans trooped back to camp, relieved at the change and proud that they had not done what they had come close to doing, refusing to carry out orders.[18]

On the twenty-fifth the battle was over, with Brunete again in rebel hands. Both sides were claiming victory in what was still another stalemate. The Loyalists had gained an area about 3 miles deep along a 10-mile front, but had lost many more men than the enemy. What was more important, they had not dislodged the rebels from the gates of Madrid, and the diversion of troops and aircraft from the northern front was only temporary. Leaders of the Americans like Steve Nelson were proud of their men. The inability to seize the strategic heights was blamed on factors other than the Lincolns' fighting abilities; the lack of coordination between tanks and infantry, the mistake at headquarters that sent the Americans against Villanueva de la Cañada when they should have been pressing the offensive onward, and Franco's overwhelming superiority in aircraft, tanks, and artillery were the real reasons the offensive was stalled. Brigade officials called the campaign a victory, because it "demonstrated the great advances made by the Republican Army in training, discipline, equipment and staff work," ignoring the fact that victories are not usually counted in terms of things like improved discipline. Yet after the long vigil at Jarama, many of the Americans were heartened by the fact that the Loyalist government had at long last been able to undertake an offensive, even an unsuccessful one. For by now they were soldiers enough to know that wars are only won by offensive actions.[19]

The first week in August the Americans were back in Albares again, swimming in the muddy Tajuña, training halfheartedly, sometimes making the streets of that old village echo with the unfamiliar crack of ball against bat and the strange warlike cry, "Kill the umpire!" There were fiestas with the townspeople and regular meals again, and the Lincolns had water and wine to drink when they were thirsty. Though Albares was a fine spot for relaxing, for reknitting the unraveled nerves of weary troops, it did not provide enough diversion, and the Americans happily thronged into Madrid. There they wandered down the broad boulevards and through the Puerta del Sol, sat under awnings in sidewalk cafés on the Gran Via and attended American movies, which they sorrowfully learned had been dubbed into Spanish. Some men played at being tourists by visiting the front lines of the beleaguered city in University City, while others sought out wounded comrades in hospitals, or dropped by Ernest Hemingway's room at the Hotel Florida, where tidbits of imported foods and a "bottomless flask" were attractions as great as the writer himself. The Florida was a kind of center for home-less Americans in Madrid, for it was here that most of the American correspondents lived; in their bathtubs many of the troops washed in the first hot water they had felt for months, and in their rooms the Lincolns smoked the mild cigarettes that they missed so desperately at the front. Another reason for going to the Florida was the dining room, where meals were always served on a table covered with spotless linen and gleaming with sterling silver. Yet here many an American soldier was more than a little disconcerted to find, as did Mike Goodwin, that in spite of the appointments, his entire meal consisted of one solitary plate of garbanzo beans.

Madrid was a more dangerous place than Albares, for several times a week rebel batteries on Mount Garabitas shelled the downtown areas, killing and wounding Madrileños by the hundreds. The Lincolns were used to artillery fire by now, but it annoyed them more on their leaves than it ever did on the battlefield. In the capital many of them saw the shelling firsthand, for one of the Americans' favorite domiciles was the luxurious Hotel Alfonso, whose price had plummeted downward since the enemy's chief target had become the huge Telefonica building directly across the street. Madrid was a wartime city, where no tobacco could be bought and good food was in short supply, but bustling, noisy Spanish crowds still filled the streets, the chaperoned girls lovely in their crisp summer dresses. In the balmy summer nights there were many places for the soldiers to amuse themselves, music halls and theaters, restaurants and bars crowded with women who did not have chaperones and who were willing to entertain anyone for a price. The dark shadow of war may have hovered around the edges of the city, but most of the Lincolns would have agreed with the judgment of Moishe Fishman, well-traveled seaman, who wrote that Madrid was "one of the truly fine cities of the world." On leave there, Fishman found that "life goes on almost as normally as it did before the war." In spite of the siege or maybe because of it, there was an exciting atmosphere in Madrid that all the young Americans felt. Even Edwin Rolfe, who had to spend endless frustrating days battling with Spanish printers—who could not read a word of English—as he attempted to put out weekly editions of the

Volunteer for Liberty, came to love the city, its people, its boulevards, its gardens and cafés. To the committed Rolfe, Madrid was still the rallying point, the one center of the world that continued to defy the onslaught of fascism. It was a good place to be if one were committed, and Rolfe put it thus: "Madrid was still the livest city in the world, the best to wake up in."[1]

Back at Albares, life was lazy. The Americans were learning for the first time the reason for the long Spanish afternoon siesta, for in the steaming summer days it was almost impossible to move outdoors during the afternoon hours. In Albares, as in all the Spanish towns where they were quartered during the war, the Lincolns were learning about a way of life different from anything they had ever imagined. Young Americans abroad for the first time are always startled to find how different life can be from that at home, how varied are the ways that people go about living and working, loving and dying. In his heart, many a young American believes that the great world cannot be very different from the streets of St. Louis or Des Moines, or the valleys of Shenandoah or Willamette. Perhaps the men of the Lincoln Battalion were especially prone to this fallacy, for they were one-worlders who had a kind of intellectual stake in the unity of mankind. High-school teacher Leo Gratschow could easily find himself discovering in Spain the similarities of the human race. He had sailed an ocean and crossed the mountains and now he found that he was still the same and the world was still the same, and he wrote that there are "Flies in Spain; chicken and eggs, green things growing; horizons and sunsets; pregnant women; earth and humanity here as well as in the U.S.A. . . ." The experience was only reaffirming what he had already believed, that "this is one world and humanity is one."[2]

Of course, the similarities were real, and yet there were vast differences between the United States and Spain. In many ways Madrid resembled Chicago or San Francisco, since metropolitan areas all over the world have many things in common, crowds, apartment buildings, traffic jams, and slums. Yet most of the Lincolns were from urban areas, and in Spain they spent weeks and months in villages like Albares, towns with houses of adobe and streets of dust, where life contrasted so drastically with what they had always known that even the most self-conscious one-worlder had to recognize the difference. Wilfred Mendelson, the New Yorker, was one of many who looked for similarities but had to admit the towns of Spain were unlike anything he had ever seen. He noted the ever-present plodding burros, the peasant women walking slowly along with bundles balanced on their heads, the small, cool, unlit shops selling wine and food, the bedraggled plaza with its gushing fountain where children filled huge jars of water, the goats wandering through the streets followed by shepherds with weathered faces. And yet the unfamiliarity of the scene quickly vanished for Mendelson, and within three weeks he could write, "Nothing is strange; it has all become a part of me."[3]

Spain, its countryside, its people, and its indefinable spirit became part of many of the Americans who fought there, though most of them could never really express what they felt for the land. They only knew they had come to love it and love its people, and in their letters they expressed this love in the well-worn clichés about the brotherhood of man. Some, talented with the brush or pen, tried to capture the distinct Spanish mood that they felt. To the artist Fred Weiss there was something about Spain that justified any sacrifice he might have to make. Partly it was the violent colors of the sunbaked country, the red clay of the earth, the intense light that made the countryside shimmer on the clearest of days. Yet this was only the outward sign of a conflict Weiss felt to pulsate through the Spanish land, a conflict between sensuality and religion, a violence expressed in the music and wild dancing of the Gypsies, in the lonely wail of the *cante hondo* he had heard sung beneath the starlit skies near Córdoba. Others could not see the passion, but were charmed by the slow tempo of Spanish village life, and some wrote of wanting to come back to live in Spain after the war. One New Yorker even picked out the town where he would settle, a small fishing village on the Mediterranean, a picturesque cluster of white houses and sandy beaches, surrounded by palm trees, orange groves, and fields of wild poppies.[4] Perhaps this man, used to the bustle of Manhattan, did not wonder how he would occupy himself in such a town, but his dreams were as unrealistic as those of many other dedicated youngsters, longing for a calm refuge from the war they fought.

In truth, there was much in Spain to which the American soldiers could never have adjusted. They were left-wing activists, men from the big cities of an industrial society, and certainly they never could have understood the Spanish peasant's acceptance of life and its trials, his acceptance of abject poverty, of wooden plows and barren earth, of the natural cycle of life and death itself. If the men of the Lincoln Battalion thought about such things, they probably judged them inessential phenomena that would vanish when the Republic brought its people fully into the modern age. Few knew of the stubbornness with which a people clings to old ways and few understood that the condescension they felt toward the backwardness of the peasants was returned in kind. The Lincolns were not cultural relativists, but men who knew how the world should be run, and they would not have understood that many of the Spanish peasants did not want to be "civilized," just as few of the Americans comprehended the deep religiosity that flourished among Spaniards who burned the churches of this world because they were corrupt.

All the Americans were impressed by the Spanish landscape, though many were surprised to find how mountainous and bleak much of the country was. Still, most of them would speak favorably of its starkness and grandeur, and many commented on the sky, which seemed so large and so much bluer than any they had ever known. Long-time CP organizer Dave Doran, who was to replace Nelson as XVth Brigade commissar, wrote lovingly to his wife of the beauty for which he fought, describing Spain as "a crazy symphony of brown and green mountains, freckled by gray stones, caressed by streams, interrupted by sudden, deep canyons." For the Anglo-American writer Ralph Bates, who had served as a commissar at Jarama, Spain was a suitable setting for the war he was fighting. Bates wrote, "I felt no contrast between the landscape and the war. The fierce Prussian blue sky, the broken hills of red and ocherous rocks, the deathly gray-green of the gouged valley walls, the monotony or the violence of the earth forms, offered no contrast to the starkness of war. It was a warlike landscape, but noble, as we all of us believed our resistance to be." The fierceness of the Spanish sun startled the Lincolns, too, and Edwin Rolfe described it as being "so strong that the glare . . . blinds not for a moment, like the American sun, but continually, from the minute you enter it until you leave it behind."[5]

A country is more than its landscape, and for the Lincolns, it was the Spanish people who interested them most of all. Like all soldiers, they found that in the towns they were always surrounded by small children, begging rides on brawny shoulders, wanting to finger their weapons. Always they were impressed by the youngsters who clenched their fists, raised their arms in the Popular Front salute and yelled *"Salud camarada!"* Even when Edwin Rolfe realized that the children often expected a reward of fruit or cake for the patriotic gesture, he was not dismayed, excusing their actions with the thought, "the little buggers have known terror and hunger, worse than any in America have known." Sometimes, as he sauntered to the village fountain to fill his canteen, a Lincoln might be stopped by a villager and read a letter from his son at the front, and even though he might not understand the language, he would listen politely. On occasion a peasant would offer an orange to a soldier, or ask him to share some *vino tinto* from a wineskin. Once in a while a Spaniard whose knowledge of geography was nonexistent, and who lumped all *Americanos* together, would ask a Lincoln to look up a relative in Montevideo or Buenos Aires when he returned home.[6]

In general, relations between the Americans and the Spanish people they met were unruffled, for the Spaniard is noted for his cordiality to strangers and, in return, the Lincolns rarely behaved boorishly. This was because the Spanish civilian was the man the troops had volunteered to defend, and also because the Americans came so much to admire the Spaniard's uncomplaining diligence in the face of adversity, the way he calmly plowed his barren fields right up to the lines where warfare raged. Actually, many a Lincoln seems to have idealized the Spanish peasant, thinking him part of the revolutionary masses to which the future belonged. In truth, he did not really know the Spaniard, and what he saw was the peasant of revolutionary mythology.[7] What the peasant thought of the American, this foreigner who was marching through his life, cannot be known, though undoubtedly the parochialism of many made them indifferent to much of the war and its clash of ideologies. In person, the Spaniard was usually polite and helpful, though it is likely that many in their hearts wished that the foreigners helping to scar their lands would leave. Still, it was only rarely that Americans would come upon a peasant who would openly blame them for bringing warfare to his world and who would spit out contemptuously, as one did to Steve Nelson, "Fight your war in Madrid."[8]

Some of the Americans did make friends with people in the towns, and a few lucky ones experienced the traditional hospitality of the Spanish family. David M. White, whose preconceptions about the country were one by one being destroyed, found that this one happily withstood the test of reality. Disappointed to find the Spaniards short rather than tall and slender, and depressed because his idea of colorful Spanish peasants had been demolished by the reality of women always clad in somber black, White found dinner in a Spanish home to be a sheer delight. In the house of a poor village barber, he ate soup and bean stew, a few shreds of lamb and a salad, all out of a common plate set in the middle of a rough-hewn wooden table. The food was washed down with lots of wine, and it was digested with plenty of friendly conversation, and the meal ended with the family insisting that White return again.

The twinge of guilt he felt at taking rationed food from the family's mouth was easily overcome by White's thorough enjoyment of the experience and the company.[9]

Of all the Americans, the Negro troops had the most personal reasons for appreciating the Spanish people. As they had found their skin color to be no handicap within the battalion, so they were happy to learn that the Spanish villagers had nothing against them because they were black. One, who was startled to find himself being treated as an equal by the townspeople, stated simply, "I like this place." Californian Alpheus Prowell enthusiastically wrote home that although in four years of night school in Oxnard he had never been in the house of a white classmate, here in just a few weeks he had been invited into the homes of white people. What's more, in Spain he could, if he wished, date white girls, unafraid that they might ask him if "soap and water would take the blackness out of my skin." In view of the Americans' poor dating record in Spain, it is doubtful if Prowell actually did take out many girls, but the simple fact that he could was extremely important to him. Interestingly, Prowell put his finger on the peculiar prejudice of the Spaniards, noting that Catalonians did not want their daughters to marry men from Andalusia. But to this kind of discrimination—based on the fact that southern Spaniards are thought to have Gypsy blood, and to be dirty and shiftless—he was blind. In Los Angeles, Prowell had earned $7.50 a day and in Spain his pay was only $2.80 a week, yet, as he wrote, "I was miserable in L.A. Here I am happy." Prowell even found it a bit strange when a Spaniard liked him for helping them, for, as he said, "They do not dream of how much they are helping me." Perhaps the most succinct statement of the Negroes' feeling in Spain was that of Luchell MacDaniells, who had left a WPA writer's project to make the journey. Said MacDaniells, "I would rather die here than be slaved any more."[10]

The Lincoln Battalion was back up to a strength of 500 men by mid-August. Some soldiers wounded in earlier battles had returned from hospitals, and a large number of new troops had come up from Tarazona. Among them was a section of machine gunners composed entirely of seamen and commissared by Bill Bailey, who only two weeks before had hiked through the midsummer snow-drifts of the Pyrenees. Also with the newcomers was Gabby Klein, slight yet wiry, the young man whose constant complaints and criticisms during training at Tarazona had prompted brigade officials to pull him out of his company and send him to the front.

Recently there had been some reshuffling in the XVth Brigade, which now consisted of the Lincolns, the British, the 24th Spanish, and the Dimitrov Battalions. Steve Nelson, his reputation enhanced by his role at Brunete, had moved from battalion to brigade commissar, and chief of staff for the brigade was Major Robert Merriman, who had left Tarazona for the front again. Commander of the Lincoln Battalion was Hans Amlie, the mining engineer and sometime Socialist from Wisconsin. Tall and spare, Amlie was a man of few words who had earned the respect of his troops leading a company at Brunete, where he had been wounded. His commissar was John Quigley Robinson, a seaman from New York.

After three weeks at Albares, orders for the brigade to move out came unexpectedly, so unexpectedly that Major Merriman had to send off a messenger to Madrid to round up the 200 soldiers still on passes. It was on August 19, a bright summer day, that the Lincolns were carried in trucks down to the coast at Valencia, where they camped in the bull ring for two days, then boarded trains with machine guns mounted on the roofs and rode northwest into the ancient area of Aragón. Back in Madrid, messenger David M. White had arrived in the early morning hours of August 19, and both he and Edwin Rolfe had gone from hotel to hotel, banging on doors, rousing soldiers, and dragging them bleary-eyed and grumbling into the warm Spanish sun. They were piled into trucks, given loaves of bread and tins of meat and sardines, and sent off after the brigade, which they did not catch for two days. By then all the Lincolns knew they were on their way to take part in the second major Loyalist offensive of the war.[11]

The region of Aragón which the Americans were entering contained some of the wildest, driest, most barren areas in Spain, endless ranges of rocky red hills and windswept valleys with dust as fine as talcum powder. The only things growing in that land were in flat and startlingly green river valleys. The greatest of these was that of the River Ebro, 10 miles wide as it approached the city of Zaragoza. Most of the towns of the valley climbed the walls of the cliffs that surrounded it, as if the Spanish valued the fertile farmland too much to waste any of it by covering it with their homes. It was down this Ebro Valley that the Loyalists were aiming their new offensive. The object of the attack was Zaragoza, which the rebels had held since the beginning of the war, but where there was thought to be much underground Loyalist sympathy. As in the Brunete offensive, the government was still attempting to aid the Basque armies in the north—where the situation was very critical as Franco's forces closed in on Santander—by causing a diversion of troops and material. Still another reason for the offensive was the fact that the Aragón front seemed ripe for an easy breakthrough. Here there was no continuous line of trenches, only a series of strongly fortified points in the main towns on the roads toward Zaragoza, the provincial capital.[12]

More than military reasons for the offensive were given to the men of the Lincoln Battalion. Their commissars told them that they were being sent to activate a front which had been largely inactive since the beginning of the war because the POUM and Anarchist militias in the area had never wanted to take the offensive against the enemy. The Communists had long criticized certain elements of the Anarchists in Aragón called "uncontrollables," men who had gone out and forced collectivization of the lands upon the peasants rather than spending their time fighting Franco. To the Communist Party, winning the war was at this time more important than pursuing the social revolution, and thus it was also at odds with the POUM, which was calling for immediate collectivization of everything. Not only was the POUM supposed to be full of fascist spies, but the story was widely repeated in the International Brigades that its militia had played soccer matches with rebel troops near Huesca. So the Lincolns were entering Aragón with the dual idea that they were to help seize Zaragoza and at the same time counteract the bad example of the POUMists and Anarchists.[13]

The Lincoln Battalion, along with the other units of the XVth Brigade, descended from the troop trains at the poor, dirty village of Hijar, built on a steep hill over the trickle that is the Rio San Martín. There they received a shipment of new Russian Dictoryev light machine guns, then moved on to Azaila, another huddle of buildings surrounding a plaza where a few scraggly trees were bent and weighted with a heavy coat of dust. The troops crossed the dry river, Aguas Vivas, and marched toward the front across a countryside as desolate as most of them had ever seen, and then they made camp on the open plateau. After a couple of days they moved into the front lines, replacing an Anarchist battalion whose commanders exhibited a barely concealed hostility toward Steve Nelson and the other leaders of the Internationals. In shallow trenches the Lincolns settled and waited for the offensive to begin.

Dawn came quietly on August 24. There were no aircraft in the sky and no artillery to splinter the morning air, for the government wanted the attack to be a surprise. Among the men, young Gabby Klein, his stomach in a turmoil, pressed against a ridge of earth, hiding as he had been taught to back at Tarazona, waiting for the enemy guns to open up. As the darkness paled, he noticed the black figure of a man against the sky, standing above the ridge, facing toward the enemy. Klein yelled at the man to get down and was chagrined when the figure strode toward him and it turned out to be his commanding officer. The officer waved in the direction he had been facing and told Klein not to worry yet, for they were still over two miles from rebel positions.

As light flooded the world, five small Republican

bombers droned across the clear summer sky and dumped bombs onto the town of Quinto, the American objective. Across a flat wasteland the Lincolns could see only part of the town, a jumble of hundreds of adobe buildings at the edge of the Ebro River valley, leaning against each other on the steep slopes toward a bluff where a huge stone church dominated everything in sight. Close to and also above Quinto was a large, bare hill named Purburell, where the enemy was deeply entrenched with machine guns commanding the approaches to the village. At the base of the bluff ran a major highway, and once Quinto was taken there would be only one more strong point between the Loyalists and Zaragoza, 25 miles to the northwest.

In the full light of morning, the Lincolns were ordered

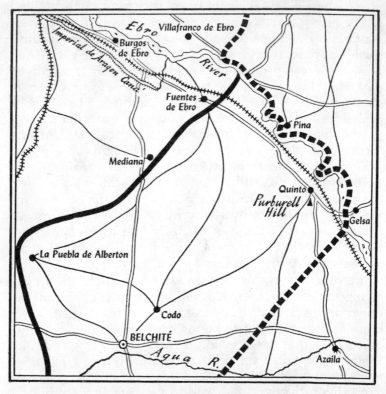

THE ARAGON OFFENSIVE

Lincoln Casualty in Aragon Offensive

from their trenches, and as they marched toward Quinto, the calm summer day was shattered by the noises of war as the first waves of Loyalist troops swept forward. Moving with his comrades-in-arms, Gabby Klein lost his nervousness, for the buildings of Quinto seemed so far away. Then without warning the sky was screaming with the sound of machine-gun fire, and Klein dived forward and hit the dirt. He was on top of a small knoll, and bullets were tearing up the ground around him. He wanted to crawl back, but his limbs were paralyzed with fright and he could only lie there, rigid beneath the enemy fire. When it slackened, he heard the voices of comrades, urging him to move, and then he found that his arms and legs could still function, so he crawled back down the hill.

Stopped by the enemy, the men of the Lincoln Battalion could see other Loyalist troops, the Dimitrovs, flanking Quinto and going up the heights to attempt to knock out machine-gun emplacements. The Americans were ordered back, started a march in one direction, and then retraced their steps. For a good part of the day they simply sat in barrancas, out of range of enemy guns, able to catch glimpses of the battle, while nervousness and fear slowly built within them. Such a time, just before combat, was always the worst part of the war, for these were the hours when thoughts of wounds and death could not be banished from the mind, when endless cigarettes and wisecracks could not drive the awful possibilities of injury away. And to the Americans from commissar Nelson down to Private Klein, August 24 was one of those terrifying, draggy days when the sun seemed to be screwed into the sky, as immobile as a light bulb in a ceiling.

Finally, at three o'clock in the afternoon, Loyalist artillery began to plaster Quinto, and Hans Amlie received word from brigade to get his men ready to advance. When the Lincolns moved out, they did so as perfectly as troops in an army training film, going forward in fanlike sections with tanks on each side of them. Drenched in sweat, the Americans double-timed to keep up with the ponderous vehicles. The tanks exploded into noise, their 47 mm. guns roaring with destruction. Running alongside, the Lincolns felt invincible. They came toward the enemy fortifications and saw some rebel troops fleeing back into the town. The tanks tore holes in the barbed wire and the Lincolns raced through, pulling pins from grenades and hurling them into trenches, opening up their rifles to kill the few rebels who remained. Guns blazing, the tanks chased the enemy into the streets of Quinto. The infantry followed, but then was ordered to pull back outside the town, for the sun was already behind the hills and dusk lay over the Ebro River valley. The last action of the day came with a section of Lincolns sprinting through machine-gun fire to enter positions deserted by the enemy behind the walls of an outlying cemetery. That night some of the troops kept watch from behind the shelter of tombstones, while others slept quietly on ancient graves.[14]

Before dawn on the twenty-fifth, the Americans left their positions and swarmed into the town. In Quinto's steep, narrow, twisting streets the men of the Lincoln Battalion were baptized in the art of street fighting, as they learned to scan the rooftops and windows for snipers, to use their bayonets, and to pitch grenades through shattered windows and down cellar stairs. As the Americans cleaned up Quinto, one large building with thick walls, bristling with machine guns, remained as a center of enemy resistance. Volunteers were called for, and ten men said they would help reduce this stronghold. Leading them was Carl Bradley, CP organizer of Bethlehem Steel, who had once spent four years in the U. S. Navy, and one of the ten volunteers was Henry Eaton from Los Angeles. Bradley and his men were given bottles full of nitroglycerin, and they crept as close to the fortress as they could, while Loyalist artillery was brought up. When its defenders withdrew from the windows under heavy shelling, the Americans raced forward. Two were shot down on the way, but others got close enough to hurl the bottles "in well directed pitches that came from good baseball arms" through the windows of the building. Violent explosions erupted inside and flames licked through the windows of the structure. Again the men came forward with the deadly bottles and threw them in. Then they managed to roll a gasoline drum with a fuse into the fortress, and soon after it exploded, rebel resistance inside Quinto was at an end.

There was still the church above the town and the strong hill of Purburell, and while other units took care of the hill, the Dimitrov and Lincoln Battalions moved on the heavily fortified church. As they did so, Henry Eaton mused on the ironic symbolism of the fact that the rebels always made their last-ditch resistance in churches. Of course, these were always the most solidly constructed buildings of the Spanish towns, the best for defense. Yet it almost seemed as if the rebels, when they withdrew into one, hoped the Loyalists would have to destroy the building to get them out, thus fulfilling the charge that the Republicans were church-wreckers. In point of fact, both sides in the war utilized churches when it was convenient to do so for defense, and both armies were willing to bomb an enemy-held church to rubble. The Quinto church, edging on a sheer bluff and approachable only over the flat terrain of the plateau, was no exception to this rule. Machine guns in its towers swept the 200 yards of naked ground before it to keep the infantry at bay. Now artillery was brought up to close range and fired point-blank at the building until holes began to appear in its walls and its towers began to crumble. As its defenders withdrew from their positions, infantry surrounded the building and captured it, and the Americans were surprised to learn that within, rebel troops were far outnumbered by women and children of Quinto, who had been cowering in this house of God for safety from the Russian troops they had been told were attacking their town.[15]

Quinto was in Loyalist hands on August 27, and so far the offensive was going well for the government. The towns of Mediana and Codo, closer to Zaragoza than Quinto, had fallen, too, and forces were pressing onward to the capital of Aragón. American losses had been slight, while 350 rebels had been killed and more than 1,000 taken prisoner at Quinto. All levels of command had praise for the Americans. General Walter, chief of the 35th Division—to which the XVth Brigade belonged—announced that the troops taking Quinto had "fulfilled their tasks to perfection," while General Pozas, head of the entire Army of the East, cited them for the "heroism and fighting spirit shown in the brilliant action of the taking of Quinto." The Americans probably wanted rest more than praise, for although not badly hurt, they were nervous and on edge from the street fighting. But right after Quinto fell, they were moved eight miles northwest, close to Fuentes del Ebro. Another brigade was assaulting that town, the last stronghold on the highway. Plans called for the XVth Brigade to mount trucks and tanks as soon as Fuentes fell, and race down the highway in a flying column to lay siege to Zaragoza. But Fuentes did not fall and after the Americans had huddled in gullies for three days, the idea had to be abandoned.[16]

Still the Americans were not allowed to relax. Though the government offensive had swept 10 miles past it, the small, well-fortified crossroads town of Belchite, which lay on another approach to Zaragoza, was stubbornly holding out, and the XVth Brigade was called upon to help the Spanish troops surrounding it. It was 20 miles to Belchite, and to get there the battalion had to march across a savage, primitive country as desolate as the face of the moon, with mesas like those in the American West, deep gorges where no rivers ran, a horizon of red hills 30 miles away, the earth molded into hard clumps that had never been broken by a plow. From a distance of 10 miles, the troops first saw the town, set in a cultivated green valley. The towers of two churches dominated its skyline, and the dust and smoke of artillery explosions partially obscured its buildings. Dark was falling when they marched through the olive groves and replaced Spanish troops in trenches 400 yards away from Belchite's northern edge. Immediately, they went forward, crouching low, creeping all the way to the tree-lined road that bordered the town. A hundred yards away were the low walls that surrounded Belchite and to their right the tower of a large church bulked black against the darkening sky. In the morning the Americans were crouched behind a small ledge that sheltered them from machine guns in the church to their right. With the light of day, Belchite exploded with the noise of enemy machine guns, and the Lincolns found they were under fire from a church they had not noticed the night before; one on the left farther up the sloping hill of the town, from whose tower enemy gunners could enfilade their positions. The outlying buildings of Belchite were bristling with snipers, and the trenches of the Americans were so shallow that they were only safe if they lay flat. For those who had been in the Washington Battalion, it was like Villanueva de la Cañada all over again, for they had to lie motionless through the dragging hours of the September day as the sun burned slowly across the sky, while machine guns raked the earth around them and the dust of Aragón filled their eyes and mouths.[17]

In the evening the Americans withdrew from their untenable positions and moved back a couple of hundred yards. Russian anti-tank guns were brought up the next day, and Steve Nelson directed them to knock snipers and machine guns out of the church towers and house windows, but as soon as the guns were silent the rebels reappeared at their posts, and infantry assaults up the slope to the walls were not attempted, for the volume of fire would have made them suicidal. For three days government artillery bombarded Belchite until house after house crumbled to the ground. The town's water supply was cut, so that its occupants must have been suffering from the intensely hot days even more than the Loyalists, but still the rebel defenders stubbornly and gallantly held out. Already the Loyalist offensive was slowing and being stopped, and rebel counterattacks were beginning all over the Aragón front. One relief column was fighting its way toward Belchite, and rebel aircraft were flying sorties over the town, dropping bundles of food and messages telling the defenders to keep from surrendering, for help was on its way. Major Merriman was forced to post lookouts to watch for the relief column, afraid of suddenly having to face enemy troops on both sides. Finally, on September 2, army headquarters demanded that Belchite be taken, and Merriman had no other choice than to send infantry to do the job.[18]

The Lincolns broke into small groups. Carl Bradley led one section of 30 forward, creeping with his men to the tree-lined road, lying there while the artillery pumped shell after shell into Belchite until smoke darkened the air. Then he signaled his men and they dashed across the narrow road and sprinted up the gentle slope toward the walls that were 200 yards away and looked to Bradley like 200 miles as enemy machine guns rattled in anger, tearing up the earth around him. He ran and his heart began to pound as if his chest would burst open; he charged across the fields, deaf to the blast of Lincoln machine guns that were trying to drive the enemy back from his positions. Some of Bradley's men stumbled and fell to earth, picked themselves up, and lunged forward again, while others fell as bullets tore through them, some dead on the spot, others wounded. As he raced forward, Bradley could see the yoke and arrows of the Falange stenciled on official buildings growing larger and larger, and then at last he reached the low walls and clambered over them. Right behind him were his men, only 20 of them now left to scatter into the narrow streets and huddle in the doors of buildings, safe at last from enemy fire.

Other groups of Americans followed Bradley's, breaking into Belchite from the north and east, while more Loyalist troops were entering in a similar fashion from other directions. Now battles began to rage in the streets and outlying buildings, as men fought from house to house, breaking into basements, crossing patios, and even engaging in hand-to-hand combat on wrought-iron balconies as the rebel defenders disputed every inch of ground. In small squads the Americans pushed through the town, inching their way down streets that were often no more than a yard wide, hugging the walls as they watched for snipers.

Carl Bradley led one group of ten slowly forward, four on each side, and two watching for attacks from the rear. The buildings seemed empty as they moved and for a time the streets were ominously silent. Suddenly bullets began to whine and ricochet around Bradley. One of his lead men pitched forward into the dust of the street and the others drew back. Knowing they could not advance, Bradley ordered his men to set up positions to halt any enemy thrust. In the cellars of deserted houses they found heavy sacks of grain and they piled them into a barricade across the street, dubbing their position with the grisly title, "Dead Man's Point." From behind the barrier they found the enemy in windows and on rooftops, and now the American rifles began to speak with authority. For a while, Bradley got his men to advance by pushing the heavy bags of grain slowly forward. But a real assault through the streets began to seem impossible, and he sent his men into the houses. Here they moved from one to another by digging holes in the thick adobe walls, eventually reaching points from which they could fire on the enemy and force him to abandon his positions.[19]

Robert Merriman, Steve Nelson, and the other brigade leaders knew that the key to Belchite was the main cathedral on the north edge of town, a building impossible to approach because in front of it lay an open plaza, while behind it lay the walls of Belchite, a solitary factory building, and the sloping fields, and all these approaches were commanded by machine guns in its high tower. As the Americans inched down the streets and tunneled through buildings toward the cathedral, a group of them still outside the walls worked their way down a ditch toward the factory next to the church. Ben Sills, who had spent exactly six days in Spain before going into action at Quinto, crawled with a group of others to the doors of the factory. They flattened themselves against the ground as anti-tank guns wheeled up within a couple of hundred yards and blasted holes in the walls of the building. The earth trembled violently under Sills and the noise pierced his ears with pain, but when the guns stopped firing he found himself on his feet, hurling a hand grenade before him, waiting for the explosion and then pushing his way into the factory, only to find it empty, to learn that the enemy had withdrawn. Surprise and relief mingled inside him, yet as his adrenalin drained away, he found that in spite of the silence of the factory, the earth was still trembling. He turned to ask a comrade what was going on, and only then did he notice that it was not the world but his own limbs that were shaking. Like the others who had crouched beneath the anti-tank guns, Sills was to find himself continually trembling for the next two days.[20]

Close to the cathedral on all sides now, the Americans, supported by a Spanish battalion, tried to rush across the open plaza toward the building, but they were driven back by withering enemy fire. They regrouped in nearby buildings and then tried a second assault that also failed. These were costly maneuvers and among the men who fell dead in them were Henry Eaton and Samuel Levinger. Now Major Merriman thought of calling upon artillery again to oust the defenders from their posts behind the cathedral's thick walls, but the big guns could not be brought into the narrow streets. A third assault on the huge structure was led by Merriman. As he ran forward a grenade exploded nearby, and a few splinters tore into his face and arms. Comrades shouted at him to go back but he refused, and with blood streaming from his wounds he led his troops forward until they swarmed into the cathedral, driving the rebels out into the plaza and down the open streets where many of them were shot down and the survivors at last surrendered. Only then did Merriman let himself be led back to the medics to dress his open wounds. It was September 3, and Belchite seemed to belong to the Loyalists.[21]

But the battle continued to rage, for many rebels stubbornly held out in the central buildings of the town, and the weary Americans were to see two more days of street fighting. When a few of the enemy began to desert their positions and come over as willing prisoners, the assistant brigade commissar Dave Doran brought up a sound truck which boomed the Spanish national anthem through the streets of Belchite, drowning out the crackle of gunfire. For a short time the sound of battle faded away, as the martial strains of the *Hymno de Riego* blared over the dust-choked streets of Belchite, penetrating shell-torn walls and crumbling cellars, falling impartially on the ears of grimy American Internationals and dogged rebel warriors, hidden in second-story rooms, their food and water long since gone, their ammunition running low. After the music came silence, and then the harsh, public-address system voice of a Spaniard attached to XVth Brigade headquarters, reading a speech hastily written by Dave Doran. The voice asked the rebels to surrender, saying their promised relief column had been smashed. Claiming they were acting against their own interests and those of the people of Spain by opposing the Republic, the voice threatened that if they continued to fight they would find that in Belchite death awaited them.[22] The national anthem boomed through the calm air once more and then the silence of a warm summer afternoon fell over the town.

It did not last long. Linked together, almost united for

one long moment by the sound of the Spanish voice, while the sky and sun proclaimed the aching beauty of summer that all men can share and the beating of the heart of each reminded him of the mortality that all men have in common, the large group of men huddling in Belchite quickly splintered into its two incompatible components. As rifles began to stutter again, some of the rebels did surrender themselves to the Internationals, and members of the commissariat like Nelson and Doran congratulated themselves on the effectiveness of warfare by words. Yet the fight for Belchite was not yet at an end, and the men of the Lincoln Battalion still had the job of going through the streets, house by house, to subdue the last resistance.

They went in small squads, the men weighted down with rifles and sacks of grenades, some of them carrying bottles of gasoline and arms full of dry twigs for starting fires. One of the groups was led by commissar Bill Bailey, feeling like an experienced street fighter after all the action he had seen in the past couple of weeks. Happy the battle seemed over, carefree and careless, the men with Bailey spread out, knocking on the doors of houses and asking the occupants to come out into the streets. Bailey felt loose and happy, too, until, as he stood in a street, he saw a comrade knock on a door which immediately swung open. Behind it was an enemy soldier holding a pistol, which he calmly pointed at the American and fired into his face. Bailey's comrade spun to the ground, instantaneously dead, while other Americans gunned the rebel soldier down. But after that, Bailey and his men were more careful as they moved through Belchite, calling people into the streets, yelling that the Loyalist government had taken the town. Sometimes people did emerge from the houses, but in most cases the Americans had to pitch grenades through the windows. In a few cases when their aim was bad, the grenades bounced off walls into the streets, and Bailey's men scattered screaming in all directions. Later, Bailey would shiver to think back on these incidents and wonder, "Why we weren't all killed, I don't know. One fascist with a rifle on a roof could have picked us off at times like that." But there were fewer

and fewer rebels with ammunition as the Americans pene-
trated deeper into Belchite, and finally, to hurry the mop-
ping-up process, they spilled gasoline on the walls of the
last enemy strongholds and set fire to the buildings,
watching the defenders burn to death or taking them
prisoner as they fled from the flames. In one such case,
Donald Thayer of Wisconsin was careless enough to set
himself on fire, but the flames of his clothing were quickly
smothered and his name did not have to be added to
casualty lists.[23] On September 6, with a pall of black smoke
towering above the town, the Loyalists could finally call
Belchite their own.

Weary from ten days of steady action, the Lincoln Battalion was moved a few miles behind the lines for a rest,
leaving Belchite a mound of smoldering ruins in which not
a single house or building had escaped some destruction.
Behind them, too, the Americans were leaving what Herbert Matthews was to call a "stain on [their] otherwise
admirable record," for evidently someone had ordered the
summary execution of a number of rebels who had been
taken alive. Morale was very high, for the men knew they
had been instrumental in capturing, in General Rojo's
words, "the most strongly fortified point" on the Aragón
front. Casualties had been heavy, with some 50 per cent
of the Americans being killed and wounded during the
campaign. Many were saddened by the loss of Steve
Nelson, seriously injured by a sniper just before Belchite
fell, but all could take heart in the fact that the government offensive had captured 350 square miles of territory,
and all were overjoyed that the Lincolns had borne the
brunt in taking the two most important points in the
offensive.[24]

History would duly note the American accomplishments,
General Rojo commending their "superiority" and "passion," while others stated that Quinto and Belchite were
the main triumphs of the entire Aragón campaign.[25] Contemporary reactions to their victories were enthusiastic,
too. In Tarazona, George Poole of Buffalo, in training with
the Mackenzie-Papineau Battalion, found that all his

countrymen were filled with pride at the well-publicized news of what their fellow Americans had done. In Madrid, Edwin Rolfe was convinced by news from Belchite that an entirely new phase in the war had begun, one in which "the offensive has definitely passed over to our side." As he wrote home: "We know we're going to win, and there's a feeling here that we're going to win much sooner than we expected several months ago. We have a real army now. . . ."[26]

Correspondents came up to visit the Americans in their reserve positions. Hemingway, touring the front on September 14, found the Lincolns resting in an olive grove along a little stream, the "yellow dust of Aragón" blowing over them. He gave them his highest praise by writing, "Since I saw them last spring, they have become soldiers." Herbert Matthews was there, too, and he found that "like all good fighters they knew they were good, and were proud of the fact that they had made the American Battalion as famous as the Thaelmann, Garibaldi and Dimitrov" battalions.

Matthews and Hemingway were right. The Americans were good soldiers and they knew it. They had just fought the best battles they were to fight in Spain. They were to see many more months of war, were to seize other objectives, were to defend many positions tenaciously. But never again were so many Americans to be in the forefront of such a successful Loyalist attack, and never would they seize objectives so well. As Herbert Matthews so accurately worte of them after Belchite: "Now they are at their apogee."[27]

After Its Capture, Belchite Shows the Scars of War

Jarama, Brunete, Quinto, Belchite . . . the list of places where the Lincoln Battalion had been in action was slowly lengthening, and now American graves dotted the landscape in Aragón as well as Castile. There were new-comers in the ranks and a good many veterans, and those who had been through one or more battles were learning to live with what the whole world called "the horrors of modern war." In mid-September 1937, Hemingway could write that the romantics and cowards among the Americans had pulled out, saying "Those that were left were tough, with blackened, matter-of-fact faces, and after seven months they knew their trade." [1]

After what they had been through, there is little doubt that the Americans did know their new trade, yet at a distance of thirty years it is difficult to judge with any precision the fighting abilities of the men of the Lincoln Battalion. It can be said that they neither triumphed regu-larly against overwhelming odds nor collapsed under enemy attack. Almost always the Americans were under-equipped in terms of heavy machine guns, and usually they lacked the effective support of both artillery and aircraft. Yet the Lincolns managed more than once tenaciously to hold defensive positions, such as on the Brunete front or later at Teruel. On the offensive the men of the battalion moved well, if not always with the insane bravado that characterized the initial assault on Pingarrón, at least with the courage and conviction that were shown at Brunete, Quinto, and Belchite.

Though observers' opinions tended to vary according to their sympathy for the Loyalist cause, most commentators seemed to agree that the American in Spain was a "tough fighting man." Hemingway once wrote that "They fought as well as American fighting men have ever fought anywhere," and he claimed that the XVth Brigade was "one of the best in the army." But it must be noted that this author's reputation for understatement was not earned by the things he wrote about the Spanish Civil War. Shortly after the capture of Belchite, General José Miaja, commander of the Spanish Army of the Center, termed the Americans "brave, courageous and fine warriors," and said he wished there were more of them in Spain. Of course, Miaja was not in much of a position to criticize the performance of the International volunteers. Yet the gratuitous comment of an International Brigade official once contained enough criticism of the Lincolns to make it seem as if his judgment of their fighting abilities was honest. Noting that the Americans did not really understand Spain, its politics and problems, and saying that their lack of discipline made them "the most difficult to handle of all the nationalities in the International Brigades," the officer still called them "grand soldiers," who, "when they go into action . . . fight like hell."[2]

What the Americans thought of themselves as fightingmen is not an easy thing to determine, for they seem to have been steeped in the Anglo-Saxon tradition of taciturnity. One can never imagine someone raised in this tradition making the kind of statement that Spaniards enjoyed, such as Loyalist General Vicente Rojo's claim that "The Spanish Civil War was a great war because it was fought by Spaniards." Occasionally, an American wrote a letter home that made it sound as if the Lincolns were the finest fighting unit assembled since the days of the Roman legions. Yet it was more characteristic for them to joke about how strangely heroic their exploits sounded in the party press and to write, as did Abe Sasson of Los Angeles, that a picture of their battles as glorious was "recognizably a lot of crap." When interviewed by the press, they were uniformly reserved, usually saying things like, "No one enjoyed front line battle. But there was a job to be done. . . ." In their public statements most of them agreed with Donald Thayer, who wrote, "No one of us believes himself a hero." But in the privacy of his thoughts many an American believed what Alvah Bessie wrote about his comrades-in-arms: "They were no iron men, but they were heroes."[3]

For an American of the political left to become a hero, or even a worthwhile fightingman in the Spanish Civil War, was quite a feat. The Americans differed from their European comrades in having no background of compulsory military training. More important, all segments of the American left had been condemning militarism for years, and this anti-militarism had been a most popular left-wing cause, especially among the young. The idea of pacifism as a means of securing world peace was widespread in the 1930's. Tens of thousands of students had signed the Oxford Pledge, which stated that they would never bear arms, even in defense of their own countries. Many of these youngsters were then drawn into the orbits of various left-wing organizations that espoused pacifism. Now, ironically, some of them were voluntarily on Spanish firing lines. To a totally committed pacifist such men were hypocrites, but in reality they were youngsters who wanted world peace and who had learned that against an aggressive, armed enemy, pacifism does not secure peace. Ed David of Coeur d'Alene explained their position by saying, "We knew that as long as the Francos and Hitlers and Mussolinis could invade and despoil democratic nations there could be no peace. So we went and fought for peace."[4] A fighting pacifist may seem a contradiction in terms, but in the thirties and forties the choice was often not between pacifism and war, but between going peacefully into a concentration camp or struggling against your enemies.

Having accepted the need for militarism in the battle

against the politico-military powers they detested, the Americans in Spain went on to master as best they could their new trade as soldiers. Some of the least military-minded, like Ed Rolfe, found themselves glorying in "the feeling of complete adequacy, of self-assurance" that military training gave them. It was not the soldier's trade that they liked so much, but, as Rolfe said, "the use to which the trade was being put." But training was only one step in the making of a soldier; after he finished at Tarazona, each American had to take the giant step to the battlefield. There he found that his first—and major—enemy was fear, the fear of dying, or of being seriously wounded, and along with this the fearful question that gnawed at each man until he had undergone enemy fire: Will I be a coward? There was no way of answering this until the inexperienced soldier was crouched in the trenches waiting for his first action to commence. When it did, when angry bullets filled the air and artillery began to roll like thunder, the ideology which had brought a man across the Atlantic and through training to the trenches quickly vanished.[5] Suddenly he was experiencing a moment when beliefs meant nothing, when language vanished, when friends, training, loved ones, and desire were as evanescent as a summer cloud. Action was all, and those who did not flee knew they could take the shock of war.

Following the initial noises was the test of combat itself. Always difficult, it was never more so than when the new soldiers had to launch themselves into an assault. In the trenches a man could hug the earth and feel the warmth of comrades close at hand. But once over the top he was terribly conscious of the softness of his flesh and the hardness of steel that was seeking the flesh as a resting place. Each time an advance was called, anxiety returned and, as Saul Wellman put it, an assault was always a matter of "conquering fear with conviction and faith." Yet once having launched themselves into battle, the Americans lost their fear, not because they were heroes but because the concentration and physical energy that combat demanded left no room for it. Combat was a busy time, and without thinking of danger men fired their weapons, moved quickly from place to place, carried ammunition back and forth, hurriedly dug trenches, and dashed into no-man's-land to drag wounded comrades to safety. Often it was only after an action, when he was at rest in a reserve position, that a soldier would begin to "think of the battle and remember the bullet that passed through your coat or of the mortar that landed too close for comfort, or of the men you killed. . . ."[6] After an engagement, fear sometimes returned as men remembered the risks they had taken and as they pondered on the closeness of death.

The more a soldier saw of warfare, the more he developed confidence in himself. Once full of unknown terrors, the battlefield became familiar. Every experienced soldier came to know that the bullets he could hear were already past, that bombs dropped from the air rarely injured men on the ground, that well-dug trenches provided good protection against artillery. Yet if a man were kept at the front long enough, a new kind of fear began to assert itself, for as experience showed that he could survive in battle, it also made it impossible for him to ignore the fact that casualties in Spain were heavy. As one veteran put it, "The thought that—'This is my time'—increased with each succeeding action." Added to this was a growing physical and mental debility brought on by hearing too many screams, seeing too many open wounds, hiding in trenches from too many airplanes and too much artillery. From having to live too long on the knife edge of danger, men were drained of the resources that would allow them to answer a call to duty; a good many were afflicted by this disease, which one Lincoln described in himself by saying simply, "My nerves are on the bum since that last battle."[7] Ideally, such a man should be withdrawn from the lines for a rest. But in Spain, where replacements were often lacking, troops weary of battle—sometimes to the point of being unable to function—would continue to be used at the front. It was little wonder that later in the war a few of these soldiers would break and flee under the pressure of prolonged combat.

Death is the ultimate reality of war, as of life, and though the men of the Lincoln Battalion learned to live with it as a daily companion, death was still something they never totally hardened themselves to. As one American wrote, the fact that death was a commonplace did not "stop the lump from coming to your throat when you bury a comrade."[8] Yet despite the endless deaths of comrades and all the friends they had seen torn to bits by machine guns or mortars, the veteran Americans were able to return to battle time and again. And they were able to carry on not simply because of ideological commitment, but because they used a reasoning that soldiers have always used, a reasoning nowhere better expressed than by Edwin Rolfe, who wrote,

> . . . we knew that a number of us would be killed and even more wounded; but we all had the sublime conviction that we would escape death or wounding, that we would be there at the finish, exhausted but completely alive. . . . It doesn't work out that way, but soldiers must think in those terms if they are to be soldiers at all. You can't weigh your chances of survival before going into an attack or before stiffening yourself against an enemy attack; that would spoil you for action. You've got to be sure, sure as you've got a rifle in your hand, sure as you have eyes and ears, sure as you're alive, that you're going to remain alive, that you'll be there kicking when it's over.[9]

The fears and reality of injury and death were not the only things that made the Spanish experience an ordeal. War was such a constant state of upset, confusion, and abnormality that the Americans never fully adjusted to it. They were plagued by many things; the monotonous or wretched food; the lack of meals during actions when supply lines were broken; orders that were given, then canceled, then given again; the necessity of digging trenches that were immediately abandoned; the extremes of Spanish weather; the dust in summer and the mud in winter; the blanket rolls thrown on rocky ground; the sleepless nights before an action; the lack of sanitary facilities; the continuous war between men and lice that men could never win; and the inexplicable and maddening lack of American cigarettes, which caused one American to say, "If we got enough American cigarettes . . . we would wade right through the fascists without rifles." [10]

Men are not supposed to enjoy war, and yet in spite of the difficulties of life in the trenches the Americans learned to take many kinds of satisfaction in combat. To a man, they were proud of having mastered the various tools of war. It was good to be able to hit a moving target with a rifle, and tossing a grenade into an enemy machine-gun nest gave the feeling of a job well done. No matter how weary to the bone a soldier might be from days of combat, when an enemy position was captured or one of his attacks at last repulsed, the most exhausted American would feel a surge of triumph.

While all the Lincolns knew such moments of joy, there were special kinds of satisfactions that white-collar workers, students, and intellectuals found in Spain. Accustomed to a soft life at home, middle-class Americans took pleasure in the fact that muscles which had been soft for years were now hard, that flab had disappeared from their bodies. For men of the left like the Lincolns, the activist proletarian was the true hero of the 1930's, and in Spain nonworkers found themselves coming closer to this ideal. To a salesman with soft palms, calluses from holding a shovel proved that he was one of "the people." To an advertising man with a sunken chest, shoulders and arms newly muscled from lifting crates of ammunition showed that he was now a "true proletarian." For teachers, writers, and artists, used to feeling ineffectual in times of crisis, there was a deep satisfaction in learning that they, too, could march endlessly, go nights without sleep, brave machine-gun fire, and calmly kill enemies. There is little doubt that middle-class Americans who believed the proletariat was the wave of the future had often felt guilty because of their own easy lives and envious of the rugged activism of laborers. In Spain they were ridding themselves of envy and expiating that guilt as they toughened their bodies and fought alongside the real workers in the ranks.[11]

Of course, the men of the Lincoln Battalion rarely, if ever, admitted that they enjoyed combat. They were great complainers, who never stopped grumbling about the miseries of warfare and their unhappy lot. Yet occasionally one would admit that trench life had done him no real harm, that in fact it had toughened him both physically and mentally. Most would have agreed with the sentiments of Edwin Rolfe, who wrote home that although he was not always happy and content in Spain, still he "would not have missed this for anything in the world."[12]

Above all, the Americans in the International Brigades enjoyed a pleasurable feeling of usefulness. George Kaye of Los Angeles spoke for many when he wrote to his parents, "For the first time in my life I've got a feeling of accomplishment. . . ." A Pennsylvania miner claimed, "I have never felt so useful since I was a-feuding with the National Guardsmen in the Coal Strike [sic] at home." They felt useful because they were men of the left, with intellectual and emotional commitments to a certain kind of world and way of life, and they had come to Spain to fulfill these commitments. At home they had worked for social reforms as members of the Communist Party or other political groups, in labor unions, artists' leagues, or on student committees. Often they had been frustrated, for their struggles had been against the general inertia of the American political system or against entrenched enemies with the weight of society behind them; the police on picket lines, university administrations, factory owners. In Spain many Americans felt they were meeting their opponents on an open field, with arms to defend themselves and destroy what they hated. To a worker who had been clubbed by police, it was satisfying to shoot down a rebel soldier, especially since that soldier represented to him the same exploiting class that fought unionization in the United States. To Jews who had felt anti-Semitism, to men whom the Depression had kept out of work for years, to Negroes who knew Jim Crow, to students who had been unable to finish college for lack of funds, it was satisfying to bring their quarrel with the powers-that-be out into the open, to strike a blow against what oppressed them and for their own beliefs. As Joe Dallet wrote home to his wife, who was also in the Communist Party: "All the dirty work you did for years, cranking leaflets, passing them out in snow or sun, visiting contacts, etc., was not in vain. Everything we worked for for years is coming true in steel."[13]

The men of the Lincoln Battalion may have changed themselves from civilians into soldiers and taken satisfaction in their new role, but there was one aspect of army life that they never fully adjusted to—the need for military discipline. It was not at all the necessity for discipline in combat that they disliked; cases of insubordination in the face of the enemy were rare. Rather, they did not show, in the words of one brigade officer, "much superficial respect for officers or ranks," and they could never understand the little disciplinary niceties that are so close to every professional soldier's heart.[14]

In the early days of the war, some of the Spanish militias had been so informal that men had elected their officers. Though this had never been done in the International Brigades, the Americans had always shown a rough egalitarianism, with men and officers on a first-name basis. For the first year of the conflict, neither Spanish nor International units had used the salute; in the early, revolutionary days of the war it had been abandoned as too "bourgeois" for a People's Army. Then, as the Spanish Republic suppressed the militia system and built a real army in the name of military efficiency, all the traditional forms of military courtesy were reintroduced. In the fall of 1937, the Americans were asked to begin saluting their officers with the clenched fist of the Popular Front and addressing them by their rank and last name. At first many refused, while others took to raising their unclenched fists so slightly that it looked as if they were waving hello rather than saluting. Annoyed by this recalcitrant behavior, brigade commissars mounted a campaign to have the salute accepted. Editorials on the subject blossomed in the pages of the *Volunteer for Liberty*, commissars gave lectures on the need for military courtesy, and some popular men were called in by officers and asked to act as a good example for the others. The party line was itself egalitarian; a salute, it maintained, was not a sign of deference from one class of men toward another; rather, it was no more than a friendly greeting between comrades and equals. Reluctantly, the men of the Lincoln Battalion accepted this line of reasoning, and they grudgingly began to salute their officers. Even then, they rarely called officers by their last names, and the troops talked back to superiors often enough to show that the courtesy was no more than skin deep.[15]

Success with the salute may have spurred brigade officials on in another disciplinary attempt in the winter of 1937–38, this one to make the soldiers shave the beards that many of them had grown. Perhaps the men in the ranks felt that, like Samson, their strength was in their hair, for this campaign ran into a stone wall. Though commissars mentioned hygienic reasons for shaving, though the *Volunteer* used ridicule, saying that when a beard reached a certain length it became "increasingly difficult to insert food into the mouth owing to the invisibility of the orifice. Much of the food is lost on the way and tends to attract hyenas," the Americans remained adamantly hairy. One volunteer replied with a letter to the editor that mentioned the noble role of beards in history, pointing to Marx, Engels, and Lenin as "proud bearers of a hirsute chin." Then he stated flatly: "With a beard to chew on and to cover you at night you are invincible." The commissars continued their campaign, but the final word on the subject came in doggerel from a trooper who pointed out that, after all, Gillette was a capitalist, and to use his product would certainly be anti-Marxist. His verse concluded triumphantly:

> By the beard of the prophet that never was sheared,
> I'll stick to my dirty old lousy beard.[16]

Bearded or cleanshaven, it did not take long for every American in Spain to learn that in some ways the worst part of any military organization, as of war itself, was the continuous waiting, the long, nervous periods between actions when there was time to drift into fantasy, nostalgia, and desire to see home and loved ones again, the periods of inaction during battles when, without speaking of it, each man in the back of his mind inevitably began to calculate the percentages of his own chance for survival. During these periods they read and reread the letters from home. They tried to remember what it was like to take wives or girlfriends out to dinner in clean restaurants, to have drinks and good food and then be alone with them somewhere. Fathers often thought of their children as well as their wives, wondering if they would ever see the day when their youngsters would graduate school or get married. Such longings for home, such thoughts about loved ones, did not mean that the soldier was ready to leave the war in Spain. Rather, as Edwin Rolfe realized of his own desire to see his wife, this was simply the normal, healthy reaction of a soldier far from home.[17]

While they waited during lulls in action, the Lincolns wrote letters home, for that was another way of feeling close to family. Usually the letters were full of observations about Spain and its people. Often the men told about leaves to Madrid, about the unaccustomed pleasure of taking a hot shower or sleeping in a hotel room between sheets for the first time in months. Sometimes stories about military exploits were included, though for security reasons the military censor would excise all place names. At other times the soldiers could be playful in their letters, as was Dave Doran, who wrote to his wife when Belchite fell:

> At least I am learning how to fight so well now that
> I am sure you will get a husband, upon my return,
> existence with whom will be one battle after another.
> Truthfully, I would rather fight with you anyway.

Occasionally, not wanting to show their real feelings, not wanting those at home to think they were weakening in their determination to defeat the enemy, the letters of the troops were full of fiery clichés like: "The world proletariat

223

is historically destined . . . to face and prevail against the forces of reaction." Or a man would refer to the "bright, new world" that would exist once the struggle in Spain was won. But often they were self-conscious enough to realize that some of their letters sounded like *New Masses* editorials. Al Handler, who wrote such militant letters, excused himself by saying, "You have no idea how real a slogan becomes when you live this close to the struggle." Ed Rolfe, whose letters were not of that sort, explained that though some of his comrades' missives sounded like "leaflets and pronunciamentos," this only arose because of their "earnestness and intensity." Everything they wrote, said Rolfe, was "truthful and deeply felt." [18]

A longing for home was a constant factor for the Americans in Spain. One wrote that his homesickness sometimes became "physically painful," and another found to his surprise that after weeks of hot, cloudless days, he was homesick for something he never knew he could miss, "a good drizzly gray sloppy dirty day in New York. . . ." A desire for details of life in America filled the soldiers' letters. They complained that they were fed up with news about strikes and politics and said they hungered for personal news of friends and loved ones. What they wanted to hear, said New Yorker Wilfred Mendelson, was "the local dirt, the stuff that will carry us back to the boardwalk rail or now on to the watermelon infested beach. Tell us about the boys you girls are dazzling . . . about the sun and the stars, the movies and the ice cream vendors." A San Franciscan pleaded, "Give us some news on who's who at home. Does Kay still love me, or rather Edna? Do tears run down her eyes when you speak of me?" Ed Rolfe expressed a common desire when he wrote his wife asking her to tell him

> . . . how you feel, what you're doing, what you think about, dream about, what you ate for breakfast, whether you tripped across yourself while walking down the street yesterday, or a month ago.

And he concluded, "Make it real, so I can feel I'm participating in these things." It was important for the men in Spain, living in a strange world as unreal as life and as real as death, to know that with all the dangers and discomforts of their daily lives, with all the knowledge that they might never leave Spain, back home in America there was the old, safe world they had left, where there were "bacon and eggs, milk shakes, good coffee, you, and all the little things that make life pleasant." Most important was the knowledge that someone at home loved and wanted the man in Spain, that someone would eventually provide him with a safe haven from the war he fought. As Dave Doran wrote his wife during an icy December battle in 1937, "In the cold I know that somewhere I can go where there is rest and warmth. It's this promise of a future that your letter breathes, and fills me with a new spirit. . . ." [19]

To compensate for the absence of loved ones and old friends, new friendships developed rapidly under the trying conditions of war, where the sharing of a cigarette, or stale water in a canteen, or a midnight conversation on guard duty would suddenly create a strong bond between two human beings. Alvah Bessie found that after just one battle the men in his unit were "closer than men who have known each other a lifetime." Ed Rolfe thought this happened because "in a military unit, far from home, expecting that sooner or later one will face bullets and shells and their shrapnel," men seemed to become more sensitive to and aware of the world and other people around them. Under such circumstances, they quickly discovered how much they had in common. Rolfe found there was something about the dangerous life of wartime that quickly exposed the character of men, so that they were "seen in sharp relief, like mountain ridges on a plaster-cast map." [20]

Without saying it, Rolfe was getting at something that the men of the Lincoln Battalion came to feel. Sooner or later they realized that Spain was providing them with a test. The confusion and upset of war, the life-and-death nature of combat, and the loneliness of the soldier far from home—all these were testing the depth and strength of the idealism that had brought a man to Spain. Day in and day out, each man's stamina, courage, and dedication were being assessed by his comrades. More important, war was providing each man with a test of his own self-image; only he could know if his actions squared with the vision he had had of what he would do in Spain. That some soldiers did not live up to their own standards became most glaringly apparent in the cases of men who not only deserted the ranks, but also went on to turn against their former comrades and to claim that the cause they had supported was not worth fighting for.[21]

For some of the more militant troops, the test that Spain provided had a special Marxist twist. Wilfred Mendelson as a Communist claimed the real test of every volunteer was "to prove how strong is the tie between his idealistic romanticism and dialectical materialism." If the tie were strong enough to carry him through battle then, Mendelson felt, a man "begins to throw away all his old values about life and people. One really adopts for the first time a world view. . . ." Stripping it of left-wing jargon, one might describe this test by saying, as has Murray Kempton, "Spain was a reality; no one who went there and was shot at could ever be the same again." Examples of this were apparent enough in the ranks of the Americans. Often, leaders in movements at home became nonentities in Spain, while young newcomers shot to the top. As Joe Dallet wrote his wife,

> Spain is a funny place. Some of the best people at home crack up badly here and some of the least significant ones from home come through with flying colors. You can see men changing before your eyes, and they say that up front the changes come so fast you can't even see them—they just have happened, that's all.[22]

Perhaps nobody is the same after being shot at. Certainly, each man in Spain found that the experience was changing his view of war. Kenneth Shaker of Springfield, Massachusetts, might offhandedly say: "One's attitude

Troops Out of Action Grab a Meal Behind the Lines

toward war generally is much more enthusiastic before he encounters war's hardships than after he has been through one encounter," but there was more to it than that. However much they had denied it, the Lincolns had come to Spain with at least a trace of the feeling that war is a romantic adventure, a feeling that probably nobody in the Western world since the time of Homer has been totally able to escape. In Spain, amid the mud, sweat, blood, and dust of the battlefields, the romanticism left them at last. They found little heroism in war, and less glamor. Ed Rolfe best phrased this poetically:

> *Needless to catalogue heroes. No man*
> *weighted with rifle, digging with nails in earth*
> *quickens at the name. Hero's a word for*
> *peacetime. In war*
> *There are but three realities: enemy, rifle, life.*[23]

By being close to it for so long, the Americans came to hate war with a passion, to hate, as Abe Sasson wrote, "The whole bloody business, the useless slaughter, the wrecking of so many lives and the stupidity of great reserves of human energy wasted in the frantic industry of killing." The unending deaths in this conflict were horrifying, exasperating, and frustrating to the point that sometimes it was even hard to see what good would come of it all. One day a young soldier exploded: "What a fuckin' bloody thing war is. Just because people have different ideas they have to kill each other for it." [24] In the late 1930's, nobody knew better than the people in Spain that war was a terrifying way of settling differences of opinion. But the men of the Lincoln Battalion would have said that war had been thrust upon them by their enemies. They were in the same position as the rest of the Western world, which would soon be dragged to war against its will, except that the Lincolns had chosen where to fight their war.

The Americans in Spain were, for the most part, men young enough to be learning from their experience. Spain was changing them and war was changing them. They were learning to kill and to take the risks of being killed, to regard life at once as something infinitely precious and at the same time a very cheap commodity. They were becoming more mature, were, as one wrote, "losing their schoolboy attitude" toward life. This maturity was coming in the realization that the world is an unfair place where victories are not always won because one fights hard and well. They were learning that though they charged a hill, took a town, and saw their comrades slaughtered under enemy guns, the battle still might be lost elsewhere, through a mistake at headquarters, because another unit failed in its mission, or perhaps because the enemy was simply too strong. In Spain many of the Americans were being struck by the immense complexity of things, and by the fact that they individually had so little control over events. They were learning something else in Spain, too, another thing that was maturing them. They were learning what years later Albert Camus was to say the whole Western world learned from Spain, that you can be right and still be defeated, that morality and power are two different things that do not always go hand in hand. The men who went to Spain had always felt that to die in a struggle to make the world a better place was a noble and fitting way to die, that the better world justified the sacrifice. In Spain they were learning that sacrifices can be made in vain, and they had to comfort themselves with the knowledge that the struggle was more important than the end.

If the Americans were learning these truths, they did not all learn them, nor did they learn them all at once. Nor, when at last they learned them, did they despair and give up the fight, though a few did both and though all had moments of internal struggle when they sat up and wondered, How the hell did I get here? They had come to Spain for a cause, and the cause still existed. The best among them absorbed the new truths, grudgingly accepted the idea of death without victory, and rededicated themselves to the struggle. This acceptance and rededication was some measure of their maturity. Sam Levinger, the student who fell at Belchite, had written shortly before in a poem:

> *Comrades, the battle is bloody and the war is long;*
> *Still let us climb the gray hill and charge the guns,*
> *Pressing with lean bayonets towards the slope beyond.*

As Murray Kempton has said, "These are tired words, and they have absorbed all the agony which is the truth of life. They are resigned, but they are undefeated."[25] Throughout the Spanish Civil War, for more than a year after Levinger's death, the Americans were to continue fulfilling his words. From Pingarrón until their final battles, the men of the Lincoln Battalion threw themselves wholeheartedly into any fight to which they were called. The war was long and the battles were as bloody as battles could be, and yet the Americans continued to climb the hills and charge the enemy guns to fulfill their commitments to their own beliefs.

After the capture of Belchite the Lincoln Battalion, along with the other units in the XVth Brigade, took a well-earned rest. The Americans were out of the front lines for over a month, staying in small towns or camping on the Aragón plateau. For a few days they were in the hills near Grañen, where they were tantalized by the sight of the spiny church towers of Zaragoza visible across the open plain. Some of the high country was beautiful, with oak and elm trees splashed with a riot of autumn colors and the smell of pine sweetening the brisk air. But most of the countryside in which they camped was "lonely and barren, with savage, treeless hills, fold on fold, to the horizon," and the troops suffered from a wind that never stopped blowing and a fine gray dust that filled their eyes and throats. In September the nights were already cold in Aragón, and the Lincolns huddled inside blanket rolls during the hours of darkness, or walked their posts on guard duty under starlit skies with hands stuffed deep into their pockets. As in all such periods of inaction, the battalion seethed with rumors; now came the definitive story—for someone had seen the orders—that the brigade was to lead an assault upon Zaragoza; soon this was followed by the absolutely authentic story—for someone had seen the orders—that the entire division was going down to Valencia for a seashore holiday.

230

One topic not subject to rumor was the weather, for each soldier could see with his own eyes that it was becoming increasingly nasty. In late September autumn rains came to Aragón. Soldiers suffer from rain, and like men in all armies the Lincolns did not suffer in silence. They griped and cursed to each other, and a disgruntled Archie Kessner complained in a letter to his parents in Los Angeles, "Everywhere is a sea of mud. . . ." No matter how he tried to shelter himself at night, Kessner found his blankets annoyingly damp when he awoke. No matter what Kessner did during the day, whether he helped build fortifications or stood guard, whether he peeled potatoes in the field kitchen or simply spent his time trying to keep dry, he found that by nightfall he was covered with mud from head to toe, and he went to sleep at night with the sinking knowledge that the next day would bring more of the same. Yet the rain was a partial blessing for the Americans; at least on cloudy days they were sure that no enemy aircraft would plague them. As Kessner admitted, "Almost all of us hope for rain, because even being miserably muddy all the time is preferable to the dread of 'avion'." And as the rains continued, new, authentic rumors circulated, these affirming that no attack was possible during the wet season.[1]

On the Aragón front itself there was little significant action after Belchite fell to the Republic. The XVth Brigade's action there had been the last major victory of the Loyalist offensive; though moves toward Zaragoza continued, none achieved success. Rebel counterattacks that had won back some territory seized by the Republicans were also at an end. Government troops now stood guard over the ruins of Belchite, Quinto, Mediana, Codo, and half a dozen other tiny villages captured from the rebels, but the lights of Zaragoza, which Anarchist units had set out to capture more than a year before, still twinkled like stars in the night, ever beyond the grasp of the Loyalists. Through September the two exhausted armies faced each other warily, each rebuilding its shattered units. Like the Brunete offensive, that in Aragón had fallen short of total

231

success. Not only was Zaragoza still in the hands of rebel troops, but the dream of aiding the Basques on the northern front had vanished. Though the offensive had caused General Franco to shift his German Condor Legion away from the north, still his armies had inexorably gone on to capture Santander, and during September they were slowly but surely swallowing the remaining Republican territory in the Asturias. Even the most ardent Loyalist partisan had to acknowledge sadly that the complete disappearance of the northern front was now only a matter of time.

Late in September the Mackenzie-Papineau Battalion, whose 625 men in more than two months at Tarazona had received the longest training of any Internationals, moved to Aragón. While the Dimitrovs were shifted to another brigade, the MacPaps joined the Lincolns, the English, and the 24th Spanish to keep the XVth at a strength of four battalions. Despite the Canadian name, three quarters of the MacPaps were Americans.[2] Commanding the new battalion was twenty-three-year-old Captain Robert Thompson, an Oregonian who had recovered from a wound received at Jarama in February. Of fourteen staff and company officers under Thompson, two were Spanish, one was Canadian, and the remainder were from the United States.

When the fresh soldiers joined their American comrades in an olive grove near the small, battered town of Azaila, 16 miles from Belchite, the contrast between the untried troops, with their clean uniforms, and the mud-splattered veterans was startling. As George Poole of Buffalo noted, "We were the clean-shaven schoolboys, and they were the dirty and bearded veterans with hard, reserved looks in the eyes." Back at Tarazona, Poole and his comrades had followed the exploits of the Lincolns with admiration and envy. Now, face to face with their heroes, they were disappointed to find them scruffy men who answered questions about war with uncommunicative grunts. Yet these soldiers who were taciturn toward outsiders did discuss military actions among themselves. Mike Goodwin, transferred to the Lincolns because the leaders of the MacPaps considered him a bit of a troublemaker, found many of the veterans "bitching" about the mistakes made in taking Belchite. Startled by this, he soon learned that after every action men in the ranks played Monday morning quarterback; there were always soldiers who knew better than the commanders how the war should be run or the individual battles fought. In September the complaints were that the XVth Brigade, weary from taking Quinto, had been forced to capture Belchite alone, while ten to twenty thousand Loyalist reserve troops in the area had not been thrown into action.[3]

After the arrival of the MacPaps, the brigade went on a 25-mile hike to the front at Albalate, where the troops awoke one morning to find their blankets stiff with frost and the earth covered with a thin, crunchy layer of ice. New rumors about an offensive ceased when the soldiers retraced their steps to the olive grove near Azaila. The rain stopped for a few days and then started again, and the MacPaps began to look as muddy as the Lincolns. Some men were put to work digging trenches, others went on brief maneuvers, and in the evening there were endless card games for entertainment. October came and leaves on the lonely trees in the highlands turned crisp and brown and began to scatter in the wind. Then one day orders did arrive, and the XVth Brigade went down into the Ebro River valley, bivouacking on October 10 next to Quinto. In a last attempt to reactivate the Aragón offensive, the Republican high command was again going to try seizing Fuentes del Ebro, where more than a month before the Lincolns had waited in vain to become part of a flying column that was to besiege Zaragoza. In this action, the XVth Brigade was to be the spearhead. Once Fuentes was taken, the Loyalists would be able to roar down the highway toward the capital of Aragón.

October 13 was designated assault day. On the night of the twelfth the brigade was just a short truck ride from the jump-off point. While the troops checked their gear and carefully oiled rifles and machine guns, a problem that had been brewing among the MacPaps for a long time suddenly boiled over. It centered around battalion commissar Joe Dallet, party steel organizer from Ohio and onetime playboy. Nobody really liked Dallet, and none less than the men subject to his commands. For Dallet was aloof and arrogant, a strict disciplinarian who broke up card games, put men on punishment details, and fined them for breaking minor rules. For weeks there had been idle gossip that some soldiers might refuse to follow him into battle. Now, on the eve of the Fuentes attack, brigade headquarters belatedly decided to investigate the problem.

Runners went out to all companies, and commissars and officers engaged in trying to soothe their men in preparation for the assault found themselves summoned to a meeting. They gathered grumpily at headquarters, two dozen men in the dim light of an oil lantern, their minds already on the next day's battlefield, annoyed that they had been called away from their troops. Dallet was there, too, a slender young man with bushy, tousled hair. The problem was quickly stated, debate was thrown open, and officer after officer rose to have his say. Most of them mercilessly tore into Dallet, criticizing his manners and methods, while he sat alone, defiantly sucking a foul-smelling pipe. Some party members called for Dallet's dismissal on the grounds that losing contact with the feelings of his men was a cardinal sin for a commissar. Others among these politically conscious men rose to refute them, and then Dallet took the floor and attempted to defend himself. Saying he knew he was not liked, he claimed the disciplinary measures that made him hated had been crucial for making his men combat-ready. And now, Dallet said, he was ready to prove his own abilities by leading his troops from the trenches. His defense only stirred more debate, and soon everyone was interrupting, recommending, shouting, and refuting, apparently forgetting the next day's battle. Only as the night hours slipped toward morning did the storm of words subside, leaving the participants exhausted and Dallet sitting isolated, embittered, and alone. After all the talk, brigade leaders decided that removing a commissar before a battle would be unwise. Then, at three o'clock the meeting broke up and the officers hurried back to their men, who were already up and preparing to move.[4]

From its first moments, the assault on Fuentes del Ebro was dogged by mistake and misfortune. Supposed to reach attack positions while it was still dark, the Americans found dawn breaking over the valley as they left their trucks and hurried forward. Enemy machine guns cut into them and several deaths and injuries were sustained before the troops disappeared into the safety of the trenches. Stretched out along a two-mile front, nervous because the enemy now had to know an attack was in the offing, the men of the brigade waited through a long morning for promised artillery fire and air raids that were to soften up the well-prepared cement and steel rebel fortifications, 400–700 yards away across open fields. For a long time the bombardments did not materialize. This had happened to the Americans more than once and, as before, men began to wonder about planes that rarely showed and artillery barrages that often fizzled out. On these occasions the thought flickered through the minds of some that the Loyalists were woefully short of aircraft and big guns, that the bombardments might be promised merely to keep up their morale. But when such unsettling thoughts occurred to the Americans, they tried to put them out of mind.

Finally, at about ten o'clock, two government batteries fired a few salvos at the enemy and then fell silent. At noon, 18 single-engine government bombers made one run high over enemy lines, dumping their loads and disappearing. Down in the trenches the troops waited for tanks that were to lead them toward the enemy. The day was warm and the men beat off swarms of mosquitoes that filled the air of the lush valley. In the early afternoon, just as many were beginning to feel that the assault had been called off, some three dozen tanks rumbled into view. Riding on their decks and clinging to their turrets were men of the 24th Spanish Battalion. Stopping briefly to lob a few 47 mm. shells at the enemy, the vehicles suddenly lurched forward, crashed through the XVth's trenches—

crushing a couple of Spanish members of the brigade—and roared off toward enemy lines. The Americans rose and left their trenches, but the tanks raced ahead, cracking through the rebel positions and disappearing into Fuentes, leaving the infantry behind to advance unprotected into the lethal fire of the reclosed enemy lines. Such an attack had to be a disaster, and it was.[5]

True to his word that he would set a good example for his men, Joe Dallet early in the attack, leaped out of the trenches to rally the MacPap First Company, falling back after its commander and commissar had been killed. Running ahead of the men and waving them on with his pistol, Dallet was cut down almost immediately by rebel machine guns. When first aid men rushed to his side he waved them away, insisting they care for others first. Then, as he began to crawl back to his trenches, a burst of enemy fire ended his life. Still, the men he had rallied, the other MacPap companies, and the other battalions of the brigade fanned out into a storm of fire and pushed forward until the most advanced troops were hidden in dips of earth just beneath enemy fortifications. All over the open fields the injured lay in agony, many, like Archie Kessner, pestered to the point of madness by flies settling on open wounds. By the time the advance ended, fully 300 dead and injured brigaders dotted the fields before Fuentes. More than half the toll was in the MacPap Battalion, which had borne the brunt of the enemy's firepower. As dusk slowly darkened the valley, brigade officials were quite aware that the assault had been a dismal failure.

How great the failure was only became apparent when the Americans learned that the men of the 24th Battalion who had dismounted behind enemy lines had been surrounded and virtually annihilated, while more than half the tanks had been either destroyed by anti-tank guns or captured in Fuentes. The official story, patiently explained to the men by their commissars, blamed the debacle on insufficient artillery and the skimpiness of the air strike, while the ill-coordinated maneuver with the tanks was chalked up to some unspecified "betrayal" among high-up

Fortifying Near Fuentes del Ebro

officials. But many Americans were never convinced such a betrayal had occurred; many believed that the Loyalist command had simply underestimated the strength of the enemy troops holding Fuentes, and one popular story soon making the rounds had it that nobody had informed the tank commanders to move slowly enough so that foot soldiers could follow them. Despite the commissars, many veterans felt afterward that Fuentes had been no more than a typical military foul-up, similar to the wrong orders received at Brunete, or to a dozen other mishaps, both great and small, that a soldier sees in any war.[6]

For eleven days after October 13, the XVth Brigade remained in its trenches close to Fuentes, sustaining a few casualties from snipers and mortar shells. The failure to take the town had been the last gasp of the Aragón offensive, and now there was nothing for the Americans to do but consolidate their positions, digging trenches, setting up new machine-gun posts, and laying transmission wires. At night, patrols were sent into no-man's-land, some to drag the bloated bodies of the dead from the field of combat. On October 24 the XVth was relieved by a Spanish brigade, and the troops returned to positions next to Quinto. A few days later, the men were ordered into company formations one afternoon and visited by Colonel Stephen Fuqua, the American military attaché in Republican Spain. Proud of their unit, the troops tried to look as straight and military as possible while Fuqua made a short speech. Though his words were noncommittal, men like Bill Bailey felt that Fuqua was really trying to say—without implicating his government—that he was proud of their military record. The colonel did not even mention the American embargo of the Spanish War, but somehow all the troops felt cheerful after his departure. Talk spread through the ranks that his visit had been a preview to some change in American policy, perhaps even support of the Loyalists.[7] This was probably the most fanciful of all the rumors the Lincolns heard during the course of the war.

By the beginning of November, the XVth International Brigade was back once more in the little villages around Ambite, just east of Madrid. The Lincolns were again in Albares, quartered in the houses of the town, sleeping on straw mattresses thrown on stone floors. Not far away, the MacPaps inhabited a huge, icy castle in Pezuela de las Torres. The diet of the troops was beginning to show the deprivation that all of Republican Spain was suffering; potatoes, rice, and beans were plentiful, but meat and fresh vegetables were in short supply. Griping over the quality of the food was constant during this period, and as a protest against the monotony of the diet, almost all the men in the Mackenzie-Papineau Battalion fell out on sick call one morning, for the hospitals were believed to house stores of fresh meat. This minor revolt was quickly settled by the commissars, who got the troops to vote part of their salaries toward the purchase of foodstuffs, and for a while the quality of food improved. Then a particularly severe epidemic of dysentery hit the MacPaps and the sick call lines lengthened with men who had legitimate complaints.

Yet in spite of the lack of meat or the presence of

sickness, life was pleasant in the quiet little towns as the Americans rested, took furloughs, mingled with the villagers, and engaged in a kind of desultory training. Mike Goodwin, who still had seen little fighting because his company had hardly advanced at Fuentes, later remembered the late fall of 1937 as the "most delightful" period he spent in Spain, for he enjoyed his off-hours rambling through the town, which seemed so "picturesque," learning to speak Spanish with the friendly villagers and watching them slaughter pigs for the holiday fiestas in the open streets. Visiting during this period, Herbert Matthews found the morale of the Americans high, and he described them as "cheerful and full of fight," adding, "they needed this rest and it's doing them good."[8]

Those who received their first passes into Madrid, like tall, husky, twenty-two-year-old Sgt. Martin Sramek of the MacPaps, found the Spanish capital in a holiday mood. November 7–14 was being celebrated as the first anniversary of the defense of the city, and Spanish flags waved from electric poles of streetcars and hung from balconies, while brightly colored posters plastered the walls of buildings. Left-wing Spain was simultaneously celebrating the twentieth anniversary of the Russian Revolution, and huge picture posters of Pablo Iglesias, founder of the Spanish Socialist Party, and of Carlos Marx, were to be seen everywhere. In Madrid to enjoy themselves, Sramek and four comrades spent their money on food, women, liquor, and on warm clothes and new boots. After a few days, they returned broke to their battalion to brag at length about the delights of Madrid. But Edwin Rolfe, who had lived there for months, probably had a more accurate view of the capital city in this period. In spite of its flags and decorations, Madrid seemed strangely quiet in November 1937, and to Rolfe the city's people looked unusually somber. The quietness was real, for artillery bombardments of the city, once a daily occurrence, had ceased. Indeed, from all over Spain war communiques reported quiet on all fronts day after day. To Rolfe such silence seemed ominous. He feared the lack of action was no more than a ploy, an attempt to lull the Republic so that it would be unprepared for a surprise attack.[9]

In the towns near Ambite the troops were put on stand-by orders late in the month; the men packed their gear and got ready to move at a moment's notice. Thanksgiving came, and it was lugubriously celebrated not with turkey but with a dinner of boiled cabbage livened by a few shreds of burro meat. Then the orders were canceled and the soldiers unpacked. They all knew by now that the northern front no longer existed. On October 21, Franco's troops had taken Gijón, the last Loyalist stronghold in the north, leaving the 65,000 men of the insurgent Army of the North with their 300 pieces of artillery and 250 tanks free to fight elsewhere. Though expected, the final collapse of this front depressed the troops. Official rationalizations that the Republic would ultimately be stronger because now it could concentrate its military power neither convinced nor particularly cheered them. Everyone in the Republican camp began to expect a new rebel offensive in the Madrid area, and this helps to explain the somber faces of the Madrileños. But when November passed without any major military engagement and the heaviest snowfall in 20 years blanketed much of central Spain in December, most of the Americans began to think there would be no real fighting until the next spring. In the Mackenzie-Papineau Battalion, Sgt. Sramek found some new men grumbling over the inaction and worrying that they might never get to see combat.[10]

On December 10, the XVth Brigade left the Madrid area for Aragón once more. On trains the men were carried through Albacete, down to Valencia, then north and inland to Caspe. From there the troops marched under cloudy skies and through hilly country to the tiny villages of Alcorisa, Agua Viva, and Mas de las Matas, all situated on rivers some 50 miles southeast of Belchite. Overseeing this operation was the brigade chief of staff, Robert Merriman, who had as one of his new assistants Major Humberto Galleani, transferred from the group of Italian Internationals he had joined a year before. Dave Doran, longtime

YCL organizer, was now brigade commissar, for Steve Nelson's groin wound was so serious that he was being repatriated to the United States. Doran was not a pleasant, affable person as Nelson had been. Like Joe Dallet, Doran lacked rapport with those he commanded. His arrogant ways seemed to many Americans to belong more to a regular army than one composed of volunteers. Obviously given his position because of his party background, he was heartily disliked by many from the start. Yet showing himself brave under fire, Doran eventually earned the grudging respect of some brigaders, though he never replaced Nelson in the hearts of his men. For lanky Phil Detro, now commanding the Lincolns, respect and popularity had come easily. A curiously apolitical figure, the twenty-six-year-old Detro had quickly proved he had learned a lot in six years of National Guard service. At Brunete he had been wounded leading the First Company of the Washington Battalion against Mosquito Crest. Recovered and healthy, he had been appointed commander of the Lincolns just before Fuentes; since that battle, New York elevator operator Fred Keller had served as his commissar.[11]

As the Americans settled into the little Aragón towns and began to anticipate the festivities of the Spanish Christmas season, news came through that let them know they were still very much part of a war. In the cold, pre-reveille dawn of December 22, they were jolted from sleep by the sound of cheering and singing in the streets. They awoke to see their Spanish comrades dancing with joy and to hear the news that amid heavy winter blizzards the Loyalist government had successfully completed a surprise offensive, capturing the important provincial capital of Teruel that the rebels had held since the beginning of the war. It was a nice Christmas present for all partisans of the Republic, and the Americans poured into the streets to yell and pound their Spanish comrades on the back. The news was especially welcome and heartening because it showed that in spite of the fall of the north, the Republic was still strong enough to seize the offensive. So optimistic did the news make some men that Edwin Rolfe wrote home to his wife, "It may be . . . the beginning of the end for Franco." In the offensive the government had taken Teruel without the help of any International Brigades. This seemed to be a good sign, for it showed Rolfe that the Army of the Republic was at last coming into its own, that soon it would be able to stand up to Franco without the help of the Internationals.[12]

But the Americans were being prematurely sanguine. What had happened was this: Teruel, a walled city of 20,000, built on a high hill, with gorges around it and higher hills beyond, had been on the point of a rebel salient thrust deep into Loyalist territory. It seemed the logical starting point for a rebel drive to the sea to split Republican Spain in two and cut Madrid off from Barcelona. At least, so the Loyalist high command had long feared. Now, with some inkling that Franco was planning an assault through Guadalajara aimed at Madrid, the Republicans, knowing Teruel was defended only by a small garrison, decided both to forestall Franco and to nip off the rebel salient. Massing a huge army, which excluded the Internationals for reasons of political propaganda, the Loyalists moved upon Teruel on December 15.[13] In the midst of a snowstorm the city was quickly and easily surrounded, but behind its old walls rebel defenders tenaciously held out. When news came to the Americans that Teruel had fallen, the enemy was actually still in possession of various large government and religious buildings of the town; they did not surrender until the first week in January. Meanwhile, Franco began rushing all available forces toward Teruel. Soon rebel aircraft controlled the skies, and on the ground the Republicans were outmanned and outgunned. Blizzards lashed the area and the temperature dropped to $-18°F$. In blankets of snow that cut both armies off from their supply depots, rebel troops began to push the Republicans back in an effort to seize La Muela del Teruel, the high ridge to the west of the town. By December 30, three of the six small towns west of Teruel that the government had captured had already been retaken by Franco's forces.

In their little towns, the men of the XVth Brigade knew none of the details of the battle. They were busy attending the many dinners and parties of the Spanish holiday season. Chocolate bars, candy, and other things to eat arrived in mail from home, and ample supplies of cognac added to the warmth and spirit of the fiestas. Entertainment was supplied by the men themselves, and then for a couple of days by Paul Robeson, who came to visit them. Through Christmas Day and beyond, morale was high—indeed, it would probably never be so high again, for victories after Teruel would always come in a context that foreboded ultimate defeat. But for a few brief days the presents, the liquor, and the good news kept the Americans suspended in a fragile bubble of optimism. After December 25, the soldiers were looking forward to a New Year's Eve dance with the American nurses of a mobile International hospital stationed at Alcorisa. But it was never to occur, for on the morning of the last day of the year orders came for the brigade to move to the Teruel sector. In an attempt to stop the huge rebel counteroffensive, the Republic was once more calling on the Internationals.

On New Year's Day the British, Spanish, Lincoln, and Mackenzie-Papineau Battalions crammed into trucks. For hours their convoy bumped across rutted, frozen roads through bleak gray hills, while snow flurries cut visibility to nothing and icy winds sliced through the canvas truck tops. Shortly before midnight the convoy stopped at Argenté, 20 miles north of Teruel. The night was bitter cold and snow drifted slowly down and danced in the headlights of the trucks as the Americans descended and then spread out into the fields to make camp.

George Poole shivered inside his overcoat as he marched along with his section of the MacPaps. He pitied the men around him who had only short jackets, and those who wore rope-soled sandals on their feet. Assigned a position, Poole and his comrades began to gather wood to build a fire. But word came down that no fires were to be allowed; the brigade was too close to the front and the commanders did not want to give enemy artillery a target. The way to keep warm was to dig, and Poole attacked the ground with his shovel, only to find it virtually impossible to break through the frozen crust of earth. He and his comrades took turns stabbing at the ground, working and sweating

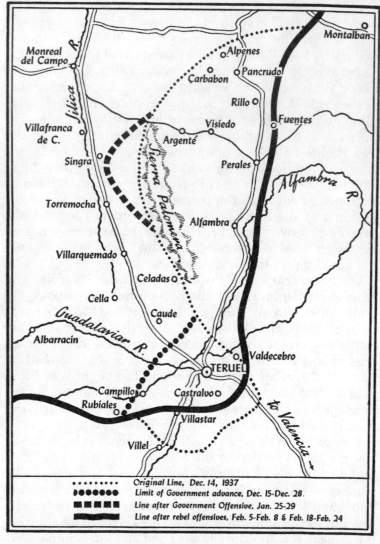

Original Line, Dec. 14, 1937
Limit of Government advance, Dec. 15-Dec. 28.
Line after Government Offensive, Jan. 25-29
Line after rebel offensives, Feb. 5-Feb. 8 & Feb. 18-Feb. 24

TERUEL

and cursing the Spanish Army and Franco and the weather and their commanders. All around them Poole could see figures in the dark, men wandering through the slanting snow, moving their arms to keep warm and scrunching into their coats until only noses and eyes peeped out. As Poole began to despair of having a trench to sleep in, officers called the men together and led them back to Argenté.

The town was showing the scars of war. Snow softened the jagged outline of smashed tiles and broken bricks heaped together in piles of rubble, but still it was a dismal collection of buildings, with no roofs and caved-in walls. To the Americans it seemed a terribly lonely place—indeed, all but a handful of its 1,500 residents had been evacuated. Picking their way through the cluttered streets, the soldiers managed to find a few buildings that still had roofs, and they settled down, some of the lucky ones like George Poole finding piles of straw to sleep on. Because each man had only one blanket, they doubled and tripled up, huddling against each other for warmth. In the morning the men awoke before it was fully light. All were hungry, but the only things available to eat were sardines that had been distributed the day before, and the cans were frozen solid. Poole and his comrades prepared breakfast by putting the cans into their pockets and crawling back under the blankets. By the time they were thawed out, a kitchen truck had appeared, and Poole ate the fish with bread, washing them both down with hot chocolate. Plenty of cigarettes came up with the truck, too, and armed with these the Americans marched out to the flatlands over a mile from Argenté. There they dug slit trenches and sat through the freezing hours of daylight, smoking and waiting for orders, unable to move because of the necessity for camouflage, flattening themselves against the snow time and again as enemy aircraft roared incessantly overhead. By the end of the day the medics were already treating soldiers for frostbite.[14]

Thus began a month of winter war that was to test the Americans as they had not been tested before, a war in which they fought the elements and sickness as much as enemy troops, a war in which continuous skirmishes against lice, which thrived in the cold, seemed to absorb almost as much time as battles with the rebels. Teruel had always registered the lowest temperatures in Spain, but no native could remember a month as cold as January 1938. Often the temperature reached 20° below, and an arctic wind howled day and night. Herbert Matthews, there for the *New York Times*, later recalled: "It was the cut of the wind which was so especially distressing. Nothing was protection against the icy blasts that came shrieking down from the north, penetrating any amount of clothes. Our eyes filled with constant tears from the sting of it; our fingers swelled and became numb, and all feeling went out of our feet except an overwhelming iciness. We gasped for breath, and could not stand in one spot to look through our field glasses, for the wind buffeted us like a prizefighter boring in. . . ." [15] If it was so bad for a correspondent, who could often retire to a warm house at night, how much worse it must have been for the man in the trench.

Teruel was later called Spain's Valley Forge, but the Continental Army never had to meet British troops in the snowdrifts, while in Spain the Lincolns battled a superior enemy through most of the icy month of January. Not only were the Loyalists defending Teruel now vastly outnumbered—some reports claim by as much as two to one—but as the rebels pushed them slowly back toward the gates of the city, they were completely outgunned. Franco's forces had brought up dozens of new field batteries, and these were manned by German gunners who laid down pattern bombardments so precise that government commanders "estimated that at the height of the attack there was no five-yard square [of the front] that had not received its shell." When weather permitted, rebel aircraft filled the skies, and the combined bombardments were the heaviest any American had seen to date, so heavy that the crests of chalk hills were lowered by as much as six feet and George Poole claimed that they "made anything we had seen before seem like something among friends." [16]

During the first weeks of Franco's attacks in January the

Moving up to Altas Celadas

MacPaps remained dug in near Argenté, while the Lincolns marched 13 miles south to Cuevas Labradas, sleeping one night in a damp, smoky railroad tunnel cut into granite cliffs above the town. Then they hiked west 5 miles through snowy, submountainous terrain to Altas, on the crest of the Sierra Palomeras, overlooking the rebel-held town of Celadas. Like the MacPaps near Argenté, the Lincolns were in a position to defend the Teruel-Belchite road, the only connection from Teruel north into Aragón. Almost immediately the men of the battalion named their position the North Pole, for from the first day frostbite took a greater toll of the Americans than did enemy guns, some 20 men being treated for it in a week. At the same time, only one man was killed and about ten wounded by enemy artillery. Though the Lincolns skirmished briefly with rebel troops, they were mainly spectators during their time at Altas. On January 5 and 6, they could see long lines of enemy troops, dark against the gleaming winter landscape, moving out of the range of their guns and assaulting hills to the south in wave after unending wave, and being turned back by Loyalist guns. Then the temperatures dropped so low that no action at all was possible, and the troops spent a few quiet days before being relieved on January 11.

Back in the railroad tunnel near Cuevas Labradas, the Americans watched the steel gray skies turn blue for two days, as a strong winter sun appeared and temperatures soared. Some sunbathed with their shirts off, and all spent long hours picking lice from the hairy recesses of their bodies. Food was plentiful now, for enemy stores had been found in Teruel, and the troops stuffed themselves on chicken, pork chops, and mashed potatoes; one morning they were even treated to real American doughnuts with their coffee. At the same time there arrived a shipment of American chocolates and cigarettes, sent by the FALB, and supply sergeants brought up a load of woolen socks and overcoats, so that when Herbert Matthews visited them on January 13 he could write, "I have never seen them in better spirits and health."[17] But this idyll was short-lived. In mid-January continuing rebel pressure caused the entire XVth Brigade to be called into action again.

As a cold wave descended, the MacPaps came down from their positions and turned west a couple of miles north of Teruel. The other battalions followed them until the brigade was stretched across the valley that cradled the Teruel-Zaragoza road. In one set of hills the MacPaps dug trenches, while the 24th Spanish took up positions that ended on the key ridge, La Muela. It was in these posts that after January 17 the brigade met the full onslaught of the rebel drive, which decimated the Germans of the XIth International Brigade before reaching the XVth. It was here that the Americans bore the brunt of massed rebel artillery—the greatest concentration of it since the beginning of the war—here that they suffered from the silent, deadly mortars that caved in trenches and tore men and guns to bits until one day all five heavy weapons in the MacPap machine-gun company were out of commission.

Trucks Bear Lincolns to Battle Near Teruel, January, 1938

Finally, it was here that the MacPaps, in positions lower than the rebels all along the line, took an enormous toll of attacking infantry, lost close to 250 men, and ultimately had to cede ground as hordes of enemy troops threatened to inundate them. When the offensive stopped momentarily on January 22, the rebels were in possession of La Muela and other heights overlooking Teruel, but the XVth Brigade had helped keep the city from their grasp. For their role in its defense, the MacPaps, along with the British Battalion, were specially commended by Juan Modesto, commander of the 5th Army Corps.[18]

While the MacPaps were battling in the hills, the Lincolns were holding down positions along the railroad line from Zaragoza, just outside the walls of Teruel. Some of them slept in buildings at night, and they sent out raiding parties that ransacked the clothing stores of the deserted town, exchanging their tattered uniforms for a strange assortment of new clothes; men with ragged pants could now be seen sporting vests and neckties, while a few were observed walking around the trenches in patent leather dancing shoes and others wore huge sombreros. Though they engaged in little close combat, the Lincolns sustained casualties from the same combination of massed artillery and trench mortars, while their sharpshooting snipers managed each day to pick off a few rebels moving through the blackened terrain. The major casualty in this period was Captain Detro, mortally wounded one day while crossing a street between two positions without using a shallow communicating trench. Altogether, during the last two weeks of January, the Lincolns reported 80 casualties, most of them among the machine-gun and rifle sections that had been detached and sent forward to bolster the MacPaps.[19]

Still in the forward lines, the decimated MacPaps spread themselves so thin after January 22 that no men at all were available for improving the trenches. The troops merely lay low during the daytime "workouts," as the men now called artillery barrages. A warm spell made things easier, but then almost everyone in the brigade, from Merriman on down, was hit by a flu that made temperatures soar and noses runny and red, while hacking coughs filled the air. Late in January, the Americans learned that reports from Franco sources printed in the world press had recently claimed that the XVth Brigade had been wiped out. At first amused, the men became annoyed when they realized the news must be causing anguish to relatives at home. Their mood improved when Matthews came up to see them on the twenty-ninth and sent out a cable story to tell the world that the XVth was still very much intact. Intact it was, but after a month of being frozen, battered, and pushed back, the Americans were tired of this winter war. And after seeing the masses of enemy troops, artillery, and aircraft, they were losing their optimism about the possibility of holding Teruel. George Poole spoke for many when he wrote of this period: "We ate well . . . and we waited for them to collect more aviation and artillery men . . . to smash through."[20] As January turned to February 1938, the main question in the minds of the Americans was, Who would have the almost impossible task of stopping the next thrust at Teruel? That such a thrust was coming soon nobody could doubt.

Actually, unknown to the Americans, it was the Loyalists who counterattacked north of Teruel during the last week in January, and this caused rebel pressure on the city to ease for a few days. Just as this was becoming apparent, the entire XVth Brigade was relieved on February 3 by El Campesino's Spanish troops, and the Americans marched southeast on the main highway toward Valencia. They halted behind the concrete fortifications near La Puebla de Valverde, 12 miles from Teruel. On the fifth, the Lincolns boarded a train that carried them down through mountains and immense coastal orange groves to Valencia. Two days later, just as the MacPaps were crowding into boxcars at the start of the same journey, telegrams were received ordering them back to battle. On their way from Valencia toward Madrid, a dismayed battalion of Lincolns found their train reversing direction, lumbering back over the route they had just taken. The forces of Francisco Franco, stopping Loyalist thrusts north of Teruel, had counter-attacked heavily, breaking government lines and seizing Argenté, Perales, and Alfambra, the last two on the main road from Teruel to Belchite. Now they were sweeping down toward Teruel, menacing the hilltop town from three sides.[21]

When it was assembled again, the XVth Brigade was sent by truck some 50 miles north of Teruel to the tiny village of Cortes de Aragón. From this point, the XVth and XIth International Brigades were to lead a diversionary movement toward enemy lines behind Segura los Baños, designed to make the rebels pull back their advancing troops in the Teruel sector. If successful, the diversion might provide a jump-off point for a full-scale assault on the Zaragoza-Teruel road, the main line over which the enemy was pouring men and materials in its drive to recapture the provincial capital. But first the Americans had to worry about Segura, a region of wild, rocky, steep hills on top of which the rebels had entrenched themselves behind forests of tangled barbed wire.

When the brigade reached the area on February 15, it was snowing again. The next evening the troops were given rations for two days and canteens full of cognac, and the battalions moved out in the snowy night. In the dark the Americans were silent. When he had to give orders, Sgt. Sramek had them passed down the line in whispers from man to man in his section. Led by Spanish peasants from the area, the MacPaps, ahead of the other battalions, spent what seemed like hours crossing a broad, open valley. Winds roared down from the dark heights above, blowing snow and sleet into the soldiers' eyes. Yet the snow helped conceal the troops' movements, and they crept forward, finally reaching boulder-strewn hills to the rear of the enemy's positions. The men of the battalion deployed and waited for orders to move. Then, just as they began a silent assault upon a hill named Mount Atalaya, the Lincoln Battalion slipped past them in the dark, on its way toward the Sierra Pedigrossa.

When orders came, Sramek led his men in a painful crawl upward, feeling carefully for solid rocks that would not begin to slide. His men went forward slowly, working their way up the slope through the long hours of the night, cutting through barbed wire as they went, until they approached the summit. Then, as the first light of day made the steep hills above Segura stand out in jagged relief against the sky, the Americans pulled pins from hand grenades and at a signal all stood up, hurling the grenades before them and charging upward. The surprised defenders managed to swing their machine guns into action before the MacPaps were upon them, and suddenly wounded and dying Americans dotted the slopes. While the rebels unleashed their trench mortars and rocks began to shatter with their fire, the dispersed MacPaps pulled back to re-form their broken ranks.

Sheltered by a dip of earth only 100 yards from the enemy, Sramek was trying to get his section in line for another charge when a sledgehammer seemed to smash against his knee and he went down. Blood spurted from his leg, a dark stain rapidly spreading on his pants. A first aid man went swiftly to work on him, tightening a tourniquet about his thigh. Just as he finished, a burst of machine-gun fire riddled the medic's body and he died on the spot, leaving Sramek helpless and alone as his men started back toward the enemy, scrambling upward, small rocks slipping under their feet and throwing them off balance. Yet they came up through the barbed wire and into the muzzles of roaring machine guns until they swarmed over the crest and into the enemy trenches. Then the MacPaps could settle back to watch the Lincolns assaulting and taking their hill, out of rifle range across a broad valley. Because they had not begun their attack until daylight, the Lincolns had more trouble than the MacPaps, but by early afternoon Monte Pedigrossa belonged to them. At the end of the operation—which included the taking of a couple of more hills—some 120 rebels, 200 rifles, 13 machine guns and 3 mortars had been captured by the brigade. Though Sramek, left with a tourniquet on too long, was about to have his leg amputated at a hospital, and though the commander of one Lincoln company had been killed, casualties had not been heavy. The action at Segura had been a complete success.

Barely had the XVth Brigade consolidated its new positions, when it had to face the inevitable counterattack. Rebel aircraft rained bombs upon them, and high on their naked hilltops the Lincolns and MacPaps were perfect targets for enemy artillery. Yet they were soldiers who had learned a lot about warfare, and while the enemy plastered their positions, they left the trenches and lay back on the slopes behind the protective crests of the hills. Then, when the barrages ended and they saw the enemy infantry move forward and begin to climb toward them, they returned to the trenches, turned the captured mortars and machine guns against the rebels, and beat back their assaults. The first attack ended with 100 enemy lying dead on the hills above Segura, but soon they were back with reinforcements. For three days and nights the Lincolns and MacPaps held their hills, stopping the rebels before they could even get close to the trenches.[22]

While the XVth Brigade held above Segura los Baños, rebel forces stepped up the pressure around Teruel. Francisco Franco poured men and equipment into the sector, until the Loyalists were outnumbered on all sides of the provincial capital and were in danger of being trapped there. By February 19, the rebels were at the gates of Teruel. On that day the Americans were pulled from their trenches and rushed south until they were at Valverde once more. They were put to work preparing new defensive positions, and for the next couple of days heard the continuous boom of enemy artillery from beyond the snowy hills, where the insurgents were methodically reducing Teruel to rubble. On the twenty-second, the noise stopped and an ominous silence filled the air. It was the sad signal that the Loyalists had completely evacuated Teruel.[23]

Before the men really had time to think about it, the Republic had made its justification for the loss, and the commissars duly explained to the troops that Teruel was a victory, for it had taken Franco two months to recapture what the government had captured in just a few days. Yet as the Americans pulled out of their positions and headed down the highway toward Valencia, they knew in their hearts that the official line on Teruel was a grand rationalization. The hopes of late December, that Teruel was to be a turning point in the struggle against fascism, had been shattered. In early February, Earl Browder had visited the soldiers on their way to reserve positions and had lectured to them, saying that they would be in Spain until Franco was out of Spain.[24] As they marched toward Valencia through slush, and a slight warmth in the air foretold the coming of spring, many of the Americans were beginning to have the grim feeling that Franco was not going to be out of Spain for a long, long time.

When Teruel fell once more to Spanish rebels and the dispirited men of the Lincoln Battalion climbed aboard trains taking them to rest areas far from the front, the young soldiers had time to reflect on the unsuccessful campaign the Republic had just waged. The high hopes of the Christmas season were gone now, and there remained only the grim memories of battle and defeat, of comrades killed and wintry positions abandoned, of bitter cold that had sapped their strength and caused old wounds to throb with pain. As the crowded railroad cars rattled slowly toward the rear, many tried to put the battle in its larger context, as part of the struggle against fascism. For though they were activists, committed to a daily world of struggle and sudden death, the Americans often thought of the issues of the 1930's that had brought them to the trenches of Spain. Unlike conscript soldiers, the Lincolns shared no national patriotism that kept them on the firing line. As volunteers for a war in which the major ideologies of the world seemed locked in a death struggle, they were forced to keep large social and political issues always in mind.

In this war, especially in its moments of rest—and

sometimes doubt—the Americans needed, as Ed Rolfe wrote,

> *something to think about, words that will prod*
> *the war-weary brain back to life from forgetfulness . . .* [1]

Such words were readily supplied by the commissars, always anxious to convince the American that he had been right in volunteering, yet usually reaffirming that his job was still a long way from being done. But more often the words were those of the soldier himself, in newspaper articles, in interviews, in letters home, or in the endless bull sessions that took place in trains or trucks, in the trenches, at night among troops huddled around tiny fires, in bombed-out houses far behind the lines. The words were not freshly coined. Often they were no more than cliché-ridden slogans conveying ideas that a later generation may find amusingly naïve. Yet such words meant a great deal to the men who spoke and heard and believed them, for the thoughts they conveyed served to define the volunteers' role in the important struggles of the decade. Fortunately, enough of the words remain to give insight into the mind of the American in Spain, to outline his beliefs and hopes, to show the context of ideas in which his continued presence on the battle line took place.

Because the soldiers in Spain were essentially young men and, more important, because they were deeply involved in the daily risk of death, it is not surprising to find that they engaged in little idle philosophic speculation. They did little agonizing over the nature of man or of political commitment, though their presence in Spain was obviously based upon the belief that the human condition could be improved and that commitment was necessary for bringing about such improvement. Abstract, philosophic ideas do not appear in their writings, except, fittingly enough, those concerning life after death, a concept emphatically rejected in numerous eulogies. William P. Smith, Jr., in a poem on the dead, was typical in saying:

Troops Reading a Wall Newspaper

I cannot say that they've been torn
To some far place and there reborn to live again . . .

And yet the Americans in Spain rejected Christian immortality in favor of a worldly immortality in which posterity would remember the deeds they had done in Spain and commend the cause for which they had died. As Joseph Rosenstein wrote in a memoriam to those who had fallen at Pingarrón:

And when the far-off tales are told, of the brave and the
    quick and the dead,
A thousand minds will flicker back to Jarama, from which
    there soon
Came the new dead. The climbing flesh is gone, but only the
    flesh.[2]

Apart from this one digression, the thoughts of the men of the Lincoln Battalion were practical ones, concerned with the political and economic problems of Spain, the United States, and the world at large. Such thinking was their mental bread and butter, but this seems only fitting for men who were risking their lives for a political cause. Visitors to the battlefields never ceased to marvel at the fact that even during military engagements the Lincolns would display a passionate interest in events in the outside world. Riding with a twenty-year-old truck driver who had just narrowly escaped death in a retreat, Vincent Sheean once found himself being lectured on the meaning of recent international developments, and he saw something amusing about the soldier's "fierce earnestness and his capacity for forgetting every immediate detail . . . in the high preoccupation of *Weltpolitik.*" Another correspondent, trying to interview a group of wounded Americans at a hospital, found them more interested in the plight of Czechoslovakia than in the course of the Spanish War. During the battle of Brunete, Louis Fischer came upon a soldier, stationed in a farmhouse just behind the lines, who appeared more concerned about the organization of workers at "Little Steel" than the progress of the offensive.[3] Such attitudes were only prevalent because the Americans were true internationalists who thought of their battle in Spain as part of a worldwide struggle. To the Lincolns, union developments at home or in England, the fate of France or of Czechoslovakia, the foreign policy of the Soviet Union, and Japan's invasion of China were all important, for fascism had to be defeated in all its manifestations throughout the world.

The political thinking of the men in Spain took place within the framework of beliefs they held as men on the left wing of American life. All shared the "conscience of the thirties," believed in the rights of labor, oppressed minorities, and the common man, felt the necessity for human solidarity and collective action, upheld the needs of "the worker" against the property rights of the "owning classes." Having lived through the virtual—if only temporary—collapse of capitalism in the United States, having suffered from the ensuing Depression, having seen the march of Europe to the right in the 1930's, the Lincolns felt that depressions were inevitable and that fascism was the ultimate stage of capitalism, one which had to be resisted by force. These common beliefs of the left wing in the late thirties were, of course, fostered by Marxist political parties. Yet the acceptance of such ideas by the Americans does not imply that they were real Marxists; their acceptance was more the product of an emotional reaction to what they saw wrong with the world than of a closely reasoned agreement with Marx. Since few Lincolns had ever read Marx or any Marxist thinkers, their knowledge of such thought came from exposure to the left-wing press. Because journalistic Marxism gave an explanation for the ills of the world, and because this explanation accorded with the facts as they perceived them, the volunteers embraced the ideas without caring about any underlying intellectual structure. Once they had accepted this viewpoint, the Lincolns clutched it fiercely and dogmatically, and as some men later realized, they tended to become inflexible in their thought patterns. Many of the troops were unused to the world of ideas anyway, and it was not hard for them to swallow the left-wing viewpoint whole. Some had doubts, of course, but most could think the full sum of wisdom was contained in the *Daily Worker*.[4]

There is little doubt that many of the men in the Lincoln Battalion foresaw the inevitable arrival of socialism throughout the world. But this is not to say they were revolutionaries, ready to go to the barricades to overthrow the capitalist order. Since they were primarily concerned about curing immediate social, political, and economic ills, the volunteers had done little thinking about the socialist state. This is hardly surprising, for even members of the Communist Party were not encouraged to think about socialism during the Popular Front era. The party was itself devoted to reform rather than to drastic upheaval in the United States, and it was giving support to the New Deal. Perhaps a few men in the battalion hoped that a revolution would destroy all the institutions they did not like at home, but this was certainly not the common state of mind. The typical volunteer was optimistic enough to have the vague feeling that the United States could change without violence, and he looked upon the New Deal as a first step being taken in the direction of a socialized state. Those who did foresee violence thought it would come when the political right rose to defend its interests against social change, as it had in Spain.

Concomitant with the left-wing viewpoint in the thirties was often a heavy-handed and serious approach to issues. Certainly the author of the Jean Harlow obituary which appeared in the *Volunteer for Liberty* exhibited an intense humorlessness in writing:

> Jean Harlow, well known motion picture actress, died in Hollywood a few days ago.
> Although she was often compelled to act in insipid or even reactionnary [sic] roles, she always succeeded in relieving the boredom or vileness of the plot by superb acting. Jean Harlow was one of that little bunch of actors who for years worked towards the unionization of the motion picture industry. Before her death she saw the craft organized and in militant action.

While other Americans might have been tempted to forgive Miss Harlow's pictures for physical reasons, the Americans in Spain would forgive her "reactionary" roles simply because she had helped to organize a union. Certainly, not all the Lincolns could have been impervious to the star's charms, but all would have agreed that the battle for unionization in the United States was the counterpart of the struggle in Spain. Time and again men would write home things like, "The boys who stayed in the United States are doing a very important job there. We aim to beat fascism here, they intend to do it there." Or one would write to a fellow union member, "We do not consider that you are fighting in the rear . . . we feel that we are all fighting at the front together: while we, with our guns, hurl fascism back in Spain, you, with your organized strength halt reaction at home. . . ."[5]

By "fascism" at home the Lincolns did not simply mean William Dudley Pelley and his Silver Shirts. In their minds,

Gabby Klein and
Vaughan Love in
Front of Their Hut

"fascism" in the United States was espoused by the people
who had "compelled" Jean Harlow to act in "reactionary"
roles, that is, in the form of the traditional "big interests"
which controlled the economic life of the country. These
forces owned the factories, which had been converted into
"armed fortresses, manned by gangsters, labor spies and
provocateurs, who mislead or by threats force thousands
of misguided workers to act as scabs." These "fascist"
forces in the United States were supposedly hoping for a
Franco victory, for—the reasoning ran—if the rebels won
in Spain, the right would be strengthened throughout the
world, and in America the "big interests" would redouble
their efforts to break the labor union movement.[6] This
inability to differentiate—willful or not—between the
ideology of American industrialists and that of Hitler and
Mussolini is the most striking example of the inflexibly
applied Marxist doctrines of the volunteers. Certainly, it
shows the Manichaean streak in their thought, their rigid

division of the world into the forces of good and evil.

Despite the great power of the "big interests," the men of the Lincoln Battalion were not pessimistic over the future of the United States. In the press, they followed the spreading organization of labor—above all, the CIO—with pleasure, writing home such remarks as: "Their progress is thrilling. We won't know the U.S. when we return." Publications like the *Volunteer for Liberty* were full of news about successful strikes at home, and the soldiers welcomed these as signs of increasing democracy. Similarly, every move of President Roosevelt toward legislation for a minimum wage or a 40-hour week was greeted with approval. Their attitude toward the American government, traditionally thought to be in thrall to the "big interests," was a cautious one, tinged slightly by optimism. The troops thought that the American people, aroused over the destruction of democracy in Germany and Italy, were at last electing men "at least more favorable to labor than in the past." Under the influence of public pressure, previously "cowardly and even reactionary public officials" had been forced to legislate laws favorable to unions, such as the Wagner Act. Even the Supreme Court, "the last citadel of reaction," had come under enough pressure from FDR's packing plan, so that "it did not dare to declare the Wagner Act unconstitutional." [7]

If the internal policy of the American government won the grudging approval of the Lincolns, its foreign policy always fell short of their hopes. The touchstone was Spain. Though the United States was not involved in the farcical Non-Intervention Commission, still Congress, under Roosevelt's prodding, had embargoed both sides in the war. All through their stay in Spain, the Lincolns called for the sale of arms to the legitimate government of the Republic. They wrote letters home to friends, urging them to work through labor unions, student groups, Popular Front organizations, or political parties to put enough pressure on the government so that the embargo would be lifted. At home the left responded to their appeal, but the pressure it generated did not at all budge the government of FDR, whose worry about the Catholic vote overrode any impulses of sympathy he may have had for the beleaguered Spanish Republic.

When the men of the Lincoln Battalion looked at the rest of the world, their vision was colored by the same left-wing orientation. Their opinion of Hitler, Mussolini, and fascism in general preceded their arrival in Spain. To some, fascism had previously been an abstract concept, "something to which we were opposed in principle," while now, after exposure to it, "We have learned what fascism is in reality . . . we have seen it with our very own eyes. . . . Fascism is utter savagery, barbarism and destruction. . . ." Others, like Rubin Schechter of Los Angeles, came to feel that fascism was simply the latest form of the evil that always plagued mankind. As he wrote to his mother,

> Our enemy is old. He cannot bring new life to mankind, only poverty, pestilence and death. . . . Fascism is his last straw and it will break our backs unless we rid the world of this beast of prey.

If fascism was old and barbarous, it was certainly not confined to Europe. The Americans considered Japan a fascist power, and they thought its invasion of China under the guise of "anti-Bolshevism" to be typical of "fascist aggression." Feeling a kinship with the people of China, they exchanged telegrams of fraternal greetings with partisans there.[8]

Fascism was so evil and destructive that one response to it was a kind of bitter humor. Exasperated with Italian claims of defending high civilization against the encroachments of godless communism, one soldier struck back with a cartoon in the *Volunteer for Liberty*. Here was a huge, bloated Mussolini, grasping two dead Ethiopians by the neck, while Franco and Hitler lurked nearby. To a Japanese soldier carrying a bloody sword, obviously about to dispatch some helpless Chinese civilians in the background, Il Duce is saying: "So you too are going into this civilization business I see." In common with the rest of the Western world, the volunteers found Italy and its leader to be good subjects for humor. Mussolini often bragged of the troops he had in Spain, always claiming that they were genuine "volunteers." To this came the cartoon answer showing a boy and a teacher in an Italian school standing in front of a blackboard. The caption read as follows:

> TEACHER: 90,000 soldiers plus 25,000 technicians. How many Italian soldiers does that make?
> CHICO: 40,000 volunteers.[9]

As would be expected from men with a Marxist world viewpoint, the Lincolns did not look upon England and France, the old bourgeois democracies of Europe, with much favor. As the traditional continental strongholds of capitalism they were naturally viewed with misgivings. But if they had helped Spain, they would have been forgiven their other sins. The sponsor of nonintervention, England was plainly and simply the old imperialist empire, out only to protect its own worldwide economic interests while oppressing numerous colonial peoples. France—with her in-again, out-again Popular Front government during the Spanish Civil War—might have been looked upon more favorably had she not appeased Germany in the Rhineland, adhered to nonintervention, and kept the Pyrenees frontier closed to arms movements through most of the war.[10]

In this world of the late thirties, where fascism was spreading like a dark cloud and the old democracies seemed in the hands of men too timorous or reactionary to take action, the men of the Lincoln Battalion saw only one country that offered light and hope to the world: the Soviet Union. Favorably disposed toward Russia before coming to Spain, many Americans became more enthusiastic about the Soviets while there. Part of this was due to the continuous diet of pro-Russian propaganda fed to everyone in the International Brigades. But more important was the fact that between the soldier and his enemies stood only his rifle, supplied by Russia. The machine guns that

A Group of Lincolns

protected his positions and covered his advances were Russian too; so were the government aircraft, tanks, and artillery that he saw. Knowing the vital importance of such weaponry, the soldier was bound to grow in his admiration for the one country openly supplying arms to the Republic.[11]

In the brigade press and the lectures of commissars, Russia was always bathed in a rosy light. Coupled with the actual Russian aid, the propaganda had a marked effect upon the Lincolns. Typical of the view presented was a caption below a picture of Soviet sailors holding rifles with fixed bayonets, which read: "The Soviet Union does not want war, but these sailors are ready to defend their land of socialism against any imperialist threat." Articles played up the promotion of culture by the Soviet government and the great advances made in industrial and agricultural production. A Russian polar expedition became a way of both lauding the Soviets and beating capitalism over the head; though it was admitted that Robert Peary had been the first to reach the North Pole, still his discoveries had been kept out of the hands of "the people," while the Russian expedition was naturally for the benefit of everyone. Unfortunately, the specific nature of the benefits the common man was going to reap from this voyage were

265

not mentioned. On the twentieth anniversary of the Russian Revolution, the *Volunteer for Liberty* exploded into praise for the Soviet Union, saying: "It lifted itself by its own bootstraps from a land lacking industry and culture to one of the technically most developed countries . . . surpassing the expectations of all and realizing the ideals of the world's greatest thinkers." [12]

The Spanish Civil War came at the time that the shadow of Stalin's great purges fell across the world Communist movement. Though a few of the men in Spain were shaken with doubts at the news of the Moscow Trials, most accepted the version fed to them in the party and the brigade press. Even if they had had access to anti-party publications, most of the Lincolns would have discounted their stories, for they were true believers whose faith in Stalin was firm. As John Gates later wrote, "Stalin . . . did seem like a god to us. As the leader of the one big power which was helping democracy in Spain, we did not believe him capable of any wrong." The Americans could accept the purge trials because, as Franco had boasted of a fifth column in Spain, it seemed logical that there would be one in the Soviet Union. They could not conceive that men of the stature of Radek and Bukharin would confess to grave crimes unless they had actually committed them. That coercion might have been used to force confessions was literally unthinkable. According to Gates, his comrades could not have believed "such vileness" could be committed by the man who was helping Spain. [13]

As Stalin was the friend of Spain, so his enemies were the enemies of the men of the Lincoln Battalion. Thus the chief object of hate in their world—even more so than Hitler himself—was the leader of "counter-revolution," the "internal wrecker" of the world Marxist movement, Leon Trotsky. A cartoon run many times in the *Volunteer* showed the dark, distorted head of a Trotsky who was grotesque, hideous, and insane-looking. Usually it was captioned simply: "What is it?" Trotsky was a convenient scrapegoat for everything that went wrong, both in Spain and outside the country, and most of the internal troubles of the Republic were blamed on Trotskyist sabotage. Edwin Rolfe, normally the mildest of men, was by the fall of 1937 writing that though he had once thought of the Trotskyists as merely a "group of nuts," now he felt that the "Moscow trials and their stinking pro-fascist actions here should convince anyone who is really for the workers that they're fit only to be spat upon, crushed." [14]

Virtually all of the men in the battalion viewed the war in Spain, and the complex internal issues connected with it, exactly as did the Communist Party. No doubt their ideas were strongly influenced by the publications they read and the pro-party lectures they heard. But there were more reasons than propaganda for agreeing with the Communist line, which called for vigorous prosecution of the conflict, the creation of a strong, centralized war machine in the form of a "People's Army," and the suppression of social revolution for the duration of the struggle. Though this anti-revolutionary program of the Communist Party has ever since been criticized in many quarters as a betrayal of Spain by Communists in general and Joseph Stalin in particular, there is ample evidence that it was a far more sensible policy than that advocated by the other left-wing parties, notably the Anarchists and POUM.

Basically, the Communist Party did not wish to alienate various elements in the Republican camp, the middle classes and peasants who might support Franco if the Republic were to collectivize both land and the means of production. In truth, a full-scale revolution had taken place in parts of Spain in the first months of the war; workers had seized factories, union committees had ousted local governments, peasants had appropriated the lands of absentee owners. Because of the complexities of the situation and the importance of the war news, and also because many pro-Loyalist correspondents did not wish Spain to appear as revolutionary, little news of the social upheaval was reported in the world press. The American volunteers who came to Spain knew as little about the revolution as anyone else, but even if they had known, they probably would not have approved.[15] After all, they were not revolutionaries but men committed to stopping the growth of fascism. Thus they were primed to accept the anti-revolutionary Communist line.

By the time the Americans reached Spain, the Communist, Socialist, and centrist elements in the government were attempting to suppress the revolution. Meanwhile, the Anarchists and members of POUM, wherever they were in the majority, were going ahead with it. In small Catalan towns revolutionary Anarchist committees enforced collectivization on the lands of unwilling peasants. True to their principles, they occasionally gathered all the paper money in a village and burned it in the central plaza, while those from whom it had been wrested unhappily watched their life savings go up in smoke. In a few cases, Anarchists tore up the railroad tracks entering towns on the theory that this assured their complete independence from central government. Such extreme actions certainly were alienating bourgeois and peasant supporters of the government and helping to create internal enemies that the Republic could ill afford.[16]

News of the revolutionary actions of the Anarchists and POUM filtered to the Lincolns through publications and lectures. Since the POUM was thought to be Trotskyist, its tactics were considered typical pro-fascist disruptions. The Anarchists, as the largest Loyalist party, could not be dismissed like the tiny POUM. Rather, the Americans were told that certain elements among them, the "uncontrollables," were serving to ruin the war effort by spending their time promoting revolution rather than fighting fascism. Because little fighting had taken place on the Anarchist-controlled Aragón front before the government offensive there, the charge seemed true. Indeed, military matters were the weak point of the Anarchists, and the Lincolns did not have to think them traitors to think them wrong. Opposed to a centralized, unified army, the Anarchists wished to retain the independent workers' militias that had formed in July 1936. Yet heroic as they were in street fighting, such militia units had proved ineffective in the

THE MIND OF THE VOLUNTEER

field. In part, they were undone by their egalitarianism. Not only did militiamen elect officers, they sometimes cast ballots before military actions, and a negative vote might mean that one or more units on a front would not fight. Admirable in its libertarianism, such a policy is obviously self-defeating for an army, and the American troops had no sympathy for it. Even George Orwell, who as a member of a POUM militia had to flee the country for fear of being jailed as a Trotskyist, and whose writings are the chief exposé of the counterrevolutionary actions of the CP, admitted that the militias would have to be drastically reorganized. Orwell also insisted that the revolution and the fight against Franco should be pursued at the same time. But for the Lincolns, presented with a picture of Anarchists and POUMists who did not fight because they were busy spreading revolution, the choice in favor of the CP policy was most natural. Ready to agree that disrupters of the war effort should be stopped, perhaps even done away with, few Americans shed tears when the government suppressed the POUM and absorbed Anarchist militias into the People's Army.[17]

Acceptance of the Communist line on internal Spanish affairs was general among the troops, but not universal. Certain men in the ranks never were fully convinced by the party's arguments. Undoubtedly, they were few in number. Unquestionably, they did not voice their doubts in public and records of their beliefs are scanty. Yet evidence does remain to show that some men interested in revolution did get to Spain, where they became disillusioned with the pro-bourgeois attitudes of the Communist Party. One who was actually a party member felt he had enlisted with the understanding he was "to fight not simply against Franco, but for a social revolution in Spain." Soon after arriving he became disgusted because the Communists were ignoring "the real revolutionary spirit which was strong and vibrant in the country." Afraid to voice his doubts in public for fear that a man critical of the party would be sent on a suicide mission, he continued to fight in the lines, although he had the feeling that the Spanish people had become hostile to the Internationals because they knew the CP was "selling out" the revolution.[18]

A more interesting—if less typical—dissenter from the party line was the twenty-two-year-old Jewish volunteer whose parents had been radical long before his birth. As a youth he had learned American history from a Marxist point of view, and at the age of ten he was already handing out party leaflets to workers at factories. Active in the Young Communist League in the mid-thirties, he managed to maintain associations with some Trotskyist friends. Then the first purge trials convinced him that Stalin was betraying the Russian Revolution. Hating Stalin and disgusted with the party because "free discussion was dead in Communist movements," he still felt strongly enough about the cause of Spain to swallow his distaste for the CP and join the Lincoln Battalion. In the war he was faced with a dilemma. On the one hand, he saw in Spain "the complete betrayal of revolutionary Marxism by Stalinism." Yet this negative experience was made ambiguous because he "also saw the Communist youth of the world in its most energetic and heroic role." Torn internally by hate for the Communists and love for the cause they fought, he was left "practically in a state of numbness." Rather than trying to resolve the problem, he decided, "The hell with thinking about it—I'll just roll along."[19] Of course, the longtime Communist associations of this young man made him more sophisticated about left-wing politics than the majority of the Lincolns. Perhaps a few others fought with similar reservations about the CP, subordinating distaste for Stalin to the importance of the cause. But for most Americans, the cause of the Spanish Republic was inseparable from the anti-fascism of the Popular Front and the Communists.

When the men of the Lincoln Battalion thought about the conflict in Spain, they felt, in spite of what they considered to be Trotskyist sabotage, in spite of a certain amount of contempt for headquarters soldiers and commissars, in spite of occasional resentment that they were often thrown into the breach because Spanish soldiers seemed unreliable, that the war itself was something noble and clean. They felt much like Hemingway's hero, Robert Jordan, who thought of himself as taking part in a crusade, for like Jordan, in the cause of the Spanish Republic they found "something you could believe in wholly and completely and in which you felt an absolute brotherhood with the others who were engaged in it." The troops were proud of their own role in the war and they certainly nodded approval when the chief International Brigade commissar, Luigi Gallo, wrote on the first anniversary of the brigades: "The deeds which they [the original brigaders] performed and which we continue to perform here, have already become the great epic of our times. . . ." [20]

If the International volunteers saw the war as noble and just, some could also see it through the glasses of Marxist rhetoric. Thus one believed the war to be something the world had long awaited, "an armed expression of the class struggle." The struggle was not toward revolution, however, but had only occurred because fascism was the attempt of "international capitalism to destroy the strength of the proletariat." George Kaye of Los Angeles also sounded a Marxist note in writing that he was happy to be participating in this war because he was "actively engaged in helping humanity pass to a higher state of society. . . ." where there would be a "life of happiness" for all. [21] If such sentiments do not seem consonant with the defensive nature of the Spanish War and the pro-bourgeois stance of the CP, it only means that traditional Marxist rhetoric was not always readjusted to fit current programs.

For the men of the Lincoln Battalion, at least until late in the conflict, the Spanish Civil War was a time of optimism. In the infectious atmosphere of Republican Spain, it seemed as if a brave new world were just over the horizon, for here an oppressed people had awakened from the sleep of the ages. In new government schools they were at last learning to read and write, while they clutched in hand weapons that would defend them against the old enemies that wished to keep them enslaved. The great Western ideals of freedom and equality had come alive in Spain at last and, as one American wrote home, these were the kind of ideas that could not be killed with bullets.[22]

As the volunteers looked around them, they were proud to be part of this social transformation. And their pride extended to more than just Americans. It included, according to Henry Eaton, the thousands and thousands of radicals who at this critical juncture in history had marched to the front "to give their lives for their beliefs. . . ." In doing so, they were betting on the future, and events in Spain were making that future look bright. Optimism filled the soldiers for many reasons, because the peasants could be educated even in wartime, because the Republic was defending itself against fascism, and because the strength of the workers of the world, shown in the growth of the International Brigades, seemed to prove that the international working class was at long last ready to defend itself; never again, after Spain, would the "big interests" dare to turn the military loose on the workers. For a while, after the capture of Belchite, optimism overflowed the soldiers' cups, and many considered victory to be near. As Matthew Mattison of New Hampshire wrote in September 1937: "The world at large is too activated, too conscious and aroused by what has been taking place everywhere these last few years to allow the forces of destruction to trample unchallenged on all that it considers to be right and just."[23]

Such optimism cannot exist in a vacuum; still less can it thrive in a world of defeat. After the loss of Teruel it became increasingly obvious that the war could not be won in Spain alone. Then Mattison's sentiments that the world was too aroused to allow a rebel triumph in Spain became the hope of all the Americans. Actually, hope for total victory in Spain alone was a fleeting mood that rose after successful battles like Belchite. Most of the volunteers had always looked to the world at large for aid. From the very beginning, they had thought of their role as an expression of international solidarity with the people of Spain, as a kind of holding action while the Republic developed its own army and while world opinion came around to supporting it. They were convinced—and perhaps this is a

Alvah Bessie and Edwin Rolfe

measure of their American optimism and naïveté—that England, France, and the United States would eventually see it was in their own interests to help the Spanish government. But, as Wilfred Mendelson said, it was first necessary to show victory was possible before the "weak capitalist powers" would step in to help; thus the Internationals were in Spain to show that battles could be won against the forces of fascism. At the very least, the Americans had often hoped that a world war between the fascist countries and the Western democracies would get under way, and that aid to Spain would come about as part of a larger conflict. As the months dragged on and things began to look worse upon Spanish battlefields, the Lincolns continued to hope in vain either for the end of nonintervention or for the outbreak of a world war.[24]

The individuals who fought in the Lincoln Battalion did not necessarily come to Spain with rigid beliefs. Many of the young men who joined the Internationals "to give fascism a punch in the nose" had been quite hazy in their political views beyond a general distaste for Hitler and his cohorts. In Spain, there occurred what some would later call their "political development."[25] That is to say, most of them came to hold the sorts of ideas about the world that have been outlined here, came to see the world through red-tinged glasses. If some had had few political opinions before the war, most of them were highly politicized by the time they left Spain. And though a few reacted against the CP either because of the way the brigades were run or because they felt the social revolution was being betrayed, most of the Lincolns became more pro-Communist than ever, believing more firmly than before in the Marxist view of the world.

Depending on the point of view, one may deplore or applaud this increased radicalization of the Americans in Spain. Either way, one must admit that this movement was due to much more than the propaganda that inundated the troops. Rather, the shift was due to the experience of war itself. As conditions of the thirties had driven them to volunteering for Spain, so the view from the battlefields tended to drive them further left. From where they stood the Lincolns could see that the CP was the most efficient and vigorous group prosecuting the war. It had been responsible for creating the best Spanish military units, such as the famous Fifth Regiment; it had brought the Internationals to Spain; its generals, like Lister and Campesino—partly because of the party's propaganda machine —were becoming the best known of the war. Even Orwell, when a member of a POUM militia, chafed at the fact that his party and the Anarchists were "standing still," while the Communists "were getting on with the war," and he was seriously thinking of joining the International Brigades at the time he had to flee the country.[26] If a regular army officer like General José Miaja joined the CP because it seemed the most effective war party, it is little wonder that the American volunteers were deeply impressed with the party's accomplishments.

Even more important in the increased radicalization of the Lincolns were the actions of the Western powers. The Non-Intervention Agreement, the collapse of the Popular Front in France, the appeasement of fascism, the remilitarization of the Rhineland with French acquiescence, the effecting of German *Anschluss* with Austria and the sellout of Czechoslovakia at Munich all tended to confirm the validity of the dim view the Communists had always taken of the capitalist countries. At the same time, Russia's continuing complaints against nonintervention, her offer to help Czechoslovakia, and her support of Spain with military equipment made the Soviet Union seem more than ever the one country in the world—outside the Spanish Republic—that was interested in seriously opposing fascism. Even the Americans who did not join the CP—and a goodly number never did—were having a lesson burned into them in the crucible of the Spanish War. The conflict was teaching them that only communism and Soviet Russia stood as bulwarks against the spread of fascism throughout the world. It was a lesson the Americans were to learn well, so well that many of them would go on believing it far into the future, even in times when it no longer was true in fact.

At the beginning of March 1938, the men of the Lincoln Battalion were back in Belchite. The town no longer smoldered as it had on that hot September day when they had marched away from it some seven months before, but still it looked like an exhibit in a festival celebrating the horrors of war. No building in Belchite had totally escaped the marks of battle, and whole areas of the town had simply been flattened. The main cathedral was crumbling, while the single, slender, pointed tower of another church incredibly remained erect, though gaping holes made it so fragile and airy that it seemed ready to crash to earth at any moment. The streets of the town were clogged with piles of rubble, adobe bricks, pieces of roof tile, splintered wooden beams, broken glass, and twisted wrought-iron railings, with occasional crumpled helmets, discarded canteens, blackened rifles, or the burned-out hulks of military vehicles.

When they came to Belchite, the men of the Lincoln Battalion did so expecting a period of rest and quiet. There was no inkling of military action in the offing, and after the hardships of Teruel, this suited the soldiers well. Numbering more than 500 again, the battalion was commanded by David Reiss of New Jersey, who had been chief of the machine-gun company at Teruel, while Eric Parker, former commissar at Tarazona, had taken over that position with the Lincolns. At night the troops were billeted in the

Bathing in an Irrigation Ditch

few houses that remained standing. To keep warm in the
wind that never stopped blowing through the drafty buildings, the men ransacked the deserted town for rugs and
blankets and slept snugly rolled in them. During the day,
when air raids were feared, they spread out in the fields
around the town. Here they taught the many newcomers
how to use their rifles and the machine guns that were in
short supply. Around Belchite, as far as the eye could see,
spread a yellow desert, ending in distant red mountains
that rimmed the huge valley and cut the troops off from
the rest of the world. In that vast visible expanse no other
military units were to be seen, and for a few days the
Americans could well imagine that they were alone in a
deserted land which armies had fought over centuries
before.

The first week in March was a pleasant period for the Lincolns. The wind lost its sharpness, the air became almost balmy, and the soldiers could feel the softness of spring. Then the sun broke through the high, thin layers of clouds and the Americans lolled in fields during the day, letting the warmth soak into their bodies and drive away the lingering memories of the weather of Teruel. A few of the braver ones stripped and took dips in the icy water of flooded irrigation ditches. A few miles away over the hills to the south the English Battalion was resting at Lecera, while the Spanish and MacPap Battalions were just to the east, in the tiny, mud-colored village of Letux.[1]

On March 9, flights of enemy bombers lumbered over Belchite heading east, and when the faint rumble of artillery was heard, uneasiness touched the troops. Still, they enjoyed the sun, and in the evening the Lincolns gathered in ruined buildings to talk and read newspapers. Many of them went to sleep early, while in one house a large group of men stayed up long past midnight, absorbed in a poker game in which the stakes were unusually high. The biggest winner for the evening was twenty-two-year-old Mike Goodwin; altogether, he raked in 3,000 pesetas, the equivalent of a full month's pay. As he fell asleep that night, Goodwin was already planning how to spend his winnings on his next leave to Madrid. He could not know that this was to be his last bit of luck for a long time, or that he would not make it to Madrid until a quarter of a century later.[2]

Reveille came earlier than usual the next day, so early that the men of the Lincoln Battalion immediately knew that something unusual was happening. They fell out in the dark with their arms, rubbing open bleary eyes and yawning themselves awake. Formed into companies, the troops began to march through the narrow, deserted streets without any idea of where they were going. The battalion passed through Belchite and hurried through the olive groves outside it, on the highway going west. In the dark they saw Spanish units coming back along the roads, and some stragglers moving in small groups. Four miles from Belchite, the Lincolns turned off the road to the left and climbed into a range of low, barren hills. Amid the scrub brush and boulders the troops hurriedly scratched out defensive positions. The companies of the battalion were stretched out across the hills with the third company on the far left flank, and some of its men on a hill 200 yards in front of the main body of troops. As the stars faded, the Americans in the first light of day could see west and north over the empty landscape to range after range of shadowy mountains. Behind them, on a very high plateau, sat the single, large building of a deserted monastery. As pale fingers of light began to tint the long valley before them, it seemed for one evanescent moment as if this were the calm beginning to another peaceful spring day.

Then, as Mike Goodwin later said, "All hell broke loose." Daylight suddenly revealed that far from being empty, the valley before the Lincolns and the hills beyond were swarming with enemy. Not yet really dug in, the men of the battalion dived for cover as the rebels opened up against them. Small-arms fire peppered their positions, but it was quickly drowned as the thunder of artillery erupted in the distance. Above them air bursts shattered the sky and kept them quivering against the ground, while flat trajectory shells began to tear their hilltops to bits. One shell ripped into the command post of the battalion, killing Reiss and Parker and wounding most of their staff, disrupting communications both with brigade headquarters and with the troops in the trenches. The Lincolns could now see the enemy coming out of the distant hills, moving across the plain toward them in battle formation with no Loyalist artillery disrupting their advance. They could also see the English and Spanish Battalions of the brigade across the highway, suffering from the enemy barrage. Suddenly, the sky was black with aircraft. German Heinkels and Messerschmidts roared over the defenseless Lincolns to unload bombs, then dropped so low to strafe that the Americans could see the white faces of the pilots as they flashed by. Now enemy tanks were rolling across the plain, stopping and smokily belching shells at the Americans pinned to the rocky ground. Meanwhile the rebel infantry held back, obviously waiting for the artillery, tanks, and aircraft to pulverize the Loyalists before moving in.

Until midday the Lincolns remained in their positions, firing their small arms ineffectually against a foe that was softening them up and moving with great deliberation. Then three of the companies quietly left their trenches and hurried back toward Belchite. In the confusion of the destroyed headquarters and the enemy barrage, word went out to the third company on the left flank almost as an afterthought, and by the time it began to pull back, the rest of the battalion was gone. Some of its personnel were able to retreat, but others, stuck in forward posts like the machine-gun crew that Mike Goodwin was with, felt terribly deserted and alone. Still under heavy artillery fire, Goodwin and those with him could see columns of enemy troops moving across the flatlands toward them, while enemy tanks rolled down the road to Belchite, disappearing behind the high plateau with its monastery. Now they were surrounded and their chance for orderly retreat had been cut off. Under the pressure of the situation command completely broke down, and men, in terror for their lives, flung away weapons and dashed from the trenches to try to escape. Mike Goodwin and three others stumbled down the shoulder of a hill that screened them from the rebels and made it into a gulley on the plain. They began to work their way forward, hoping it would bend in the direction of Belchite. When the gulley turned the wrong way, Goodwin peered over the edge and saw thousands of enemy troops swarming around them. Deciding to wait until evening to make a dash to freedom, the four Americans huddled in the ravine. Two of them carried rifles, and the four soldiers spent the afternoon debating whether they would fight if the enemy came upon them, or if perhaps they should commit suicide to avoid the torture that they felt sure awaited them if they were captured. When a rebel patrol found them at dusk, Goodwin and his comrades quietly surrendered. They were among a large number of Americans taken prisoner on March 10, 1938.[3]

Back in Belchite, everything was chaotic. The town had been heavily bombed and by late afternoon it was under fire from artillery. Attempts to re-form defensive lines had been made and then abandoned. Soldiers wandered around the streets of the town, darting into buildings to find personal belongings, gathering clothes, books, packets of letters from home. Supply sergeants hurriedly grabbed men to load trucks with food and equipment, and arguments broke out as officers tried to get ammunition for their men, only to be told that other officers had ordered the ammo dumps transferred farther toward the rear. Meanwhile, shells were bursting in the streets. Communications with higher headquarters had been broken, and as enemy tanks rumbled into Belchite from the west, there was no time to plan an orderly retreat. In the confusion of early evening darkness, the Americans formed up on the eastern outskirts of town and then split into two groups. One, led by John Gates of the brigade commissariat, began a march east toward Azaila, while the other, under Major Merriman, started south toward Lecera, where brigade headquarters was thought to be located.[4]

As they trudged off into the rolling hills, leaving Belchite behind them a dull, burning glow under the stars of the Spanish sky, the men of the Lincoln Battalion still had only the smallest inkling of what had happened. Soon it would become clear. What they had been caught in was the virtual collapse of the Aragón front, as the troops of Francisco Franco, attacking the day before in overwhelming numbers, had smashed through the Republic's lines in many places and had overrun them in others. Panic had struck the Loyalist Spanish troops, many of whom were young, fresh, and inexperienced. The stragglers the Lincolns had encountered had been from the many units whose soldiers had thrown away their arms and fled the onslaught. Their flight was not surprising, for they were being overrun by a motorized enemy in what the world would soon call a *blitzkrieg*. Not only did the rebels have total control of the skies over the Aragón front, and not only did hundreds of Italian and German tanks lead the offensive, but also the rebel infantry—outnumbering the Loyalists probably four to one—was largely riding to war in trucks.[5] Soon the Lincolns would learn the advantages of motorized infantry over the foot soldier, for in the next week every time the Americans tried to make a stand they would be flanked by the faster-moving rebels, and when they did fight, their opponents would be much fresher than the footsore, weary Internationals.

While the Lincolns had marched west to defend Belchite early on March 10, the MacPaps had been sent to Azuara, a small town farther south. There they had spent the day, being punished in their trenches by rebel bombardments. In the evening they had begun to pull back too, having to leave behind two full machine-gun crews that had been cut off from the battalion. On March 11, in the late afternoon, they reached Lecera, a collection of mud huts set in the middle of a brown, windswept plain where a few thin sheep morosely grazed. A few brigade officers were still in Lecera, but Merriman's group of Lincolns had already passed through. As night fell, the MacPaps went into defensive positions behind the adobe walls of Lecera to cover the retreat of other units in the 35th Division. They watched as the XIth and XIIIth International Brigades filed slowly past. Then, just after midnight, they began their own forced march toward Albalate, 20 miles to the rear. At dawn, the exhausted MacPaps found the Lincolns in the line there, tired from their own long trek, hurt and shaky from the continuous attacks of enemy aircraft that they had suffered.

There was no chance to make a stand at Albalate. News came that the motorized enemy had swept by and the Americans had to start marching again, 10 miles over the rugged hills to Hijar. The soldiers were now weary to the marrow of their bones, and some fell out of the line of march. Others trudged silently along and began to throw things away. First they got rid of heavy equipment, machine-gun barrels and carriages, boxes of grenades, cartons of

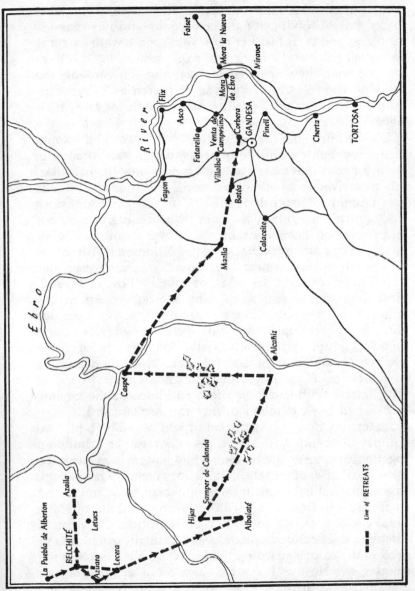

THE RETREATS

- - - - Line of RETREATS

ammunition. Then they dropped the contents of their packs, tins of food, extra clothes, books and newspapers, canteens, and their blanket rolls, until some were carrying only their rifles and a few rounds of ammunition. Officers insisted that they keep their weapons, but among the soldiers who fell out of the line of march and then continued alone or in small groups, many did throw away their rifles.

On the thirteenth the Americans reached the hills south of the bombed-out village of Hijar, which was already in enemy hands. Members of the English and Spanish Battalions arrived from other directions, and soon the brigade was a jumble of Spanish, English, Canadian, and American troops mixed irregularly together. While some men stayed and fought off enemy infantry and Moroccan cavalry attacks, others straggled back to the Kilometer 70 marker on the Hijar-Alcañiz highway, where a defense was supposed to be set up in the midst of a flat, yellow wasteland. Here their ranks were swelled by a group of Americans who had been serving time in military prisons on various charges. Brought up to the front under armed guards, and without weapons themselves, the complaints of these newcomers added to the general demoralization beginning to affect the Lincolns. Only half the regular troops at Kilometer 70 still had their rifles, and because the kitchen trucks had been bombed during the retreat, all the men were terribly hungry. As the cold night of the high plateau country descended, the soldiers shivered and huddled together, regretting the blankets they had thrown away. To avoid a collapse of morale, commissars raced 15 miles back to Alcañiz, bullied recalcitrant supply sergeants, and forced their way into storerooms without proper authority to take blankets, clothes, weapons, and ammunition. They found kitchens and rounded up cooks and brought truckloads of food to the troops guarding the highway. Momentarily the sagging morale was bolstered, and for a day and a half 200 men held their positions at Kilometer 70. Then they learned once more that a mobile enemy had bypassed them, driving onward to Alcañiz.

Now the retreat was still more grim. The men were exhausted as they pushed along the 15 miles of arid, sandy country toward Alcañiz. The roads were jammed with truckloads of soldiers and civilians fleeing the oncoming rebels. There were donkey-drawn carts, packed with family belongings, peasants in work clothes, and prematurely old Spanish women in their black dresses. Groups of Spanish soldiers, their uniforms in tatters, most of them without rifles or officers, crowded the highway. More of the Americans fell out, but the majority managed to keep together and at last they could see Alcañiz, climbing its rocky hills above the green valley of the River Guadalope, while on a height, dwarfing the town, sprawled the crumbling battlements of a medieval castle. But whatever joy there was in reaching their destination turned quickly to dismay as the Americans saw, through the naked branches of the trees lining the highway, that rebel artillery fire was exploding over the town, and as they learned that Alcañiz was being evacuated and that they were to proceed 20 miles farther on to Caspe.

The march to Caspe was a nightmare. The men of the XVth Brigade went up and down hills until the muscles in their legs had tightened into knots and each step was painful. They went along the roads and sometimes crossed the countryside through terraced olive groves. Rebel aircraft were overhead, and often the Americans had to scatter among the trees as planes swooped to attack. Once more men who could not keep up the pace were left behind to make their way alone as best they could, and many ended up as prisoners. Once more belongings and heavy weapons were abandoned until many of the soldiers were without rifles and only a few of the strongest men still lugged machine guns. There was a barely submerged panic among the troops as they fled toward Caspe, full of fear that the rebels would once more beat them to their destination. On March 15, when the ragged columns stumbled ahead of the enemy into the town, the soldiers were, in the words of one of them, "demoralized almost to the point of tears."[6]

By the time the Americans reached Caspe, the XVth Brigade had almost ceased to exist. Of the more than 500 Lincolns who had defended Belchite, only 100 were still together. The MacPaps numbered about the same, and the entire brigade, including staff officers, consisted of fewer than 500 men. Along the 75 zigzag miles of their retreat from Belchite were scattered the bombed trucks, wrecked mortars and machine guns, innumerable rifles, and the many dead of the brigade. Along the way there were pockets of men, some of them haphazardly attached to other units, fighting desperate rearguard actions, while many others wandered in the hills of Aragón, lost and alone. This fragmentation of the Americans was not unique, for the motorized onslaught had shattered all Republican units and scattered their members over the map. As Loyalist General Vicente Rojo wrote: "On March 15, in the vast space between Caspe and Calanda there was not one single organized unit . . . and a front of sixty kilometers was entirely open for invasion to the coast." [7]

When the weary XVth Brigaders entered Caspe, they found that commissar Dave Doran had been placed in charge of the brigade and the entire sector. Doran was now at the nerve center of the region, and it was his job, in the words of Sandor Voros of his staff, "to withdraw no further than he must, to contest every foothold, to improvise some position." In the confusion of the collapse and retreat all over the front, the commissar received little news from higher headquarters, and his decision of how and where to fight had to be based on the sketchiest information. Yet sensing that time was important for reestablishing Loyalist lines, and knowing that some unit had to make a stand somewhere, Doran rose to the occasion and ordered his men to meet the enemy. Rather than simply defend Caspe, the undermanned, underequipped Americans advanced to attack their foes.

As the enemy forces came down from the hills toward the town, the men of the XVth Brigade moved out to meet them, and all around Caspe there were bitter skirmishes. But the rebels had too many men, too many tanks, and too much artillery. Forced back into the town, many of the Americans were literally torn to bits as rebel tanks rolled through the streets, blasting infantry from point-blank range. Pushed out of Caspe in the afternoon, the Internationals fought their way back in, and then, at night, led by a few Loyalist tanks, they swept forward, throwing grenades and yelling like madmen until they overran the enemy's positions in the hills. But there were only 250 men of the XVth Brigade now, too few to hold the new trenches for long. The next day they were overwhelmed by enemy fire and almost surrounded by infantry, and it would have been suicidal not to abandon their positions. By the time night fell on the seventeenth the insurgents were in Caspe, and on the eighteenth the decimated American unit was marching east again, this time toward the border of Catalonia. Though the troops were bone-tired and more than a bit downcast, they might have been cheered to know that General Rojo considered the stand at Caspe one of the important factors in stabilizing the front and closing the enemy's previously open highway to the sea.[8]

The remnants of the XVth Brigade stopped in Maella for a couple of days, then pushed on to Batea, 25 miles southeast of Caspe. Spanish divisions and other Internationals were now holding the enemy, whose attacks had slackened off. Eight days had carried the rebels 60 miles from their starting point, and for the moment they had to stop to reorganize overextended supply lines, giving Republican forces a breather. When at this point a group of more than 100 trainees arrived from Tarazona to fill up the ranks—this was to be the last such group—they found the men of the Lincoln Battalion outside Batea, scattered over a hill wooded with scrub pine. Among the newcomers was the author Alvah Bessie who, like his comrades, was neatly dressed and cleanshaven, and had his pack stuffed with such military necessities as writing paper, envelopes, needles, thread, and shoeshine equipment. Proud of the discipline of the Internationals he had seen, Bessie did not know what to make of the 100 disorganized men sprawling on the hillside. For the Lincolns were a total mess. In

Bessie's words, "They had week-old beards; they were filthy and lousy; they stank; their clothes were in rags; they had no rifles, no blankets, no ammunition, no mess kits, no packsacks. They had nothing but the rags in which they were dressed and the filth with which they were covered." Bewildered by the sight and by the fact that the veterans did not even bother to greet them, the recruits were most shocked by the conversation of the Lincolns, which sounded like treason. For the troops were cursing their commanders, Merriman and Doran, and all the stupid mistakes—real and imagined—that they had made, and a few of the men talked openly of desertion. The newcomers joined them and sat on the hill and listened to the veterans complain and growl at one another. When one clean recruit began a party-line speech suggesting that throwing away their rifles had been unwise, a bearded soldier answered him with a grunted four-letter word. And another veteran suggested where he and all the rest of the newcomers could shove their own rifles—if and when they got them.[9]

In their reserve location near Batea, in the midst of vineyards that were just beginning to be flecked with green, the men of the XVth Brigade spent their days talking and complaining. News came that the French, responding to the pleas of the Spanish government, had opened the border at last, and that war materials of all sorts were pouring into the Republic. In the distance there was the sporadic sound of artillery, but rumor had it that Spanish troops were holding firm outside Alcañiz and Caspe. Two or three times a day flights of rebel aircraft droned overhead, but they never bothered the Americans. Food was scarce and the Lincolns were always hungry. Meals, which were brought up in trucks, arrived at irregular hours. A breakfast of weak coffee often came at 10 A.M., while lunch, no more than a couple of scoops of rice, a few shreds of salad, and a piece of bread, was at 2:30, and a similar dinner reached the troops long after dark, sometimes as late as 11 P.M.

While they loafed near Batea, the Americans received special editions of the *Volunteer for Liberty* that Edwin Rolfe had rushed through the presses. Three of them came up within a week, all full of huge, headlined slogans that were obviously meant to instill new fight into the men. The troops read "No Pasarán," "Do Not Yield an Inch of Ground to the Enemy," and "Now Is the Time to Strike Back," and looked at each other and their total lack of weapons, and in the words of one of them, "Their contempt for the rear-guard generals exploded into laughter, the best morale builder in the world." Other factors helped to revive morale, too. Many of the Americans who had disappeared in the retreat began to find their way back to the brigade. Though losses had been heavy, they had been far less so than the 100 Lincolns who marched away from Caspe had feared. Besides the new group of volunteers, many fresh Spanish troops were incorporated into the brigade's ranks. Once again men came up from desk jobs at headquarters and from hospitals. Though many of these were flabby, or not fully recovered from wounds, they helped swell the ranks of the battalion until it had more than 400 men. Finally, meals began to arrive on time, the food itself was more edible, and occasional rations of cognac were given to the troops. Though Alvah Bessie still heard a lot of beefing in the ranks, its tone became less bitter and more good-natured as the days went along.[10]

Rainy days began on March 22 and the Americans moved into Batea and built fires on the stone floors of buildings to keep themselves warm and dry. On March 25 came news that a renewed rebel offensive had started three days before, and rumors circulated that the brigade would soon be called back into action. With this disturbing news in mind, the troops threw themselves wholeheartedly into a fiesta on the night of the twenty-fifth. A huge bonfire was built on the hill near Batea and the men ate well, drank cheap French champagne, and fraternized with the young men and girls of various socialist youth organizations who had made a pilgrimage from Barcelona to spend the evening with them. The next afternoon, some of them nursing hangovers, the Americans began a 15-mile march past the crossroads town of Gandesa to the hilltop village of

Corbera, for, as Doran explained, without weapons they were useless as enemy troops approached. Commanding the Lincolns in this move was Milton Wolff, a tall, gaunt, twenty-two-year-old New Yorker who had been in every action since Brunete and had worked his way up to the rank of captain. At their new camp the soldiers waited a couple of days before at last receiving new military equipment. In the early hours of the morning they were issued Russian and Czech rifles, machine guns, and hand grenades, and fresh clothing, blankets, and ponchos. When they filed through Corbera before dawn on March 30, listening to the faint boom of artillery, the men of the Lincoln Battalion were well-equipped soldiers going back to war.[11]

In their new drive the forces of the Spanish rebels were advancing along a broad front, more than 200,000 men moving against perhaps 80,000 Loyalist defenders. In the middle of this attack several troop columns aimed at the town of Gandesa, where a number of important roads converged. The XVth Brigade was being sent out along those roads to help stop the advance, ostensibly to take over defensive positions from other troops. What the Lincolns did not know was that the front had already buckled and broken before the rebels and that they were moving toward a fast-advancing enemy, not one that was being held in check by Loyalist defenders.[12]

The troops went down the paved road heading due west, the sky paling overhead and etching the Sierra Pandols jagged and dark away to the south. With rhythm in their stride, with no morale problem now that they were going to work, the Lincolns raised the dust in the streets of Gandesa, swung past the two cafés on its sad, deserted main plaza, and headed on. When the sun came up, the day quickly grew hot. As he marched along, Alvah Bessie felt the straps of his heavy pack biting into his shoulders and, like the veterans around him, he began to shed some of the things in his pack, blankets, tin cans, extra underwear. Five miles beyond Gandesa there was a fork, and while the MacPaps and English continued down the main highway toward Calceite, 12 miles away, the Lincolns took the smaller road on the right and went 6 miles, just beyond Batea. Enemy aircraft overhead, artillery rumbling and bombs falling in the distance, and the ruts of the war-torn road impeding the march, it took the men a long time to reach their destination. As Bessie wrote: "We marched and flopped all that day, feeling the sweat in our armpits, the dust on our faces, our feet swelling in our bad shoes." It was not until just before dawn on the thirty-first that the Lincolns took up positions in the sandy hills between the two roads from Caspe and Nonaspe into Batea.

For a couple of hours the soldiers were allowed to sleep. But before the sun had burned the morning mist from the wooded hills, they were roused by officers and led forward to engage the enemy. The Lincolns tramped over the rolling country for about a mile before they were fired upon. Then they dropped to the ground and infiltrated forward. During all of March 31, the Americans engaged in small-arms fire with the rebels, pushing the enemy back off a couple of hills. That night there was little sleep for the Lincolns as the rebels peppered them with machine-gun fire through the hours of darkness. The next day was a scorcher. The soldiers were already weary with lack of sleep, and the heat further sapped their strength. They lay on the ground fighting to keep their eyes open, holding their lines, and waiting for an attack that never came. Finally, the world began to grow dark. The troops were ordered from their trenches and formed into companies, and then they went down from the hills and back along the road toward Batea. Only gradually did the tired men moving along in the dark realize that once more they had begun to retreat.[13]

Just before the pullback had begun the American commanders had received frightening news. At Calceite, the armor-led rebels had smashed through Republican lines. The English and MacPaps, not yet at the points they were supposed to defend, had been overrun and scattered to the winds and the enemy was now racing toward Gandesa. On hearing the news, Doran had wanted the Lincolns to fight to the last man where they were, but Merriman had overruled him and ordered the retreat. As they went back over the roads at night, the officers of the Lincoln Battalion still did not know the full story of the disaster, for they had not heard that rebel forces had also driven through Villalba de los Arcos, to their east, and were now in the process of closing in upon Corbera. With the roads to the south and east now in rebel hands, the battalion was entirely behind enemy lines.[14]

Tramping along the dusty roads in the dark, the American troops were so tired that every time they halted for a rest, men fell asleep instantaneously and had to be dragged to their feet to go on. The officers of the battalion were hurrying them, trying to get the troops to Corbera, which was still supposed to be in Loyalist hands. One company of the battalion was going ahead of the others as an advance guard, its 80 men marching in tactical formation, strung out for several hundred yards along the sides of the narrow dirt road. In the hour before dawn, with the hills still merging into a black sky, the few lights of a town came into view. The Lincolns went on, seeing soldiers, wrapped in blankets and holding rifles, sitting quietly along an embankment. And they went on, until they saw a field full of sleeping men, some of them in pup tents. And they went on, until suddenly somebody realized that nobody in the Republican Army had ever been issued a pup tent, and one American began to run, and then another, and then the whole company was suddenly scattering wildly through the fields. Rifles flashed in the darkness and shots rang out and hysterical voices screamed: "Halto los Rojos!" but the tired Americans were suddenly full of energy again as they dashed through the rebel encampment, tripping and falling over sleeping soldiers, jumping down from one terrace to another through the olive groves as they scrambled to get away. Those who did manage to escape, like Alvah Bessie, wandered off through the hills and aimed their footsteps in the general direction of the Ebro River, 20 miles to the east. Most of the men caught in the camp were never heard from again.[15]

The three remaining companies of the battalion kept together, but the officers now knew the roads were not safe, so they struck out across country. By dawn the battalion was in the green hills a mile north of Gandesa. The Americans could see truckloads of troops and tanks rolling down two highways toward the town. Three miles farther to the left, enemy columns were converging on the hilltop of Corbera. The one road that seemed open was on the opposite side of Gandesa from them, the road which ran southeast toward Tortosa and the sea. There were still Republican forces holding Gandesa, for the Lincolns could hear the crackle of small-arms fire and see the rebels as they cautiously moved toward outlying buildings of the town. As they watched the fight, Major Merriman made the decision to attack the rebels from behind, fight into Gandesa, and join the Loyalists there.

At ten o'clock in the morning the Americans came down, spread out in the vineyards, and moved on Gandesa. But the enemy must have seen them when they were still in the hills, for the roar of entrenched machine guns greeted their advance. Two of the companies had to pull back under heavy fire, but on the right part of the third forced its way through a breach and made it into the town. The majority of the Americans retired to the hills. They had no hope now but to wait until darkness and then try to break across the Corbera-Gandesa road and reach the open highway to Tortosa. Laying low through the hours of afternoon, the Lincolns anxiously awaited nightfall. Just as the sun was disappearing in the west, some 400 Moorish cavalrymen, with banners waving and swords lifted, rode up the hill in an insane frontal assault, and the Americans shouldered their rifles and fed belts of ammunition into their few remaining machine guns, slaughtering the horsemen as they came. The Moors fled, and in the long minutes of dusk, enemy artillery opened up against the hill; but before it found the range, night at last came. The Americans rose from their positions and in single file slipped off the hill. As they started out, each felt terror slowly rising within him until, as Captain Wolff said, "there wasn't a man . . . who didn't feel death walking by his side."

Well might they feel that way, for that night and the

next three days were the most disastrous the Americans spent in Spain. In the darkness on that night of April 2, the battalion began to come apart even as the men clambered down from the hills. Everywhere there were enemy patrols, and the world was alight with the dozens of fires of rebel encampments. Since the Lincolns did not dare raise their voices, there was often no way of keeping in contact with one another. One company was detached from the others almost immediately, and its men wandered on in small groups. The two other companies went forward until they stumbled into an enemy camp in the vineyards near Corbera at midnight. As the men scattered in the dark, shots rang out and some fell wounded, while others were taken prisoner. It was in that melee that Dave Doran and Robert Merriman disappeared, never to be heard of again.[16]

After that there was no more Lincoln Battalion, but only bands of men roaming through the hills, trying to reach the Ebro River, which they vaguely knew to be some 10 miles to the east and where they hoped to find safety. Many of the MacPaps were also wandering in the hills. After having come apart at Calceite, part of the battalion re-formed at Gandesa for the unsuccessful stand there. Then, with the English, they withdrew down the Tortosa road, fighting a rearguard action and helping to hold one important highway junction for 48 more hours.[17] Still other MacPaps were lost, and like the Lincolns, were trying to reach the Ebro. But there was no safety to be found in the whole sector, for the rebels were everywhere, and the terrified Loyalist command, its army in shambles, had already blown up all the bridges across the river. So the Americans wandered on in the night, scaling and dropping from steep terraces, lying low when enemy troops were near, walking endlessly in the hills until they dropped from fatigue. Day came, and then another night. Some of the Americans were so tired they lay on the ground and awaited capture. Others were so hungry they gnawed at the bark of trees, and a few were fed by sympathetic peasants. Many were shot and bayoneted by rebel patrols.

Weary Troops Halt for a Moment During Retreats

Some were taken prisoner and then managed to escape and flee once more. One broke under the pressure, began raving like a madman, and had to be left behind by his comrades. Others blundered onward through another day and night, sometimes recognizing a landmark and realizing they had been wandering in circles. Those who had their wits about them hid and watched which way enemy troops were going and followed them, for they knew the rebels had to be heading for the front. At last many of the Americans reached the river, only to find the bridges gone and the springtime waters of the Ebro swollen and fast-flowing. Some who could not swim simply sat down to await capture. Others plunged into the icy waters of the 200-yard-wide river, and with their remaining strength battled the roaring currents. For a few it was a losing fight, but others dragged themselves naked and freezing onto the eastern shore of the Ebro, at last safe from the enemy. They were picked up and brought to Mora la Nueva, where the remnants of the XVth Brigade had gathered. Shattered, disconsolate, yet happy to be alive, they waited there, usually in vain, for their missing comrades to turn up. When they counted heads the second week in April, about 100 Americans were left in the Lincoln Battalion.[18]

While the remnants of the XVth International Brigade gathered above Mora la Nueva on the eastern shore of the Ebro, waiting for more survivors of the Aragón debacle to make their way back from behind enemy lines, the troops of Francisco Franco drove on toward the Mediterranean. Stiffening Republican resistance south of the river slowed the rebel thrust, but on April 15 the troops of General Alonso Vega's 4th Navarrese Division entered the fishing town of Vinaroz and waded waist-deep into the sea. Now Republican Spain was split in two, land communications between Barcelona and Madrid were severed, and world observers settled back with the belief that essentially the war was over, that the ultimate victory of the rebels was now only a matter of time.

Press reports to the United States all through the retreats had been full of news of the Lincoln Battalion, its stands and counterattacks, and then the first week in April the wire services carried stories about daring escapes from behind enemy lines and the slow regathering of survivors in Catalonia.[1] Widely known now as tough fighting men engaged in battling for a cause of which most Americans approved, the Lincolns in April 1938 were to achieve a new notoriety. In France and in the United States, men who had deserted the ranks of the battalion during the retreats and had escaped from Spain began to be interviewed by the press of the world. Many of the stories they told of their experiences as International Brigaders differed significantly from those the press had previously carried and seemed to shed new light on the Americans fighting in Spain. In fact, in some quarters the men of the Lincoln Battalion have never fully emerged from the shadows cast upon them by various deserters in the spring and summer of 1938.

The first such American to make headlines was John H. Honeycombe, who on April 7 was interviewed by an Associated Press reporter in Perpignan. Saying he had been a political commissar and a Communist, Honeycombe told how he had fled after the collapse of the Republican forces near Gandesa, hitchhiking and walking five days to reach the frontier. He admitted having gone to Spain to fight for his "ideals," but said that these ideals had been shaken because of all the killing and because it was obvious that the Republic was "finished." Honeycombe's story thus contained nothing unusual, for during the retreats it was quite natural to feel that the end of the war was near. Controversy only arose after his interview with a *New York Times* correspondent on April 8, when Honeycombe's tale differed significantly in its emphasis. Adding new facts, the deserter now claimed that 8,500 Americans had been killed in Spain and that only 500 remained in the country, not because they wanted to be there, but because they were held as virtual prisoners by the International Brigade command. Drawing a somber picture of demoralization in Loyalist ranks, Honeycombe said many Americans had been shot for insubordination. To the *Times* he admitted to having been in a Loyalist jail, supposedly because he had asked to leave Spain after his original six-month enlistment was up. During the Aragón retreats, he claimed, he had been sent—along with some other prisoners—to the front. There they had been all put in the trenches without arms, and at that point he made his getaway.[2]

While Honeycombe went off to Marseilles to try for a job on a ship back to the United States, friends of the

Lincoln Battalion attacked his story. The *Daily Worker* denounced him as a "miserable deserter" and stated he had never been a commissar, and this was also affirmed by David M. White, now back in the States. On April 9, Herbert Matthews found the men in the battalion at Mora la Nueva fuming over Honeycombe's allegations that they were all "anxious to leave" Spain. Lt. Alvin Cohen of the brigade staff claimed that Honeycombe had been in jail for desertion and said it was a lucky thing for him that he made it all the way to France on his second try, for "when soldiers desert twice they get shot."[3]

Soon other deserters began to turn up with stories similar to that told by Honeycombe. On April 10, two Americans who "figured the war was lost" and had "decided to beat it" during the Aragón retreats arrived in Bordeaux looking for jobs on a ship bound for home. In San Francisco on the twenty-second, José Maria Sandoval spoke of his own desertion from Spain, where, he claimed, hundreds of men were being kept in concentration camps. Arriving in the United States on May 30, Robert H. Searl told a story of harsh discipline, alleged that people had tried to convert him to communism, and said that many soldiers were in prison on suspicion of espionage. Not a prisoner himself, Searl had during the retreats been forced at gunpoint to return to a shattered front line with no rifle and only two hand grenades for defense. In subsequent months, more deserters made headlines with tales of hardships suffered in Spain and often with complaints of inhuman discipline and terrorism in the International Brigades. As in the case of Honeycombe, officials of the brigade and well-wishers usually tried to discredit both the deserter and what he said. The Friends of the Abraham Lincoln Brigade, for example, claimed that Sandoval had been rejected in Figueras as physically unfit, and was only angry because the FALB refused to give him money.[4] But too many cases were reported for the battalion to deny that a number of desertions had taken place.

Actually, there was nothing new about desertions from the ranks. As in any war, there had been deserters almost as soon as there had been soldiers. But until Honeycombe started giving interviews, such men had been content to slip quietly away. As early as February 24, 1937—a little more than a week after the battalion first went into action —the American consul in Valencia reported to Washington that a deserter wished help in returning to the United States. Two weeks later, five more Americans were asking for similar aid. Though the consul pointed out that the deserters were in danger of arrest by the Spanish government, the Secretary of State answered that as long as the men were in Spain, there was nothing the United States government could do other than endeavor to keep Spanish authorities from imposing severe punishments on them. Some of these deserters were arrested and undoubtedly punished. Later in the war the consul at Barcelona managed to have a few such men released from Spanish jails into his custody, and he then helped them to leave Spain. But as late as April 1938, the Secretary of State was advising consuls against helping deserters unless they were "able to obtain discharge from military service . . . and permission of Spanish authorities to leave Spain."[5] Since such discharges and permissions to leave would have obviated the original need to desert, it is clear that America was simply washing its hands of the problem of soldiers trying to escape from Spain. Any such aid came as the result of individual actions of American diplomats and not as part of official government policy.

There is no way of knowing exactly how many Americans deserted from the ranks of the International Brigades. Men who were there have always insisted that there were "few" desertions, and this seems to have been the case.[6] During the course of the war only 13 went to American counsuls for aid, though most Lincolns must have realized the United States government was not prepared to do anything for them since they had crossed into Spain with passports stamped as invalid for travel there. Desertions seem to have occurred in batches, usually after brutal military actions in which casualties were heavy. The first six to appear at a consul did so shortly after the Pingarrón massacre, the next four immediately following the Brunete offensive, and three more just after the unsuccessful attack at Fuentes del Ebro.[7] After the Aragón retreats, Honeycombe and some 20 others received publicity upon reaching France or the United States. So it seems that desertion was a sporadic affair until many men became disillusioned during the collapse in March 1938, and decided that they had seen enough of warfare and of Spain.

The two deserters who received the most publicity sprang to nationwide attention on August 10, 1938, when they told Martin Dies's House Committee on Un-American Activities that "hundreds of their former comrades wanted desperately to come home but were being held 'virtual prisoners.'"[8] Abraham Sobel and Alvin I. Halpern, both of Boston, testified at length in Washington, D.C., about their own motivation in going to Spain. Then they outlined the methods used by the CP to recruit members of the Lincoln Battalion, and revealed the details of the underground railroad used to smuggle the Americans to Spain. Both were critical of the severe discipline in the International Brigades and went on to affirm that many Americans had faced firing squads either for trying to escape or for opposing Communist policies.

Because of their anti-Communist viewpoint and the great deal of inside information they were able to impart, Sobel and Halpern made sensational newspaper copy. But for anyone later reading their full remarks, the value of the testimony of the two men seems questionable at best. Though they were aided and encouraged by committee members, they still said some strange and revealing things. At one point, Sobel sounded like a petulant child. Describing various hardships, he said that in Spain "human life and misery are never thought of," obviously ignoring the fact that life is cheap and full of misery in any war. Although he had gone to Spain for idealistic reasons, after being robbed of $30 on his second day there Sobel quickly realized that he had come to fight for "a bawdle of crooks and selfish, rotten, cowardly and downright cruel Spanish bastards." Certainly such remarks show a terrible over-reaction to a theft that, after all, could have taken place anywhere in the world. What's more, because he had undergone extremes of heat, cold, and lack of food, Sobel admitted he had vowed to "make the Communist Party pay 'through the nose'" for what he had suffered in Spain. Unfortunately, nobody on the committee thought to ask whether his testimony was part of that payment.

Halpern's remarks raise as many doubts. After giving the bizarre explanation that he had gone to Spain because his job in America kept him busy seven days a week and he had become tired of working, he actually lapsed into incoherence in some of his testimony. Moreover, he did not know the name of various brigade officials, calling Dallet and Doran "Dalred" and "Durant." While claiming that anyone who opposed Communist leadership had been shot, he spoke of his own opposition to the CP, and then, even to the friendly committee, could not successfully explain exactly how he had escaped the firing squad. Interestingly, both Halpern and Sobel agreed that most of the men in the Lincoln Battalion were not Communists, and would, in fact, be good anti-Communists if they ever returned from Spain. Halpern, in fact, urged that the American government take steps to help bring his former comrades-in-arms home again.[9]

The reaction to the testimony by people friendly to the Lincoln Battalion was swift and typical; more of an attempt was made to discredit the men than to deal with the issues they raised. The *Daily Worker* claimed that Halpern had demanded blackmail money from the FALB to keep from selling anti-Loyalist stories to the Hearst press. Twenty-one hospitalized Americans in Spain signed a letter which denounced Sobel and Halpern as cowards, drunkards, and looters. The FALB released photostats of statements the two had made just after leaving Spain, full of favorable comments about the Lincoln Battalion; here the implication was strong that the two men had "sold out" to the HUAC. Veteran Eugene Morse, home in Minneapolis, wrote to a local paper to say that having found warfare too tough and then deserting, Sobel and Halpern were "trying to blacken the name of all the American volunteers in Spain—to excuse their own miserable conduct." Another ex-Lincoln who knew Sobel may have come closer to the truth. From a hospital bed in Cleveland, Albert Bires wrote more understandingly of the deserters' problems than did other veterans, saying: "Sobel did very good work in Spain. He was a very good anti-Fascist. . . . I believe the false statements he made to the Dies committee were made to cover up his desertion from the army." [10]

The testimony of Sobel and Halpern, and the statements by Honeycombe and some five other deserters, contain the sum total of serious public complaints made during the war against the way the American units of the International Brigades were being run. Certainly it is significant that so few men lodged such charges. The typical deserter did not at all denigrate the battalions in Spain. Probably ashamed of their own desertions, such men remained silent about their experiences. The Sobels, Halperns, and Honeycombes, however, may very well have been trying to assuage their own shame by making it seem as if the cause had become tainted. Yet however few made such statements, and even if they were as disreputable as their former comrades maintained, these deserters brought to light certain important issues that were to come up before the HUAC again in 1940, and from time to time in succeeding years. Desertion, cruel discipline, Communist terrorism, concentration camps, and political executions cannot be taken lightly. Anyone dealing with the history of the Americans in Spain must face these important problems.

Desertion is the easiest issue to deal with. In one sense, it does not really need to be explained. Every war produces men who flee the rigors of trench life and combat. In Spain, where the Internationals were usually underequipped, often underfed, and frequently kept in the lines longer than is good for soldiers, there was even greater cause for desertion. Certainly, the desire for the comforts and safety of home was always strong among the Americans. As committed a Communist as Edwin Rolfe occasionally wrote to his wife that he was anxious to return to the United

States. In other letters he would speak of his internal struggle, the conflict between "you and home" and "Spain and duty," that often went on within him "in the wee small hours."[11] Such a struggle raged within most of the Americans, but not many let it get out of hand. What changed the soldier who thought longingly of home into a deserter was some unknown quality within the man himself, though the catalyst usually seems to have been a particularly bloody battle. Or perhaps the confusion of battle merely provided the cover for the American looking for an opportunity to escape.

When Honeycombe and others mentioned that they had originally been promised only a six-month enlistment, they were probably telling the truth, even though that may not have been the real reason for their own desertion. At least early on in the war, many Americans had been promised such an enlistment. Originally, International Brigade officials thought six months' service would be adequate, but soon they realized that this was no way to get maximum use out of their manpower, and the promised rotation of men never went into effect. The first official Republican statement that the International volunteers were to remain in Spain "until the end of the present campaign"— obviously a euphemism meaning the duration—did not appear in the *Volunteer for Liberty* until November 1, 1937. Since it came at the end of a lengthy government decree, it is possible that many of the troops were not aware of such a policy until Earl Browder announced it to them at Teruel. Still, by then it must have been obvious that this was to be the practice, for apart from the badly wounded and a chosen few healthy men, nobody had been discharged and allowed to leave Spain. Most of the troops accepted the new policy and the reasoning of the commissars, which held that fighting fascism was not a part-time job. But others may very well have been demoralized by the prospect of an unlimited stay in Spain.[12]

While complaints about the length of enlistment may have been legitimate ones, those about severity of discipline in the XVth Brigade were unwarranted. Among the

Americans, discipline was no more severe than in any army. It must be remembered that the charges were made by men unused to military life, some of whom found any regimentation oppressive. Several American officers were severe disciplinarians, and Joe Dallet was certainly not the only martinet. Yet it must be remembered that Dallet's strictness earned him the enmity of his men and almost led to his dismissal as commissar of the MacPaps. John Gates, last commissar of the XVth Brigade, also could be severe, and he later admitted that in tense periods he sometimes jailed men who disputed his word. Dave Doran, always willful, once threw a man who swore at him in prison, though after a proper apology he let the soldier go. But along with Dallet, Doran, and Gates were men like Nelson and Merriman who were always considerate toward those whom they led. And some officers were as lax as Milton Wolff, the last field commander of the Lincolns, who ignored his men's conduct when they stumbled drunkenly around the camp. Wolff's only concern was that the troops be sober during battle. Other leaders punished drunkenness, but at Tarazona this offense only drew a fine of three days' salary and confinement to barracks for the same period. Near the front, drunkenness was considered worse; one tipsy sergeant who frightened a whole town by yelling "air raid" in the middle of a night found himself spending a short term in the guardhouse after having been busted to private.[13]

Occasional drunken behavior was not the only disciplinary problem. There were men in the ranks who groused a lot and those whose complaints overflowed into mild insubordination. If this happened at Tarazona, they often found themselves being quickly sent to the front. At Jarama in the early days, soldiers were put on work details for breaches of discipline, and this common form of military punishment continued to be used. Occasionally, men working in rear positions were sent to the front lines as punishment. One trooper, sentenced to front-line duty, argued that he was not worthy of it, for being a foot soldier in the war against fascism was too great an honor for the likes of him. Unimpressed by this line of reasoning, his commanders shipped him off.

More problem was posed for brigade officials by the men in the ranks who were real troublemakers. A few individuals always seemed to be creating problems. Some were chronic drunkards, others could never carry out orders. A few loudmouths always talked back to officers, some soldiers committed crimes against fellow Americans or the civilian population, and others were so lazy that they did not wish to do any hard work. Such offenders could be dealt with in various ways. To get them out of sight, brigade officials might ship them off to *"inutiles de guerra"* camps near Barcelona. These had been set up to hold "Men judged unfit for war by reason of their incorrigible lack of discipline, their bad spirit, their demoralizing influence on others, their cowardice or their doubtful loyalty." Though there was no cruelty at these camps, they must have been unpleasantly boring places, for nothing was provided to occupy the troops, who spent their days lying around and grumbling about their unhappy lot. One soldier who spent a few days at the *"inutiles"* camp at Badalona reported the inmates engaged in an unending series of complaints against the brigade leadership. They charged that officers were arbitrary, dishonest, and unjust, and claimed they had been discriminated against. A few openly stated they had been persecuted by officers because they were not Communists. Interestingly, their charges brought no punishment or persecution from the directors of the *"inutiles"* camps.[14] Yet at other places such complaints might not have been tolerated. Serious offenders, such as soldiers who tried to desert, found themselves in strictly run punishment battalions, where heavy labor occupied their days. Some were even clapped in military stockades where complaints were no more tolerated than in any other prison in the world.[15]

The ultimate penalty in military—as in civilian—life is death, and there can be no doubt that some Americans shot other Americans in Spain. In one case, a man who had served faithfully in many battles finally cracked up, fled during an engagement, and made it all the way to the French frontier. There he decided he had made a mistake, and rather than cross the border he returned of his own free will to the battalion. He was immediately tried, and his execution was announced to the troops the next day.[16] Others were shot for desertion, too, though there is no way of knowing how many. During the retreats on the Aragón front, there were at least four executions for cowardice in the face of the enemy, including those of some Spanish troops attached to the XVth Brigade.[17] In another case, two Finnish-Americans attached to the MacPaps were tried and executed, allegedly for raping an old Spanish woman. There was also an incident of a death penalty being ordered but never carried out. During the March retreats, an American captain and a lieutenant became detached from the Lincolns and ran into a German International Battalion whose commander insisted they march with his men back to the front. The Lincolns did not want to, but when the officer ordered them at gunpoint, there was little they could do to resist. The first night with the Germans the captain deserted, and he soon found his way back to the XVth Brigade. When the story came out, he was tried and condemned to death by an American court-martial, despite a long record as a leader and organizer for the CP in the United States. The night before his scheduled execution, friends helped him escape, and he successfully made his way to France.[18]

Although Americans were shot for desertion, there is no reason to believe that the death penalty was invariably inflicted for this offense. Men who fled the battalion after the February 27 debacle at Pingarrón Hill were not even questioned when they returned, and others who took off during the course of the war received no worse than imprisonment. In October 1937, just before the battle of Fuentes del Ebro, half a dozen Americans stole an ambulance and were captured trying to make it across the French border. Someone in headquarters decided to let the men in the ranks vote on their punishment, but Dave Doran wanted to nullify this democratic procedure, for he instructed the battalion and company commissars to speak in favor of the death penalty. Refusing to buckle to the pressure of the commissars, the majority of volunteers voted against death for the deserters, and eventually they were accepted back into the ranks.[19]

Executions for desertion in the face of the enemy, however deplorable, are not something peculiar to the International Brigades; probably every army in the world has made soldiers face firing squads for such reasons. The more serious charge made by deserters and other critics was that men in the Lincoln Battalion were executed for political reasons, because they opposed either Communist ideology or the way the party was running the brigades. Scholars have documented the fact that the great purges in Russia spilled over into Spanish Communist elements, and have shown that "Chekas" were used to eliminate political opponents of the CP in Spain.[20] It is also well-known that André Marty got rid of people he disliked on the grounds that they were spies or Trotskyists. Whether the atmosphere of the purges and the terror filtered into the ranks of the Americans in Spain is another question, but it would take a most fervent and unseeing partisan to say that the Americans were totally immune to the epidemic of political executions.

It is chilling to read the words of one anonymous Lincoln, who wrote home, "disrupters and individualists are given short shrift over here. . . ." Since both "disrupters" and "individualists" were terms often used by the Communists to denote those opposed to the party line, one must pause to wonder what the "short shrift" consisted of. Part of it may have been the *"inutiles de guerra"* camps, or the labor battalions. In one known case, an American suspected of being a Trotskyist was held incommunicado in a Spanish jail for some time, but finally he was released and allowed to return to the United States. In some cases, undoubtedly very few, the "short shrift" may have consisted of execution, and it is possible that no more than ideological differences accounted for such an act.[21]

This sort of execution could occur because although the

International Brigades were supposed to be following regular Spanish Army procedure in their courts-martial, they did not always do so. The line of authority between the Internationals and the Spanish government was, in practice, never a clearly defined one, and International commanders were not always held accountable for their actions before the government of the Republic.[22] Moreover, the men running the Lincoln Battalion were not accustomed to military life and procedures. They were more used to the kind of drumhead court that party cells were noted for. In one brigade court-martial, witnessing Spanish officers from division headquarters were so outraged at the high-handed way in which Doran was running things that they stopped the trial, denounced him in front of other American officers, and went on to accuse the Americans in general of showing by this kind of action that they did not realize that Spain was fighting for democratic ideals. The men on trial at the court-martial were freed, but there were other courts held when no Spanish officers were around to intervene.[23]

Even more irregular proceedings occurred. Among the Americans in Spain, some people were scheduled for liquidation because their unorthodox political beliefs seemed to be disrupting other troops. How many times this happened it is impossible to tell. Only one such case has turned up, and it is an instance in which the proposed execution misfired. But it gives an insight into the kind of thing that could—and undoubtedly did—happen in Spain.

Just before the action at Teruel, when the Lincolns were still camped in small towns in Aragón, a company commissar began hearing some anti-Stalinist talk among his men. Puzzled and disturbed, he called in some close friends in the ranks, asked them what was happening, and was told that one soldier had been attending Anarchist meetings, and that others were coming under the influence of the doctrines he had adopted. Worried that the ideas could spread, he went to the brigade headquarters secret service man, probably a member of the Servicio de Investigación

Militar (SIM), a new Spanish secret police organization charged with the duty of investigating spies, and responsible, many observers feel, for much of the "terror" in Republican ranks. Alternately referred to in a kind of lugubrious humor as the "Gestapo agent" or the "Kremlin agent" by the Americans, this man told the company commissar that he should already have acted individually to "wipe out" the troublemaker, and he urged him to get on with the job quietly and as soon as possible. The commissar did not like the idea of killing one of his own men, but he felt it to be his duty. During the action at Teruel the next week, he went out on patrol with the deviant soldier, intending to shoot him in the back of the head. But in the dark of the night the wind blew up a blizzard and the men became separated. The commissar returned to camp, hoping the task had been taken care of by the weather; however, the soldier was brought in the next morning suffering from severe frostbite. He was immediately evacuated to a hospital and later returned to the United States, never realizing how fortunate his frostbite had been. The important and disturbing note is that his execution without trial had been approved of by someone in a position of leadership.[24]

From such a case one should not be misled into positing a "reign of terror" among the Americans. That other instances of similar events have not been uncovered does not mean they never occurred, but surely they were extremely rare. In point of fact, all the evidence from sources hostile to the Internationals seem to boil down to four men who *may* have been executed for political reasons, and though such cases are deplorable, four hardly constitute a "reign of terror."[25] On the other hand, there is evidence that brigade leadership tolerated quite a bit of dissidence in the ranks throughout the war. Men who grumbled about the "incompetence" and "stupidity" of their leaders in the spring of 1937 at Jarama or during the retreats in Aragón were not even reprimanded, and complaints of party control in the form of publications the soldiers were given to read and lectures they had to attend were commonplace and drew no penalties. Though the Communist Party existed in the ranks and though members attended meetings throughout the war, the brigades had been formed in the spirit of the Popular Front and nonparty views were tolerated. Party secretaries in the companies undoubtedly wielded more influence on policy than their ranks might warrant, but they did not use their powers to liquidate nonparty members; if they had done so, perhaps half the Lincolns would have been done away with. How much disagreement with the party line—which was synonymous with the International Brigade line—might have been tolerated before one was labeled a Trotskyist it is difficult to determine. Certainly the soldiers would have known this themselves, and those with violent disagreements probably kept their mouths shut rather than risking reprisals.[26] Such self-censorship probably occurs in any war, for it is the rare army that permits foot soldiers the luxury of criticizing the nature and purposes of the struggle being fought.

The desertions, the drumhead courts-martial, the executions for cowardice and those for political reasons cannot be ignored, but they should not be overemphasized. The fact is that desertion among the Americans was a rare phenomenon, affecting about 1 per cent of the men. Discipline was no harsher than in other armies, and the complainers at the *"inutiles de guerra"* camps and the labor battalions show that execution was certainly not the rule for men who did not like to work and fight, for those who deserted, and those who were in opposition to Communist ideology. That men in the Lincoln Battalion fighting against fascism occasionally resorted to heinous, extralegal means to ensure ideological conformity is a black stain upon their record. It is a stain upon individuals, men corrupted by the real and almost unlimited power they now possessed as military officials. It is a stain, too, upon the kind of mind that demands conformity—among the Americans in Spain there were undoubtedly many men with such mentalities, men who believed that the ends justified any means. Yet political executions were a rare thing, and, as in the case of the commissar who tried to kill another man on patrol, they were hidden from the men in the ranks. The average American knew of executions for desertion and cowardice, and of these he may have halfheartedly approved. He probably had heard rumors of political executions, but they were likely to be stories of what André Marty was doing at Albacete. Whether he would have approved of political executions is problematic; certainly many of the Lincolns did not. Yet the main concern of the American was winning the war, and he obviously would have wished to remove— though not necessarily execute—anyone standing in the way of that objective. For better or worse, many Americans in the Lincoln Battalion subordinated everything, sometimes even their own sense of justice, to what they considered the battle of the century, the fight against fascism on the battlefields of Spain.

In early April 1938, the morale of the men of the Lincoln Battalion reached its lowest ebb. After all the running from the enemy, the brave but unsuccessful stands, the fragmenting of the battalion, the hungry and dazed wandering behind enemy lines, the tired battles with the rushing waters at the Ebro, there was no will to resist left among the Americans. The 120 Lincolns who had survived the debacle gathered in gullies behind Mora la Nueva. They were unshaven and filthy, their clothes torn, their bodies full of lice, their feet swollen and bloodstained. Command had broken down, and for several days the Americans were less a military unit than a mob of homeless men. Supplies of wine were plentiful, and the soldiers drank until they were drunk enough to forget the horrors of the retreat and the many friends who were missing. They lay in the hills and drank, and many talked openly of desertion, of stealing trucks and driving to the French border, or of hiking to the coast, seizing sailboats, and making for Marseilles. One American became so drunk that he grabbed a rifle and attempted to shoot another, just because he wanted to kill someone. Another soldier kept bursting into tears and repeating: "They killed all the good guys, they killed all the good guys." [1]

There was good reason for the demoralization. It was

not just the defeat the Republic had suffered, but the magnitude of it, not just the loss of comrades, but the cold fact that 70 per cent of them were missing. In the Aragón retreats, the Lincolns had seen for the first time how much the balance of men and material had shifted against them. They had been indelibly impressed by the overwhelming superiority of their enemy not only in personnel, but in the all-important weapons of modern war, trucks, tanks, artillery, and aircraft. In truth, after the spring retreats few Americans would ever again be able to believe in the possibility of their own victory.[2] And now even hopes for international intervention on their behalf had been buried. During the early stages of the retreats, Adolph Hitler had bludgeoned Austria into *Anschluss,* and France and England had acquiesced in this violation of the Treaty of Versailles. The Internationals were disheartened that their example of willingness to fight and die to prevent the spread of fascism had not been followed, and they knew now that Republican Spain would never receive outside aid.[3]

With the senior officers still missing, Lt. Aaron Lopoff, a former company commander, took charge of the battalion during the first week in April. Trying to instill some discipline into the men, Lopoff was aided by improvements in the Republic's services and supply. On April 8 a shower truck visited the Lincoln Battalion, and the men cleaned themselves and shaved, and then donned newly issued clothes. Though food rations were still scanty, there was plenty of tobacco for a change, and the supplies of wine seemed endless. Yet spirits were still not very high. Commissars tried to improve the morale with pep talks and rumors that Franco's drive to the sea had been stopped, that the Republic had started its own offensive in the Madrid area, and that new shipments of military goods were on their way from Russia. But the soldiers greeted all this news with "a bucketfull of salt." Battle had deadened them to the influence of promises and soothing words, and even, it seemed, to objective facts. A large fleet of new Russian aircraft overhead did little to infuse new spirit into the Americans, though they did take some heart from the return of Captain Wolff to the battalion on April 12; he was the last man to escape from behind enemy lines.[4]

A fiesta scheduled for April 14 in the tiny hamlet of Darmos preceded a return to work. Stuffed full of rice and burro meat, nuts and chocolate, and still drowsy with wine, the Americans set off at 4 A.M. and marched three miles to the Ebro. There they began to dig positions into the sandy hills above the river, all the while grumbling at the stupidity of holding a fiesta just before the troops had to move out. For two weeks they remained along the river. On either side of them were other International battalions, as decimated and despondent as the Lincolns, and it is a measure of the Republic's weakness that such shattered units had to be sent into the lines, even on an inactive front. Behind the Americans was a battery of Loyalist artillery, and occasionally it exchanged a few rounds with some unseen rebel guns. Once in a while, the shots of snipers whined and echoed across the river valley. For the time being, that was the extent of the Lincoln's military action.[5]

The ranks were filling up again. Since there were no more men training at Tarazona, which, like the base at Albacete, had been closed down, the new Lincolns were men who had previously held jobs in the rear. Some, like Edwin Rolfe, volunteered for front-line duty. But others were simply ordered to the battalion, and many were men previously thought unfit for war. Some were in their forties, too old for trench life. Others had once deserted and had been put in work battalions. A few had seen so much action that they had been retired to *"inutiles de guerra"* camps. There was no morale among the newcomers, and brigade officials made little attempt to enforce discipline. Soldiers who had lived through the retreats were not at all pleased with their comrades. Alvah Bessie disgustedly described the Lincolns at this time as, with some exceptions, "a pretty crummy bunch," who were "unfit, either physically or psychologically, for the front." Most worthless were the newcomers, like the man who went around falsely claiming he had a bad heart or the youngster who accurately described himself as "dumb, yellow and worthless." Bessie, like many veterans, thought it a mistake to have brought such men to the front.[6]

If the sudden presence of so many worthless men in the ranks was unsettling to the veterans, so was the infusion of large numbers of Spanish youngsters. At the end of April, just after the battalion returned from the river to the area near Darmos, more than 400 Spanish recruits between the ages of sixteen and twenty were incorporated into the unit. The declining fortunes of the Republic had put an end to foreign enlistment, but the International Brigades had become a famous rallying point for pro-Loyalist propaganda throughout the Western world. So the names of the brigades were kept intact, even though, as in the case of the Lincolns, the membership became three quarters Spanish. Previously, there had been Spanish companies in the battalion and Spanish sections within the companies, but in May 1938 the Spanish and foreign troops were thoroughly integrated. In the Lincoln Battalion there were now some Spanish officers, though because of experience the Americans were still the backbone of the unit.[7]

At first, relations between the Americans and Spaniards were good. At a May Day celebration in the fields near Darmos the men engaged in contests, ran foot races, played soccer, boxed, and fired competitive rifles, sharing their prizes of chocolate bars and cigarettes. The young Spaniards looked up to the seasoned American warriors, who in turn were friendly out of natural instinct, rather than because the commissars had urged them to become the "comrades, brothers, teachers and friends" of the newcomers. Yet it was not too long before the flower of friendship between the two groups withered, and each nationality came to socialize mostly with its own kind. The main barrier between the Americans and Spanish was one of language. Though the *Volunteer for Liberty* had often urged the Lincolns to learn Spanish as their "anti-fascist duty," most of them had been unwilling or unable to do so. Feeling that their time in Spain was limited, there was even less incentive to learn it now. On their part, few of the young Spaniards spoke any English. This language barrier quickly became food for each nationality's latent chauvinism. Spaniards and Americans looked down on each other for not speaking their own mother tongue. Perhaps such condescension over language would have been surmountable, had not other factors worked to keep the soldiers apart. Age was a barrier between the two groups, the average American being in his mid-twenties, the average Spaniard no more than eighteen; many of the Spanish, as some Americans scornfully noted, had not yet begun to shave. There was a great difference in backgrounds, most of the Lincolns coming from cities while the Spanish were the sons of peasants. Finally, there was a political barrier, for while the Lincolns were highly politicized left-wingers, the Spanish—to the Americans' way of thinking—were naïve conscripts who did not understand the world-shaking issues at stake in Spain. On their side, the Spanish harbored a resentment toward and a lingering suspicion of all foreigners who were fighting over their homeland.[8]

In early May, when feeling between the two nationalities was still good, the Americans did play the role of instructors to the new men. The commissariat prepared a program of political education, with lectures on the history of Spain that emphasized its "revolutionary" tradition, on fascism and the world struggle to contain it, on the International Brigades and the past actions of the Lincoln Battalion, and even on the history and geography of the United States, all given in Spanish. Native officers and the few bilingual Americans conducted classes in reading and writing to help eliminate illiteracy among the youngsters. Together, men of both nationalities suffered from the cold rain that fell for almost two straight weeks, and from the ever-present Spanish lice who showed no particular chauvinism of their own. And all the men joined in bitter complaints over the monotonous diet of garbanzo beans, tasteless meat, and almonds that the mess sergeants presented to them twice a day.[9]

On May 17, the 700 men of the Lincoln Battalion were issued ammunition, and along with the other units of the

XVth Brigade, they began to move. For three days they marched and then rode in trucks northeast to Tarrega. In this area the Republic was launching a small offensive, designed to recapture power stations—that lighted Barcelona—along the Segre River at Tremp and Balaguer, and perhaps even to take Lérida back from the rebels. First at Tarrega and then at Mollerusa, the Lincolns waited for a week, listening to the distant sound of artillery, watching flights of friendly and then enemy aircraft pass overhead. The Spanish troops were alternately jumpy and on edge or in hysterically good spirits, singing and dancing about like children. Quarrels continuously broke out among them, while older Americans like Bessie looked on with attitudes of paternalism, feeling: "It is shit that such babies should have to know this sort of thing." Then he grimly added: "It is shit that *anyone* should have to know it." In a few days the Lincolns piled into trucks once more and rode 70 miles south, knowing that the offensive had been a failure.[10]

They returned to the area from which they had come. The entire XVth Brigade was now 10 miles from the Ebro, in the fields surrounding the village of Marsa, with its crooked dirt streets and single, unimpressive church tower. They were camped at the south end of an immense valley, at the foot of high, granite peaks, with a view of blue mountains to the north. The vineyards around the troops were ripe and green. Beneath hazelnut and almond trees they dug trenches to live in, roofing them with branches, layers of cloth, soil, and leaves. It was silent countryside, its stillness broken by the call of birds and the hum of insect wings. The Lincolns found it beautiful, the valley lush green in the sunlight, with white clouds piling up behind the granite mountains in the afternoons and spilling over them like frothy waterfalls. Summer came to Catalonia and the sun blazed in the sky day after day, bronzing the faces and bodies of the soldiers, making them look more like men on vacation than warriors taking a rest.[11]

Some of the newer men in the ranks, like Ed Rolfe, did not even feel that the word "warrior" applied to them. So far, Rolfe had fought more battles with linotypists in Madrid than he had with enemy soldiers, and in letters home he complained that he had felt closer to the front in the capital city than he now did in the trenches. With the battalion, his chief problems were keeping clean and fighting boredom. The former was accomplished by occasional dips in nearby icy streams, the latter partly by helping in the educational program for Spanish troops. Boredom with the battalion's food was relieved when Rolfe and his friends made occasional unauthorized raids on the patches of sweetpeas, baby potatoes, asparagus, and artichokes that gew in small quantities among the rows of olive trees. Boredom with the news of the world and Spain was broken only occasionally in this period, as in late June when word came that Joe Louis had in one round knocked out that perfect representative of the master race, Max Schmeling.

Despite the beauty of their surroundings, their comfortable routine of training, eating, and sleeping, the men of the Lincoln Battalion were far from happy as June of 1938 rolled toward July. Rumors were circulating that under the auspices of the Non-Intervention Commission all the foreigners were to be withdrawn from Spain, and in spite of their dislike of the commission, the Americans seized upon the rumors and discussed them continuously. Almost to a man, they now wanted to return home. As Bessie noted in his diary, "Many feel that they have a justifiable grievance—that they came as volunteers, have been here a long time, have gone through a lot and are entitled to go home." Since they were not allowed to leave, Bessie found a growing feeling among the troops that they were being held against their will.[12]

Many factors were working to create dissatisfaction among the soldiers. Still haunted by the grim memories of the retreats, the veterans knew that the Americans, like the other Internationals, no longer represented a fighting force of any consequence. They were well aware that the 150 Americans with the Lincoln Battalion, the 50 with the MacPaps, the 20 on the brigade staff, and the 200 in transport, medical, artillery, and other units would play no decisive role in the future course of the war. All the men realized that they were being retained "solely for their moral effect and propaganda value." This made them resentful over the big buildup given in the party press to the men who had been allowed to return home—these men were considered "phonies" for whom the American Communist Party had gone out of its way to pull strings. Especially galling to Communists and non-Communists alike was the fact that the party press was hiding the truth that the Americans were no longer a real fighting force. Joe North of the *Daily Worker* continuously wrote pieces denying that the Americans had been decimated and putting their number at the usual 3,000 mark. With such lies being told, some Americans felt they had even outlived their usefulness as propaganda.[13] If the party could turn 200 troops into 3,000, it could just as easily bring the Lincolns home and write articles as if they were still in Spain.

The undercurrents in the Lincoln Battalion, the restlessness, the dissatisfaction with the party and its press, and the feeling of the men that they deserved repatriation, could not remain hidden. Grumbling among the troops became more and more open, until it reached a point where brigade officials could no longer ignore it. Some men were punished for talking about repatriation, but that did not end the problem. Brigade commissar John Gates had to call a mass meeting of the American Internationals at which he laid down the law, saying they would stay in Spain as long as the Loyalist government felt it needed them, and claiming that soon the brigade would return to action, and that when it did, they would be expected to maintain "its tradition of sacrifice and courage." The men heard this speech with mixed emotions. Realizing it would look strange for anti-fascist fighters to run when things were going against them, they still could not banish their desire for repatriation. As Bessie commented, "They still believed in Spain; they still felt that in fighting for her they were helping to stem the tide of international Fascism . . . but they were only human. They were tired; they were homesick; they were a bit afraid." Men in such a condition cannot be made fearless by speeches, and Bessie found himself worrying that some of his comrades might desert if they were thrown into action again.[14]

In mid-June, the command of the XVth Brigade passed into Spanish hands. After nearly two years, Lieutenant Colonel Vladimir Čopic relinquished his position, being replaced by Major José Antonio Valledor, a wiry Asturian. Though Čopic had never been well liked, though Valledor was much more of a human being and less of a prima donna than the colonel, the changeover brought a twinge of sadness to many of the veterans. The action symbolized the dissipation of the brigades, the dimming of the bright hopes they had raised in many hearts. In this vein, Bessie confided to his diary, "The IB's, which might have been developed into a great force whose strength, whether used or not, would be felt all over the world, have petered out . . . we are a spent force, actively disliked in certain quarters, distrusted in others, considered indifferently in others."[15]

Partly as a morale builder, battalion officials threw a July Fourth fiesta in Marsa. The Americans feasted on ham, French fries, pudding, and hot chocolate, and received extra rations of cigarettes. Helping them celebrate were some 30 newcomers, the last group of American volunteers to arrive in Spain, men who had been hurriedly trained at the new International Brigade base at Montblanch, in Catalonia. Among the new troops were San Francisco longshoreman Archie Brown and ex-CCNY student Wilfred Mendelson. Also infusing spirit into the ranks were eight Americans who had been wounded and sent home, and had then decided to return to Spain for another shot at their enemies. One of them was Joe Gordon, the man whom Steve Nelson had helped to get to an eye specialist a year before. A last newcomer enjoying the fiesta was Jim Lardner, who had joined the battalion in early May.

After the Independence Day celebration, training took on a new intensity. The soldiers spent their days marching, spreading into combat formations to infiltrate fields, and crawling across the ground until their bellies were sore. A new maneuver had troops pretending they were in boats, crossing dry streams, and assaulting ridges beyond. This set off speculation that an offensive back across the Ebro was imminent. Busy in mid-July, the men of the Lincoln Battalion were still not too occupied to drink when they could and to continue to hope for repatriation. Adding to their annoyance was a cigarette famine, and the leaves of hazelnut trees that they rolled and smoked were hardly a good substitute for tobacco. By now the Spaniards' respect for them was gone—these very sober youngsters totally disapproved of the drunkenness of the Americans. Hardly a day passed that each American was not asked hopefully by a Spanish soldier if he were going home soon. A couple of ugly squabbles over which nationality was getting more food served to make the split in the battalion even worse. Yet this lack of communication should not be overexaggerated. Many soldiers treated others as individuals rather than members of a national group, and some close friendships did develop between Spaniards and Americans.[16]

Among the rank and file there was still a lot of grumbling, but certainly not all the Lincolns were demoralized. Some, like Alvah Bessie, were always skeptical of the chances for repatriation under the Non-Intervention Commission. Others took heart from the reports of strife between Spanish rebels and their German and Italian Allies. Evidently annoyed over mass bombings of cities like Barcelona, Spanish rebel soldiers fought in bar rooms with foreign troops. This dissension culminated in Falangist General Yagüe's speech praising the courage of the Loyalists—"because they are Spaniards"—and denouncing the Germans and Italians as "beasts of prey." Though Yagüe was removed from his leadership position, the hope for some sort of reconciliation had been implanted in a few of the Lincolns. Others, especially among the newcomers like the militant Wilfred Mendelson, actually looked forward to the next battle with Franco's troops. Mendel-

A Boat Sinks Crossing the Ebro

son thought the coming struggle would seal the fate of world peace, for, if Franco broke through, "War will be forced upon the European democracies in a life and death struggle for independent existence." Some men, while downcast about the Internationals, still retained the impossible hope that in her own interests, France might yet intervene to save the Spanish Republic.[17]

On midnight of July 21 the XVth Brigade broke camp. Carrying full packs, the troops marched at a good pace down the roads until dawn, moving 15 miles. They slept in olive fields during the day and tramped another 15 miles through hills and silent villages the next night. At dawn on July 22, the Lincoln Battalion slipped into a deep gully a few miles to the north of Mora la Nueva. There the soldiers rested their sore feet, and there they were told by the commissars that a large offensive was about to get under way. The objective of the Lincolns was to be Gandesa, 13 miles across the river. An extra incentive was given the men when they learned that Gandesa was now a rebel supply center, housing stores of food, cigarettes, and beer.[18]

Ever since the forces of Francisco Franco had sliced Loyalist Spain in two in mid-April, the rebels had been extending their territory southward toward Valencia. In July they began a great push toward that port city, and Republican leaders rightly felt that if Valencia fell, Madrid would be cut off from the coast and hopelessly surrounded. To counter the insurgents the Republican war council planned an offensive along the Ebro River about 65 miles from the Mediterranean. It called for a crossing of the Ebro and, if possible, a thrust all the way across the rebel salient in an attempt to restore land communications between Catalonia and the rest of Republican Spain. One hundred thousand men and all the available artillery were put together in a new Army of the Ebro to carry out the attack. As before, the XVth Brigade was attached to the 35th Division, this time along with the XIth and XIIIth Internationals. Of some 12,000 men in the division, fewer than 3,000 were actually non-Spanish troops.[19]

The operation began quietly, just after midnight on July 25, the first groups of Loyalists rowing silently in small boats across the river on a moonless night, then spreading out and overwhelming rebel outposts. The Republican troops swiftly pushed forward, surprising the enemy.[20] Yet Franco's air force responded quickly, and by the time the Lincolns were pushing through bamboo stands along the river and scrambling into boats just as the sun was coming up, planes were flying low over the valley and dropping bombs. No damage was done to the Americans; the battalions landed intact on the south bank, and the men immediately began to move. It was a broiling July day, and the Lincolns marched at a swift pace down the dirt roads until they were choking with the white, powdery dust. Stopping occasionally to drink from their canteens, they went on through the wooded, hilly country without seeing the enemy, though his artillery, which could be heard everywhere, had already hit the MacPaps.

On the night of the twenty-fifth the Lincoln Battalion

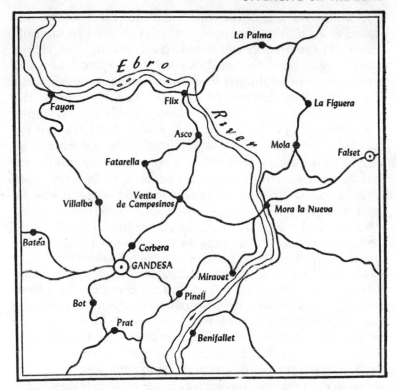

THE EBRO OFFENSIVE

rested in the hills overlooking the town of Fatarella. The
men were hungry because food trucks had not been able
to cross the river, but the long day's march had left them
exhausted, and for a few hours they slept well. At four
o'clock they were up again, and they moved quickly into
Fatarella, capturing it after a brief skirmish. The town had
been a supply depot, and the Americans found plenty of
cookies, chocolate bars, and an immense supply of tobacco.
By noon the soldiers were marching on the road toward
Gandesa, over the same countryside where some of them
had fled for their lives after the breakup of the battalion
in April. Now they were happier, and their complaints
about military life and the desire for repatriation were gone
in the joy of once more being on the offensive.

A little over a mile beyond Fatarella, the Lincolns received word that an enemy force was scattered in the hills ahead. The battalion deployed, swarmed up the slopes against weak rebel fire, and in a short time had taken 250 prisoners. Many soldiers were surprised to see how much like themselves the rebels were; in Bessie's words, the prisoners were "a ragged, dirty crew, mostly very young— tired, thirsty." While the prisoners were led back toward the river, the Americans marched on. They camped the night of the twenty-sixth in an open field, and their first real casualties of the offensive occurred in the darkness, when a guard fired on what he thought was an enemy infiltrator. Immediately the whole line came ablaze, and it was several minutes before the companies of the Lincoln Battalion realized they were firing on each other. Three wounded men were the result of this mistake.[21]

The next day the going got rougher. The old, familiar pattern was repeating itself as Franco, dropping his offensive against Valencia, began rushing troops to contain the rapidly growing Loyalist bulge south of the Ebro. Soon the insurgents would outnumber the attacking Republicans three to one on the Ebro front, and their superiority in firepower would be as great as during the April retreats. In truth, the whole offensive was the last, desperate gesture of a Republic that refused to give in to the inevitable, a Republic that was asking its soldiers to fight with courage alone, since it had so little to give them in the way of material support.

On the morning of the twenty-seventh, while the MacPaps and other battalions closed in on Gandesa, the Lincolns learned how quickly the enemy had recovered from his surprise. Two miles from camp the battalion came upon rebel-held hills. Again the troops went into battle formation and drove the rebels back. But there were hills beyond with entrenched machine guns, and as they opened up, many of the Spanish troops refused to advance toward them, and there were sections in which the few Americans had to go forward alone. It was another scorching summer day and the Lincolns felt drained of energy. But rest was denied them, for still another enemy ridge beckoned. The Lincolns went on toward it, the officers yelling at the young Spaniards and pointing guns at them in half-successful efforts to make them aid in the attack. Hit hard by enemy fire, the battalion staggered forward and took the hill. Casualties were heavy, and the wounded were dragged back and attended to by first aid men. There were no ambulances to evacuate them, because the bridges across the Ebro had been bombed out. Many of the wounded, like Wilfred Mendelson, died without a doctor ever looking at them.

The brigade was now close to Villalba de los Arcos, where the first company had blundered into an enemy camp during the retreats. On the twenty-eighth when they tried to push forward across the Villalba-Gandesa road, the Lincolns ran into a stone wall. At 6 A.M. the soldiers started through a wooded valley toward enemy positions over 400 yards away, but they were hit by firepower that slashed them to ribbons. Machine guns and trench mortars cut into the ranks, then rebel artillery came into play, and before long a squadron of Heinkels swooped in to tear up the valley. Again, many of the Spanish troops would not move forward, and some of those who did quickly dropped to the ground and lay in the underbrush. Soon the Lincolns were forced to withdraw. They tried to advance later in the morning and again in the afternoon, but each time they were stopped. Determination alone could not conquer rebel guns, and the Americans had to pull back with the bodies of their comrades scattered in the fields. In the late afternoon, the Lincolns had to face counterattacks that almost reached their own lines, and that night enemy troops swarmed up their hill again. The next day brought more of the same, and by the evening of July 29 the battalion was a shadow of what it had been five short days before. Only 400 of the 700 Lincolns who had crossed the Ebro were still in action, and they were a weary crew; 50 of the 300 missing had been killed. Losses of the Americans had been proportionally higher; of 40 Internationals in Bessie's company, only 13 were still in the lines.[22]

On July 30 the Lincolns were pulled back, and for two days they were in reserve positions, sleeping all day on a hillside, the continuous roar of artillery close at hand. The offensive seemed to be going well, and Bessie was heartened to learn that pressure had been relieved on the Valencia front. What was more, 3,000 prisoners had been taken and dozens of small towns recaptured. But the rebels still held Gandesa. Unless their line was broken there, the whole offensive would bog down. For two days the XIth and XIIIth International Brigades had been trying to storm into the town from the north, but rebel firepower had bled them white. The MacPaps and British Battalions had also suffered heavy losses trying to take a hill just west of Gandesa. Other units were being brought up to help over-run this key center, and the Lincolns were among them. On the night of August 1, the battalion moved into hills less than a mile from the point where four highways converged in a cluster of mud-colored buildings sur-rounded by a jumble of fortifications. Expecting to be called upon, the Lincolns were not used in the series of assaults on Gandesa. Instead, they became spectators at a particularly bloody sort of contest.

Early on August 2, the men of the 59th Spanish Battalion came through the lines and charged forward. As they watched, the Lincolns saw a battle that caused them to name the area before them the Valley of Death. Franco's troops stopped the Loyalists, counterattacked, were stopped in turn. Aircraft of both sides flew sorties all day long, bombing the narrow valley, while artillery ranged in from everywhere, pounding it to bits. The struggle raged with charges and counterattacks, with more soldiers being thrown into the breach, and hundreds falling beneath the storm of steel. Dozens of wounded men were carried back through the lines while machine guns hammered and echoed, but many more remained trapped on the battle-field. In the heat of the Spanish sun the stench of death was rising, and in the hills the Americans gagged on its nauseating sweet smell.

Late in the afternoon rebel artillery zeroed in on the

Carrying Wounded Back Across the Ebro

positions of the men of the Lincoln Battalion, and now they
began to undergo their own ordeal. Ed Rolfe found himself
clutching the earth as shells screamed overhead and exploding trench mortars crumbled the walls of the gullies
where the troops huddled. Darkness came, but the shelling
did not slacken. Now the enemy was using tracers in his
machine guns. To Rolfe it was strangely beautiful to see
the red streaks float through the air, but others were
frightened by the sight. As mortar shells crashed into the
gullies and men shrieked in agony, panic and confusion
struck the battalion. Soldiers hugged the rocky earth and
refused to move to help wounded friends. Others moaned
in fright and huddled together like sheep, while through
long hours Rolfe could hear the piercing voices of young
Spaniards wailing: *"Madre mia!"* or *"Socorro, socorro!"*

The next day was strangely quiet, but the troops were
jittery and quarrels broke out in the chow lines. Gandesa
had not been taken, and the back of the Ebro offensive
had been broken. Yet though the Loyalists had been contained, the battle of the previous day must have hurt the
rebels badly, for they showed little stomach for any quick

counterattacks. The Lincolns were pulled back, then sent on a night march to new positions just east of Gandesa. The troops spread out into fields pitted with shell and mortar craters. In the new positions, mess trucks reached the Americans and they ate hot food for the first time in more than a week. For three days they remained in the war-torn fields, watching rebel aircraft fly back toward the Ebro to bomb their supply lines, occasionally serving as targets for enemy mortars. But the days were mostly quiet, and the Lincolns slept in the hot sun and gathered in the shade of stunted nut trees to win huge sums from one another in endless poker games.

On the evening of August 6, the Lincolns were relieved by Spanish troops. They formed on the Gandesa-Corbera highway and began a 10-mile hike to the rear. In the moonlight the troops climbed a steep hill and went through the awful rubble of what had once been Corbera, which had been bombarded to pieces by both armies. Now it stank with death, for many unburied bodies lay beneath the crumbled walls of the buildings. The hike ended before daybreak in some broad, terraced olive fields not far from Mora la Nueva. Here the men of the battalion were in rest positions for a week, always hearing artillery in the distance. The troops were ordered to dig deep circular trenches around the base of the trees, but because they felt they were soon going back into action, they dug very little. Enemy planes were overhead often, and a couple of times dropped billowing clouds of leaflets, asking the Americans to surrender and come over to the enemy, saying they would be treated with "justice and liberty." The soldiers found the leaflets amusing and complained that Franco was using scab labor, for there was no union label on the printed sheets.[23]

On August 15 the brigade went back into action. There were only 350 of the 700 soldiers who had crossed the Ebro, and fewer than 100 Americans still with the Lincoln Battalion. They climbed into the Sierra Pandols, the craggy granite mountains south of Gandesa. Burned repeatedly by incendiary bombs, they looked as desolate as the face of the moon. On the hills there were no real fortifications or trenches, no cover from airplanes or artillery. The Lincolns simply spread out over the rocky peaks, lay without food or water during the daylight hours for ten days on top of the naked hills—and hung on. Franco's counteroffensive was aimed through this region, and the rebels were using a new formula of battle: "Artillery conquers the ground, infantry occupies it." So the Americans were forced to endure some of the heaviest barrages of the war. The toughest day was August 19, when artillery and mortars pounded the Lincolns for seven and a half hours without letup. In Bessie's view, this was: "The worst day, so far, of this life. . . . The strain, unbearable, the shells, thousands, falling in groups of 3, 4 at second intervals . . . fog of dust and ears ringing . . . hour after hour of the same, hour in and out, the body utterly exhausted and indifferent to conscious fear, but strained to the snapping point . . . sweat and internal pain, waiting, waiting for the shells and mortars, falling to right and left, above and below, to finish us off. . . ." Bessie was not finished off, but many others were, and when the roar of explosions stopped, the uninjured men went on trembling for hours. Some, like Bessie himself, never fully recovered the use of their hearing after the barrage. Though the softening up on the nineteenth was not followed by an infantry attack, there were a number of bitter struggles on the peaks of the Pandols, and for their "tenacious resistance," the Lincolns were cited by brigade and commended for their heroism.[24]

When they came down from the Sierra Pandols on August 27, the ranks of the battalion were thinner than before and the morale which had held during the battle began to disintegrate. While they went into reserve positions still within the sound of war—for the Loyalist bulge south of the Ebro was slowly shrinking—the most depressing news about Hitler's threats on Czechoslovakia began to reach them. Some of the Americans talked of repatriation incessantly. Others did more than talk, slipping away quietly in the night. Yet on September 6 the Lincolns went back into the lines near Corbera, and for five days held onto one hill against heavy attacks, while Spanish troops in droves surrendered to the enemy or simply fled the battlefield. Once more they returned to reserve positions, while enemy airplanes filled the sky and his artillery was as close as if they had been in the front lines.[25]

Meanwhile, far from the sound of gunfire, on the quiet shores of Lake Geneva, Spanish Prime Minister Juan Negrín rose to address the League of Nations on the afternoon of September 21. He announced that the Spanish government was immediately and unilaterally withdrawing all foreign volunteers in its armies. The decision to remove the International Brigades may have come from the Comintern in Moscow, but it seems more likely that it was prompted by the fact that the weary foreign troops could do the Spanish government more good as propaganda than as soldiers at this point.[26] Negrín undoubtedly hoped that if he withdrew the Internationals, Franco might have to withdraw his German and Italian "volunteers" or suffer the consequences of being the only side using foreign troops in a domestic war. In the latter case, some of the parties to the Non-Intervention Agreement just might lift their embargoes to Spain, allowing it to buy vital war materials. Since there were few effective Internationals left, the Loyalists were sacrificing little, and they stood to gain much. But at the time of the Munich agreement on Czechoslovakia, Negrín's hope that the Western powers would stand on principle proved vain.

Whatever the reasons for the withdrawal, they would have mattered very little to the Americans, on their way back to the front lines on September 21. On the twenty-second, news of the imminent withdrawal reached brigade headquarters. Commissar Gates decided to keep the information from the troops until relief actually arrived. But the news leaked out, and on the evening of the twenty-second and all through the twenty-third, a day when the Americans were pounded ceaselessly by enemy artillery and bombers, the soldiers fought with the knowledge that this would be their last battle. Each death seemed more bitter than ever to the men, now that they knew they were going home. Yet several Americans, including Jim Lardner, were killed on the last day of fighting, while many of the Spanish troops again broke and ran under enemy assault. Finally, relief arrived near midnight, and the XVth Brigade at last marched away from the front. At daybreak on September 24, the troops shuffled slowly across the wooden plank bridge over the Ebro River. The sun rose and the waters of the river shimmered in the cool dawn. The Americans in Spain had seen their last battle.[27]

A week after the Americans crossed the Ebro for the last time, word came of the conference at Munich that had sealed the fate of Czechoslovakia. With Western capitulation to Hitler on that issue, the Lincolns knew there was now no longer the slightest hope that any country would help the Spanish Republic. Camped in Marsa again, the soldiers were anxious to leave Spain, and some feared that a general European war might get under way and prevent their return home. Though farewell fiestas were staged to promote amity, the gulf between the American and Spanish troops was now too huge to bridge. Even personal friendships were strained as some Spaniards accused their International comrades of deserting them. Such accusations did make many Americans feel twinges of guilt, but for the most part the Lincolns believed they had fulfilled their commitment to the cause, and they realized the Internationals were no longer of any use to the Republic. Yet even this knowledge could not make them fully comfortable with the native troops, and the Americans were not sad when the XVth Brigade, now all-Spanish, marched back across the Ebro to war.[1]

Remaining at Marsa through October, some 200 Americans journeyed to Barcelona on the 29th for a farewell parade. Smoke was still twisting slowly skyward from the rubble of buildings flattened in air raids when the festivi-

Lincoln Battalion Officers After the Last Battle (left to right): Lt. Larry Lustgarten, Lt. Rico Rusciano, Captain Donald Thayer, Lt. Emmanuel Lancer, Major Milton Wolff, Commissar George Watt, Company Commander Harold Smith, Commissar Archie Brown

ties began in the late afternoon. Along the Diagnol, the broad boulevard that slants through the center of Barcelona, hundreds of thousands of civilians stood on the curbs, perched on benches, leaned from balconies, and hung from trees to watch the soldiers of the Spanish Army swing past. Then, while government fighter planes thundered over the rooftops, hundreds of men clad in rags and smiling and waving to the crowds marched by—the Internationals. The spectators went wild with cheers. Girls rushed forward with bouquets of flowers, pressed them into the soldiers' arms, and kissed the men goodbye. Little boys darted into the streets and were picked up and carried on broad shoulders. In the crowd lining the streets, thousands of people wept and yelled and shouted farewells. Marching together, the

200 men of the Lincoln Battalion felt their hearts swell with joy and pride, and in the noise they felt a reaffirmation of their faith that all men are brothers. And if the Americans marched out of step that day, it was because, as Herbert Matthews cabled home, "These men learned to fight before they learned to parade."[2]

After the Barcelona farewell, the Lincolns went north to Ripoll, 25 miles from the French border, where they waited through the month of November. They were visited by the League of Nations Commission, which was engaged in counting the volunteers before they left Spain. In the middle of the month they learned that the Republican troops had at last been pushed back across the Ebro. The thought that it had taken Franco four months to recapture what the Republic had seized in four days did not comfort them much. They were too anxious to leave Spain and more worried than ever that the end of the war might trap them there.

During November 1938, two things were holding up the departure of the Americans, lack of passports and of money for their transportation. Passports had been a problem before, as wounded men on their way to America had been unable to get theirs back from either International Brigade headquarters or the Loyalist government, both of which denied knowledge of their whereabouts. Earlier in the year, a representative of the American Communist Party had tried unsuccessfully to persuade Loyalist officials to return the documents. In October, party chairman Earl Browder came to Spain for the same purpose, but only succeeded in having a few of them returned. American diplomatic officials in November made one last attempt of their own to retrieve the documents. Evidently they achieved some success, for many of the Lincolns did have their passports returned before their departure. For those who did not, consular officials journeyed to Ripoll and issued temporary identification cards. Then they stamped available passports to make them good only for direct travel to the United States. Meanwhile, the Republican government took upon itself the expense of returning the Lincolns home, adding $25 pocket money for each man.[3]

In Ripoll there was nothing for the Americans to do, and though the commissariat still functioned, holding lectures and discussions, the men were endlessly bored. At the end of the month, 327 Americans were issued a strange assortment of out-of-date civilian clothing and taken on a slow-moving train to Puigcerda. There they formed for the last time into a military column on December 2 and then marched across the border into La Tour de Carol, France, where they watched rebel aircraft bomb the railroad station they had just left. They were fed a good meal for the first time in months and hurried aboard a train. Evidently worried both about this large band of trained "revolutionaries" entering France, and also about the kind of reception the Internationals might receive from the left-wing workers of Paris, the French government sealed the train and routed it around Paris directly to Le Havre. The schedule called for a sailing on the *Normandie* on December 3, but French maritime workers had chosen that day to begin a strike, and the Americans were held as virtual prisoners in immigrant barracks outside the port city. Three days later they were taken by train to Cherbourg and put aboard the *Paris* for the trip home.[4]

Other Americans who had been in hospitals or attached to various special units were still stranded in Spain, some as far south as Valencia. In December, many of them went through the same routine of crossing the border and being taken by sealed train to a French port. Yet in late January, there were still 200 Americans in the Barcelona area as the armies of Francisco Franco closed in. On January 23, as rebel forces reached the outskirts of the city, the Spanish Communist Party issued an appeal to the Internationals to help defend Barcelona. Among the Americans, in a little town just north of the city, a violent debate ensued and finally almost half of them decided to remain to fight to the end. These who did so formed themselves into a company and went to bed that night with the idea that they were going to die in Spain. Only the next morning were they told that the Loyalist government did not want them back in battle. They boarded one of the last trains to leave Barcelona before it fell, and on January 26, 96 of them crossed the frontier. The remaining Americans, along with 1,000 other Internationals, were reviewed at the border by André Marty on February 7, after which they all marched into France singing the "Internationale." By then thousands of refugees were pouring into France from Catalonia, and some Americans were herded with them into concentration camps on the beaches of southern France, where they remained for several weeks until foreign service officials were able to have them released.[5]

That was still not the end of Americans in Spain, for more than 90 were being held prisoner by the rebel government. Mostly captured in the retreats of March 1938, they had been imprisoned along with other International captives at the old monastery of San Pedro de Cardenas, near Franco's capital of Burgos. Though they lived in cramped quarters, with poor sanitary facilities and no opportunities for recreation, the Americans were not really mistreated during their captivity. Food was scant, all the men lost weight, and they suffered because there were only five toilets for 600 prisoners, no medical facilities, and no tobacco whatsoever. They kept up morale by starting a school, with men giving lectures in history, political science, and languages, and they held bridge tournaments and entertainment programs. Even so, time hung very heavy for the men at San Pedro. Behind the scenes, American Ambassador to Spain Claude Bowers went into action in October 1938 to have them freed. Negotiations with the rebel government were long and involved but finally, in April 1939, 81 of the Americans were released, probably as a gesture of goodwill by Franco toward the United States. Another 10 were held a few months longer and then they, too, were at last repatriated.[6]

The veterans of the Lincoln Battalion returning to the United States in the winter of 1938–39 were not the first soldiers to come back from Spain. As early as the summer of 1937, wounded and disabled men had returned in small numbers. Under the auspices of the Friends of the Abraham Lincoln Battalion, headed by David McKelvy White, a number of the early returnees toured the United States, speaking to all sorts of groups in an effort to raise money. The three O'Flaherty brothers from Boston, who had all served at Jarama, and Robert Raven, who had been blinded there, were among the most popular of the touring speakers, and the money they gathered was used to purchase cigarettes, magazines, candy, overcoats, and blankets for the men in the trenches.[7]

In April 1938, the FALB announced that 222 men were already back from Spain and said that half of them were being given $15 a week by the organization because they could not find jobs. Two months later, the FALB began a drive to bring home 250 to 400 more wounded Americans. Supporting the drive was a committee boasting such names as William Rose Benét, Lillian Hellman, Quincey Howe, and Congressmen Thomas Amlie and Jerry O'Connell, and among many donors were Mr. and Mrs. Henry Luce, who gave a total of $450. During the summer of 1938, groups of wounded Lincolns were brought home by the FALB, and $10,000 to transport the final 83 men was put up by the financier Bernard Baruch, who explained his action by stating, "They were willing to fight for something they believed in, and I had the money to bring them home." With floods of men returning after the withdrawal of the International Brigades in the winter of 1938–39, the FALB increased its efforts to raise money. Membership—anyone who donated $1 or more was considered a member—reached 50,000. Dances, cocktail parties, and memorial meetings for the veterans raised the total collected by the FALB to over $400,000, half of which was spent on rehabilitation of the men who came back from Spain.[8]

For most of the individuals involved, the return to civilian life in the United States was difficult. If he were with one of the big groups, there would be a cheering crowd waiting to welcome him at the dock in New York, and maybe a parade with a brass band to lay a wreath inscribed: "In memory of those who died for democracy," at the eternal light in Madison Square.[9] Then the crowds would disperse and he was alone with wife, friends, or family. After the excitement of seeing those he had missed for so long, after the realization that he was safely out of Spain, there was the inevitable letdown. For though not quite finished, the Spanish War was as good as over, and the ex-Lincoln knew he had fought a losing battle. The force he had gone to fight against, fascism, was more belligerent and bellicose than ever. Spain belonged to Franco now, and Austria and Czechoslovakia were part of Hitler's empire, while in the Far East, sections of China were controlled by Japan. When he thought about it, the veteran felt that a bigger war was coming, for he still believed a showdown with fascism was necessary and inevitable.

But first he had practical problems to face. If he needed medical treatment, as did 75 per cent of the returning veterans, he went to the FALB, which took care of doctors' bills and hospitalization.[10] Some of the Lincolns had simple needs, like new glasses or minor dental work, while others who had come home in stretchers required surgery and were confined to hospitals for months. Some men, like blinded Robert Raven, or Yale Stuart, who had lost an arm, were saddled with permanent disabilities and needed retraining before they could support themselves again. For all the Americans, in need of medical care or not, the problem sooner or later became one of finding a job, something not very easy to do in 1939, when 10 million were still unemployed.

Some of the men who had been in Spain had no trouble finding work. Many seamen, like Bill Bailey, simply scraped together the money to pay back union dues and soon shipped out. Skilled workers, carpenters, plumbers, printers, were often back in their trade before long. One artist returned to a WPA project and one journalist resumed his post on the *New Republic*. Alvah Bessie used his Spanish experience as the basis for a book which Scribner's soon published; then he became drama editor for the *New Masses*. Edwin Rolfe began a history of the Lincoln Battalion commissioned by Random House. A number of the men who had been students reenrolled in schools, and those who had been on the CP payroll simply went back to work for the party, where their prestige had been enhanced. Some who had joined the party because of Spain and had shown their mettle there were employed by the Communists for the first time.

Other veterans had trouble finding positions. Some were barred from companies where they had worked, either because management was not much impressed with the reliability of workers who took time off to fight wars abroad, or because it was not in sympathy with the ideals of the Popular Front. Many of the ex-Lincolns had never worked before, and 1939 was not a very good year to start looking for a first job. Still, the FALB and the Communist Party tried to use their influence to find employment for veterans. Articles were run in the party press, urging employers to give them preference in hiring. Labor unions sympathetic to the left were asked to take in ex-Lincolns; some of them, like the United Electrical, Radio and Machine Workers, did so. At its April 1939 convention, the ILWU approved a resolution urging its locals to hire veterans, since some of them had been expelled by the "reactionary leadership" of their own unions.[11]

In time, perhaps after weeks, perhaps after months, the men who had fought Franco in Spain readjusted to civilian life and found ways of supporting themselves. Yet it was impossible for a person concerned with international politics really to settle down in 1939, when the world was hurrying toward war. The men who had gone to Spain were political men, and most of them swung back into political activity soon after their return. As early as December 1937, 20 veterans had been arrested for disorderly conduct as they picketed a store selling Japanese-made products on Times Square. They were soon freed by a judge who thought they were not lawbreakers, but simply men "sincerely in favor of a cause." Two days after their case was dismissed on January 13, 1938, Spanish veterans led 1,000 pickets in Long Beach, California, protesting the loading of scrap iron to be shipped to Japan.[12] On Lincoln's Birthday 1938, 75 veterans gathered in Washington, D.C., for a conference that endorsed Roosevelt's "Quarantine the

Aggressors" speech and asked for a lifting of the neutrality law. One delegation carried a petition to the White House, while another group entered the Italian Embassy to demand withdrawal of Mussolini's forces from Spain. On February 14, the Lincolns picketed the embassy, and an airplane trailing a streamer reading: "Quarantine the Aggressors" flew back and forth over the capital.[13]

While the war raged in Spain through 1938, the men who had returned home continued to protest, picket, and demonstrate against fascism and for collective security. On May Day, 150 veterans wearing berets, some of them confined to trucks because of their wounds, took part in a workers' parade down Broadway, "in an uproar of shouted songs and slogans, beating drums and blaring horns." October found 25 carrying a Spanish Republican flag to a demonstration of 7,000 people outside a German-American Bund meeting in Chicago, and then taking part in an ensuing riot. After most of the Lincolns were home, in January 1939, 31 Spanish veterans were wildly cheered at a Communist Party rally in Cleveland, which then heard former commissar John Gates demand a lifting of the Spanish embargo. The next month New York veterans picketed the Italian consul—the last agitation of the Americans during the Spanish War.[14] At the end of March 1939, after a two and a half year siege, rebel troops entered Madrid, and on April 1, the Spanish Civil War was at an end.

Although they had come to expect it, the final collapse of the Spanish Republic was a disappointing blow to the men who had fought in the Lincoln Battalion. Yet for people of the left, 1939 was not a year to brood over failures. Too much in the world was calling for attention. The ex-Lincolns were used to collective action in movements against fascism. Their Spanish experience had created a special bond between them. When the call went out for them to join a veterans' organization, it was as natural for them to do so as for a World War II veteran to join the American Legion. The driving force behind the formation of the Veterans of the Abraham Lincoln Brigade was the Communist Party. But the party could not create the VALB—any more than the battalion itself—by a conjuring trick. The men who joined the organization and came to its meetings did so because they were interested in working with others to carry on the fight against fascism on the domestic scene, and at least in part to share their precious memories of Spain.[15]

How many of the more than 1,500 Americans who returned from Spain actually joined the VALB it is impossible to tell.[16] Theoretically, any veteran was a member as long as he paid the nominal dues of the organization. In point of fact, the VALB office had a mailing list with the names of most of the ex-Lincolns. Even if they lived outside an area where there was a post and never paid dues, Spanish veterans were often sent publications of the organization and were, in an informal way, considered members. For in spite of a constitution, by-laws, and all the other paraphernalia of such organizations, the VALB was always very loose and amorphous in structure.[17]

Not all the ex-Lincolns associated themselves with the new organization. Those who had deserted did not want to meet former comrades, even though the VALB was willing to forgive desertions as long as they were not combined with press allegations of the Honeycombe variety.[18] A few men who had spent time in labor battalions left Spain embittered about the whole experience. Others had been bored, annoyed, and disgusted by the continuous pro-Soviet propaganda within the brigade and never again wanted to be associated with an organization in which Communists predominated. Some had been horrified by executions and had come to consider their comrades and the whole organization immoral. And, of course, there were men among the veterans who simply did not like joining organizations, loners whose commitment to Spain was to be the only collective action of their lives.[19]

The Communist Party was interested in supporting an organization of Spanish veterans because large segments of American opinion looked with favor on what the Lincolns had done in Spain.[20] Presumably, their admirers would listen with attention to the voice of their organization. In 1940, Earl Browder recognized their symbolic importance by saying the people of the United States looked upon them as the "conscience of America." A measure of their importance and popularity can be seen in the actions of Attorney General Robert Jackson, when the FBI, under prodding from Martin Dies, picked up 17 people accused of Loyalist recruiting in Detroit and Milwaukee on February 7, 1940. Nine days later Jackson ordered the indictments against them dismissed, stating, "no public injury seems to have been suffered from the fact that individual Spanish sympathizers who had become so heated over the foreign conflict as to want to fight, left this country to do so." [21]

Organized originally in December 1937, the VALB really got under way after the main body of veterans returned and its leaders decided to capitalize upon its popularity by taking stands on all sorts of national and international issues. From the beginning, the viewpoints it took were always the same as the Communist Party line. Whether this was actually dictated from above is irrelevant, for most of the leaders of the VALB were Communists or sympathetic to the party, and a large proportion of the active members were friendly to the party, too.

From its beginning, the VALB shared another characteristic of the party: it expelled members for ideological differences. The first time such differences hit the organization was in the fall of 1939, when the Stalin-Hitler pact shattered Communist parties and alienated friends of the Soviet Union all over the world. In October 1939, the official organ of the VALB—called, like their Spanish journal, the *Volunteer for Liberty*—took the party-line stand that the war in Europe was "an imperialist war" toward which the United States should remain neutral. Two months later, at its first real national convention, the VALB ended its main resolution with the phrase that the American Communist Party had adopted with regard to the war: "The Yanks Are *Not* Coming!" Some members, who could not believe that because Stalin had signed a pact with him

Hitler was now worthy of their support, tried to start an organization within the VALB called, clumsily enough: "Veterans of the Abraham Lincoln Brigade, Anti-Totalitarian." The new organization received little support, soon languished, and its sponsors were immediately expelled from the VALB.[22]

Similar internal conflicts arose over the Russian invasion of Finland, which the VALB supported, and over Hemingway's *For Whom the Bell Tolls*, which, because of its bitter portrait of André Marty and because it showed Loyalists committing atrocities, was condemned as "an attack on the cause of peace, progress and democracy." Yet most of the veterans who disagreed with these policies did not try to set up rival organizations or issue public pronunciamentos, as did Ralph Bates in the pages of the *New Republic* when he condemned the Soviet invasion of Finland. Most dissident members simply stopped coming to the VALB meetings or associating with its members. And there is little doubt that the majority of men in the VALB did approve of the Stalin-Hitler pact and the Soviet invasions of Poland and Finland. As Milton Wolff and Fred Keller wrote, they had complete faith in the Soviet Union as a "defender of peoples fighting for their freedom."[23] To most of the men who had fought in Spain, Stalin could do no wrong. Of course, they did not suddenly acquire a liking for Germany. They still detested fascism, but they agreed with the party line that England and France had been trying to turn Hitler against Russia, and they applauded the Russo-German pact as something which would free the Soviet Union from the fear of invasion. As for Poland and Finland, they believed the governments of these two countries to be hopelessly reactionary and thought that by invading them, Russia was both saving them from Nazism and extending the area of freedom and socialism.[24]

Though they believed these things, many of the veterans, even the good Communists among them, were uneasy. They had been opposed to Hitler and fascism for so long that they never were comfortable supporting the Nazi government, even if they were helping the Soviet Union at the same time. During the time of the phony war, when Britain and France seemed more interested in conducting operations around Finland than in attacking Germany, their suspicions that the democracies wanted to transform the war into one against the U.S.S.R. grew. When the Nazi invasion of Russia on June 22, 1941, changed the party line, the veterans quickly did a sharp about-face. What had been an imperialist struggle was now a "battle for world democracy." Immediately the *Volunteer for Liberty* clamored for the United States to "throw its might into the battle by a[n] . . . immediate declaration of war." Milton Wolff, last field commander of the Lincolns, rushed into print with a pamphlet titled *Western Front—Now!*, which demanded not only an American declaration of war, but also an immediate invasion of the continent to take the pressure off the Red Army and make Germany fight a two-front war.

The day after Pearl Harbor was attacked, Executive-Secretary Jack Bjoze wrote to President Roosevelt, offering him the military services of the entire membership of the VALB, though how he would have delivered the scattered veterans had the offer been accepted remains a mystery. When the United States entered the war against Japan and then Italy and Germany, the men who had gone to Spain had the rare opportunity of feeling at one with their society. Even more than during the Popular Front period, their radical beliefs now accorded fully with the desires of the American public, and they could throw themselves into the struggle wholeheartedly and be good radicals and good Americans at the same time. The Communists among them could similarly be Soviet and American patriots in the struggle against fascism.[25]

The most militant of the men who had fought in Spain rushed to enlist in the American armed forces, and within a few months 500 of them were back in uniform, while 300 others served in the merchant marine.[26] Their reception by American military officials was a mixture of indifference, hostility, and even absurdity. All enlistees had to fill out forms listing prior service, and many ex-Lincolns were told by impatient sergeants to stop kidding; obviously they were too young to have fought with Teddy Roosevelt in the Spanish-American War. Most of the veterans were called in for interviews by military intelligence. In many cases the questioning was perfunctory, and some men like Mike Goodwin found their interviewers interested in their military exploits. More often, the officers questioning the men were unnecessarily nasty. Gabby Klein was repeatedly asked which Russian officers he had served under in Spain, and he was called a liar when he said he had seen no Russian officers. Jack Lucid and others were called in for repeated interviews by officers who let them know that they suspected them of disloyalty to the United States. After the questioning the men were left alone through basic training, only to find that when their units shipped out for the front, they were kept behind. Some were put to work on permanent menial details, in storerooms cataloguing supplies, as gardeners tending to grass and shrubbery, or on permanent KP. A few had even less pleasant experiences, like Lucid, who was sent to Camp Ripley, Minnesota, and there put into a work company which contained 50 American fascists and some 15 Communists, who brawled and fought against each other whenever they got the chance. Though many of the left-wingers repeatedly petitioned their commanding officers for transfer to combat units, their requests were invariably denied.[27]

Evidently there was no general American military policy behind all this. Individual intelligence officers must have decided that men who had been in Spain were security risks and best kept from the front. For while some ex-Lincolns were thus mistreated, others were not bothered because of their past. A few were actually welcomed by their superiors, used as military instructors because of their experience, and even applauded for having the foresight to fight fascism before America realized its danger. Camp newspapers were full of feature stories about such men. Typical was an article in the Camp Livingston, Louisiana, *Communique* on newly commissioned Second Lt. Saul Israel Birnbaum, a Spanish veteran described as a "fighter for the principles of democracy." After telling in glowing terms of his military actions in Spain, the newspaper stated:

"Now Uncle Sam's Army is getting the benefit of his experience in battle and his knowledge of Hitler's tactics." A similar story in the Camp Crowder *Message* described Pvt. Herman Hollander as a man who had gone to Spain for his ideals, not as an "adventurer or thrill seeker." It quoted favorably Hollander's opinion that it was too bad the democracies had not supported the Loyalist government, for the "destruction of fascism could have been so easy. . . . If France and England and America, too, had given us just a small amount of what they were forced to create for this war. . . ."[28]

Among the ex-Lincolns not marked as disloyal on the whim of an intelligence officer, a number were soon in combat. They fought in all theaters and many served with distinction: Jerry Cook landed in France on D-Day; Lt. Morris Cain won a silver star for braving machine-gun fire and leading trapped Americans out of an encirclement near St. Lo in 1944; Sgt. Anthony Toney won the Distinguished Flying Cross for action in the South Pacific; Sgt. Gerald Weinberg won the same award for bombing raids over Ploesti and was later killed when his Liberator was shot down; and Ernest Kozlowski was killed on Leyte leading his platoon in an attack on an enemy strongpoint, to give a few examples.[29]

Two of the Lincolns won the army's second highest medal of valor, the Distinguished Service Cross, in the battles in the malaria-infested swamps near Buna that stopped the Japanese advance in New Guinea. One was Sgt. Hermann Bottcher, a German-born American who had lost his United States citizenship for enlisting in the International Brigades. Though wounded several times, he personally wiped out several Japanese machine-gun nests and then rallied his men to hold an almost untenable position against repeated counterattacks. For his valor, Bottcher won not only the DSC, but also a battlefield promotion to captain. In 1944, he was killed in the battle of Leyte. The other Lincoln to win the DSC was Sgt. Robert Thompson, who swam a river under fire, towing a rope to which the rest of his troops clung when crossing.

Thompson then led his men to wipe out two machine-gun positions, ensuring the bridgehead and an American advance.[30]

Because many of the Spanish veterans felt they were being systematically discriminated against by the American military, VALB Executive-Secretary Jack Bjoze wrote an open letter to President Roosevelt in early 1943, asking that the policy be changed. The liberal press quickly picked up the charge and documented it. *P.M.* named two Lincolns denied commissions after going through OCS and told of Sgt. John Gates, left behind when his unit was shipped to Europe. Drew Pearson added the story of Morris Brier, second in his OCS class, who at the last minute was kept from graduating. The *New Republic* gave additional case histories and then mentioned Bottcher's exploits, saying "his example seems to suggest that the army may be losing some of its best fighters by keeping the other men at home." Finally, Democratic Congressmen John Coffee, Chet Hollifield, and Warren Magnuson wrote a letter to Undersecretary of War Robert P. Patterson asking whether the charges were true. Patterson answered "No," and said the War Department was not concerned with whether someone had served in Spain. He also named five Spanish veterans who had already received commissions. While Patterson's statement that there was no general policy on Spanish veterans was probably true, the War Department obviously tried behind the scenes to rectify the cases of discrimination. Soon after the publicity, John Gates was sent to Alaska and then to France, parachuting east of the Rhine shortly before the end of the war. Jack Lucid, who had stewed for many months at Camp Ripley, suddenly was shipped to North Africa, and then he took part in the invasions of Sicily and Italy, fighting at Salerno and Monte Cassino. Other veterans who had been held back had similar experiences.[31]

The Spanish veterans who became best known in World War II were the four officers attached to the OSS in Italy—Irving Goff, Vincent Lossowski, Irving Fajans, and Milton Wolff. At least three of them were Communists, and this led to later charges that the party had consciously infiltrated the OSS. According to Goff, however, the initiative came from General Donovan, head of the OSS, who met Goff shortly before the war, learned he had been active in espionage work behind Franco's lines in Spain, and decided he could be of use to the United States. The others were brought into the organization on Goff's suggestion, when Donovan asked him if other Spanish veterans would fit into the OSS setup. Goff was active in the Italiam campaign, going behind enemy lines, collecting intelligence information, giving radios, arms, and money to partisan groups. His connections with Italian Communists like Luigi Longo and Palmiro Togliatti, both of whom had been with the International Brigades in Spain, were valuable, for much of the Italian resistance was Communist led. Conducting a guerrilla warfare school to train Italians for partisan activity was another of his jobs, and for his service, Goff was awarded the Legion of Merit.[32]

Inevitably, there were members of Congress who found out about Communist officers in the service and took exception to such people holding commissions. In February 1945, a House Military Affairs subcommittee began looking into the question, and eventually it found 16 men in the army "whose backgrounds reflect Communism in some form." Goff, Fajans, and Wolff were mentioned for their YCL and VALB connections, while Lossowski and three others were named as members of the "Communist-dominated" VALB. The men were defended by Undersecretary of War Patterson, who said the sole test of an officer's fitness was his loyalty at the time his commission was given, not what he had done in the past. Major General Clayton Bissell, head of Army Intelligence, also spoke for the accused, telling the committee: "These officers have shown by their deeds that they are upholding the United States by force and violence." General Donovan, approached and told that Irv Goff was on the honor roll of the YCL, snapped: "For the job he did in Africa and Italy, he's on the honor roll of the OSS."

The House Committee released its findings without

comment, but at least one member of Congress was not prepared to let the issue drop. Representative John E. Rankin of Mississippi not only wanted the Communists thrown out of the army, but he also called for the removal of War Secretary Stimson, Assistant Secretary McLoy, and Undersecretary Patterson. Other representatives defended the Communist officers. Republican John Folger of North Carolina called Rankin's statements "deplorable," and Democrat Adolph Sabath of Illinois said Rankin objected to the men only because they had offended various reactionary or fascist groups in the United States.[33]

Despite their brave words in defense of the officers, the chiefs of the War Department must have been worried by possible repercussions of the investigation. Irv Goff, on his way to the OSS in the Far East in May 1945 for a mission in China, was suddenly reassigned to Fort Ord, California. Soon the other OSS officers joined him there. Before their discharge they received a letter of apology from Donovan, who said that the whole matter had unfortunately been taken out of his hands.[34]

After V-J Day the veterans of two wars came back to the United States. They were mostly men in their thirties now, and some of them were beginning to drift away from the radicalism of their youth. In the anti-Communist atmosphere of postwar America, a number found it convenient for business and social reasons to forget that they had ever fought in Spain. Others were still militant, and they returned to work in their labor unions or within the Communist Party. Some, like Bill Bailey, found themselves being excluded from unions they had helped to build, as labor organizations like the Maritime Workers became conscious of their own "internal security" and sought to bar radicals from their ranks. Of those barred, many took refuge in the ILWU, which under Harry Bridges's leadership retained an uncommon militancy.[35]

For those Spanish veterans still interested in a left-wing approach to the problems of the world, the VALB existed as a mouthpiece. But it did not speak for all the men who had fought in Spain. As early as its 1940 convention, its membership chairman had complained that only one third of the Spanish veterans actually supported its activities, and by 1946 the percentage was much smaller.[36] Only in New York, where the largest number of veterans lived, did a post continue to function. When the VALB now took stands, it was the leaders in New York who did so, without reference to the membership. Probably the majority of veterans agreed with the stands taken, but if they did not, there was nothing they could do about it. As Jack Lucid pointed out, among such left-wing movements it was quite common for all decisions to come from the top.

In the cataclysm of World War II, the fight in Spain had lost much of its importance, and the VALB consequently spoke with a voice that fewer people cared to listen to. Probably the last time the Lincolns were able to elicit support from a number of prominent Americans was at their Fifth National Convention on September 21–22, 1946, in New York City. On that occasion, former Secretary of the Interior Harold Ickes sent congratulations and said of the veterans: "They were among the first to see the menace of fascism. . . . In the last decade they have been in the forefront of all the battles for democracy, and they deserve the best that this country has to offer." At the same time, greetings came from Herbert Lehman, Gene Kelly, Lillian Hellman, Edward G. Robinson, Carey McWilliams, and Congressman Vito Marcantonio. Evidently officials of the U.S. government did not share Ickes's enthusiasm, for on December 7, 1947, the Department of Justice listed the VALB as an organization of questioned loyalty to the United States.[37]

At its 1946 convention, the VALB's objectives were outlined by national commander Milton Wolff who, among other things, said the veterans would campaign to free all of Franco's political prisoners, and within the United States would work "to cooperate with all organizations and groups interested in promoting peace, democracy and civil liberties." To the men running the VALB, these objectives seemed best achieved by a support of the party line on the various issues of the postwar world. When President

Truman enunciated his doctrine for Greece, the VALB accused him of betraying FDR's program "for peace and security," saying: "The President has donned the mantle of England's Emperors, of Hitler and Mussolini and declared himself the conquering saviour of the world." The Marshall Plan was anathema to the VALB, and when the President intervened in the Korean War with American troops, the veterans sent him a letter equating Synghman Ree with Francisco Franco and urging nonintervention.[38]

Toward the Franco regime the Spanish veterans were uncompromisingly hostile. In 1945, the VALB got 250 prominent Americans, including Van Wyck Brooks, Dorothy Parker, William Shirer, James Thurber, Sigmund Spaeth, and Louis Untermeyer, to sign a petition demanding that the United States sever diplomatic and economic ties with Spain. When John Coffee's resolution to this effect was introduced into the House of Representatives, the VALB helped write speeches for radical Representative Vito Marcantonio supporting the measure, one of them maintaining that escaped Nazis were helping Franco to develop an atomic bomb. Meanwhile, David M. White wrote a pamphlet to show that Franco was not a neutral, but had been an open friend to the Axis, and he claimed that Nazi forces within Spain were already plotting another world venture. In 1947, Milton Wolff published a pamphlet on the same theme, and then alleged that the United States had not broken relations with Franco—all members of the United Nations had withdrawn ambassadors from Spain—because American big business had investments there and because the State Department liked Franco's anti-communism.[39] In following years, the VALB publicized similar ideas again and again.

As for the individuals who fought in Spain, their stories become increasingly difficult to follow in the postwar years. As they grew older, many of them made their peace with society and, for better or worse, meshed their political and social beliefs with the vast, middle-of-the-road consensus that is the mainstream in America. Others remained philosophical radicals, but with wives and growing families to support, dropped out of active participation in political affairs. Many went on as labor organizers, as party workers, or as general activists, taking part in such things as the Wallace campaign in 1948, demonstrations to save the Rosenbergs, and anti-HUAC activities.[40]

Of those who gained notoriety after World War II, almost all did so in a negative sense. Their stories are not pleasant ones to tell, and yet they are instructive in showing how the United States, in its anti-Communist moods, has mistreated its native radicals. In the main, the stories of the ex-Lincolns are those of trials and hearings. One of them, Alvah Bessie, was among the Hollywood Ten, sentenced to prison for contempt of Congress after refusing to answer questions before the House Un-American Activities Committee. Two more, John Gates and DSC winner Robert Thompson, were among the Communist Party leaders convicted under the Smith Act in 1949 of belonging to a group of persons "who teach and advocate the overthrow and destruction of the government . . . by force and violence." Though in this trial the "clear and present danger" doctrine was changed to one of "sufficient danger of a substantive evil," the Supreme Court upheld the convictions, $10,000 fines and five years in prison for Gates, and only three years for Thompson because of his DSC. Steve Nelson and Irving Weissman also were convicted under the same law. At a 1952 trial in Detroit, Saul Wellman was similarly convicted, but the Supreme Court later reversed the decision. Even then, Wellman, who had fought at Bastogne and had been discharged after a piece of shrapnel ripped into his chest, was asked because of his "disloyalty" to return $9,581.85 in disability that he had been paid by the Veterans' Administration. Further benefits to him, Thompson, and another Spanish veteran were also canceled. Only after much agitation and outcry by such liberal columnists as Murray Kempton and James Wechsler, and after the American Civil Liberties Union took Wellman's case to court, were the benefits restored.[41]

Other agencies of the American government engaged in harassing the Spanish veterans, though this seems to have happened as a by-product of the general anti-Communist crusade. FBI agents sometimes dropped in on Lincolns and asked them to give names or serve as informers. When veterans were uncooperative, as almost all of them were, the agents might go to their employers, tell them of the veteran's activities, and cause him to lose his job. Though it is difficult to prove, this seems to have happened only to men who remained active in the CP, and not to those who had drifted away from such movements and casually received the *Volunteer for Liberty* or got together with other veterans from time to time.[42]

It is not surprising to find that the House Committee on Un-American Activities has also enjoyed investigating VALB members over the years. Though there was no systematic calling of members after the 1940 hearings, ex-Lincolns often turned up in the course of the committee's inquiries into Communist activities. HUAC's attitude toward them was probably best expressed by Congressman Fred E. Busby of Illinois, who as a friendly witness in 1948 stated, "Now anybody . . . knows that the Loyalists in Spain and the Abraham Lincoln Brigade were definitely 100-percent Communist outfits."[43] The most fanciful of assertions about the veterans which the committee seemed to swallow were made by professional Communist-hunter Walter M. Steele in 1947, when he maintained that the VALB was now part of a Red Army Reserve with headquarters in Moscow and branches all over the world. Steele stated that 15,000 men were in this organization, though he admitted that some might be in the Friends of the Abraham Lincoln Brigade rather than the VALB. With all its investigative expertise, the HUAC did not seem to know that the FALB had been dissolved in 1939.

Most of the Spanish veterans called before the committee were asked about many of their activities, before, during, and after Spain. To those who were uncooperative—and this meant virtually all the veterans—the HUAC members were often unpleasant. Still, they got little testimony out of VALB members. Steve Nelson in Washington in 1949 refused to answer almost every question put to him, as did Sterling Rochester and John Tisa in Philadelphia in 1952, and Neils Kruth in Albany two years later. A couple of vets who did testify talked only about their own activities and refused to implicate others. The only Spanish veteran really friendly to the committee was Robert Gladnick, who, at the New York City hearings of May 1953, talked at length and named about 20 ex-Lincolns as members of the Communist Party. Though few people have ever had the last word before the HUAC, Dr. Lawrence Markert, a biologist teaching at the University of Michigan, managed to do so. In Lansing in 1954, Dr. Markert refused to answer all questions about his Spanish activities or about the Communist Party. Trying to get him to admit the party advocated the overthrow of the government, Gordon H. Scherer of Ohio exploded: "In the Spanish War didn't the Communists use force and violence?" Answered Dr. Markert: "I presume if there was a war that force and violence were used."[44]

By the early 1950's, the VALB leadership began to feel that the veterans were being persecuted by the American government. Noting that the United States and Spain were now military allies, Executive-Secretary Moe Fishman claimed in 1953 that the government was trying to destroy the VALB "because with our organization out of the way, the administration is certain it will be easier to bring about a fuller alliance with Franco Spain."[45] To the outsider, this view seems more than a little paranoid and egocentric, in view of the fact that the VALB had a minuscule influence on public opinion by the time of the Korean War. Rather, its members were being hurt only as part of the general drive against Communists.

As part of the organization's activities, the VALB collected money to defend the various veterans standing trial under the Smith Act. In 1952 it agitated on various issues, taking stands against the American alliance with Spain, the admission of the Madrid mayor to the States for a world conference of mayors, the sending of the New York City Center Ballet to Madrid, and the admission of Spain to UNESCO. The next year, after the signing of the U.S.-

Spanish military pact, the VALB issued a statement saying American bases in Spain might be used to "launch an abominable war of aggression against the Soviet Union," and warning solemnly that "we are drifting to war and fascism, with McCarthyism and McCarranism at home and to alliances with Francoism abroad." [46]

In 1954 the ax fell on the VALB. Under provisions of the Subversive Activities Control Act of 1950, Attorney General Herbert Brownell ordered the VALB to register as a Communist-front organization. The case went before the Subversive Activities Control Board, and hearings were held in May, September, and October 1954 in New York City and Washington, D.C. The government trotted out 16 witnesses, a number of whom were what might be termed "professional ex-Communists." The VALB responded with 5 witnesses of its own. During the hearing, the VALB busied itself collecting money for its legal defense. A number of New York veterans gathered to pass a resolution insisting they were fighting not only for the life of the organization, but also "to protect every man and woman who fought for the Republic of Spain from political and economic persecution." [47]

When the SACB hearings, which filled 4,576 pages with testimony, ended and the board reached its decision in May 1955, it admitted that "many veterans of the Spanish War are not members of the [VALB] . . . or in any way represented by it." Yet because many of its members and officers were in the CP, and because the VALB had supported the Communist line for years, the SACB decided that the VALB was "directed, dominated, and controlled by the Communist Party of the United States . . . and . . . is primarily operated for the purpose of giving aid and support to it and the world Communist movement." [48] The SACB then ordered the VALB to register as a Communist front. The case was immediately appealed to the courts and the decision was upheld on the slow road to the Supreme Court.

The harassment by the American government, the jailing of several veterans under the Smith Act, and the SACB decision did not seem to intimidate the VALB, though in 1955 its executive-secretary admitted that its supporters were dwindling. On December 8, 1955, leaders of the organization sent a telegram to the American delegation to the United Nations, asking that the United States vote against the admission of Franco Spain. Soon the Soviet Union, which so many of the veterans had worshipped for so long, was to help silence the VALB's opinions on world affairs. When Russian tanks rolled into Budapest in 1956, the American Communist Party began to crumble away, and the de-Stalinization that followed provided a virtual death blow. By the time John Gates, editor of the *Daily Worker*, formally resigned his membership on January 10, 1958, most of the Lincolns who had been party members had quietly left the movement. Though there were internal reasons for the exodus from the party, Hungary and de-Stalinization were the kiss of death. In resigning, Gates said he had not given up the ideals that had attracted him to the party, those of democracy and socialism, but that he did not "believe it is possible any longer to serve those ideals within the Communist Party." Many other veterans had left for similar reasons, just as many who were not party members had over the years slowly become disillusioned with their former pro-Russian beliefs.[49]

While a direct connection cannot be proved, it seems likely that the breakup of the party had something to do with the VALB's decision to continue its existence not as a political pressure group, but simply as a "social, welfare and historical organization." It was also partly due to a belated recognition that the VALB "has long lost whatever political character it formerly possessed . . . as an anti-Fascist center influencing life itself." Leaving behind its feelings of persecution, the organization admitted that this development "flows primarily from life itself and not from the attacks upon us."[50]

Older men, perhaps wiser men, the ex-Lincoln Brigaders in the late 1950's had come to realize that because of the cold war and their own uncompromising left-wing beliefs, the capital they had accumulated as an anti-fascist organization had now been spent. They were still anti-Franco, and in succeeding years the issues of *Volunteer for Liberty* reported news of happenings in Spain, of strikes and political arrests, and it agitated in its own limited way for a release of political prisoners still in Franco's jails. In 1962, a delegation of 22 veterans and their families attended celebrations on the twenty-fifth anniversary of the Spanish Civil War, held in East Germany. Many veterans were impressed with the chance to see socialism at work at last and all enjoyed themselves at the memorial meetings. But at least one came back admitting that the East Germans were trying to hide the fact that people were escaping to the West. In the summer of 1963, the HUAC senselessly harassed Executive-Secretary Moe Fishman over a few bundles of clothes the veterans had collected to send to Franco prisoners. The next summer the VALB organized a demonstration of 150 people at the Spanish Pavilion of the New York World's Fair, where the participants wore buttons calling for "Amnesty for all Political Prisoners in Spain." [51]

For the most part today, the people who still receive the *Volunteer for Liberty*—and perhaps there are 600 of them —are aging men who occasionally get together with the friends who once shared the greatest adventure of their life with them. Through the VALB they maintain a vague contact with one another. When the Supreme Court at long last decided on April 26, 1965, that the VALB did not have to register as a Communist front, it did so on the grounds that the case was "stale" because so many of the organization's members had died off and because the evidence on Communist control dealt mainly with the 1940's. [52] Of course, it was the slowness of the courts that helped make the case "stale," and yet the decision was fitting. It would have been absurd to decide that the VALB was a Communist front at this point, when its members had less to do with the Communist Party than at any time in their history.

The Americans who fought under the banner of the XVth International Brigade were sometimes referred to by the Communist Party as latterday Lafayettes, paying off the debts contracted by the United States during the American Revolution. Perhaps they occasionally did think that because Europeans had fought for American freedom, it was only right for Americans to do the same in Europe. This attitude may show naïveté, but from more than one point of view the Lincolns can be considered naïve. Certainly the men of the Lincoln Battalion were naïve enough to believe that on the battlefields of Spain they could help stop the growing fascist threat to world peace and freedom. It was this belief that was their strength, that allowed them to transmit desire into action, that helped place them among the first battlers against aggression while the timid democracies buried their heads in the sands of appeasement. If this be naïveté, it has much to commend it.

Of course, the members of the International Brigades did not expect singlehandedly to defeat Franco's armies. All they hoped to do was to help slow down the enemy until a Spanish Loyalist Army was created, and until the democracies saw that it was in their own interest to end the farce of nonintervention and sell arms to the legal

Spanish government. On this score, the Lincolns suddenly sound less naïve than the hardheaded diplomats of Western Europe. In retrospect it seems clear that it was in the interests of France and England to draw the line against fascism somewhere. Spain would have been as good a place and time as three other well-known instances of appeasement—the remilitarization of the Rhineland, *Anschluss*, or the sellout of Czechoslovakia at Munich. Certainly it would have been a better place than Poland in 1939. Appeasement in Spain, as elsewhere, only whetted the appetites of the dictators and brought much closer the day when Hitler would turn on the democracies. Even without Western aid and with only erratic support from Soviet Russia, the battle against Franco lasted more than thirty-two months. Six months after its end, World War II erupted. It is likely that if the Loyalists had held out those six months, until September 1939, the Allies would have aided the Spanish to get rid of Franco as a member of the Axis powers.

While fighting their defensive action against the Spanish rebels and hoping for nonintervention to end, the volunteers of the International Brigades became tough, effective soldiers. They were among the real shock troops of the Republic. The XVth Brigade was in the vanguard of three of the four major offensives of the war, and at Brunete, Aragón, and the Ebro, the American battalions reached the farthest limits of Loyalist gains, doing as much as any battalions to aid the doomed government cause.

In later years it would become common in some circles to speak of the volunteers as "dupes" in a cause that Stalin betrayed, because some historians would show that the Soviet leader was not really interested in winning the war, and thus never gave the Loyalists as much aid as he could have. But surely this is irrelevant. The question is whether or not the cause of Spain was worth supporting, and not who else supported it or for what reasons.[1]

Perhaps the impulse to see the volunteers as "dupes" springs from an unwillingness to come to grips with their honest radicalism. Not liking the idea or term "radical,"

Americans rarely apply it to their own past. Yet the United States has had many radicals in its history, and in the thirties radicalism certainly flourished. The question to be asked about the Lincolns is whether the events of the decade, seen from their perspective as laborers, students, Jews or intellectuals, justified their politics or world-view. The same question can be asked about other radicals in American history. Looked at this way, the actions of the Lincolns, as of many earlier radicals, becomes understandable and even commendable. Seen from their point of view, the late 1930's was a time when the future of the world hung in the balance. To help tip the scales, they put their bodies on the firing lines of Spain, in the belief that individuals help to create the future. It is true that many died and the cause was defeated, but this is perhaps less important than the fact that the Lincolns showed that Americans can and should commit themselves in times of crisis. Doing so, men create history. As Hemingway wrote late in the war, the action of the Lincoln Battalion is "already a part of American history. It is a fine part, and all who had a share in it can be proud within themselves as long as they live."[2]

At the time of the war, as later, the Lincolns were sometimes criticized as "Bolsheviks" or "Reds." This is only to be expected. More surprising is the fact that praise for them came not just from the far left, but also from many other quarters. Newspapers that thoroughly disagreed with their politics often commended their actions. The Asheville *Citizen*, for example, applauded the Lincolns because they were willing to die for their ideals, stating: "One does not have to be a political radical to respect such men."[3] The Lewiston *Morning Tribune* took the same approach when Edward Robel, a local young radical, was killed in Spain. It said, "You may not agree with the advanced economic and social views held by this young man . . . yet you must admire and respect this unselfish devotion to an ideal which he was prepared to defend to the death."[4] The legislature of the state of Kansas, investigating the death of university student Don Henry, disapproved of party recruiting on the campus, but said: "We have the deepest respect for Don Henry's idealism and courage."[5] The idealism and courage of the Lincolns remains idealism and courage, no matter what has since been discovered about other parties in the Spanish Civil War.

For the men who went there, the Spanish War was the highpoint of their lives. All of them looked back on it in later years as the most clean, noble, and glorious thing they had ever done.[6] Herbert Matthews, as a noncombatant covering the war for the *New York Times*, best expressed the mood of them all in writing: "nothing so wonderful will ever happen to me again as those two and a half years in Spain. . . . In those years we lived our best, and what has come after and what is to come can never carry us to those heights again."[7] Of course, men who go to war in their youth often look nostalgically back on that time when they were touched with fire, and certainly the Lincolns were victims of this. Yet because they acted under no compulsion other than their own convictions, because they volunteered for a cause that was good and right and just, there seems to be particular truth in how they later felt. Many would agree—in spite of certain blemishes on the Lincolns' record—with Louis Fischer's estimation: "The Brigade's life stands as an untarnished epic."[8]

There is still another reason why the men who went to Spain should look upon their past so fondly. In the 1930's the world struggle was very simple to them. When they came back from Spain they were defeated, but uncompromised. Yet when their arch enemy, fascism, was itself buried in World War II, things became more complicated. Those who remained radicals found the gap between themselves and the rest of America widening more and more. Even that, and the attendant investigations, jail terms, and the SACB decision might have been bearable. But eventually, after Hungary and de-Stalinization, they saw that the party with which they had allied themselves no longer carried out the ideals in which they believed. When the men of the Lincoln Battalion lost faith in Soviet Russia—whether they did so in 1940, 1957, or in between

—and rejoined American society, they found the world terribly complex. To them, the evils of communism and the purity of American capitalism were not as apparent as to some patriots. Russia was not Germany, and communism could not be opposed with the same singlemindedness that fascism had been. The world they looked out upon was one in which they could be less sure than ever before that their ideals of democracy and, yes, socialism, could triumph. For to them it was not always apparent now exactly which country was upholding these ideals and to what extent.

The record of the VALB in the postwar world has nothing of the cleanness of the Spanish struggle itself. Perhaps this is the way of all veterans' organizations; certainly, the American Legion has come to stand for ideals other than making the world safe for democracy. The cold war was one factor, and America's anti-communism was another, but even Americans relatively unaffected by the latter were not much interested in defending the VALB when it was listed as a Communist front. The VALB's uncritical support of the Soviet Union had lost it many friends. Of course, many ex-brigaders disapproved of the VALB actions and many Americans still have a warm spot for the Lincolns in their hearts. But they think of the battalion on the hot Castilian plain near Brunete, in the twisting, narrow streets of Quinto and Belchite, in the icy snowstorms of Teruel, and on the naked hills overlooking Gandesa, where the Lincolns reached the climax of their glory. When the last soldiers tramped through Barcelona in October 1938, and the cheers of the Spanish people thundered about them, the men of the Lincoln Battalion were marching into an unhappy dénouement.

APPENDICES

In Chapter IV, estimates are made as to the occupations, ethnic origins, ages, and places of residence of the men who went to Spain. Here is how these figures were arrived at. In all my research through books, pamphlets, newspapers, magazines, letters, and diaries, and in my interviews with veterans, I extracted every bit of information I could find about the backgrounds of the men. The final roster contained 1,804 names, or over half of those who went, certainly a good sample. Unfortunately, for some of the men I could find no more than a name. When it came to occupations, the roster contained 447, some 15 per cent of the total; for age, the list contained 291 names; state of residence was more readily available, and 1,336 names made up that roster. The figures given in Chapter IV are projections based on this available information. Though approximations, they are the best figures obtainable; estimates of this sort made elsewhere seem to have been simple guesswork.

Occupations

The figures given for various occupational groups in Chapter IV are projections based on the table below. For example, since the 89 seamen represent 20.6 per cent of the total known occupations, the projection is that 618 (or approximately 600) of the 3,000 Lincolns were seamen. Similarly, the 79 students formed 17.9 per cent of the total, resulting in an estimate of 530 (or approximately 500) students in Spain.

While this is the general way projections have been made, certain correctives have had to be applied. Some occupations seem clearly to be overrepresented, and meaningful projections cannot be made. Lawyers, engineers, and teachers are more important to middle-class newspapers than are steelworkers, and the volunteering of such professional men—especially in a left-wing cause—would be more newsworthy; stories of them would thus be more likely to find their way into publications. This would also be true for left-wing and Communist publications, which always liked to play up the number of "intellectuals" in their ranks. Similarly, newspapermen whose own publications would be sure to note their going, and artists of various sorts who tend to be in the public eye, also would be more likely to have something written about them. In such cases, projections have not been made; I have simply assumed that a number of people in these categories went to Spain. In some cases, very individual correctives have had to be applied. Though the table shows 25 teachers, representing 5.73 per cent of the total (or 171 in Spain), I feel this is probably exaggerated because most of the names of teachers appeared in one single publication, *WPA Teachers in Spain.*

One other caution. Obviously it is difficult to make meaningful projections for occupations which appear only two or three times. Thus in Chapter IV the projections are made only for occupations that show up in significant numbers on the full list, given below:

Occupation	Number	Per Cent
Seamen	89	20.6
Students	79	17.9
Teachers	25	5.73
Miners	15	3.44
Longshoremen	14	3.12
Steelworkers	14	3.12

Occupation	Number	Per Cent
Doctors	13	2.9
Newspapermen	11	2.46
Writers	11	2.46
Artists	10	2.24
Truck drivers	10	2.24
Labor organizers	9	2.00
Cafeteria workers	8	1.75
Garment workers	8	1.75
Lumber industry	8	1.75
Auto industry	7	1.56
Engineers	6	1.34
Lawyers	6	1.34
Newspaper boys	6	1.34
Cannery workers	5	1.2
Cooks	5	1.2
White-collar workers	5	1.2
Actors	4	0.9
Bakers	4	0.9
Accountants	3	0.67
Auto mechanics	3	0.67
Carpenters	3	0.67
Electricians	3	0.67
House painters	3	0.67
Pilots	3	0.67
Salesmen	3	0.67
Taxi drivers	3	0.67
Waiters	3	0.67
Composers	2	0.45
Machinists	2	0.45
Printers	2	0.45
Oil Industry	2	0.45
Radio and telegraph operators	2	0.45
Sculptors	2	0.45
Textile industry	2	0.45

The following occupations all turn up once, making 0.24 per cent of the total: Aircraft industry, artist-entertainer, barber, building trades, choreographer, CIO worker (industry unspecified), dancer, drugstore worker, elevator operator, FBI employee, fur worker, grocery clerk, highway construction, hod carrier, laundry worker, meat cutter, metal trades, locksmith, municipal worker, musician, plumber, policeman, projectionist, radio announcer, radio parts factory, railroad worker, scrap iron worker, shipping clerk, shoe salesman, singer, small boat operator, traveling salesman, WPA construction worker, wrestler.

Ethnic Background

I determined that some 30 per cent of the Lincolns came from Jewish homes in the following way: my list contained 371 obviously Jewish names, or approximately 21 per cent of the total roster of 1,804. However, the fact is that not all Jews have such names to begin with, and in America it has become common for Jews to change their names to more Anglo-Saxon sounding ones. Moreover, many men changed their names simply to go to Spain, often choosing common American names. Estimates of the percentage of Jews in the ranks made by interviewed veterans range between 25 and 40 per cent. For these reasons, then, I feel my figure of 30 per cent is certainly warranted.

The presence of members of other groups, Italian-Americans, Finnish-Americans, and the like, is also derived from names. The absence of Mexican-Americans and Chinese is inferred from the fact that they are never mentioned in anything written about the war, and it is well known that Communist publications loved to crow about members of minority groups supporting their efforts. The one Japanese-American is mentioned so often that certain Franco publications have assumed there was a whole Japanese contingent. Though I found actual mention of only 49 Negroes, I assumed there were more of them, though not the 200 which the CP often mentioned. Today, all interviewees agree there were fewer Negroes than claimed at the time.

State of Origin

With this information on 1,337 of the men, I feel that I have quite a good sample. Only South Carolina, Delaware, and Wyoming are void of representatives. Perhaps if information were available on every Lincoln, these states would be represented, too.

The complete list is as follows:

New York	499	Kansas	5
California	124	Kentucky	5
Illinois	109	North Carolina	5
Pennsylvania	98	Montana	4
Ohio	74	Nevada	4
Massachusetts	61	Tennessee	4
Michigan	48	Texas	3
New Jersey	41	Georgia	2
Wisconsin	38	Louisiana	2
Washington	23	Maine	2
Minnesota	20	Mississippi	2
Missouri	19	Nebraska	2
Connecticut	19	New Mexico	2
Oklahoma	16	North Dakota	2
Maryland	12	Utah	2
Colorado	11	West Virginia	2
Oregon	11	Arkansas	1
Indiana	10	Idaho	1
Florida	9	South Dakota	1
New Hampshire	9	Arizona	1
Iowa	8	Vermont	1
Rhode Island	8	Delaware	0
Virginia	8	South Carolina	0
Alabama	5	Wyoming	0
District of Columbia	5		

Ages

This list, containing 291 names, seems to agree with various estimates and with common sense, that the men were mostly in their twenties. The age given may have been either at the beginning, during, or at the end of the conflict. The relatively large number of men over forty is probably misleading, and one should hesitate to make a projection based upon it. As with professional men, older men volunteering for war would have made better "copy" for newspapers and magazines:

Age	Number	Age	Number	Age	Number
18	1	27	25	35	1
19	6	28	11	36	6
20	14	29	8	37	7
21	19	30	6	38	3
22	33	31	13	39	2
24	21	32	8	40	1
25	24	33	5	Over 40	22
26	16	34	11		

Breaking this into groups and percentages we get:

Age	Number	Per Cent
Under 20	7	2.4
20–24	115	39.2
25–29	84	28.6
30–34	43	14.7
35–39	19	6.5
Over 40	23	7.9

"TERROR" IN THE LINCOLN BATTALION

During the course of my research into this subject, I grew to feel strongly that political executions were exceedingly rare among the Americans in Spain. Originally I had made the assumption that the "terror" in Spain must have spilled over into the International Brigades in general and the XVth Brigade in particular. Yet the American veterans interviewed, even those who were quite frank about CP activities, usually claimed to know of only one or two executions, and to a man they maintained that these were for desertion. Their opinions seem corroborated by the fact that American government agencies investigating the Lincoln Battalion—and quite obviously interested in discrediting it—have turned up such meager evidence of "terror" in the ranks.

In 1938, Abraham Sobel and Alvin Halpern told the HUAC that "many men" had been shot for opposing party policies, but they did not name a single individual. When pressed on the point, Halpern said they were not actually shot, but that they had "disappeared." In view of the generally garbled and often incoherent nature of both Halpern and Sobel's testimony, it is hard to put much faith in anything they said, and the fact that they named no victims seems significant. Two years later, in further HUAC investigations into the Lincoln Battalion, the parents of two soldiers supposedly executed by battalion officials testified. One was the mother of Vernon Selby, the other the father of Albert Wallach. Another name introduced to the committee as the victim of an execution was Paul White. Yet Humberto Galleani, friendly to the committee and rather critical of the way the CP ran the brigades, claimed White had been executed not for political reasons but for attempted desertion. William McQuiston, an ex-Lincoln totally hostile to everything having to do with the brigades, mentioned that three Finnish-Americans were executed. In 1964, veteran Bill Bailey told me that there were only two Finns, and he said they were shot for having committed rape, and not for political reasons.

When the Subversive Activities Control Board got around to investigating the VALB in 1954, extensive testimony on the wartime period was taken. Among 16 anti-VALB witnesses, only 3 political executions and 1 "disappearance" of a political opponent of the CP are mentioned; the names in these cases are Marvin Stern, Harry Perchick, and again Paul White and Albert Wallach. All this testimony boils down to 7 or 8 men: Stern, Perchick, Wallach, Selby, White, and the Finns (either 2 or 3). If the Finns were executed for rape and White for desertion, that leaves 4 *possible* political executions mentioned by basically anti-VALB sources.

Now all this evidence may not be conclusive. It is possible, for example, that some political executions went unrecorded, that men were done away with silently by commissars in the same way as was attempted at Teruel. At the same time, it is equally possible that in the unexplained cases above, the men were simply killed in battle or executed for desertion. Reading the testimony of the hearings mentioned above, one is inclined to believe in a minimum of political executions, for the hostile witnesses are so totally hostile to the VALB that surely they would have mentioned anything they knew of to damage it.

There is one other source from which one can infer that political executions were not commonplace in the Lincoln Battalion. In his memoir of the war, Sandor Voros presents a totally unsympathetic account of the leadership of the brigades, and he feels that he and other idealists were basically dupes of the CP. In all the unpleasant things he has to say about his Spanish experience, Voros only once touches on the subject of "terror." Here he says that during the retreats of March–April 1938, "the terror" was on, and he mentions Internationals being "ruthlessly executed" on Kremlin orders, particularly Poles, Slavs, Germans, and Hungarians. When speaking of the Americans, Voros accuses commissar Dave Doran of catching "the bug," holding courts-martial, and condemning comrades to death for "cowardice, for deserting their posts, for abandoning their duties." Lamentable as such condemnations may be, they are hardly evidence of terrorism; probably every army has shot men for cowardice or desertion. At any rate, at this time no executions were actually carried out among the Americans; according to Voros, this was because the commander became afraid that news of them would reach the press and hurt the world image of the Republican cause. Thus, Voros's evidence of "terror" turns out to be no evidence at all. Since he was a commissar on the staff of the brigade, he certainly would have been in a position to know of acts of terror. Yet nowhere else does he mention any. An inference of their absence thus seems warranted.

Certainly all the evidence above does not conclusively disprove "terror" in the Lincoln Battalion. But the burden of proof is on those who assert its presence, and it seems clear that they have not proved their case. To me it is obvious that whatever "terror" there was in the Lincoln Battalion—and deplorable as such activities are—it in the end boils down to a few possible cases. The idea of any kind of widespread massacre is farfetched and untrue.

A Note on Sources

Because a number of the recent, scholarly works on the Spanish Civil War have contained valuable, extensive bibliographies, and because many of my sources appear in footnotes, it would be both redundant and a parade of useless pedantry to include another lengthy bibliography here. Suffice it to say that I consulted everything on the war, the International Brigades, the Lincoln Battalion, and the background of the thirties that seemed necessary or pertinent for understanding the subject. Still, because so much of the source material for a study of a Communist Party enterprise is not readily available in general libraries, being found rather in ephemeral pamphlets, in private collections, or in the minds of men still living, this bibliographic note is for the serious student of this subject, to give an idea of which sources helped me most in understanding the men of the Lincoln Battalion.

For anyone interested in general bibliographies on the war, adequate ones can be found in both Hugh Thomas, *The Spanish Civil War* (New York: Harper and Brothers, 1961) and Gabriel Jackson, *The Spanish Republic and the Civil War, 1931–1939* (Princeton, N.J.: Princeton University Press, 1965). A bibliography focusing on the Internationals is available in Verle B. Johnston, *Legions of Babel* (University Park, Pa., and London: The Pennsylvania State University

Press, 1967), while Allen Guttmann, *The Wound in the Heart: American and the Spanish Civil War* (New York: The Free Press of Glencoe, 1962), contains one covering American reactions to the conflict, and Richard P. Traina, *American Diplomacy and the Spanish Civil War* (Bloomington, Ind.: Indiana University Press, 1968) has one on the sources of U.S. diplomacy.

Histories of the Abraham Lincoln Battalion number three, two of them written by participants. Edwin Rolfe, *The Lincoln Battalion* (New York: Random House, 1939), is a well-written, interesting account with a great feeling of immediacy. Because it was written just after Rolfe's return from Spain, it lacks historical perspective, and it is occasionally marred by party-line distortions, such as the claim that Guernica was bombed by the Italian Air Force (the book was completed during the time of the Stalin-Hitler pact). Yet it is the basic work on this subject, and a very good one even after almost thirty years. Much less satisfactory is Arthur H. Landis, *The Abraham Lincoln Brigade* (New York: The Citadel Press, 1967), which despite its recent appearance contains no better historical perspective. Actually, this weighty tome (some 650 pp.) is not so much a history as a chronicle. Ignoring sources like diaries and letters, Landis seems to have written his work largely from some 70 tape-recorded interviews with veterans of Spain. Rather than digesting these, the author frequently presents long and often redundant sections of them for the reader. Not only does this make the book hard to read, but it tends to confuse rather than enhance the narrative. Only as a sourcebook on the Lincolns is Landis's work valuable, and this largely for the military actions rather than the ideology, feelings, or motivation of the men, which are virtually ignored. The third history is Cecil Eby's very recent *Between the Bullet and the Lie* (New York: Holt, Rinehart and Winston, 1969). Often good in describing events, the author does not place those events in a meaningful historical context. Eby is vague with regard to the radicalism of the thirties that explains so much about the Lincolns, and his hostility to the CP is so blatant that it interferes with any deep understanding of the Americans who went to Spain.

Memoirs by participants are helpful, but there are surprisingly few of these. By far the best is Alvah Bessie, *Men in Battle* (New York: Charles Scribner's Sons, 1939), a perceptive, honest, and readable work by a dedicated man who was not blind to the problems and faults of the soldiers and leaders of the brigade. Less good, but still important, is John Gates, *The Story of an American Communist* (New York: Thomas Nelson and Sons, 1958), while Steve Nelson, *The Volunteers* (New York: Masses and Mainstream, 1953) must be used with care because it was compiled from the author's notes by someone else. Sandor Voros, *American Commissar* (Philadelphia: Chilton Company, 1961) contains a lot of information, but the author's current anti-Communism leaves some of his judgments suspect. Works by journalists who saw the Lincolns often during the course of the war also shed light upon them. The best are Herbert Matthews, *Two Wars and More to Come* (New York: Carrick and Evans, 1938) and *The Education of a Correspondent* (New York: Harcourt, Brace and Company, 1946), Vincent Sheean, *Not Peace But a Sword* (New York: Doubleday, Doran and Company, 1939), and Louis Fischer, *Men and Politics* (London: Jonathan Cape, 1941).

Letters written home from Spain provide much insight. A good number of them were published at the time in newspapers (which will be considered below) or in various books or pamphlets, usually under left-wing sponsorship. Since such collections had a point of view to sell, I approached them with a good deal of suspicion. Yet the internal evidence in almost all of them shows that they are authentic. Whether they are representative is, of course, another matter; but since my study led me to the conclusion that the volunteers for Spain shared a community of beliefs, the problem of how typical such letters are seems of less importance. The only such collection which can be called a book is Marcel Acier (ed.), *From Spanish Trenches* (New York: Modern Age, 1939), which contains letters by volunteers of many countries. Among pamphlets made up exclusively of letters from Americans in Spain are the following: Joe Dallet, *Letters from Spain* (New York: Workers Library, 1938); *From a Hospital in Spain: Letters from American Nurses* (New York: n.p., 1937); . . . *from the cradle of liberty . . . to the tomb of fascism* (Philadelphia: The Communist Party of Eastern Pennsylvania, [?] 1938); *Let Freedom Ring* (Los Angeles: Friends of the Abraham Lincoln Brigade, n.d.); *Letters from Spain* (San Francisco: Friends of the Abraham Lincoln Brigade, 1937); *Letters from the Trenches from Our Boys in Spain* (New York: Workers Alliance of New York, n.d.).

Letters which found their way into magazines include the following: S. H. Abrams, "The International Brigades," *Canadian Forum,* XIX (August 1939), 157–158; Ben Leider, "Last Letters from Spain," *Current History,* XLVI (April 1937), 46; "Letters from Spain," *Canadian Forum,* XVII (December 1937), 310–311.

Other pamphlets, which tell the story of either one man or a group of men in Spain, also contain letters from Americans. Again, though such pamphlets were issued by organizations with strongly left-wing points of view, the letters prove themselves authentic. Included in this group are the following: Joseph Leeds, *Let My People Know: The Story of Wilfred Mendelson ("Mendy")* ([?] New York: published by his friends, 1942); *Somebody Had to Do Something* (Los Angeles: The James Lardner Memorial Fund, 1939); *Ben Leider: American Hero* (New York: Ben Leider Memorial Fund, n.d.); *WPA Teachers in Spain* (New York: WPA Teachers Union Chapter of the Friends of the Abraham Lincoln Battalion, 1938); *A Negro Nurse in Republican Spain* (New York: Negro Committee to Aid Spain, n.d.); and Joseph Starobin, *The Life and Death of an American Hero* (New York: New Age, 1938).

Other pamphlets, far less reliable as sources of information, are quite good for outlining CP and left-wing attitudes toward the issues of the war. These also provide some factual information about the Lincolns, but must be used very carefully. They include: *The American Volunteers in Spain* (New York: Friends of the Abraham Lincoln Brigade, 1938); Otis Hood and Phil Frankfeld, *Americans in Spain* (Boston: The Communist Party of New England, n.d.); Roy B. Hudson, *True Americans* (New York: Waterfront Section of the Communist Party, 1939); *The Story of the Abraham Lincoln Battalion* (New York: Friends of the Abraham Lincoln Battalion, n.d.); and Joseph North, *Men in the Ranks* (New York: Friends of the Abraham Lincoln Brigade, 1939).

Several of the American volunteers wrote narratives of their experiences in the war. Some of these were published after their return, and a few were sent home from the battlefields. Of those which appeared in newspapers, the following are the most useful: Hans Amlie, "With the Americans Fighting Fascism," *New York Evening Post,* Feb. 10, 1938; Neils Kruth, "American Boys in Spain," Ithaca *Journal News,* Jan. 20, 1939; Sam Levinger, "War Journal," Columbus *Citizen,* Oct. 4, 5, 6, 7, and 8, 1937; George Poole, "Buffalo Boy Describes War in Spain," Buffalo *News,* Aug. 27 and Sept. 3, 1938, and Syracuse *Post Standard,* Oct. 2, 1938; Frank Rogers, "I Fought for Spain," Chicago *Times,* March, 5, 6, 7, 8, and 9, 1939; and David McKelvy White, "Why Did You Go to Spain to Fight?" Cleveland *Union Leader,* Oct. 21, 24, and 28, 1937.

Similar narratives, though usually more polished in form, appeared in various magazines. They include: Ralph Bates, "Of Legendary Time," *Virginia Quarterly Review,* I (January 1939), 21–36; J. Benet, "Return from Spain," *New Republic,* XCVI (Jan. 5, 1937), 356–357; Judson Briggs, "Painted in Spain," *Direction,* I (October 1938), 18–19; Norman Dorland, "In Franco's Prison Camp," *New Masses,* XXIX (Nov. 22, 1938), 16–17; James Neugass, "Spanish Diary," *New Masses,* XXVII (June 14, 1938), 132–134; Sam Romer, "Personal Notes from Spain," *Socialist Review,* VI (September–October 1938), 4–6; William G. Ryan, "I Fought in Spain with the Abraham Lincoln Battalion to Stop Hitler," *Scribner's Commentator,* XI (December 1941), 7–12; B. Ryerson, "Foreign Volunteer in Spain," *New Republic,* XC (April 21, 1937), 17–19; David McKelvy White,

"With the Lincoln Volunteers," *The Fight,* V (April 1938); "With the International Brigade," *Nation,* CXLIV (May 8, 1937), 531–32. An account by Lou Ornitz, published in pamphlet form, *Captured by Franco* (New York: Friends of the Abraham Lincoln Brigade, 1939) overstates the brutality in a Franco prison but provides details on prison life. Similar narratives—such as Harold Smith, "Action at Brunete," and Irving Fajans, "Tourists to Lyons," to name just two—turn up in Alvah Bessie (ed.), *The Heart of Spain* (New York: Veterans of the Abraham Lincoln Brigade, 1952), an important collection of materials on the war.

Among the thousands of articles by professional writers on the Spanish War, only a few are useful for the Lincolns. They are: Louis Fischer, "Madrid's Foreign Defenders," *Nation,* CXLV (Sept. 4, 1937), 235–237; Martha Gellhorn, "Men Without Medals," *Collier's,* CI (Jan. 15, 1938), 9–10; Ernest Hemingway, "The Spanish War," *Fact,* No. 16 (July 15, 1936); Josephine Herbst, "Evening in Spain," *The Fight,* V (November 1937) and "The Starched Blue Sky of Spain," *Noble Savage,* I (March 1960), 34–56; "The Lincoln Battalion in Pictures," *New Masses,* XXX (Feb. 14, 1939).

A number of publications that appeared in Spain during the war provide a variety of writings both by the volunteers and about them. The best of these is *Volunteer for Liberty,* the official newspaper of the XVth Brigade, which was published more or less weekly. Under the same title its press run was reproduced and bound in a volume by the VALB in 1954. Also important (but difficult to locate) are the *News-Bulletin of the International Brigades* and *Our Fight,* a newssheet often mimeographed in the trenches. (Some issues of these are available in the New York Public Library collections mentioned below.) Several personal narratives appear in *The Book of the XVth Brigade* (Madrid: Commissariat of War, International Brigades, 1938), which also contains pieces by brigade officials on the course and state of the war.

Newspapers are an important source for a study of the Lincolns, especially those from small communities which often contain detailed information about local sons who left for the Spanish conflict. Such papers are also often a source of letters written home to families. Fortunately for the historian, during the war someone had the foresight to clip articles from a vast number of publications, and this invaluable collection is now on microfilm in the New York Public Library. It is catalogued as Veterans of the Abraham Lincoln Brigade, Inc., *Collection of Newspaper Clippings on the Spanish Civil War, International Brigades, Veterans of the Abraham Lincoln Brigade, Fascism, Spain, etc., 1937–1947.* Also important are two large miscellaneous collections, much of the material brought back by men from Spain, and including some rare bulletins produced on the battlefields. Both are catalogued under VALB, Inc. They are titled: *A Collection of Material Relating to the Spanish Civil War, International Brigades and the Abraham Lincoln Brigade, 1936–1948* (7 sections) and *Spain and the Spanish Civil War; a miscellaneous collection of scattered issues of periodicals gathered by the Veterans of the Abraham Lincoln Brigade* (3 vols.).

Unpublished sources on the Lincoln Battalion are difficult to find, but I was fortunate enough to come across some very important ones. Alvah Bessie's "Spanish Notebooks," a typescript copy of the four notebooks in which he kept his diary, is excellent and contains observations that do not appear in his published works. The notebooks are still in Bessie's keeping. Just as important are Edwin Rolfe's papers, which include a large number of letters to his wife, a "Spanish Diary" kept in various notebooks he carried with him in Spain, and other miscellanea. All these papers are in the possession of his widow, Mrs. Mary Rolfe. Useful too is David McKelvy White's "Sketch for a Journal—1937," an account of what he saw and experienced in Spain, handwritten just before his repatriation to America and now in the keeping of the VALB. A small collection of letters by a well-traveled seaman, Moishe Fishman, to his sister, is good for contrasting Spain before and during the war. Another valuable source is Herbert Matthews's "Originals of dispatches on the Spanish Revolution, sent to the New York *Times*, 1936–1939" (Columbia University Journalism Library). Made up of 2 huge volumes of Matthews's work before it was cut and edited for inclusion in the newspaper, these articles contain much information about the Americans available nowhere else.

Important to my study of the Lincolns were more than 20 interviews with veterans of the war. All of these were lengthy, and some took as long as a day to complete. While most veterans did not mind being named and quoted, a number felt that for personal reasons it would be unwise to identify themselves publicly with the Spanish Civil War again; they appear in footnotes under "confidential interviews." The use of such sources in a historical work presents certain problems. Basically, one is skeptical about how accurately a man can remember events a quarter of a century after they have occurred. There is no easy answer to this. It was my experience that some individuals remembered things quite well while others remembered very little. Some even remembered things which never happened. In spite of this, the interviews were worthwhile. Because I had information from a variety of sources, I was able carefully to evaluate what was told to me. Sometimes interviews helped to fill out details of sketchy events or provided important insights unavailable elsewhere. For example, no longer now as emotionally involved in the cause, many veterans were willing to talk about negative aspects of their experiences in Spain that rarely turn up in publications of the thirties (though such information does get into diaries and letters). Some of my knowledge of minor dissension in the ranks, complaints over CP control, and incidents of "terror" arose from such interviews. In short, while interviews by themselves would be close to worthless, I found that when combined with other sources they were a considerable help in forming a well-rounded picture of the battalion.

Unfortunately, interviewees could not be selected by any sort of scientific sampling technique; rather, I talked with those veterans I could find. However, they did come from a wide variety of professions (seamen, longshoremen, painters, writers, and students); were from a wide geographical area (New York, California, Washington, Wisconsin, Michigan); and included Protestants, Catholics, and Jews, and men from wealthy, middle-class, and working-class families. So in a rough way they can be considered at least representative of the volunteers.

For the postwar period, many of the sources are located in the New York Public Library. Catalogued under VALB, Inc., these include a number of volumes of press releases, proceedings from VALB conventions, mimeographed reports, news bulletins, and other miscellanea. Valuable, too, are the postwar issues of the *Volunteer for Liberty*, and several volumes of clippings on the VALB, all of which can be found in the VALB national office in New York City.

Notes

Chapter I

1. ... s, *The Spanish Civil War* (New York: Harper and Brothers, 1961), p... Robert G. Colodny, *The Struggle for Madrid* (New York: Paine-Whit... 958), p. 64.

2. Arturo ... a, *The Clash* (London: Faber and Faber, 1946), p. 195. A discussion of the b...gades' role in "saving" Madrid can be found in Verle B. Johnston, *Legions of Babel* (University Park, Pa.: The Pennsylvania State University Press, 1967), p. 56 and p. 171, n. 40. See also Jesus Perez Salas, *Guerra en España* (Mexico: n.p., 1947), p. 128.

3. Dante Puzzo, *Spain and the Great Powers, 1936–1941* (New York: Columbia University Press, 1962), pp. 67–69; Gabriel Jackson, *The Spanish Republic and the Civil War, 1931–1939* (Princeton, N.J.: Princeton University Press, 1965), pp. 248–249.

4. William Land Kleine-Ahlbrandt, *The Policy of Simmering* (The Hague: Martinus Nijhoff, 1962), pp. 14–25; Jackson, *The Spanish Republic,* pp. 254–255.

5. George Orwell, *Homage to Catalonia* (Boston: The Beacon Press, 1952), p. 48.

6. Quoted in Thomas, *Spanish Civil War,* p. 325.

7. Randolfo Pacciardi, quoted in Colodny, *Struggle for Madrid,* p. 177, n. 82.

8. Thomas, *Spanish Civil War,* pp. 239–240; Colodny, *Struggle for Madrid,* p. 60; Luis Maria de Lojendio, *Operaciones Militares de la Guerra de España, 1936–1939* (Barcelona: Montanez y Simon, 1940), p. 177; Pietro Nenni, *La guerre d'Espagne* (Paris: Maspero, 1960), p. 161.

9. Stephen Spender and John Lehman (eds.), *Poems for Spain* (London: The Hogarth Press, 1939), p. 57.

10. Allen Guttmann, *The Wound in the Heart: America and the Spanish Civil War* (New York: The Free Press of Glencoe, 1962), p. 82.

11. Quoted in Daniel Aaron, *Writers on the Left* (New York: Harcourt, Brace and World, 1961), pp. 343–344.

12. John Gates, *The Story of an American Communist* (New York: Thomas Nelson and Sons, 1958), p. 41; Bill Bailey, interview at San Francisco, July 9, 1964.

13. *New York Times*, Aug. 16, 1936; Franz Borkenau, *The Spanish Cockpit* (London: Faber and Faber, 1937), p. 73; Johnston, *Legions of Babel*, p. 159, n. 29; Hugh Taylor Lovin, "The American Communist Party and the Spanish Civil War, 1936–1939" (Seattle: University of Washington, unpublished Ph.D. dissertation, 1963), p. 155; *New York World Telegram*, July 12, 1937; *Daily Worker*, Oct. 19, 1936.

14. Louis Fischer, *Men and Politics* (New York: Duell, Sloan & Pearce, 1941), pp. 386–401.

15. *Los Angeles Times*, Dec. 23, 1936; Herbert Matthews, *Two Wars and More to Come* (New York: Carrick and Evans, 1938), p. 221; Gates, *American Communist*, p. 41; Bailey interview; Jack Lucid, interview at San Francisco, July 14, 1964.

16. Edwin Rolfe, *The Lincoln Battalion* (New York: Random House, 1939), pp. 18–26; *Volunteer for Liberty*, Nov. 7, 1938.

17. Colodny, *Struggle for Madrid*, pp. 92–106.

18. Sandor Voros, *American Commissar* (Philadelphia, Pa.: Chilton Company, 1961), pp. 348–354; Rolfe, *Lincoln Battalion*, pp. 26–30; Commissariat of War, XVth Brigade, *The Book of the XVth Brigade* (Madrid: Commissariat of War, International Brigades, 1938), pp. 70–71.

19. Colodny, *Struggle for Madrid*, pp. 106–122; Tom Wintringham, ~~~~~~~~~ *tain* (London: Faber and Faber, 1939), p. 151.

20. Jack Kalleborn letter, April 21, 1937, in Marcel Acier (ed.), *From Spanish Trenches* (New York: Modern Age, 1937), p. 174.

21. *Ibid.*, pp. 174–175; Rolfe, *Lincoln Battalion*, pp. 31–36; *Book of the XVth Brigade*, pp. 67–72; Voros, *American Commissar*, p. 354.

22. Rolfe, *Lincoln Battalion*, p. 36; Voros, *American Commissar*, pp. 354–356; Kalleborn letter, *From Spanish Trenches*, p. 175.

23. Voros, *American Commissar*, p. 356; also, confidential interview.

24. Nenni, *La guerre d'Espagne*, p. 176; Matthews, *Two Wars and More to Come*, pp. 223–224.

25. Rolfe, *Lincoln Battalion*, pp. 40–41, 50–52; *Book of the XVth Brigade*, pp. 71–72; Colodny, *Struggle for Madrid*, p. 127.

26. Confidential interview; Robert Kirby is a pseudonym.

27. Vicente Rojo, *España Heroica* (Buenos Aires: Editorial Americalee, 1942), pp. 72–73; Voros, *American Commissar*, p. 358.

28. Neil Wesson, interview at Detroit, July 22, 1964; Voros, *American Commissar*, pp. 359–360; Rolfe, *Lincoln Battalion*, pp. 54–56; *Book of the XVth Brigade*, p. 74; Matthews, *Two Wars and More to Come*, pp. 223–224.

29. Confidential interview; *The Story of the Abraham Lincoln Battalion* (New York: Friends of the Abraham Lincoln Battalion, n.d.), p. 22.

30. Jack Kalleborn letter, March 20, 1937, and Robert Munson Taylor letter, March 6, 1937, in Acier (ed.), *From Spanish Trenches*, pp. 170, 149–50; Ernest Hemingway, preface to Gustav Regler, *The Great Crusade* (New York: Longmans, Green and Co., 1940), p. vii.

   The exact number killed and wounded on this day is not known. Rolfe, *Lincoln Battalion*, p. 57, says 127 were killed and almost 200 wounded. Wintringham, *English Captain*, p. 257, says 120 were killed, 175 wounded, 108 unhurt. Voros, *American Commissar*, p. 362, claims 153 were killed.

Whatever the number, in a battalion of some 400 men this was a slaughter.

31. Hemingway preface in Regler, *Great Crusade*, p. viii; Colodny, *Struggle for Madrid*, p. 127. Pierre Broué and Emile Témime, *La révolution et la guerre d'Espagne* (Paris: Edition de Minuit, 1961), p. 235, call the attack "insane."

32. Rolfe, *Lincoln Battalion*, p. 57 (the official battalion historian) and *Book of the XVth Brigade*, p. 68, both consider the attack decisive in stopping the rebel offensive. But Thomas, *Spanish Civil War*, p. 380, and Nenni, *La guerre d'Espagne*, p. 176, show that it had already been stopped.

33. Constancia de la Mora, *In Place of Splendor* (New York: Harcourt, Brace and Company, 1939), p. 303; Alfredo Kindelán, *Mis Cuadernos de Guerra* (Madrid: Editorial plus ultra, n.d.), p. 122.

34. Confidential interview.

35. Spain, *Las Brigadas Internacionales* (Madrid: Oficina Informativa Española, 1948), p. 99; *Book of the XVth Brigade*, pp. 83-84, 98, 100.

Chapter II

1. Lewiston *Morning Tribune*, Oct. 11, 1937.

2. Murray Kempton, *Part of Our Time* (New York: Simon and Schuster, 1956), p. 5.

3. Mauritz A. Hallgren, *Seeds of Revolt* (New York: Alfred A. Knopf, 1933), pp. 58-59, 148-151, 165-170.

4. Quotes from *ibid.*, pp. 47, 58, and also from Arthur Schlesinger, Jr., *The Crisis of the Old Order* (Boston: Houghton Mifflin, 1957), pp. 204-205, 268.

5. Irving Howe and Lewis Coser, *The American Communist Party* (New York: Praeger, 1962), p. 225.

6. Arthur Schlesinger, Jr., *The Coming of the New Deal* (Boston: Houghton Mifflin, 1959), p. 396.

7. *Ibid.*, pp. 388-396; William Leuchtenberg, *Franklin D. Roosevelt and the New Deal* (New York: Harper & Row, 1963), pp. 106-114.

8. Luther Whiteman and S. L. Lewis, *Glory Roads* (New York: Thomas Y. Crowell Company, 1936), p. 24; Leuchtenberg, *Franklin D. Roosevelt*, p. 181.

9. Arthur Schlesinger, Jr., *The Politics of Upheaval* (Boston: Houghton Mifflin, 1960), pp. 16-28, 42-68, 98-104, 111-123. Quotes from pp. 107, 144.

10. "Season of Death," *To My Contemporaries* (New York: Dynamo, 1936), p. 54.

11. Aaron, *Writers on the Left*, p. 156; Paul Jacobs, *Is Curley Jewish?* (New York: Atheneum, 1965), p. 18.

12. *Part of Our Time*, p. 5.

13. Quoted in Howe and Coser, *American Communist Party*, p. 279.

14. Quoted in Schlesinger, *Politics of Upheaval*, pp. 155, 158. See also Frank A. Warren, III, *Liberals and Communism* (Bloomington, Ind., and London: Indiana University Press, 1966), pp. 50-62.

15. James Wechsler, *The Age of Suspicion* (New York: Random House, 1953), p. 36.

16. Quoted in Schlesinger, *Politics of Upheaval*, pp. 166, 176.

17. Aaron, *Writers on the Left*, p. 152.

18. *Arrow in the Blue* (New York: The Macmillan Company, 1961), p. 283.

19. Quoted in Schlesinger, *Politics of Upheaval*, p. 171. See also Ralph Lord Roy, *Communism and the Churches* (New York: Harcourt, Brace and Company, 1960), pp. 66, 142.

20. *Part of Our Time*, p. 1.

21. Quoted in Howe and Coser, *American Communist Party*, p. 280.

22. Schlesinger, *Politics of Upheaval*, pp. 176–180.

23. Jacobs, *Is Curley Jewish?*, pp. 30–34.

24. Quoted in Howe and Coser, *American Communist Party*, p. 280.

25. The commitment and dedication of the Communists is attested to by all those connected with social movements of the period. Both their friends and enemies agree that CP members were always the hardest working members of whatever organizations they joined.

26. Nathan Glazer, *The Social Basis of American Communism* (New York: Harcourt, Brace & World, 1961), p. 92; Earl Latham, *The Communist Controversy in Washington* (Cambridge, Mass.: Harvard University Press, 1966), p. 57.

27. Gabriel Almond, *The Appeals of Communism* (Princeton, N.J.: Princeton University Press, 1954), pp. 93, 100–102, 256.

28. Howe and Coser, *American Communist Party*, pp. 175–235, cover the third period of the CP. Quote from p. 242.

29. Quoted in Latham, *Communist Controversy*, p. 46.

30. Howe and Coser, *American Communist Party*, pp. 319–387, cover the fourth period, or Popular Front. Quote from p. 331.

31. Granville Hicks, *Where We Came Out* (New York: The Viking Press, 1954), pp. 35–42.

32. Glazer, *Social Basis of American Communism*, p. 154; Aaron, *Writers on the Left*, p. 156; F. Jay Taylor, *The United States and the Spanish Civil War* (New York: Bookman Associates, 1956), p. 136; Bill Bailey interview.

33. Leuchtenberg, *Franklin D. Roosevelt*, pp. 274–276.

34. Gates, *Story of an American Communist*, p. 13; Almond, *Appeals of Communism*, pp. 93, 256; Latham, *Communist Controversy*, p. 60.

35. Howe and Coser, *American Communist Party*, pp. 362–363.

36. Steve Nelson, interview at New York, Aug. 31, 1964; Morris L. Ernst and David Loth, *Report on the American Communist* (New York: Henry Holt, 1952), p. 182; Almond, *Appeals of Communism*, p. 337.

37. Hicks, *Where We Came Out*, p. 48.

38. Thomas, *Spanish Civil War*, pp. 17–110; Jackson, *Spanish Republic and Civil War*, pp. 43–230; Taylor, *United States and Spanish Civil War*, pp. 24–29; Guttmann, *Wound in the Heart*, p. 96.

39. Glazer, *Social Basis of American Communism*, p. 154; Aaron, *Writers on the Left*, p. 31; Guttmann, *Wound in the Heart*, pp. 165, 206.

40. "The Program," in Alan Calmer (ed.), *Salud!* (New York: International Publishers, 1938), p. 37.

41. Orwell, *Homage to Catalonia*, p. 48; Wechsler, *Age of Suspicion*, p. 109.

42. Taylor, *United States and Spanish Civil War*, pp. 80, 163–189.

Chapter III

1. Jack Lucid interview.

2. Subversive Activities Control Board, *Herbert Brownell, Jr., Attorney General of the United States, Petitioner, v. Veterans of the Abraham Lincoln Brigade, Respondent, Recommended Decision by Kathryn McHale, Board Member* (Issued May 18, 1955), p. 23.

3. Jackson, *Spanish Republic and Civil War*, pp. 257, 316; David T. Cattell, *Communism and the Spanish Civil War* (Berkeley and Los Angeles, Calif.: University of California Press, 1956), pp. 70–71.

4. See W. G. Krivitsky, *In Stalin's Secret Service* (New York and London: Harper and Brothers, 1939), p. 93; Thomas, *Spanish Civil War*, pp. 296–297; Puzzo, *Spain and the Great Powers*, p. 139. Franco apologists usually claim Stalin wanted to set up a Communist regime in Spain, while many International Brigaders think the Soviet leader altruistically wanted to save Spanish democracy. Both views seem highly unlikely, and Puzzo, p. 243, is more realistic in suggesting Stalin was interested in having the Western powers rejoin him in a system of collective security against the fascist countries.

5. Jackson, *Spanish Republic and Civil War*, p. 258.

6. Wintringham, *English Captain*, p. 276; Borkenau, *Spanish Cockpit*, p. 165; Thomas, *Spanish Civil War*, pp. 248, 293, 297. Johnston, *Legions of Babel*, pp. 33–39, discusses the formation of the brigades and says the Spanish government was presented with a *fait accompli* by the Communists.

7. Quote from Fischer, *Men and Politics*, p. 384. See also Cattell, *Communism and the Spanish Civil War*, p 82.

8. Lovin, "The American Communist Party," p. 161.

9. *Ibid.*, p. 192; *New York Times*, Dec. 22 and 27, 1936, and Jan. 17, 1937; Arthur H. Landis, *The Abraham Lincoln Brigade* (New York: The Citadel Press, 1967), pp. 19–20.

10. *In Place of Splendor*, p. 303.

11. Earl Browder, "The People's Front Moves Forward," *The Communist*, XVI (December 1937), 1082; Lovin, "American Communist Party," pp. 182–192.

12. *Daily Worker*, April 17 and May 1, 1937; *New Masses*, XXIII (April 27, 1937), 21; Guttmann, *Wound in the Heart*, pp. 182–184.

13. James Hawthorne, "The Yanks Under Fire in Spain," and An Anti-Fascist Volunteer, "American Fighters in Spain," both in *New Masses*, XXIII (May 4, 1937), 8–9, and XXIII (April 6, 1937), 11–12.

14. "In Memoriam, Ben Leider," *New Masses*, XXII (March 16, 1937), 6.

15. Lovin, "American Communist Party," pp. 173–175

16. *Masters of Deceit* (New York: Pocket Books, 1959), pp. 65–66.

17. *The Dove*, XII (Oct. 20, 1937). This issue of the University of Kansas "liberal journal of discussion" is devoted largely to Don Henry's exploits. See also Robert W. Iversen, *The Communists and the Schools* (New York: Harcourt, Brace, 1959), p. 144.

18. Edwin Rolfe, "Spanish Diary." This is a collection of notebooks kept by the author during his time in Spain, now among his papers owned by his widow. Similar complaints by men who claim they were forced into the army in Spain were made to the American consul in Valencia. See Department

of State, *Foreign Relations of the United States, Diplomatic Papers, 1937*, Vol. I (Washington, D.C.: Government Printing Office, 1954), pp. 495–496.

19. Iversen, *Communists and the Schools*, p. 144; Kempton, *Part of Our Time*, p. 313; Department of State, *Foreign Relations, 1937*, Vol. I, p. 232; Gates, *Story of an American Communist*, p. 41; Edward Robel letter, in Lewiston *Tribune*, Aug. 15, 1937.

20. Puzzo, *Spain and the Great Powers*, pp. 139–140; Howe and Coser, *American Communist Party*, p. 32.

21. *Nation*, CXLIV (Feb. 13, 1937), 172; *Life*, IV (March 28, 1938), 57.

22. Vincent Sheean, *Not Peace But a Sword* (New York: Doubleday, Doran, 1939), p. 259.

Chapter IV

1. Adolfo Lizon Gadea, *Brigadas Internacionales en España* (Madrid: Editoria Nacional, 1940), p. 73; Joseph North, *Men in the Ranks* (New York: Friends of the Abraham Lincoln Battalion, 1939), pp. 37, 40, 42.

2. Bridgeport *Telegram*, June 21, 1938; Oklahoma City *Times*, May 11, 1938.

3. Pittsburgh *Courier*, Jan. 14, 1939; *New York Evening Post*, Nov. 26, 1939; Columbus *Citizen*, Oct. 12, 1937; North, *Men in the Ranks*, p. 20; Landis, *Abraham Lincoln Brigade*, p. 137.

4. Murdo (S. D.), *Coyote*, Nov. 11, 1938; *Let Freedom Ring* (Los Angeles: Friends of the Abraham Lincoln Brigade, n.d.); New Orleans *Tribune*, April 29, 1938.

5. Sheean, *Not Peace But a Sword*, pp. 237–270; *Volunteer for Liberty*, May 25, 1938; Ring Lardner, Jr., "Somebody Had to Do Something," in Alvah Bessie (ed.), *The Heart of Spain* (New York: Veterans of the Abraham Lincoln Brigade, 1952), pp. 327–332.

6. From this point, all estimates of numbers of men in various occupational, residential, and ethnic groups are my own. To see how they were arrived at, consult Appendix A.

7. Schlesinger, *Coming of the New Deal*, p. 396.

8. *Volunteer for Liberty*, Sept. 17, 1938.

9. Roy B. Hudson, *True Americans* (New York: Waterfront Section, Communist Party of New York, 1939), pp. 8–11, puts the number at 500. Joe Curran, NMU organizer, claimed more than 800 seamen were in Spain. See New Orleans *Statesman*, Oct. 31, 1937.

10. Glazer, *Social Basis of American Communism*, p. 120; Donald Thayer and Ben Sills, interviews at San Francisco, July 9, 1964; Archie Brown, interview at San Francisco, July 13, 1964; Hudson, *True Americans*, p. 7; Lovin, "The American Communist Party," p. 197.

11. Bailey interview.

12. "I Fought for Spain," Chicago *Times*, March 2, 1939.

13. Joseph Leeds, *Let My People Know: The Story of Wilfred Mendelson ("Mendy")* ([?] New York: published by his friends, 1942), p. 26. Thayer interview; Kempton, *Part of Our Time*, pp. 313, 320; Iversen, *Communists and the Schools*, p. 143.

14. Louisville *Courier-Journal*, Nov. 18, 1938; Rochester *Democrat and Globe*, June

18, 1938; Lincoln *State Journal*, Dec. 3, 1938; Steve Nelson, *The Volunteers* (New York: Masses and Mainstream, 1953), p. 161; Philadelphia *Evening Bulletin*, May 4, 1938; Atlanta *Journal*, Nov. 29, 1938.

15. Columbus *Citizen*, Oct. 4, 1937; Kempton, *Part of Our Time*, p. 316; Rolfe, *Lincoln Battalion*, p. 73.

16. *Daily Worker*, Jan. 31, 1939; *WPA Teachers in Spain* (New York; WPA Teachers Union Chapter of the Friends of the Abraham Lincoln Battalion, 1938), p. 3; *New York Post*, Oct. 19, 1937; Hagerstown *Herald*, Oct. 18, 1938; Lewiston (Idaho) *Journal*, July 17, 1938; *Two Years of American Aid to Spain* (New York: Medical Bureau of North American Committee to Aid Spanish Democracy, n.d.); *Daily Racing Form*, June 25, 1957; Camden *Courier*, Feb. 25 and Aug. 1, 1939.

17. Angna Enters, "Spain and the Artist," *New Masses*, XXII (Jan. 5, 1937), 7–8.

18. Addison Star Keeler of Laguna Beach, California, and Bill Miller, of Grand Island, Oregon, seem to have been men of this sort. See Los Angeles *Daily News*, June 2, 1938, and Salem *Statesman*, Nov. 13, 1937.

19. Aaron, *Writers on the Left*, pp. 156–157.

20. Alvah Bessie, *Men in Battle* (New York: Charles Scribner's Sons, 1939), p. 182; Edwin Rolfe, "Letter for One in Russia," "Kentucky," and "Credo," all from *To My Contemporaries*, pp. 26–27, 23–25, 1.

21. Landis, *Lincoln Brigade*, p. 73, gives the figures as 60 to 80.

22. Walter Garland, quoted in Guttmann, *Wound in the Heart*, p. 100; *People's World*, Feb. 9, 1938; Glazer, *Social Basis of American Communism*, p. 180.

23. Chillicothe (Ohio) *Gazette*, Sept. 22, 1937; Nelson, *The Volunteers*, p. 161; Brooklyn *Eagle*, March 24, 1938; *Daily Worker*, Sept. 12, 1937.

24. *Life*, IV (March 28, 1938), 57; Glazer, *Social Basis of American Communism*, pp. 167–168.

25. Nelson, *The Volunteers*, p. 97; Sheldon Jones letter, March 4, 1937, in Acier (ed.), *From Spanish Trenches*, p. 146; Oklahoma City *Oklahoman*, July 30, 1938; Evansville *Courier*, Sept. 13, 1938.

26. Voros, *American Commissar*, pp. 317–320; confidential interview.

27. Hartford *Times*, Jan. 31, 1939; Lovin, "American Communist Party," pp. 194–195.

28. Herbert Matthews, *The Yoke and the Arrows* (New York: George Braziller, 1957), p. 30; Johnston, *Legions of Babel*, p. 93; U.S. House of Representatives, 76th Cong., 3rd Sess., *Investigations of Un-American Propaganda Activities in the United States; Hearings Before a Special Committee on Un-American Activities* (Washington, D.C.: Government Printing Office, 1938), Vol. I, p. 372; *New York Post*, Feb. 7, 1938.

29. In all my research I have found only one person who mentioned Spain as a means of hurrying the day of revolution, and that was Communist Archie Brown. Other ex-party members disagree with him.

30. Lovin, "American Communist Party," pp. 204–206; Gates, *Story of an American Communist*, pp. 1–13; Steve Nelson interview. Voros, *American Commissar*, p. 271, says he was sent to Spain, too, and he mentions a couple of others who were.

31. Saul Wellman, interview at Detroit, July 23, 1964, and confidential interview.

32. Duluth *News Tribune*, Sept. 3, 1938; Bayonne *Times*, May 17, 1938; *Life*, IV (March 28, 1938), 57; James Benet, "Return," *New Republic*, XCVI (Nov. 2, 1938), 356–357; Detroit *News*, Nov. 11, 1938; . . . *from the cradle of liberty . . . to the tomb of fascism* (Philadelphia, Pa.: The Communist Party of Eastern Pennsylvania, 1938), p. 8; Chillicothe (Ohio) *Gazette*, Sept. 22, 1937.

33. *Two Wars and More to Come*, pp. 17–18.

34. *People's World*, July 2, 1938; Leeds, *Let My People Know*; Joe Dallet, *Letters from Spain* (New York: Workers Library, 1938); Irving Goff, interview at Los Angeles, May 6, 1964; Brown interview; confidential interview. John Richard is a pseudonym.

35. *Not Peace But a Sword*, p. 267.

36. Kempton, *Part of Our Time*, pp. 313–314; Bessie, *Men in Battle*, p. 181.

37. Leon David letter, April 28, 1937, in Acier (ed.), *From Spanish Trenches*, p. 166.

38. Voros, *American Commissar*, pp. 344–348, is the main source. See also Rolfe, *Lincoln Battalion*, pp. 9–10; Fischer, *Men and Politics*, p. 382; *Volunteer for Liberty*, Dec. 13, 1937.

39. "To My Contemporaries," *To My Contemporaries*, pp. 59–64.

Chapter V

1. Subversive Activities Control Board, *Herbert Brownell . . .*, pp. 20–29; Krivitsky, *In Stalin's Secret Service*, p. 94.

2. Philadelphia *Evening Public Ledger*, Jan. 25, 1938; Detroit *Times*, Feb. 7, 1940.

3. Mike Goodwin, interview at Los Angeles, May 7, 1964; Gabby Klein, interview at Los Angeles, April 20, 1964; Brooklyn *Eagle*, Aug. 22, 1937.

4. Edwin Rolfe, letters to his wife, June 7 and 13, 1937; Wilfred Mendelson, letter, in Leeds, *Let My People Know*, p. 52.

5. Goodwin, Nelson interviews; Gates, *Story of an American Communist*, p. 43; Nelson, *The Volunteers*, pp. 22–23.

6. Rolfe, letter to his wife, June 16, 1937; Irving Fajans, "Tourists to Lyon," in Bessie (ed.), *The Heart of Spain*, pp. 149–150; Bessie, *Men in Battle*, p. 5; George Poole, "Buffalo Boy Describes War in Spain," Buffalo *News*, Aug. 27, 1938.

7. Fajans, "Tourists to Lyon," pp. 151–152; Bessie, *Men in Battle*, pp. 6–10; Samuel Levinger, letter to his mother, in Columbus *Citizen*, Oct. 4, 1937.

8. Poole, "Buffalo Boy Describes War . . ."; Thayer interview.

9. Matthews, *Two Wars and More to Come*, p. 229, and Rolfe, *Lincoln Battalion*, p. 84, both say 12 Americans were drowned; Voros, *American Commissar*, p. 307, puts the number at 50. Testifying to the HUAC, Abraham Sobel, who was on board ship, said 30 Americans drowned. See House of Representatives, 76th Cong., 3rd Sess., *Investigation of Un-American Propaganda Activities*, Vol. I, p. 736. The American consul at Barcelona said "over fifty." See Department of State, *Foreign Relations, 1937*, Vol. I, p. 516. It is obvious that nobody really knows how many Americans perished on the *Ciudad de Barcelona*.

10. Dallet, *Letters from Spain*, pp. 1–26; Nelson, *The Volunteers*, pp. 34–64; Department of State, *Foreign Relations, 1937*, Vol. I, pp. 499–502, 504–505.

11. Department of State, *Foreign Relations, 1937*, Vol. I, pp. 502–510.

12. Nelson, *The Volunteers*, pp. 69–70; Klein interview.

13. Details on hike from the following: Bessie, *Men in Battle*, pp. 18–24; Nelson, *The Volunteers*, pp. 70–77; Dallet, *Letters from Spain*, pp. 27–28; Rolfe, letter to his wife, June 20, 1937; Neils Kruth, "American Boys in Spain," Ithaca *Journal News*, Jan. 20, 1939; David McKelvy White, "Sketch for a Journal —Spain 1937."

14. Kruth, "American Boys"; Bessie, *Men in Battle*, p. 24.

15. Poole, "Buffalo Boy Describes War . . ."

16. Dallet, *Letters from Spain*, pp. 29–31; Rolfe, letter to his wife, June 20, 1937. Also Alvah Bessie, "Spanish Notebooks," typescript copy of the notebooks Bessie used as a diary in Spain, still in his possession.

17. Samuel Levinger, "War Journal," Columbus *Citizen*, Oct. 5 and 6, 1937; Bessie, *Men in Battle*, pp. 35–45; Nat Turner letter, April 25, 1937, in *Let Freedom Ring*; Dallet, *Letters from Spain*, p. 33; Mendelson letter, in Leeds, *Let My People Know*, pp. 49–50; White, "Sketch for a Journal."

18. Bessie, "Spanish Notebooks"; Poole, "Buffalo Boy Describes War . . ."

19. Krivitsky, *In Stalin's Secret Service*, p. 95, claims the documents ended up in Russia, whose government used them for purposes of international spying.

20. Confidential interview.

21. Poole, "Buffalo Boy Describes War . . ."; Bessie, "Spanish Notebooks"; Louis Fischer, "Madrid's Foreign Defenders," *Nation*, CXLV (Sept. 4, 1937), 235–237; Dallet, *Letters from Spain*, pp. 54–59; Frank Rogers, "I Fought for Spain," Chicago *Times*, March 7, 1939; Rolfe, letter to his wife, July 2, 1937; Levinger, "War Journal," Columbus *Citizen*, Oct. 7, 1937; White, "Sketch for a Journal." Also Edwin Rolfe, "Training Notebook," a small notebook carried by Rolfe during his time in Tarazona; in it he took notes in his various classes.

22. Confidential, Goodwin and Thayer interviews.

23. Bessie, *Men in Battle*, pp. 64–65; Goodwin interview.

24. Gates, *Story of an American Communist*, p. 29; Nelson, *The Volunteers*, pp. 59–60; Voros, *American Commissar*, pp. 338–343.

25. Archie Kessner letter, Aug. 31, 1937, in *Let Freedom Ring*; Bessie, *Men in Battle*, p. 67; Poole, "Buffalo Boy Describes War . . ."

26. Bessie, *Men in Battle*, p. 62; Rogers, "I Fought for Spain"; Rolfe, letter to his wife, July 12, 1937.

27. Bessie, *Men in Battle*, pp. 73–77; Levinger, "War Journal," Columbus *Citizen*, Oct. 8, 1937.

Chapter VI

1. Charley O'Flaherty letter, n.d., in Acier (ed.), *From Spanish Trenches*, p. 141; *Book of the XVth Brigade*, p. 98.

2. Landis, *Abraham Lincoln Brigade*, pp. 120–123, 161–162; Towanda (Pa.) *Review*, March 8, 1939; *Las Brigadas Internacionales*, p. 100.

3. Thomas, *Spanish Civil War*, pp. 381–388, 424–429; Jackson, *Spanish Republic and Civil War*, pp. 351–352, 369–370; Broué and Témime, *La révolution et la guerre*, pp. 358–366; Orwell, *Homage to Catalonia*, pp. 121–179.

4. Josephine Herbst, "The Starched Blue Sky of Spain," *The Noble Savage* 1

(1960), 86; Ralph Bates, "Of Legendary Time," *Virginia Quarterly Review*, I (January, 1937), 321–322; Ed Erik letter, April 26, 1937, Ed O'Flaherty letter, n.d., and "Hank" letter, March 28, 1937, in Acier (ed.), *From Spanish Trenches*, pp. 153, 142, 154.

5. *Book of the XVth Brigade*, p. 98; Matthews, *Two Wars and More to Come*, pp. 225–226.

6. George Seldes in *New York Post*, April 16, 1937; *New York Times*, May 24, 1937; Virginia Cowles, *Looking for Trouble* (New York and London: Harper & Brothers, 1941), p. 43.

7. Nelson, *The Volunteers*, pp. 98, 106–108; Landis, *Abraham Lincoln Brigade*, p. 166; "Hank" letter, in Acier (ed.), *From Spanish Trenches*, p. 155.

8. *Book of the XVth Brigade*, p. 184; Rolfe, *Lincoln Battalion*, p. 71; Nelson interview; Voros, *American Commissar*, pp. 270–271.

9. Nelson interview; also his book, *The Volunteers*, pp. 105–113.

10. Julio Alvarez del Vayo, *Freedom's Battle* (New York: Alfred A. Knopf, 1940), p. 126; Mijail Koltsov, *Diario de la guerra de España* (Switzerland: Ruedo Iberico, 1963), p. 142; Gates, *Story of an American Communist*, p. 47.

11. W. G. Krivitsky and David T. Cattell both hold the theory that commissars kept the army under Communist domination, but neither examined the way in which commissars worked. The full range of activities by commissars will become apparent during the course of this book.

12. New York *Herald Tribune*, May 3, 1938; Dallet, *Letters from Spain*, pp. 45, 42; "A New Situation—New Tasks," *Bulletin of the Political Commissars of the International Brigades* (English edn.), No. 3 (September 1937), 6–8. A discussion of International Brigade commissars can be found in Johnston, *Legions of Babel*, pp. 99–106. It supplements the description given here.

13. Broué and Témime, *La révolution et la guerre*, p. 357; "Bureaucracy and the Commissar," *Bulletin of the Commissars*, No. 3, 16–17; Wellman interview.

14. "The Fifth Column," *Bulletin of the Commissars*, No. 3, 14; also No. 4 (October–November 1937), 24–25.

15. Dallet, *Letters from Spain*, p. 36; Nelson, Sills interviews.

16. "Plan of Short Courses for Political Delegates," *Bulletin of the Commissars*, No. 4, 30–32; Nelson, Lucid interviews; New York *Herald Tribune*, May 3, 1938; John Dollard, *Fear in Battle* (New Haven, Conn.: Yale University, 1943), pp. 66–68.

17. Nelson, *The Volunteers*, pp. 118–120.

18. Bates, "Of Legendary Time," p. 324.

19. Johnston, *Legions of Babel*, pp. 81–82; Rolfe, *Lincoln Battalion*, p. 76.

20. Rolfe, *Lincoln Battalion*, p. 71; Nelson, *The Volunteers*, pp. 122–127; *New Masses*, XXIV (Sept. 7, 1937), 2; Milly Bennett, "Americans Fight in Spain," San Francisco *Chronicle*, March 20, 1938.

21. Steve Nelson, "In a Spanish Town," *The Fight* (June 1937), 22; Nelson, *The Volunteers*, p. 144.

Chapter VII

1. Voros, *American Commissar*, pp. 328–331.

2. Thomas, *Spanish Civil War*, pp. 299–301.

3. Landis, *Lincoln Brigade*, pp. 138–144; confidential interview.

4. Goff interview; Landis, *Lincoln Brigade*, p. 490.

5. Voros, *American Commissar*, pp. 321–323; Rolfe, *Lincoln Battalion*, pp. 85–87.

6. Nelson, *The Volunteers*, pp. 82–83. After being repatriated home, Gordon volunteered and returned to Spain again in the spring of 1938, one of half a dozen men to do so.

7. *Ibid.*, pp. 88–89.

8. Fischer, *Men and Politics*, p. 374.

9. Confidential interview.

10. Goodwin interview; Dallet, *Letters from Spain*, p. 62.

11. Found in the papers of Edwin Rolfe.

12. Confidential interview.

13. Bessie, "Spanish Notebooks."

Chapter VIII

1. Johnston, *Legions of Babel*, pp. 116–117.

2. Herbert Matthews, "Originals of dispatches on the Spanish Revolution, sent to the New York *Times*, 1936–1939," July 4, 1937, dispatch; *New York Evening Post*, Feb. 7, 1938; White, "Sketch for a Journal."

3. Wesson interview; Henry Eaton letters, July 15 and Aug. 6, 1937, in *Let Freedom Ring*; Nelson, *The Volunteers*, pp. 144–145.

4. David McKelvy White letter, in Cleveland *Press*, Aug. 10, 1937.

5. Nelson, *The Volunteers*, pp. 146–148; Matthews, "Dispatches," July 15, 1937.

6. Eaton letters, July 15 and Aug. 6, 1937, and Francis Feingersh letter, July 10, 1937, in *Let Freedom Ring; Letters from the Trenches from Our Boys in Spain* (New York: Workers Alliance of New York, n.d.), pp. 27–28.

7. Thomas, *Spanish Civil War*, p. 462; Wesson interview; White, "Sketch for a Journal."

8. Harold Smith, "Action at Brunete," in Bessie (ed.), *Heart of Spain*, pp. 181–185.

9. Manuel Aznar, *Historia Militar de la Guerra de España* (3rd edn., Madrid: Editoria Nacional, 1961), Vol. II, p. 210.

10. Matthews, "Dispatches," July 15, 1937; Rolfe, *Lincoln Battalion*, p. 92; Smith, "Action at Brunete," p. 187.

11. De Lojendio, *Operaciones Militares*, p. 340; Julian Zugazagoitia, *Historia de la Guerra en España* (Buenos Aires: La Vanguardia, 1940), p. 305.

12. Nelson, *The Volunteers*, p. 150; White, "Sketch for a Journal."

13. Rolfe, *Lincoln Battalion*, p. 95; . . . *from the cradle of liberty*, p. 20; Judson Briggs, "Painted in Spain," *Direction*, I (October 1938), 18–19.

14. Nelson, *The Volunteers*, p. 157; Matthews, "Dispatches," July 14, 1937.

15. . . . *from the cradle of liberty*, p. 24; White letter in Cleveland *Press*, Aug. 10, 1937, and Bessie (ed.), *Heart of Spain*, pp. 211–217; Eaton letter, Aug. 6, 1937, in *Let Freedom Ring*.

16 Rolfe, *Lincoln Battalion*, pp. 96–97; *Book of the XVth Brigade*, p. 160.

17. Rojo, *España Heroica*, p. 108; Kindelán, *Mis Cuadernos de Guerra*, p. 98; De Lojendio, *Operaciones Militares*, p. 242; Rolfe, *Lincoln Battalion*, pp. 99–105; White, "Sketch for a Journal."

18. Nelson interview; Landis, *Lincoln Brigade*, pp. 231–233; White, "Sketch for a Journal."

19. Thomas, *Spanish Civil War*, p. 464; Johnston, *Legions of Babel*, pp. 120–121; *Book of the XVth Brigade*, p. 130; Nelson, *The Volunteers*, pp. 173–174.

Chapter IX

1. Rolfe, *Lincoln Battalion*, pp. 107–111; Klein, Goodwin interviews; Moishe Fishman, letter to his sister, Nov. 19, 1937.

2. Leo Gratschow letter, in *WPA Teachers in Spain*, p. 32.

3. Letter of June 23, 1938, in Leeds, *Let My People Know*, p. 60.

4. Hank letter, April 12, 1937, in Acier (ed.), *From Spanish Trenches*, p. 161; confidential interview. Fred Weiss is a pseudonym.

5. Dave Doran letter, Dec. 28, 1937, in Joseph Starobin, *The Life and Death of an American Hero* (New York: New Age, 1938), p. 37; Bates, "Of Legendary Time," pp. 321–333; Rolfe, letter to his wife, July 3, 1937.

6. . . . *from the cradle of liberty*, p. 15; Rolfe, letter to his wife, July 3, 1937; Anonymous, "With the International Brigade," *Nation*, CXLIV (May 8, 1937), 531–532.

7. For idealization of the peasant, see Henry Eaton letter, June 15, 1937, in *Let Freedom Ring*, and Dave Doran letter, Aug. 7, 1937, in Starobin, *Life and Death*.

8. Nelson, *The Volunteers*, p. 176.

9. Letter of Aug. 13, 1937, in Bessie (ed.), *Heart of Spain*, pp. 216–217.

10. *Letters from Spain* (San Francisco, Calif.: Friends of the Abraham Lincoln Brigade, 1937), p. 4; Alpheus Prowell and Luchell MacDaniells letters in *People's World*, Feb. 9, 1938.

11. Robert Merriman, undated letter to Edwin Rolfe, found in Rolfe papers; Klein interview.

12. Broué and Témime, *La révolution et la guerre*, p. 382; Thomas, *Spanish Civil War*, pp. 470–471.

13. Nelson, *The Volunteers*, p. 176; Klein interview; Rolfe, *Lincoln Battalion*, pp. 113–114.

14. Nelson, Klein interviews; Rolfe, *Lincoln Battalion*, pp. 114–116; Koltsov, *Diario de la Guerra*, p. 452; "With the Yanks One Night in the Quinto Cemetery," *Our Fight*, XXXIII (September 1937), 4.

15. *Volunteer for Liberty*, Oct. 4, 1937; *Book of the XVth Brigade*, p. 247; Henry Eaton letter, undated, in *Let Freedom Ring*; Gadea, *Brigadas Internacionales*, p. 43.

16. Official information report of General Walter and General Pozas telegram, both in *Volunteer for Liberty*, Sept. 13, 1937; Rolfe, *Lincoln Battalion*, p. 121.

17. Archie Kessner letter, Sept. 13, 1937, in *Let Freedom Ring*; *Book of the XVth Brigade*, p. 261.

18. Nelson, *The Volunteers*, pp. 182–185; De Lojendio, *Operaciones Militares*, p. 354.

19. Carl Bradley, in *Volunteer for Liberty*, Oct. 4, 1937; Aznar, *Historia Militar*, Vol. II, p. 300.

20. Sills interview.

21. *Book of the XVth Brigade*, p. 265; Ernest Hemingway, "The Spanish War," *Fact*, No. 16 (July 15, 1938), 34.

22. Nelson, *The Volunteers*, pp. 186–187; Sills interview.

23. Bailey, Thayer interviews.

24. Matthews, *Two Wars and More to Come*, pp. 302, 306–307; Rojo, *España Heroica*, p. 126; Landis, *Lincoln Brigade*, p. 295; *Book of the XVth Brigade*, p. 244.

25. Rojo, *España Heroica*, p. 126; Broué and Témime, *La révolution et la guerre*, p. 382. Even Zugazagoitia, who has few good things to say about the Internationals, gives great credit to the troops who took Belchite. See *Historia de la Guerra*, p. 318.

26. Poole, "Buffalo Boy Describes War . . .", Buffalo *News*, Sept. 3, 1938; Edwin Rolfe, letter to his wife, Sept. 4, 1937.

27. Hemingway, "The Spanish War," p. 35; Matthews, *Two Wars and More to Come*, pp. 309–311.

Chapter X

1. "The Spanish War," p. 34.

2. Dollard, *Fear in Battle*, p. 7; Ernest Hemingway, preface to North, *Men in the Ranks*, and introduction to Regler, *Great Crusade*, p. vii; Matthews, "Dispatches," Oct. 2, 1937; Leland Stowe article, newspaper unknown, in Veterans of the Abraham Lincoln Brigade, Inc., *Collection of Newspaper Clippings on the Spanish Civil War* (New York Public Library).

3. Abe Sasson letter, Aug. 14, 1937, in *Let Freedom Ring*; Acier (ed.), *From Spanish Trenches*, pp. 150–151, 167; George Cady, in Syracuse *Herald*, Jan. 8, 1938; Donald Thayer, letter in Milwaukee *Leader*, Oct. 21, 1937; Bessie, *Men in Battle*, p. 108.

4. Lewiston (Idaho) *Journal*, July 17, 1938.

5. Edwin Rolfe, letter to his wife, July 21, 1937; Dollard, *Fear in Battle*, pp. 17, 89; Bessie, "Spanish Notebooks."

6. Wellman interview; Dud Male letter, San Francisco *News*, Jan. 24, 1938.

7. Dollard, *Fear in Battle*, pp. 22–23; *Letters from Spain*, p. 12.

8. Dud Male letter, San Francisco *News*, Jan. 24, 1938.

9. Letter to his wife, Aug. 25, 1937.

10. Stephen Daduk, quoted in *Daily Worker*, July 14, 1937. Complaints about trench life well expressed in George (Kaye?) letter, *People's World*, Aug. 27, 1938.

11. Hank letters, undated and April 14, 1937, in Acier (ed.), *From Spanish Trenches*, pp. 158, 161–162; Edwin Rolfe, letter to his wife, July 2, 1937.

12. George (Kaye?) letter, *People's World*, Aug. 27, 1938; Edwin Rolfe, letter to his wife, Sept. 22, 1937.

13. George Kaye letter, Oct. 21, 1937, in *Let Freedom Ring*; *Letters from Spain*, p. 2; Earl Lippo letter, . . . *from the cradle of liberty*, p. 8; Dallet, *Letters from Spain*, p. 49.

14. Wellman interview; Leland Stowe article, newspaper unknown, in *Collection of Newspaper Clippings*.

15. *Volunteer for Liberty*, May 1, 1938.

16. *Ibid.*, Dec. 28, 1937, Jan. 12, and May 25, 1938.

17. Edwin Rolfe, letters to his wife, Feb. 11 and June 25, 1938; Bessie, "Spanish Notebooks."

18. Dave Doran letter, Sept. 2, 1937, in Starobin, *Life and Death*, p. 37; Henry Eaton letter, Aug. 6, 1937, in *Let Freedom Ring*; Al (Handler?) letter, . . . *from the cradle of liberty*, p. 17; *Letters from the Trenches from Our Boys*, p. 21; Rolfe, letter to his wife, July 7, 1937.

19. Al (Handler?) letter, . . . *from the cradle of liberty*, p. 17; Edwin Rolfe, letters to his wife, June 6 and Aug. 10, 1938; *Letters from Spain*, pp. 1, 10; Wilfred Mendelson letter, July 17, 1938, in Leeds, *Let My People Know*, p. 77; Dave Doran letter, Dec. 28, 1937, in Starobin, *Life and Death*, p. 37.

20. Bessie, *Men in Battle*, p. 107; Edwin Rolfe, letter to his wife, Sept. 13, 1937.

21. For such deserters, see Chapter XIV.

22. Wilfred Mendelson letter, July 15, 1938, in Leeds, *Let My People Know*, p. 75; Kempton, *Part of Our Time*, p. 318; Dallet, *Letters from Spain*, pp. 56–57.

23. Kenneth Shaker, in Springfield *Morning Union*, Jan. 12, 1938; Rolfe, "Madrid," *Romancero de los Voluntarios de la Libertad* (Madrid: Ediciones del Comisariado de las Brigadas Internacionales, 1937), p. 82.

24. Abe Sasson letter, *People's World*, Aug. 9, 1938; Red Chilton, quoted in Rolfe, "Spanish Diary."

25. Earl Lippo letter, . . . *from the cradle of liberty*, p. 8; Kempton, *Part of Our Time*, p. 316; confidential interview.

CHAPTER XI

1. Poole, "Buffalo Boy Describes War . . .", Buffalo *News*, Sept. 3, 1938; Archie Kessner letters, Sept. 13, Oct. 4, and Oct. 9, 1937, in *Let Freedom Ring*.

2. Two of the battalion's three rifle companies were composed of Americans, and the third was Canadian, while the machine-gun company was mixed. See Rolfe, *Lincoln Battalion*, p. 131.

3. Poole, "Buffalo Boy Describes War . . .", Buffalo *News*, Sept. 3, 1938; Goodwin interview; Landis, *Lincoln Brigade*, p. 310.

4. Landis, *Lincoln Brigade*, p. 315; Voros, *American Commissar*, pp. 341–343; Wellman interview. Wellman was Dallet's assistant, and he took over Dallet's job upon his death.

5. Milo Mikela, "The MacPaps in Action," *Our Fight* (October–November 1937); Archie Kessner letter, Oct. 16, 1937, in *Let Freedom Ring*; Gates, *Story of an American Communist*, p. 51; Aznar, *Historia Militar*, Vol. II, p. 314; Goodwin, Bailey, Sills, and Thayer interviews.

6. Voros, *American Commissar*, pp. 342–343; Mikela, "MacPaps in Action"; Matthews, "Dispatches," February 1938; De Lojendio, *Operaciones Militares*, p. 358; Rolfe, *Lincoln Battalion*, pp. 136–137; Sills, Bailey, and Wellman interviews.

7. Goodwin, Bailey interviews.

8. Goodwin, confidential interviews; Matthews, "Dispatches," Dec. 5, 1937.

9. Martin Sramek, interview at Los Angeles, May 15, 1965; Rolfe, *Lincoln Battalion*, pp. 158–159.

10. George William Lighton letter, Louisville *Courier*, Nov. 18, 1938; Rolfe, "Spanish Diary" and *Lincoln Battalion*, pp. 159–160; Sramek interview.

11. Landis, *Lincoln Brigade*, pp. 336–338; *Volunteer for Liberty*, Dec. 6, 1937.

12. Charles Persily letter, Dec. 22, 1937, in *Let Freedom Ring*; Edwin Rolfe, letters to his wife, Dec. 21 and 25, 1937.

13. Thomas, *Spanish Civil War*, pp. 504–507, says Teruel was held by 4,000 men and attacked by 100,000. Broué and Témime, *La révolution et la guerre*, p. 430, put the figures at 2,500 and 40,000. Other estimates stay within these ranges. Obviously, whatever the exact figures, the Loyalists vastly outnumbered Teruel's defenders.

14. Poole, "Buffalo Boy Describes War . . . ," Syracuse *Post Standard*, Oct. 2, 1938; Rolfe, *Lincoln Battalion*, pp. 160–162.

15. Kindelán, *Mis Cuadernos*, pp. 123–126; Herbert Matthews, *The Education of a Correspondent* (New York: Harcourt, Brace and Company, 1946), p. 96.

16. Landis, *Lincoln Brigade*, p. 364; Matthews, *Education of a Correspondent*, p. 112; Poole, "Buffalo Boy Describes War . . . ," Syracuse *Post Standard* Oct. 2, 1938.

17. Robert Okin, Associated Press dispatch, Dayton *News*, Feb. 11, 1938; Bailey interview; Matthews, "Dispatches," Jan. 13, 1938.

18. Aznar, *Historia Militar*, Vol. II, pp. 399–400; De Lojendio, *Operaciones Militares*, p. 384; Landis, *Lincoln Brigade*, p. 382.

19. Rolfe, *Lincoln Battalion*, p. 172.

20. Poole, "Buffalo Boy Describes War . . . ," Syracuse *Post Standard*, Oct. 2, 1938.

21. Thomas, *Spanish Civil War*, p. 511; De Lojendio, *Operaciones Militares*, pp. 384, 390.

22. Matthews, "Dispatches," March 9, 1938; Sramek interview; Rolfe, *Lincoln Battalion*, pp. 174–176.

23. Thomas, *Spanish Civil War*, p. 515; Broué and Témime, *La révolution et la guerre*, p. 436; De Lojendio, *Operaciones Militares*, p. 393.

24. *People's World*, Feb. 15, 1938.

Chapter XII

1. "Madrid," *Romancero de los Voluntarios*, p. 81.

2. "Remember This," in *ibid.*, p. 53; "Twenty of Us," *Volunteer for Liberty*, Feb. 23, 1938.

3. Sheean, *Not Peace But a Sword*, p. 60; Lorna Lindsley, *War Is People* (Boston: Houghton Mifflin, 1943), p. 52; Fischer, *Men and Politics*, p. 402.

4. Lucid, Wesson, Thayer, and Wellman interviews.

5. *Volunteer for Liberty*, June 15, 1937; *Letters from Spain*, p. 15; *Letters from the Trenches from Our Boys*, p. 2.

6. *Volunteer for Liberty*, Aug. 28 and June 29, 1937.

7. Dallet, *Letters from Spain*, p. 43; *Volunteer for Liberty*, June 8 and Aug. 27, 1937.

8. *Volunteer for Liberty*, Nov. 7, 1938, and Aug. 16, 1937; Rubin Schechter letter, in *Let Freedom Ring*.

9. *Volunteer for Liberty*, Sept. 6 and Nov. 15, 1937.

10. *Ibid.*, June 15 and 29, 1937.

11. Klein interview.

12. *Volunteer for Liberty*, Oct. 25, July 12, June 1, and Oct. 18, 1937.

13. *Story of an American Communist*, pp. 54–56.

14. *Volunteer for Liberty*, June 22, 1937; Edwin Rolfe, letter to his wife, Sept. 4, 1937.

15. Orwell, *Homage to Catalonia*, pp. 51–52; A. J. Muste, *Say That We Saw Spain Die* (Seattle, Wash.: University of Washington Press, 1966), p. 177. In *American Power and the New Mandarins* (New York: Pantheon, 1969), pp. 72–158, Noam Chomsky argues rather convincingly that the Anarchist-POUM policy was more sensible than that of the CP. Even so, his argument does not change the picture of how the war issues appeared to the Lincolns.

16. Georges-Roux, *La guerre civile d'Espagne* (Paris: Arthème Fayard, 1963), p. 214.

17. Orwell, *Homage to Catalonia*, p. 55; Nelson, *The Volunteers*, pp. 127–132, gives the CP view of the Anarchists. Other information on American attitudes toward them from Lucid, Brown, Thayer, and Nelson interviews.

18. Henry Scott Beattie, "Spain: Another View," *Canadian Forum* (April 28, 1938), 454–455.

19. Ernst and Loth, *Report on the American Communist*, pp. 70–71.

20. Ernest Hemingway, *For Whom the Bell Tolls* (Middlesex, England: Penguin Books, 1953), p. 22; "A Year of the International Brigades," *Volunteer for Liberty*, Oct. 11, 1937.

21. *International Brigade News Bulletin*, Dec. 11, 1937; George Kaye letter, Nov. 14, 1937, in *Let Freedom Ring*.

22. *Ben Leider, American Hero* (New York: Ben Leider Memorial Fund, n.d.), p. 13.

23. Nat Turner letter, Oct. 13, 1937, and Henry Eaton letter, June 15, 1937, both in *Let Freedom Ring; Letters from Spain*, p. 14; Matthew Mattison, letter of Sept. 27, 1937, in Manchester (N.H.) *Guardian*, Dec. 7, 1937.

24. Wilfred Mendelson letter, June 25, 1938, in Leeds, *Let My People Know*, p. 62; Jack Kalleborn letter, March 20, 1937, in Acier (ed.), *From Spanish Trenches*, p. 171.

25. Wesson, Thayer interviews.

26. *Homage to Catalonia*, p. 63.

Chapter XIII

1. Landis, *Lincoln Brigade*, p. 407; Rogers, "I Fought for Spain," Chicago *Times*, March 9, 1939.

2. Goodwin interview. Goodwin returned to Madrid on a pleasure trip in 1962.

3. *Ibid.*; Rogers, "I Fought for Spain"; Landis, *Lincoln Brigade*, p. 420.

4. Rolfe, *Lincoln Battalion*, pp. 186–188.

5. Thomas, *Spanish Civil War*, p. 519; Broué and Témime, *La révolution et la guerre*, pp. 438–439; Rojo, *España Heroica*, p. 160. Luigi Gallo, inspector general of the International Brigades, later admitted the panic of many Loyalist troops during this campaign. See *Volunteer for Liberty*, June 30, 1938.

6. Rolfe, *Lincoln Battalion*, pp. 188–198; Matthews, "Dispatches," March 13 and 20, 1938; Voros, *American Commissar*, pp. 387–400.

7. Rojo, *España Heroica*, p. 151.

8. *Ibid.*; Voros, *American Commissar*, pp. 406–407; Landis, *Lincoln Brigade*, p. 433.

9. Thomas, *Spanish Civil War*, p. 524; Bessie, *Men in Battle*, pp. 82–83 and "Spanish Notebooks."

10. *Volunteer for Liberty*, March 17, 21 and 25, 1938; Voros, *American Commissar*, p. 410; Bessie, "Spanish Notebooks."

11. Bessie, "Spanish Notebooks"; Rolfe, *Lincoln Battalion*, pp. 203–206.

12. Landis, *Lincoln Brigade*, p. 448.

13. Bessie, "Spanish Notebooks" and *Men in Battle*, pp. 93–115.

14. Landis, *Lincoln Brigade*, p. 460; Matthews, "Dispatches," April 4, 1938.

15. Bessie, "Spanish Notebooks" and *Men in Battle*, pp. 115–122.

16. Matthews, "Dispatches," April 4 and 11, 1938; Rolfe, *Lincoln Battalion*, pp. 209–213.

17. Landis, *Lincoln Brigade*, p. 469.

18. Rolfe, *Lincoln Battalion*, pp. 213–215; Matthews, "Dispatches," April 4, 9, and 11, 1938; Hemingway dispatch, Minneapolis *Tribune*, April 5, 1938; Hemingway, "Spanish War," p. 55. Details on breakup of Americans can be found in many places. Because the English fought alongside the Americans, their histories are useful. See Wintringham, *English Captain*, p. 307; William Rust, *Britons in Spain* (London: Lawrence and Wishart, 1939), pp. 140–160. For a Spanish source, See Kindelán, *Mis Cuadernos*, p. 127.

CHAPTER XIV

1. See, for example, Associated Press story by Robert Okin, in Springfield *Republican*, April 11, 1938, or United Press story by Irving P. Pflaum in New York *Herald Tribune*, April 10, 1938.

2. *New York Evening Post*, April 7, 1938; *New York Times*, April 8, 1938. By June, Honeycombe's story had changed again, and he claimed 9,000 English and Americans had been in Spain, of whom only 400 were left. See Detroit *Free Press*, June 26, 1938.

3. *Daily Worker*, April 9, 1938; *New York World Telegram*, April 8, 1938; Matthews, "Dispatches," April 9, 1938.

4. New York *Herald Tribune*, April 10, 1938; San Francisco *News*, April 22 and 26, 1938; Philadelphia *Bulletin*, May 30, 1938. For later such stories, see Buffalo *Times*, July 17, 1938, or Milwaukee *Journal*, Nov. 3, 1938.

5. Department of State, *Foreign Relations, 1937*, Vol. I, pp. 482–483, 491–492; Department of State, *Foreign Relations of the United States, Diplomatic Papers, 1938* (Washington, D.C.: Government Printing Office, 1955), Vol. I, pp. 531–534, 278.

6. Thayer, Bailey, and Sills, in their interviews, all insist on "few" desertions, as does Bessie, "Spanish Notebooks." The author has found information on 13 deserters who appeared at consulates and 20 who received publicity after the collapse in Aragón. Some of the latter thought the war was over and had decided to get out of Spain while they could. This total of 33 is about 1 per cent of the volunteers. Undoubtedly there were others, but the number does seem small enough to justify the insistence on "few."

7. Department of State, *Foreign Relations, 1937*, Vol. I, pp. 482–492, 531, 556–557.

8. Seattle *Post Intelligencer,* Aug. 19, 1938.

9. House of Representatives, *Investigation of Un-American Propaganda Activities,* Vol. I, pp. 728–759. Quotes from pp. 737–738, 754, 757. Halpern's incoherence is on p. 757.

10. *Daily Worker,* Aug. 21 and Sept. 11, 1938; *New York Times,* Aug. 21, 1938; Minneapolis *Journal,* Aug. 22, 1938; Cleveland *News,* Aug. 22, 1938.

11. Bailey, Lucid interviews; Rolfe, letter to his wife, June 12, 1938. He wrote similar letters on March 13 and 19, 1938, during the Aragón retreats.

12. Rolfe, letter to his wife, May 24, 1938; Gates, *Story of an American Communist,* p. 55; Matthews, *Two Wars and More to Come,* p. 310.

13. Gates, *Story of an American Communist,* p. 62; Landis, *Lincoln Brigade,* pp. 390–391; Rolfe, "Spanish Diary"; Hans Amlie, "With the Americans Fighting Fascism," *New York Evening Post,* Feb. 10, 1938.

14. Sheean, *Not Peace But a Sword,* pp. 251–252. Here Sheean is recounting what Jim Lardner told him about his experiences in an *"inutiles"* camp. Lardner had been sent to one because brigade officials did not want him killed, but he escaped and eventually reached the front.

15. Lucid interview. In House of Representatives, *Investigation of Un-American Propaganda Activities,* Vol. XIII, p. 7808, Anthony E. DeMaio, unfriendly to the committee and very pro-Communist, admitted the brigades had "disciplinary units," which he termed "labor battalions." Bessie, "Spanish Notebooks," also mentions such battalions.

16. Bailey interview.

17. Bessie, "Spanish Notebooks," mentions four. Since this was a diary being kept at the time, it is probably more accurate than later accounts. The same number is given in Sills and Lucid interviews. Arthur Landis, a veteran of Spain and a vigorous partisan of the Lincolns, admits three men were shot for desertion late in the war. See *Lincoln Brigade,* p. 311. Gates, last commissar of the XVth Brigade, has claimed only two Americans were executed for desertion. See Muste, *Say That We Saw Spain Die,* p. 27, note 19.

18. Bailey, Sills interviews.

19. Landis, *Lincoln Brigade,* pp. 310–311.

20. Cattell, *Communism and the Spanish Civil War,* p. 118; Thomas, *Spanish Civil War,* pp. 492–493.

21. *Letters from Spain,* p. 13; Lindsley, *War Is People,* pp. 62–63.

22. Perez Salas, *Guerra en España,* p. 163.

23. Sills interview.

24. Thomas, *Spanish Civil War,* pp. 492–493; Sills interview.

25. For a full discussion of why the author thinks political executions were rare, see Appendix B.

26. Confidential interviews. See two such cases in Chapter XII.

CHAPTER XV

1. Bessie, "Spanish Notebooks"; Gates, *Story of an American Communist,* p. 60; Sheean, *Not Peace But a Sword,* p. 58.

2. Every veteran I interviewed who was still in Spain at this time expressed this sentiment.

3. Matthews, "Dispatches," March 12, 1938.

4. Bessie, *Men in Battle*, p. 143; Landis, *Lincoln Brigade*, p. 477.

5. Bessie, *Men in Battle*, p. 145; Matthews, "Dispatches," April 21, 1938.

6. Bessie, "Spanish Notebooks."

7. Matthews, "Dispatches," June 18, 1938; Thayer interview.

8. Edwin Rolfe, letter to his wife, May 2, 1938; Lucid, Sills, and Bailey interviews.

9. Edwin Rolfe, letters to his wife, May 3, 6, and 8, 1938, and "Spanish Diary."

10. Bessie, "Spanish Notebooks."

11. Edwin Rolfe, letters to his wife, May 29, June 1, and 18, 1938; Wilfred Mendelson letter, July 6, 1938, in Leeds, *Let My People Know*, p. 69.

12. Edwin Rolfe, letters to his wife, May 8, 10, 29, and June 1, 7, and 24, 1938; Bessie, "Spanish Notebooks."

13. Rolfe, *Lincoln Battalion*, pp. 247-258; Bessie, "Spanish Notebooks."

14. Bessie, *Men in Battle*, pp. 192-194.

15. Landis, *Lincoln Brigade*, p. 505; Bessie, "Spanish Notebooks."

16. Wilfred Mendelson letter, June 28, 1938, in Leeds, *Let My People Know*, p. 58; Klein and Thayer interviews.

17. Thomas, *Spanish Civil War*, p. 534; Wilfred Mendelson letter, June 22, 1938, in Leeds, *Let My People Know*, p. 59; Bessie, "Spanish Notebooks."

18. Wilfred Mendelson letter, July 23, 1938, in Leeds, *Let My People Know*, p. 78.

19. Thomas, *Spanish Civil War*, pp. 542-544; Landis, *Lincoln Brigade*, p. 516.

20. Rojo, *España Heroica*, p. 173; Gates, *Story of an American Communist*, p. 63; Kindelán, *Mis Cuadernos*, p. 139.

21. Rolfe, "Spanish Diary"; Bessie, "Spanish Notebooks"; Matthews, "Dispatches," Aug. 2, 1938.

22. Bessie, "Spanish Notebooks"; Rolfe, "Spanish Diary" and *Lincoln Battalion*, pp. 264-265; *Volunteer for Liberty*, Aug. 27, 1938.

23. Bessie, "Spanish Notebooks"; Rolfe, "Spanish Diary" and "His Name was Arnold Reid," *New Masses*, XXIX (Oct. 4, 1938), 7-8.

24. Bessie, "Spanish Notebooks"; Thomas, *Spanish Civil War*, p. 549; Rolfe, "Spanish Diary"; XVth Brigade, "Special Order of the Day," Aug. 21, 1938, in *Volunteer for Liberty*, Nov. 7, 1938.

25. Bessie, "Spanish Notebooks."

26. Cattell, *Communism and the Spanish Civil War*, p. 125, argues that Stalin ordered the Internationals out of Spain. The author feels that the exigencies of the Spanish situation were more important to Negrín than the Comintern's wishes in the fall of 1939. On the other hand, Bessie in his notebooks mentions a mid-September rumor that André Marty had been to Moscow and that the Comintern wished the brigades to leave. Still, Bessie makes it clear that the decision would be made by the Spanish government. Since Spain was receiving minimal support from the Soviet Union at this point, and since Negrín was always quite independent of the CP, it seems likely the ultimate decision was his.

27. Bessie, "Spanish Notebooks"; Rolfe, *Lincoln Battalion*, p. 293.

Chapter XVI

1. Bessie, "Spanish Notebooks"; Voros, *American Commissar*, p. 441; Lucid and Wesson interviews.

2. Gates, *Story of an American Communist*, pp. 66–67; Matthews, "Dispatches," Oct. 29, 1938; De la Mora, *In Place of Splendor*, pp. 372–373; *Daily Worker*, Oct. 30, 1938.

3. Department of State, *Foreign Relations, 1938*, Vol. I, pp. 226, 284, 333, 338–339, 343–345; Matthews, "Dispatches," Nov. 24, 1938. The passport problem is a difficult one to reach conclusions on. The Department of State's papers do not make it clear whether or not many passports finally showed up. Alvah Bessie, in a letter to me dated May 21, 1966, stated that there was a rumor at Ripoll that the documents had been lost, but that two days later hundreds of them arrived. He went on to say, "I do not know any man who went to Spain from the USA who did not get his passport back, except a couple who were illegal aliens. . . ." Bessie also totally discounts the assertions of Krivitsky, *In Stalin's Secret Service*, p. 95, and Fischer, *Men and Politics*, p. 394, that the passports ended up in the Soviet Union where the Russian government used them for purposes of international spying.

4. *Daily Worker*, Nov. 25, 1938; Department of State, *Foreign Relations, 1938*, Vol. I, pp. 344–345; *New York Times*, Dec. 3 and 4, 1938.

5. Memphis *Commercial Appeal*, Dec. 8, 1938; Goff interview; Matthews, *Education of a Correspondent*, pp. 160, 184–185; Sheean, *Not Peace But a Sword*, p. 268; *New York Times*, Jan. 26, 1938; Department of State, *Foreign Relations of the United States: Diplomatic Papers, 1939* (Washington, D.C.: Government Printing Office, 1956), Vol. II, p. 801.

6. Department of State, *Foreign Relations, 1938*, Vol. I, pp. 302–304, 330, and *Foreign Relations, 1939*, Vol. II, pp. 808–813; Goodwin interview. There is information about the prison in Lou Ornitz, *Captured by Franco* (New York: Friends of the Abraham Lincoln Brigade, 1939), but as a piece of anti-Franco propaganda, the book tries to make it seem as if conditions were much worse than they really were.

7. New York *Herald Tribune*, Aug. 1, 1937, Pawtucket *Times*, Aug. 16, 1937, and Providence *Bulletin*, Aug. 17, 1937, all describe O'Flahertys. For Raven see *Hollywood Now*, II, No. 11 (June 11, 1937). Also touring were Samuel Stember, Stephen Daduk, Humberto Galleani, Hans Amlie, and Mrs. Robert Merriman.

8. *Daily Worker*, April 21 and June 5, 1938; Brock Brower, "The Abraham Lincoln Battalion Revisited," *Esquire*, LVII (March 1962), 64–68; Bridgeport *Telegram*, Sept. 23, 1938; *Volunteer for Liberty*, Jan. 1940.

9. New York *Herald Tribune*, Dec. 16, 1938.

10. *They Did Their Part, Let's Do Ours* (New York: Friends of the Abraham Lincoln Brigade, 1939).

11. *Daily Worker*, Jan. 3, 1939; Lovin, "The American Communist Party," pp. 362–363; Goodwin, Wesson, Bailey, Thayer, Sills interviews.

12. Providence *Journal*, Dec. 23, 1937; New York *Herald Tribune*, Jan. 18, 1938; Los Angeles *Evening News*, Jan. 19, 1938.

13. Carl Bradley, "Statement of the VALB Conference for Peace, Washington, D.C. Feb. 12, 13, 1938" (mimeographed press release); "Report on the VALB Conference in Washington, D.C., Feb. 12–14, 1938" (mimeographed); Wash-

ington *Star*, Feb. 13, 1938; Washington *Post*, Feb. 15, 1938; Albuquerque *Journal*, Feb. 14, 1938.

14. St. Louis *Post Dispatch*, May 1, 1938; *New York World Telegram*, May 1, 1938; *Daily Worker*, Oct. 17, 1938; Cleveland *Press*, Jan. 23, 1939.

15. Years later, the Subversive Activities Control Board showed, at least to its own satisfaction, that the VALB was organized under a directive of the Politburo. This may have been so, but it explains nothing about why non-Communists joined the VALB. In its report, the SACB shows that some VALB officers were not Communists. See Subversive Activities Control Board, *Herbert Brownell . . .* pp. 92–98.

16. Nobody seems to know exactly how many returned from Spain; estimates vary between 1,200 and 1,800. The best source is undoubtedly Landis, *Abraham Lincoln Brigade*, pp. xvii–xviii, who says 3,300 went to Spain and more than 1,600 were killed in action. This would mean fewer than 1,700 returned. The author feels at least 1,500 came back on the basis of very rough figuring. Starting with the 222 the FALB announced were back in April 1938, he has added the 400 theoretically brought back in the summer of that year, the 327 who left December 3, the 160 five days later, the 200 at the end of January, and the 90 at San Pedro de Cardenas. That makes 1,400, and one can easily throw in 35 to 50 deserters who came home. Then there were certainly other returnees who did not get into these calculations.

17. Jack Lucid, Ben Sills interviews. The only VALB posts to last more than a year were New York, Chicago; Los Angeles, and San Francisco. Posts were briefly set up in Detroit, Cleveland, Baltimore, Milwaukee, Washington, Seattle, Portland, Pittsburgh, Minneapolis, Boston, St. Louis, and New Haven. See Subversive Activities Control Board, *Herbert Brownell . . .* p. 101.

18. Fred Keller, "Membership Report," in "Proceedings of the Third National Convention, Veterans of the Abraham Lincoln Brigade, Dec. 23-24, 1939, New York City."

19. Lucid, Thayer, and confidential interviews.

20. In December 1938, the Gallup Poll found 40 per cent of Americans were neutral with regard to the war. Of the 60 per cent with convictions, 76 per cent favored the Loyalists. Surely most of these people looked upon the Lincolns with favor. See Taylor, *United States and Spanish Civil War*, p. 137.

21. *Sunday Worker*, June 16, 1940; *New York Times*, Feb. 16, 1940.

22. Subversive Activities Control Board, *Herbert Brownell . . .* pp. 120, 145.

23. *Ibid.*, pp. 166–168; *Volunteer for Liberty*, Dec. 1940; *New Republic*, C (Dec. 13, 1939), 221–225; and CI (Jan. 15, 1940), 23.

24. Opinions of almost all men interviewed even today, when their disillusionment with the Soviet Union is fairly complete.

25. Gates, *Story of an American Communist*, p. 78; *Volunteer for Liberty*, Oct. and Dec. 1941; Milton Wolff, *Western Front—Now!* (New York: Veterans of the Abraham Lincoln Brigade, 1941), p. 13; *P.M.*, Dec. 5, 1942; Howe and Coser, *American Communist Party*, p. 406.

26. Estimate of VALB Executive Secretary Jack Bjoze, in *P.M.*, Jan. 26, 1943. Three quarters of the men I interviewed claimed to have enlisted rather than waiting to be called in World War II.

27. Goodwin, Klein, Lucid, Wellman, and confidential interviews; *P.M.*, May 23, 1943.

28. Camp Livingston *Communique*, Sept. 17, 1942; Camp Crowder *Message*, April 27, 1944. Other such articles are legion. For example, Keeler Field *News*, May 27, 1942, on Edward O'Flaherty; Scott Field *Broadcaster*, Oct. 14, 1942, on Tony DeMaio and Jerry Weinberg; Mitchell Field *Beacon*, Dec. 4, 1942, on Joe Gibbons; Army *Times*, March 7, 1942, on Joe Hecht; Air Forces *News Letter*, July 1942, on Sam Stone.

29. *Daily Worker*, Dec. 10, 1944, April 2 and Oct. 2, 1945; Gloversville (New York) *Leader Republican*, Nov. 17, 1943.

30. *New York Post*, Dec. 14, 1942; New York *Herald Tribune*, Dec. 15, 1942; *Daily Worker*, May 11, 1942; *New York World Telegram*, Jan. 7, 1943; Denver *Post*, Aug. 19, 1943; *Daily Worker*, Aug. 30, 1943.

31. *The New World*, March 18, 1943; *P.M.*, Jan. 23, April 22, and May 23, 1943; Washington *Post*, April 14, 1943; *New Republic*, CVIII (April 26, 1943); Gates, *Story of an American Communist*, pp. 84–100; Lucid interview.

32. Howe and Coser, *American Communist Party*, p. 434; Goff interview; *New York Daily News*, Nov. 7, 1943; *Daily Worker*, Sept. 13, 1945; Stewart Alsop and Thomas Braden, *Sub Rosa: The O.S.S. and American Espionage* (New York: Reynal and Hitchcock, 1946), pp. 25–36.

33. Memphis *Press-Scimitar*, July 18, 1945; Chicago *Tribune*, Feb. 20 and 29, 1945; New York *Herald Tribune*, July 20, 1945; *Daily Worker*, March 14, 1945; Alsop and Braden, *Sub Rosa*, p. 26.

34. Goff interview.

35. Sills, Lucid, Bailey, Wellman and confidential interviews.

36. Fred Keller, "Membership Report," in "Proceedings of Third Convention." At the 1946 convention there were many complaints about lack of interest of the veterans in their organization.

37. Veterans of the Abraham Lincoln Brigade, Inc., *Press Releases, Speeches, Congratulatory Messages, etc., Concerning First Post War National Convention, September 21–22, 1946*; Taylor, *United States and Spanish Civil War*, p. 116.

38. VALB, *Press Releases, Speeches . . . 1946; Volunteer for Liberty*, April 1947, July 1950.

39. *Daily Worker*, Feb. 18, 1945; VALB, *Releases, Radio Addresses, etc., on Franco Spain, 1938–1947*; David M. White, *Franco Spain . . . America's Enemy* (New York: New Century, 1945); Milton Wolff, *Fascist Spain, Menace to World Peace* (New York: New Century, 1947).

40. Goodwin and confidential interviews.

41. Alvah Bessie, *Inquisition in Eden* (New York: The Macmillan Company, 1965); David Shannon, *The Decline of American Communism* (New York: Harcourt, Brace and World 1959), pp. 196–200; Detroit *Times*, Jan. 29, 1954; *Daily Worker*, Jan. 18, 1956; *New York Post*, Jan. 18, 1956; Saul Wellman, letter to the author, January 1969.

42. Lucid, Sills, Klein, and confidential interviews.

43. House of Representatives, Special Committee on Un-American Activities, *Hearings Regarding Communist Espionage in the United States Government*, 80th Cong., 2nd Sess. (Washington, D.C.: Government Printing Office, 1948), p. 631.

44. HUAC, *Hearings Regarding Steve Nelson*, 81st Cong., 1st Sess., (Washington, D.C.: Government Printing Office, 1949); *Communist Activities in the Philadelphia*

Area, 82nd Cong., 2nd Sess. (Washington, D.C.: Government Printing Office, 1952), pp. 4434–4441, 4359–4363; *Investigation of Communist Activities in the Albany, N.Y. Area*, 83rd Cong., 2nd Sess. (Washington, D.C.: Government Printing Office, 1954), pp. 4374–4389; *Investigation of Communist Activities in the New York City Area*, 83rd Cong., 1st Sess. (Washington, D.C.: Government Printing Office, 1953), pp. 1390–1391; *Investigation of Communist Activities in the State of Michigan*, 83rd Cong., 2nd Sess. (Washington, D.C.: Government Printing Office, 1954), pp. 5371–5387.

45. *Volunteer for Liberty*, Nov. 6, 1952.

46. *Ibid.*, Jan. 9, 1953; "Statement of the VALB on United States–Franco Pact," November 1953 (mimeographed).

47. Subversive Activities Control Board, *Herbert Brownell* . . . pp. 1–7; *Volunteer for Liberty*, June 1954.

48. Subversive Activities Control Board, *Herbert Brownell* . . . p. 245.

49. Moe Fishman letter, Jan. 17, 1955, quoted in Taylor, *United States and Spanish Civil War*, p. 114; *Volunteer for Liberty*, Jan. 1956; John Gates, quoted in Shannon, *Decline of American Communism*, p. 352.

50. *Volunteer for Liberty*, Jan. 1, 1957.

51. Brower, "Lincoln Battalion Revisited"; HUAC, *U.S. Communist Party Assistance to Foreign Communist Parties* (Veterans of the Abraham Lincoln Brigade), 88th Cong., 1st Sess. (Washington, D.C.: Government Printing Office, 1963), *New York Times*, July 19, 1964.

52. Los Angeles *Times*, April 27, 1965.

CHAPTER XVII

1. Thomas, *Spanish Civil War*, pp. 604–617, is proponent of the theory of Stalin's betrayal of Spain.

2. Preface to North, *Men in the Ranks*, p. 4.

3. April 8, 1938.

4. Oct. 11, 1937.

5. Quoted in Iversen, *Communists and the Schools*, p. 145.

6. Perhaps some veterans do not feel this way, but I have never met anyone connected with the battalion who did not.

7. Matthews, *Education of a Correspondent*, pp. 67–68.

8. Fischer, *Men and Politics*, p. 544.

411

DATE DUE

AP 25 '03			

DEMCO 38-296

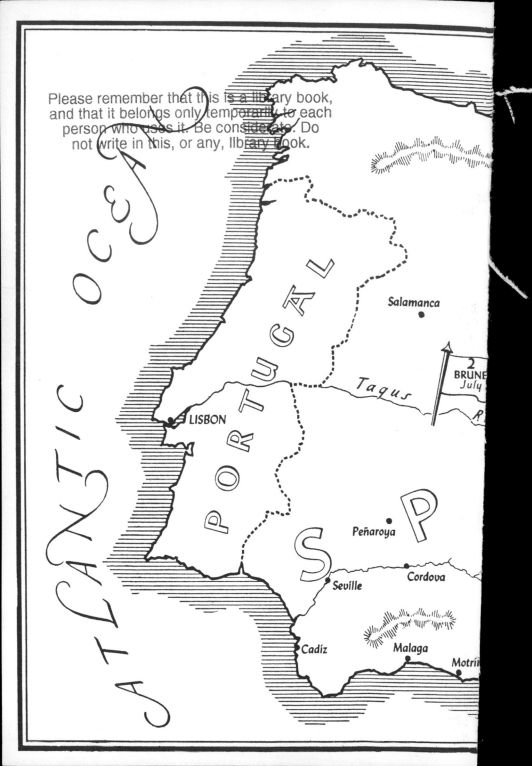

ATLANTIC OCEAN

PORTUGAL

Salamanca

Tagus R.

2
BRUNE
July

LISBON

SPAIN

Peñaroya

P

S

Seville

Cordova

Cadiz

Malaga

Motril